ISRAEL:
THE DYNAMICS OF CHANGE AND CONTINUITY

Israeli History, Politics and Society
Series Editor: Efraim Karsh, King's College London
ISSN 1368-4795

Providing a multidisciplinary examination in all aspects, this series serves as a means of communication between the various communities interested in Israel: academics, policy-makers, practitioners, journalists and the informed public.

Other books in the series:

Peace in the Middle East: The Challenge for Israel
edited by Efraim Karsh

The Shaping of Israeli Identity: Myth, Memory and Trauma
edited by Robert Wistrich and David Ohana

Between War and Peace: Dilemmas of Israeli Security
edited by Efraim Karsh

U.S.–Israeli Relations at the Crossroads
edited by Gabriel Sheffer

From Rabin to Netanyahu: Israel's Troubled Agenda
edited by Efraim Karsh

Israel at the Polls 1996
edited by Daniel J. Elazar and Shmuel Sandler

In Search of Identity: Jewish Aspects in Israeli Culture
edited by Dan Urian and Efraim Karsh

Israel: The First Hundred Years
Volume 1: Israel's Transition from Community to State
edited by Efraim Karsh

Revisiting the Yom Kippur War
edited by P.R. Kumaraswamy

Peacemaking in Israel after Rabin
edited by Sasson Sofer

ISRAEL
THE DYNAMICS OF CHANGE AND CONTINUITY

Editors
David Levi-Faur, Gabriel Sheffer
and David Vogel

FRANK CASS
LONDON • PORTLAND, OR

First published in 1999 in Great Britain by
FRANK CASS PUBLISHERS
Newbury House, 900 Eastern Avenue
London IG2 7HH

and in the United States of America by
FRANK CASS PUBLISHERS
c/o ISBS
5804 N.E. Hassalo Street
Portland, Oregon 97213-3644

Transferred to Digital Printing 2004

Website: www.frankcass.com

Copyright © 1999 Frank Cass & Co. Ltd

British Library Cataloguing in Publication Data

Israel : the dynamics of change and continuity. – (Israeli history, politics and society; v. 8)
1. Israel – Politics and government 2. Israel – Economic conditions 3. Israel – Social conditions
I. Levi-Faur, David II. Sheffer, Gabriel III. Vogel, David
956.9'4'054

ISBN 0 7146 5012 9 (cloth)
ISBN 0 7146 8062 1 (paper)
ISSN 1368-4795

Library of Congress Cataloging-in-Publication Data

Israel : the dynamics of change and continuity / edited by David Levi-Faur, Gabriel Sheffer, and David Vogel.
      p. cm. – (Israeli history, politics, and society, ISSN 1368-4795)
      Includes bibliographical references and index.
      ISBN 0-7146-5012-9 (cloth). – ISBN 0-7146-8062-1 (paper)
      1. Israel. 2. Israel–Politics and government. 3. Israel–Economic conditions. 4. Israel–Social conditions. 5. Israel–Ethnic relations. I. Levi-Faur, David. II. Sheffer, Gabriel. III. Vogel, David, 1947– . IV. Series.
DS102.95.I8615   1999   99-25984
956.9405–dc21   CIP

This group of studies first appeared in a Special Issue on 'Israel: The Dynamics of Change and Continuity' of *Israel Affairs* 5/2&3 (Winter–Spring 1999) ISSN 1353-7121 published by Frank Cass.

All rights reserved. No part of this publication may be reproduced, stored in or introduced into a retrieval system or transmitted in any form or by any means, electronic, mechanical, photocopying, recording or otherwise, without the prior written permission of the publishers of this book.

Contents

Change and Continuity: A Framework for Comparative Analysis — David Levi-Faur, Gabriel Sheffer and David Vogel 1

Courts as Hegemonic Institutions: The Israeli Supreme Court in a Comparative Perspective — Gad Barzilai 15

Israeli Constitutional Politics: The Fragility of Impartiality — Menachem Hofnung 34

Structural Change and Leadership Transformation — Gabriel Sheffer 55

Interest Politics in a Comparative Perspective: The (Ir)regularity of the Israeli Case — Yael Yishai 73

The Social Organization of the Israeli Economy: A Comparative Analysis — Daniel Maman 87

Business in Politics: Globalization and the Search for Peace in South Africa and Israel/Palestine — Gershon Shafir 103

Have Globalization and Liberalization "Normalized" Israel's Political Economy? — Michael Shalev 121

Warfare, Polity-Formation and the Israeli National Policy Patterns — David Levi-Faur 156

Consociationalism and Ethnic Democracy: Israeli Arabs in Comparative Perspective — Alan Dowty 169

From What *Edah* are You? Israeli and American Meanings of "Race-Ethnicity" in Social Policy Practices — Dvora Yanow 183

Changing Places: Jerusalem's Holy Places in Comparative Perspective — Roger Friedland and Richard D. Hecht 200

Imported Problem Definitions, Legal Culture and the Local Dynamics of Israeli Abortion Politics — Noga Morag-Levine 226

Israeli Environmental Policy in Comparative Perspective	**David Vogel** 246
The Gender and Pacifism Hypothesis: Opinion Research from Israel and the Arab World	**Mark Tessler, Jodi Nachtwey** and **Audra Grant** 265
The Promised Land of the Chosen People is not all that Distinctive: On the Value of Comparison	**Ira Sharkansky** 279
Abstracts	293
Index	301

Change and Continuity:
A Framework for Comparative Analysis

DAVID LEVI-FAUR, GABI SHEFFER
and DAVID VOGEL

WHAT IS IT ALL ABOUT?

Most Israelis and foreign observers agree that Israel's society and polity are rapidly and profoundly changing. Although their profile of the Israeli polity remains murky, they recognize that it is acquiring new cultural, social, economic, and political characteristics and that a number of these characteristics have made it similar to those of western pluralist-liberal democracies. At the same time, religious-fundamentalist, nationalist, and rightist groups have emerged that are strongly opposed to Israel becoming more similar to other advanced western democracies. For them, Israel's distinctiveness is a positive value.

The articles in this collection seek to move beyond the question of Israel's uniqueness. After all, virtually all societies are unique. Israel is distinctive, but so are Germany, the United States, China, and Japan. An emphasis on national exceptionalism per se is an intellectual dead-end. No country is unique on all dimensions. What matters is: on what dimensions is a country unique? To which countries can it be most usefully compared? And on what dimensions and to what extent is it becoming more similar and/or divergent?

The primary aim of the present volume is to employ the methods of comparative political analysis to better understand Israel and develop some theoretical insights into the kinds of changes it is experiencing. This is a particularly challenging task since until recently comparativists have been reluctant to include the Israeli case in their research, in part due to a widely shared perception of Israel's "uniqueness" and therefore its unsuitability for comparative research.

In his introductory essay to the edited volume, *Israel in Comparative Perspective*, Michael Barnett addressed the question of Israel's uniqueness.[1] He and his colleagues raised this issue in part as a way of seeking to understand why students of comparative politics so frequently ignored Israel. They suggested that it was because Israel was so hard to classify – in what conventional categories of comparative political analysis did Israel fall? It was physically situated in the Middle East, yet had relatively little in common with other middle-eastern states. It was a democracy, yet included a number of non-democratic characteristics. It was a predominately secular society, yet it was also torn by religious conflicts. It shared many of the characteristics of state socialist societies, yet it had a vigorous private sector. It was reasonably integrated into the global economy, yet had virtually no economic relations with its neighbors.

The roots of the entrenched belief about "Israel's uniqueness" are to be found, Barnett and colleagues argued, in a distinctive combination of ethnocentric self-beliefs among the Jewish people about its uniqueness, in the traditional academic organization of area studies, and in Israel's ambiguous international status and reputation, especially due to the protracted Arab–Israeli conflict. By placing a number of aspects of Israeli society and politics in comparative perspective and by examining Israel's links with other countries, the Barnett volume made an important contribution to the comparative study of Israel as well as to the study of comparative politics in general.

Our aim, however, is not merely to replicate or elaborate the findings of Barnett's volume. Rather, we wish to put special emphasis on exploring, in a comparative context, the changes occurring in Israeli politics and society. Some scholars have argued that "the extraordinary political changes of the last few years, East and West, North and South, make obsolete virtually all the conventional approaches to comparative politics."[2] While we do not necessarily subscribe to this view, there is no question that the current rate of change in many countries, including Israel, in the direction of economic liberalization and political democratization, has raised new and important intellectual issues.

If Israeli society was ever unique, and thus difficult to analyze through the lens of comparative politics, then the dynamics of globalization have clearly made it much less so. Like many other countries, Israel has been affected by profound economic, political, and social changes. They have made Israeli society and politics more "normal part of history" and less an "a-historical" phenomenon (as some Israelis still like to think of it). At the same time, this has made Israel's comparability to other polities both easier and more intellectually fruitful.

Thus, instead of only looking at what has or has not changed in Israel, we can compare changes in Israel to those that have taken place in other political systems. By adopting a comparative perspective, we not only enrich our analysis of the Israeli political system, but help students of comparative politics develop new models to explain changes in democratic regimes.

ABOUT CHANGE

An important distinction between current approaches to political analysis is between those centered on change, or which consider change as a significant element of politics, and those that emphasize continuity. The behavioral approaches and the models these approaches have generated tend to recognize the significance of political change more than do cultural, structural, and institutional approaches. The behaviorists emphasize observable and measurable behaviors of individuals or groups of persons. This is in contrast to the non-behaviorist approaches that stress the role of the more static variables of culture, structures, or institutions in explaining political outcomes and their consequences.

In addition, behaviorists are usually interested in the shorter time spans of political actions and their synoptic nature. This contrasts with the longer time spans and the emphasis on continuity that characterizes cultural, structural, and institutional approaches. Non-behaviorist approaches frequently assume that cultures, structures, and institutions develop over generations or at least decades. They also assume that once these systems crystallize, they tend to maintain their structure over time. They therefore tend to adopt a more static view of their subjects. Hence the models they propose stress the limited scope of change in the goals and orientation of political and social actors.

For the analysis in this collection of articles, change essentially means *making or becoming different*. As noted above, many existing polities, authoritarian as well as democratic, have been significantly affected by recent global trends. The most apparent sphere in which such profound change has occurred, and probably the easiest to measure, is that of economics. The increase in the cross-national flows of goods, capital, manpower, and technology has affected the largest and most powerful nation-states no less than the smaller and weaker ones such as Israel. One important consequence of economic globalization is increased interdependence. In turn, interdependence has contributed to an erosion of the economic sovereignty of states, particularly with respect to those policies that affect international trade, investment, and financial flows. Another indication of the erosion of economic sovereignty is the reduction in what can be called "Keynesian capacity" to deal with economic cycles, development, and growth. At the same time, many states are encountering greater difficulties in dealing with some crucial matters, such as sovereignty, boundaries, immigrants' inflow, and citizenship, that in the past were regarded as within their exclusive jurisdiction. Globalization also means that the boundaries between the international and domestic domains are becoming increasingly blurred.[3]

In analyzing political change, it is also important to specify its magnitude. The magnitude of change is often closely connected to the speed at which change occurs.[4] "First order" change is gradual and incrementally produced by routine processes (e.g., adjusting a line-item budget to moderate inflationary rates); "second order" change involves a moderately rapid development of new political instruments that do not radically alter the hierarchy of goals of a given political system (e.g., the introduction of new credit control measures); and, finally, "third order" change involves a fast and sweeping shift in the aims, strategy, and means for attaining goals by a political system (e.g., the switch from Keynesian economics to Monetarism in many western countries in the late 1970s). While first and second order changes can be seen as two examples of "normal policy making," third order change reflects radical transformation that may indicate a "paradigm shift."[5]

What promotes change? Many changes in political systems are motivated at least as much by modification in values as by transformation in material or economic circumstances.

> The incentives that motivate people to work, the issues that give rise to political conflict, people's religious beliefs, their attitudes concerning divorce, abortion, and homosexuality, the importance they attach to having children and raising families – all these have been changing. *One could go so far as to say that, throughout the advanced industrial society, what people want out of life is changing.*[6]

Some of the current profound social and political changes occurring in advanced industrial societies are spurred by the growth of post-materialist attitudes and preferences.

Change-centered approaches are often accompanied by predictions about "the tendency of societies to grow more alike, to develop similarities in structures, processes and performances."[7] Such predictions are not new. During the modern era, many political analysts have emphasized the *unity of capitalism* rather than the *diversity of capitalist society*.[8] Moreover, observations about convergence are common to both Marxists and mainstream analysts. Sooner or later, the proponents of these approaches maintain, the forces of change will result in the homogenization of domestic politics in advanced liberal democracies.

Convergence is not only occurring on the international and regional levels. Clear processes of political convergence are evident on the level of macro-politics as well. Thus, for example, the party maps in most advanced countries are acquiring new features: the majority of the larger parties are becoming catch-all parties, and their activities are increasingly directed toward the large number of citizens who are supposed to be located at the political center. At the same time on both the left and right one still finds smaller parties which have maintained their radical inclinations.

In contrast to Marxism's as well as to mainstream economists' predictions about system convergence, comparative institutionalists often emphasize the persistence of divergence among western democracies. "For some," it has been argued, "the very idea of convergence in the trajectories of nationalist economies has lost credibility. The differences among local capitalist states seem not only persistent but also more important and interesting than do the similarities."[9]

The path-dependency approach to political, economic, and social change offers an important analytical approach to understanding divergence. Proponents of the path-dependency approach have advanced the notion of *Multiple Equilibria* rather than *Single Optimal Equilibrium Points*.[10] Rather than assuming that a single state of equilibrium represents the optimal social outcome, the path-dependency approach posits a multiplicity of optimal points, thus resulting in divergence rather than uniformity. Multiple equilibria become possible wherever positive feedback would create sufficient incentives to remain on the same trajectory rather than to reverse the rules of the game and patterns of behavior.

"Making things different" can take place though evolutionary or radical change. Evolutionary change, which might be understood as a form of continuity, involves gradual and incremental change. It can take place over time-spans of decades and even generations. Radical changes tend to fundamentally alter systems rather than gradually reform them. This is often a rapid process, which, in extreme cases, may even occur in a matter of a few weeks or months.[11] The British polity, for example, developed through gradual evolutionary processes. Abrupt changes in British politics have been relatively rare, and the British polity still resists single major efforts to radically alter traditional structures and patterns. Frequently, the British case has been contrasted with the "revolution-ridden" development of French politics (1789, 1830, 1848, 1871, 1968). In addition to these revolutions, France had experienced 15 constitutions and approximately 20 different regimes since the great revolution of 1789. During the same period there was no major reform in the British political institutions.[12] The distinction between the French and British cases provides us with two distinct models of continuity and change.

The timing and sequence of changes are also important. The path-dependency approach can facilitate discussion of the tension between change and continuity in general, and in the Israeli case in particular. It emphasizes that *"when an event occurs may be just as important as what occurs. Because early parts of the run matter much more than later parts. An event that happens 'too late' may have no impact, though it might have been of great consequence if the timing had been different."*[13] Timing is critical to the trajectory of state–society relations. The early industrialization of England, for example, was led by entrepreneurs and facilitated by a "weak state," while many of the subsequent industrial revolutions that occurred in Europe resulted in "strong states" in Germany and elsewhere.[14] The implications of these differences in the timing of industrialization are still evident in the political institutions and political culture in the two countries.

THE OTHER SIDE OF THE COIN: CONTINUITY

Our understanding of the concept of continuity has also been influenced by the historical-institutional school that was revived in the 1980s and since has given a new vigor to the comparative study of politics.[15] Historical-institutionalism has set a new agenda for scholars of comparative politics, challenging those who have predicted the "end of history." Historical-institutional analysis emerged from a critique of the behaviorists who appeared to have neglected or at least minimized the significance of enduring social-economic and political structures and cultures. Instead of focusing on individuals' rational choice, or on collective choice, historical-institutionalists emphasize the distinct ways in which political institutions in different states mold individual and group behavior. Thus individual preferences and political strategies are explained by the examination of the structure and behavior of specific institutions of contemporary capitalism (i.e., the market), the bureaucratic state, democratic institutions, the nuclear family, religion, etc.[16]

In fact, the historical-institutional approach adds a certain depth to the analysis not only of political continuity, but also of change. According to this approach, both continuity and change are not an outcome of rational or interest-driven action by individuals. Rather, this school suggests that both change and continuity are the outcome of behaviors that are mediated by organizational factors.[17] Accordingly, institutions based on formal division of labor, relatively specific rules of behavior and clearly defined compliance patterns, and Standard Operating Procedures that structure the relationship among individuals in various units are central to the understanding of change and continuity. According to this view, institutions determine continuity and hence the scope, intensity, pace, and outcomes of change.

This approach emphasizes the various systemic and background constraints on change. The reason for this emphasis is obvious: the agents of change, themselves the products of organizational socialization, are imbued with the organizations' conservative values, corporate experience, and collective culture. Thus, whenever members face external challenges, they are bound by historically-constructed structures that change only slowly. Under such circumstances, any movement toward alternative directions is apt to be partial and gradual.

OVERVIEW OF THE CONTRIBUTIONS

The 15 essays in this collection explore the twin themes of change and continuity in the Israeli polity through the lens of comparative analysis, considering not only how Israel's politics are changing, but also the direction of these changes in comparison to other nations. Is Israel becoming more similar to other states? In what ways does it remain distinct and which factors are contributing to either trend? The essays in this issue fall relatively evenly into four categories: political institutions and organizations, political economy, ethnicity and religion, and public policy. They deal with a wide variety of issues, ranging from the changing role of the Israeli Supreme Court to the structure of the Israeli economy, from Israel's treatment of Arabs, to its environmental policy, from the leadership styles of Israel's political leaders to the conflict over control of Jerusalem, from the pattern of Israeli interest groups to the meaning of race and ethnicity. But what they have in common is the use of a comparative framework to illuminate contemporary changes in Israeli society and institutions.

While the countries with which the authors compare Israel vary widely, most compare Israel to western industrialized democracies, suggesting the extent to which Israel has become more similar to these countries. Nonetheless, it is a sign of Israel's continued complexity or ambiguity that five compare Israel to non-western ones. Maman argues that the social organization of Israel's economy strikingly resembles that of Japan, South Korea, and Taiwan, while Shafir compares the role of the Israel business community in the process of rapprochement with the Palestinians with that played by its counter-part in South Africa with respect to the dismantling of apartheid. Friedland and Hecht contrast the dispute over control of the holy sites in Jerusalem to the battles between Muslims and Hindus over control of a holy site in Ayodhya India, another nation torn by religious conflicts.

Tessler, Nachtwey, and Grant use the Arab states to test the pacifism and gender hypothesis, while Dowty's examination of the role of Arabs in Israel's democracy compares Israel to a large number of liberal democracies, both western and non-western, which have substantial ethnic minorities.

The fact that Israel can be usefully compared to other nations does not, of course, mean that it is no longer unique. After all, the very term "uniqueness" assumes a comparative framework. Moreover, a nation can be changing in ways that makes it less rather than more similar to other countries. However, the majority of the contributions conclude both that Israel is changing and that these changes are either similar to those taking place in other western democracies or are making Israel more similar to other western democracies. In short, they depict a process of change leading to convergence.

This observation emerges with particular clarity in the first group of articles which deal with Israeli political institutions and organizations. Both "Courts as Hegemonic Institutions: The Israeli Supreme Court in a Comparative Perspective," by Gad Barzilai and "Israeli Constitutional Politics: The Fragility of Impartiality," by Menachem Hofnung examine one of the most significant recent changes in Israeli government and politics, namely the growing prominence, independence, and politicization of the Israeli judiciary. This development can be seen as another dimension of the Americanization of Israel, though other countries have independent judiciaries as well. And not surprisingly, this trend threatens to provoke a political backlash not dissimilar to that experienced during various periods by the American Supreme Court. By describing the Israeli case, and placing it in comparative perspective, Barzilai and Hofnung contribute to our understanding not only of an important development in contemporary Israeli politics, but also more broadly of the political and legal conditions for judicial independence.

"Structural Change and Leadership Transformation," by Gabriel Sheffer traces the evolution of Israel's political regime from a consociational to neo-corporatist to a liberal-private one, describing how each was associated with a particular leadership style. Sheffer concludes that the style of Israel's current political leadership bears a marked resemblance to that of a number of western democracies, including the United States and Great Britain. Each are now governed by "transactional, meteoric, and bargaining leaders, whose strengths are pragmatism, a cautious and flexible reformism, and clever use of the media." Hence the important similarities among Clinton, Blair, and Netyahanyu, once again illustrating the dynamics of convergence.

"Interest Politics in a Comparative Perspective: The (Ir)regularity of the Israeli Case," by Yael Yishai is more equivocal about the significance of current changes in the structure and pattern of interest-group representation in Israel. Hence the cautionary note in her subtitle, suggesting that in this area Israel remains distinctive. The number of interest groups in Israel is significantly increasing and virtually all appear to enjoy access to power, suggesting that Israel has come to resemble the model of American pluralist democracy described by Robert Dahl. At the same time, political parties have declined in importance, Israel has become more politically and culturally diverse, and its citizens are increasingly willing to participate in challenges to pubic authority – changes which parallel those in other countries.

But Yishai cautions that each of these changes is equivocal and may reflect more of an evolutionary process than an abrupt break with the past. For example, although parties have declined, many interest groups continue to run electoral lists. Moreover, while the state has become weaker, the government still exercises substantial influence over the way interest groups are organized. From this perspective, Israeli interest-group politics remain distinctive. Thus, she concludes that Israel continues to defy ready classification as either partyist, corporatist, or pluralist since, in many respects, it remains a combination of all three.

The first two articles on the Israeli political economy also emphasize the twin themes of domestic change and international convergence. "The Social Organization of the Israeli Economy: A Comparative Analysis," by Daniel Maman argues that the net result of the substantial changes that the Israeli economy has undergone over the last three decades, beginning with the business collapse of the 1960s and the hyperinflation of the late 1970s and culminating in the rapid growth and privatization of the

1990s, has been to make business more economically concentrated. In fact, rather that moving closer to the western model of business structure, the current degree of dominance of business groups in Israeli bears a marked resemblance to that of Japan, South Korea, and Taiwan. Thus, according to Maman, Israel is changing but it is converging toward an eastern rather than western style of capitalism.

"Business in Politics: Globalization and the Search for Peace in South Africa and Israel/Palestine," by Gershon Shafir also describes convergence, though from a very different and much narrower perspective. Shafir compares the role of business in the peace process in Israel and the dismantling of apartheid in South Africa. In both cases, he finds that global economic pressures forced the domestic business community to redefine its interests as it came to understand that the lack of a peace agreement with the Palestinians in the case of Israel, and the maintenance of apartheid in the case of South Africa, represented critical obstacles to economic modernization and the strengthening of links with international capital. Accordingly, business leaders began to actively lobby for political change. His article thus highlights an important but often overlooked dimension of the impact of the international economy on domestic politics.

Michael Shalev's article, "Have Globalization and Liberalization 'Normalized' Israel's Political Economy?," offers a more complex and nuanced portrait of economic change and convergence. Shalev presents a detailed portrait of the political, social, and economic forces that have challenged Israel's long history of "embedded illiberalism." In a number of important ways, Israel, like so many other countries, has become more market-oriented: private investment has increased, state expenditures as a share of national resources have declined, the domestic market for goods has become more competitive, the state's role in directed capital flows has diminished, and, perhaps most importantly in light of the history of labor Zionism, the structure of Israel's labor market has changed significantly.

But, at the same time, Shalev cautions against exaggerating the significance of these changes. He notes that the transformation of Israeli's political economy has been both incomplete and inconsistent; in many cases, such as the sale of state-owned enterprises or the reduction in the role of the state in the economy, it has been less significant than it appears. He argues that the process of liberalization is indeterminate: there are still powerful forces in Israeli society that oppose the creation of a new economic regime. Thus the durability of Israeli's current liberalization drive is problematic. More importantly, the legacy of Zionist collectivism persists in many areas.

"Warfare, Polity-Formation, and the Israeli National Policy Patterns," by David Levi-Faur employs the framework of comparative political economy to situate Israel within the global economy. Levi-Faur notes that the pattern of economic development in western capitalist economies demonstrates a strong causal relationship between the imperatives of war and the formation of strong states. Israel, a nation which has been highly militarily mobilized and on a virtual war-footing from its inception and which, accordingly, has developed a strong state, confirms this generalization. Its pattern of military-economic development bears a strikingly resemblance to the experience of a number of European continental nations in previous centuries.

Levi-Faur also observes that the kinds of national policy patterns shaped by the historical development of capitalism both shape and constrain current policy choices. In Israel's case, this means the maintenance of statism. He writes: "we have good reason to expect that national policy patterns are self-perpetuating and that the Israeli etatism is here to stay." Thus, Levi-Faur uses a comparative framework to dissent from the conclusion that Israel is fundamentally changing.

This volume also contains three articles on ethnicity and religious decisions within Israel. Each employs a comparative framework to illuminate some important conflicts and possible future changes within Israel. "Consociationalism and Ethnic Democracy: Israeli Arabs in Comparative Perspective," by Alan Dowty notes that the marked ethnic and religious differences that characterize Israel do not make it unique. In fact, there are approximately 71 states with a dominant ethnic group defined by language of more than 50 percent but less than 95 percent. Of these states, 26, or slightly more than one-third, are classified as "free" or democratic. If one focuses on ethnic divisions, then 11 of these states practice some form of formal power-sharing.

The key factor that accounts for this variation is the size of the minority group: when the latter reaches 20 percent, formal power sharing becomes common. With an Arab minority at 19 percent, Israel finds itself precisely at this threshold. Dowty predicts that Israel is likely to move toward a policy of consociationalism which would formally integrate its Arab minority into its political system. While he recognizes that Israel will remain a Jewish state, since that after all was the reason why it was established in the first place, he concludes that the global forces of modernization are straining the relationship between Judaism and Israel, thus redefining Israel's "Jewishness" and making it more compatible with making its Arab citizens full partners.

"From What *Edah* are You? Israeli and American Meanings of 'Race-Ethnicity' in Social Policy Practices," by Dvora Yanow also places Israel's ethnic divisions in comparative perspective. In contrast to Dowty, she focuses on racial/ethnic divisions within the Jewish community. Yanow compares the relative degree of silence of public discourse in Israel on racial/ethnic differences with the increasingly willingness of Americans to confront their differences. Thus, in contrast to the United States, Israel has no affirmative action policies for its marginalized Jewish citizens. Drawing upon the American experience, she suggests that the social constructions of population categories are essentially political constructions and that political change can only occur when differences are openly acknowledged, the labels given to "minority" groups are contested, and each group is permitted to define its own history. To date, this has occurred in the United States, but much less in Israel.

If there is any city in the world which has been considered unique, it is certainly Jerusalem: it is claimed as holy by three religions while control of it is bitterly contested by two of them. Yet in "Changing Places: Jerusalem's Holy Places in Comparative Perspective," Roger Friedland and Richard Hecht argue that the experience of Jerusalem is not entirely unique. For one of India's most sacred sites, the Ramjanmabhumi/Babri Masjid in the city of Ayodhya in India, has also been the focus of long-term violent conflict between religions, in this case between Hindus and Muslims. Friedland and Hecht's essay suggests that such conflicts are not simply "symbolic." Rather they represent substantive disputes over the scope and nature of state authority and political power. Their analysis points to a kind of convergence between the Israeli experiences and that of other countries, but in this case one rooted as much in pre-modern as in modern or post-material sensibilities.

The final four essays in this volume place various aspects of Israeli public policy in comparative perspective. Morag-Levine and Vogel find only modest policy convergence between Israel and other developed countries. "Imported Problem Definitions, Legal Culture and the Local Dynamics of Israeli Abortion Politics," by Noga Morag-Levine compares abortion politics and policies in Israel and the United States. The efforts of American-inspired activists on both sides of the abortion debate issue to politicize this issue in Israel have largely failed: in marked contrast to America, abortion policy in Israel is relatively uncontroversial.

In America, the debate over the legalization of abortion has revolved around legal and political rights, making it highly contentious. However, Israelis, unlike Americans, accept the state's intrusion into numerous aspects of private life; thus the bearing of children is considered the legitimate business of the state and there is no question of a "right" to an abortion. But paradoxically, while the law and politics of abortion policy differ substantially in the two countries, the actual availability of abortion is virtually identical.

"Israeli Environmental Policy in Comparative Perspective," by David Vogel explicitly addresses the twin themes of domestic change and policy convergence. Vogel notes that while Israel's environmental policies during the state's first decades were roughly comparable to those of other developed nations, and even exemplary in the area of reforestation, during the 1970s and 1980s Israel was an environmental laggard. While it can claim some policy accomplishments, on balance, its policy implementation in the areas of pollution control, land-use planning, and conservation lagged behind those of other affluent democracies. Yet recently the forces of globalization and modernization are beginning to increase the visibility of environmental concerns within Israel – yet another sign of its "normalization."

The two final essays in the comparative public policy section, "The Gender and Pacifism Hypothesis: Opinion Research from Israel and the Arab World," by Mark Tessler, Jodi Nachtwey, and Audra Grant and "The Promised Land of the Chosen People is not all that Distinctive: On the Value of Comparison," by Ira Sharkansky both present additional evidence of Israel's lack of uniqueness. The former article compares the attitudes toward war and pacifism between men and women in Israel and a number of Arab countries, finding no differences. Sharkansky's essay is more far ranging, comparing Israel with respect to the role of religion in civic life, income inequality, and automobile fatalities. In each case, he finds no case for Israeli uniqueness. It is changing, but not in ways that are making it more dissimilar to other nations with comparable levels of economic development.

The articles in this volume suggest that Israel is changing on many dimensions. Many of these changes are similar to those occurring in other societies, leading to a process of convergence. Thus, we read of increasing judicial activism, a drift toward a more individualistic, diverse pluralist interest group politics, changes in the economic role of the state, and a shift in the style of national political leaders. The role of global pressures in facilitating convergence is perhaps most marked in Shafir's discussion of how the business classes in both South Africa and Israel led the push toward substantive policy changes on pragmatic grounds.

Yet, other authors note that change is uneven and that aspects of Israeli society or state formation are limiting convergence. Levi-Faur explains the war-related origins of the Israeli state and makes a "path-dependency" argument regarding the persistence of national policy patterns through time. Likewise, Morag-Levine portrays the futility of those who, seeking to superimpose American abortion politics on Israel, have overlooked distinctive cultural and legal patterns that pointed advocates toward alternative problem definitions. And, as Shalev writes, one of the most distinctive examples of change – the judiciary's shift toward American-style activism – is qualified by the vulnerability of the courts that stems from a lack of an overarching basic law, which in turn results from Israel's distinctive religious/secular tensions.

In sum, these articles suggest that Israel is changing, even converging with the global community on some dimensions, but that the pace and direction of change is uneven. In some areas, change is evolutionary or even glacial, slowed by tradition and entrenched institutions. Dowty suggests one such area in which change will be slow, but seemingly inevitable, namely the struggle to maintain the Jewishness of the state, while easing toward some form of powersharing with the Arab minority. This issue in turn raises a more fundamental one: to what extent will Israel define itself in terms of Jewish values and institutions, thus maintaining its distinctiveness, and on what dimensions will it become increasingly similar to other western pluralist, secular democracies?[18]

The 15 articles in this volume steer a middle ground between a nostalgia for the past that often characterizes continuity-centered approaches and the tyranny of the present that may accompany a preoccupation with change. Israel is changing, the authors suggest, but it nonetheless retains much of its particular character and traditions. Thus, the pressures of the global economy and the modernization are real, but these forces face both conscious and unconscious resistance. Israel continues to struggle with tensions of identity, sovereignty, and national autonomy in the face of the pressures of modernization and globalization as do many other nations. Here, again, Israel is "part of history."

ACKNOWLEDGEMENT

The papers in this issue were originally prepared and presented at a conference on "Israel in Comparative Perspective: The Dynamics of Change" which was held at the University of California at Berkeley, 2–4 September 1996. This conference was sponsored by The Institute of Government Studies, the Eshkol Institute at the Hebrew University, the Clausen Center for International Business and Policy at the Haas School of Business, the Center for Middle Eastern Studies at UC Berkeley, the Association of Israel Studies, and the Israeli Consulate to the Pacific Northwest Region of the United States.

We would like to express our appreciation to Michael Barnett for assisting in the review of the papers, Nelson Polsby for his encouragement of this project, Eric Shultzke for his editorial work, and Serena Joe for her editorial assistance.

NOTES

1. Michael Barnett, "The Politics of Uniqueness: The Status of the Israeli Case," in Michael Barnett (ed.), *Israel in Comparative Perspective: Challenging the Conventional Wisdom*, New York: State University of New York Press, 1996.
2. Jan van Deth, "Comparative Politics and the Decline of the Nation-State in Western Europe," *European Journal of Political Research*, Vol. 27 (1995), pp.443–62.
3. J. Roger Hollingsworth, C. Philippe Schmitter and Wolfgang Streeck, "Capitalism, Sectors, Institutions and Performance," in J. Roger Hollingsworth, C. Philippe Schmitter and Wolfgang Streeck (eds), *Governing Capitalist Economies*, Oxford: Oxford University Press, 1994, pp.3–16.
4. A.P. Hall, "Policy Paradigms, Social Learning, and the State: the Case of Economic Policymaking in Britain," *Comparative Politics*, Vol. 25 (1993), pp.275–96.
5. Ibid., p.279.
6. Ronald Inglehart, *Culture Shift in Advanced Industrial Society*, Princeton, NJ: Princeton University Press, 1990.
7. Clark Kerr, *The Future of Industrial Societies: Convergence or Continuing Diversity?*, Cambridge: Harvard University Press, 1983.
8. Hollingsworth *et al.* (note 3).
9. Ibid.
10. Paul Pierson, "Path Dependence and the Study of Politics," Paper presented at the American Political Science Association, San Francisco, Sept. 1996.
11. Richard Rose, "Dynamics of Democratic Regimes," in Jack Hayward and C. Edward Page (eds), *Governing the New Europe*, Oxford: Polity Press, 1995, pp.67–92.
12. E. Douglas Ashford, *Policy and Politics in Britain: The Limits of Consensus*, Philadelphia: Temple University Press, 1981.
13. Paul Pierson (note 10).

14. A. Gershenkron, *Economic Backwardness in Historical Perspective*, Cambridge: Harvard University Press, 1962.
15. Peter Hall, *Governing the Economy: The Politics of State Intervention in Britain and France*, New York: Oxford University Press, 1986. Kathleen Thelen and Sven Steinmo, "Historical Institutionalism in Comparative Politics," in Sven Steinmo, Kathleen Thelen, and Frank Longstreth (eds), *Structuring Politics; Historical Institutionalism in Comparative Analysis*, Cambridge University Press, 1992, pp.1–32.
16. Roger Friedland and Robert Alford, "Bringing Society Back In: Symbols, Practices, and Institutional Contradictions," in W. Walter Powell and Paul DiMaggio (eds), *The New Institutionalism in Organizational Analysis*, Chicago: University of Chicago Press, 1991.
17. G. John Ikenberry, "Conclusion: An Institutional Approach to American Foreign Economic Policy," in Ikenberry *et al.* (eds), *The State and American Foreign Economic Policy*, Ithaca: Cornell University Press, 1988.
18. This issue is explored in depth and with considerable clarity in Alan Dowty, *The Jewish States: A Century Later*, Berkeley: UC Press, 1998.

Courts as Hegemonic Institutions: The Israeli Supreme Court in a Comparative Perspective

GAD BARZILAI

INTRODUCTION

This article explores significant changes in the public status of the Israeli Supreme Court, which since the 1970s has assumed a central place in Israeli politics, and considers sources of the Court's public legitimacy. I argue that the high, even hegemonic status of the Israeli Supreme Court resembles a global phenomenon that has politically empowered supreme courts in many democracies. The high public status of the Israeli Supreme Court and its involvement in political controversies have two main causes. The first is a fragmentation and polarization of other power centers, including the legislature and the executive, while the second is a cultural Americanization and the prevalence of liberal values in some segments of Israeli society.

These causes of change have enabled the Supreme Court to mobilize three sources of legitimacy: specific, diffuse, and primarily mythical. Transforming those sources of legitimacy into institutional power *vis-à-vis* other institutions, the Court has become a hegemonic institution. This has made the court a popular target for litigation and a forum for airing sociopolitical rifts. A major condition for judicial power is the scope of its legitimacy. The Court's expanded authority cannot be comprehended without a theoretical framework comparing Israel to other nations. As noted above, changes in the status of the Court parallel those in other democracies such as France, Germany, and Italy. This article examines relations between supreme courts, public environments, and judicial legitimacy, explores the sources of judicial legitimacy, investigates the

---

Gad Barzilai is a Senior Lecturer (Associate Professor) of Political Science and a jurist in the Department of Political Science, and also teaches in the Law School, at Tel Aviv University. He is the co-director of the Law, Politics & Society Program at Tel Aviv University. He specializes in law and politics, and conflict studies.

historic sources of faith in the court, and inquires into the sociopolitical limits of adjudication.

PUBLIC ENVIRONMENT AND LEGITIMACY OF SUPREME COURTS

Judicial involvement in value-based political affairs is not unique to Israel. Courts in France, Germany, Israel, Italy, and the United States have addressed political disputes, including executive powers, emergency powers, ethnic relations, education, elections, abortion, military service and disobedience, freedom of association and expression, and property rights.[1] The growing tendency to adjudicate public disputes creates a public sphere into which more groups are subjected to the attention of the court and react to its decisions.[2] The US Supreme Court (hereafter, USSC), for example, has been defined as "one governmental agency among many,"[3] and as a significant pillar in the administrative democracy.[4] While the executive and legislative branches in democracies are linked to the general public through the procedures of elections, supreme courts often lack this institutionalized linkage.[5] Nevertheless, they often maintain visible communication with the general public.

The political nature of judicial review necessitates democratic judicial legitimacy,[6] a concern which protagonists of judicial activism and advocates of judicial restraint have emphasized.[7] Judges are less likely to be replaced or impeached than legislators or elected government officers, and the average career on the bench is frequently longer than those of elected politicians and even many other administrative officials. Public legitimacy is thus crucial if courts are to serve as messengers of democratic virtues.[8] But how can a court engage in democratic discourse and inject norms and values into a democracy without undermining its own legitimacy?[9]

The literature on judicial legitimacy is rich and varied. Some scholars have emphasized the impact of the court's legitimacy on its relations with other political institutions, arguing that public support lessens institutional vulnerability.[10] Others underscore the effect of judicial legitimacy on public compliance with court rulings.[11] My emphasis in this article, however, is on the sources of judicial legitimacy and the institutional and cultural conditions necessary for judicial domination of the political sphere.

There are three commonly proposed theories of judicial legitimacy. The first underscores the irrational aspect of public dispositions towards higher courts. Here, legitimacy is based on public myths of judicial supremacy deriving from their perceived "impartiality," "fairness," "professionalism," "morality," etc.[12] This is called mythical legitimacy, and is based on ideal symbols of the judiciary.[13] These symbols portray the supreme court as an impartial institution whose decisions are based on objective criteria of law and justice. Mythical legitimacy asserts the positive uniqueness of supreme courts in comparison to other state branches and public organizations.[14] Myths regarding supreme courts reflect national narratives. In the United States, these narratives include the reconstruction of the Union and the capitalist order of the post-New Deal welfare democracy.[15] In Israel, the narratives are Jewish nationality and the "need" to fight the perceived siege of the Jewish democracy.[16]

Fiction is a central component of myth.[17] Accordingly, mythical legitimacy is not contingent upon a specific judicial outcome, but rather on the symbolic reflections of the judicial institution. However, a salient court decision that contradicts national narratives or a series of controversial decisions might undermine mythical legitimacy. The probability of such a crisis is low, however, because supreme courts tend to articulate national narratives.

The second possible source of judicial legitimacy is diffuse public faith. This means public support for the judicial institution (e.g., public trust in the court) without specifically referring to the content or repercussions of its concrete decisions.[18] Diffuse support shares an important quality with mythical support in that both address the judiciary in terms of "faith" or "prestige." However, the dissimilarity between the two is pronounced. Diffuse support is primarily contingent upon the judicial policy and the general functioning of the court, and it does not expressively attribute to the court mythical characteristics. Mythical support is, instead, conditioned upon symbols, partly fictitious, which present a transcendent normative context to the court.

The third theory of legitimacy asserts that the general public consciously reacts to specific judicial decisions,[19] an incremental and rational process of agreement with specific court decisions breeding legitimacy based on collective consent.[20] Such a conceptualization has been entitled "hypothesis of positive response."[21] Attitudes towards court decisions tend to adapt to collective values,[22] and, sometimes, reactions to specific judicial rulings are negative. They then reflect tendencies of social dissent. In such cases one does not presume that legitimacy will always be generated. For example, some evidence suggests that the USSC decisions in Furman v. Georgia (1969) and Roe v. Wade (1973) have weakened the Court's public support.[23]

THE ISRAELI SUPREME COURT: A SYSTEMATIC ANALYSIS OF A JUDICIAL CHANGE

The Israeli Supreme Court (primarily in its capacity as High Court of Justice, HCJ) has never been only an administrative court, despite its similarity to the English model. The English model prohibits the Court from abolishing parliamentary laws. Until 1995, the HCJ had never ruled that it might cancel a Knesset's law because of its content. However, since the 1950s, and especially since the 1970s, the Court has advanced characteristics of a constitutional court, in some accordance to the German, Austrian, and American models. According to these models, supreme courts are guardians of the political order, and under specific conditions interfere in political affairs. The Israeli Court has canceled Knesset's laws because of wrong legislative procedures, and developed a bill of civil rights. Since the 1970s, its intervention in parliamentary affairs has become more intensive, and its judicial review of executive acts has been more extensive. Certain constitutional reforms have recently taken place in Israel. Two new so-called Basic Laws, Basic Law: Freedom of Occupation, and Basic Law: Human Dignity and Freedom were enacted in 1992 (with the former reenacted in 1994). Several civil rights, such as the freedom of occupation, the right to property, and the right to freedom, human dignity, and privacy can no longer be infringed unless by legislation supported by an extraordinary majority in the Knesset. The new Basic Laws empower the Supreme Court to rescind normal legislation shown to contradict certain human and/or civil rights. Overall, the reforms that they introduce may cause the Israeli Supreme Court, as a constitutional court, to develop a closer resemblance to the constitutional courts or bodies in Europe, e.g., Germany, and the USSC.

Similarities between the USSC and the HCJ are particularly clear. Both have constitutional powers *vis-à-vis* the executive and the legislature. Both have developed their authority for active judicial review to the degree that both Israel and the US might be defined as judicial-administrative regimes. Moreover, both have adjudicated public issues in the midst of deep conflicts and were crucial for the creation and empowerment of civil rights. They have broadly defined judicable issues, curtailed the scope of the "political question" doctrine and, in turn, have increased their judicial involvement in the midst of severe crises. The HCJ and the USSC should be understood in the context of the Anglo-American legal tradition. Many HCJ landmark decisions have been inspired by American constitutional law, despite (and because of) the lack of an Israeli written constitution and an entrenched Bill of Rights. Both courts have activated *a posteriori* judicial review, or rulings are not based on abstract issues of law but on specific problems raised by litigants. Finally, both courts have faced criticism of judicial activism as being undemocratic and as poor replacements of political debate by verbal legalism.[24]

This kind of western constitutionalism has not been absorbed in the Middle East. Judicial power in the region has often been subjected to authoritarian political and coercive religious institutions. The judicial review activated by the HCJ is one of the rare and prominent exceptions to this historical process. Since Israel's inception (1948), the Supreme Court has functioned within a democratic setting, enjoying relative autonomy *vis-à-vis* the political administration. Although Israel cannot be defined as a western liberal regime, its institutional sphere (in the pre-

1967 borders) has democratic fundamentals, and its cultural setting is marked by a relatively high trust in its democratic institutions.[25]

Until the 1970s, the HCJ had often resisted creating new civil rights, although a judge-made bill of rights did eventually emerge, including freedoms of expression, organization, demonstration, and occupation, all without explicit legislation. Despite Israel's protracted state of emergency, the Court posed restrictions on executive emergency legislation and reduced the probability of the government damaging individual rights. Yet, using formal-legal-administrative arguments of "political question" and "presumption of legality," the HCJ's involvement in civil-political and especially security-military controversial issues remained quite marginal.[26]

What explains the shift during the 1970s? There are two likely explanations for the increasing judicial activism and more hegemonic position of the Court. The first is the growing impact of liberal values on the political culture, combined with the lack of a written constitution in a highly divided, polarized, and fragmented setting. While social rifts have become more severe, political polarization more prominent, and political corruption more frequent, the HCJ has continued to be perceived as one of the most reliable institutions in the country, more reliable than the parties, the parliament, or the government.[27] Not only have public expectations for judicial solutions become more prevalent and diverse, but since the 1970s more politicians and pressure groups have appealed to the Court. Litigation has become a source of political pressure, a means of social communication, and a way to resolve conflicts. In 1950 there were 86 appeals to the HCJ. In 1960, there were 333, and in 1970, 381. After the 1970s, the appeals climbed dramatically: 802 in 1980, 1,308 in 1990, and 2,209 in 1994. This rate of increase in appeals to a supreme/constitutional court can be found in few other democracies,[28] and relative to its number of inhabitants Israel has experienced a massive litigation explosion.

Broad adjudication has focused public attention on HCJ rulings. Various pressure groups and political parties have been prominent in their reactions to its decisions. Media reports about judicial nominations, litigation, judicial decisions, and public reactions to salient rulings have become more frequent. In the midst of hectic public contention about the future of the occupied territories, the HCJ, since 1972, has adjudicated issues concerning military and security activities in those regions.[29] Public controversies regarding the court's judicial powers and rulings have therefore become inevitable.

The HCJ has been reluctant to intervene with the armed forces and other security organizations in the occupied territories. While the Court has recognized the right of Palestinians, most of whom are not Israeli citizens, to appeal, it tends to support arguments raised by state authorities.[30] Hawkish-right protagonists have nonetheless criticized the HCJ, claiming that the country's war management should not be based on legal texts. The Palestinians captured by the security forces, their argument has asserted, should not enjoy the legal right of standing before the court or any remedy. In contrast, the dovish-left has criticized the judicial legitimacy granted to state activities in the territories, where the Israeli rule is authoritarian and its adjudication is only an illusion of "democratic supervision." Indeed, in most cases the HCJ has dismissed the appeals of Palestinians, legitimating the military occupation.[31]

This change from a rather secondary public institution to a much more prominent one has continued in the 1980s and the 1990s. The HCJ has become more involved in regulating democratic procedures within Israel. It has molded rules regarding, among others, the validity and disclosure of political agreements,[32] specific legal criteria for excluding radical parties from participation in parliamentary elections,[33] and the legality of governmental appointments for senior administrative positions.[34] Since the beginning of the 1980s, the Israeli public has rather extensively debated HCJ rulings. Recently, international attention has been drawn to the HCJ's decision to approve the massive deportations of Hamas activists (January 1993).[35]

Public opinion has played a limited but distinct role in the expansion of judicial authority. The judges, aware of public debates and contradictory political expectations of their decisions, have been reluctant to engage controversial issues. They have used the notions of "public consensus" and "public morale" to justify intervention in appointments for administrative positions or non-intervention in decisions about the scope of military conscription.[36] Thus, the Court has leaned on public opinion to erode the doctrine of "political question" and enlarge HCJ judicial review.

HCJ's LEGITIMACY: PUBLIC SUPPORT FOR JUDICIAL HEGEMONY

The Israeli public (Arab-Palestinians and Jews) has generally acknowledged the Court's legitimacy and no organized social movement has taken on the Court. Nevertheless, judicial legitimacy is not without limits, and some questions have been raised. A 1991 study established that the Jewish public has generally approved of the Court, and the majority has clearly supported most of the Supreme Court's rulings.[37]

The Supreme Court ruling approving of the exclusion of an Arab-Palestinian political party from Knesset elections (1965) was the most popular decision (81.4%), while the ruling to adjudicate the expulsion of Palestinians from the occupied territories was the least popular (34.8%). Thus, rulings which have plainly preserved political procedures of the Jewish community were the most popular, while those aimed at including Arab-Palestinian political parties in the Jewish political game, and especially decisions that increased judicial supervision over the security authorities in the occupied territories, were the least popular.

Despite a wide range of public reactions to salient decisions (from 34.8% to 81.4% of agreement), the general tendency has favored court decisions (mean = 59.01; median = 59.10; standard deviation = 14.14; coefficient of variation = .24).

Tables 2a and 2b present public reaction to the HCJ as an institution. The public has tended to differentiate between support for the Court's decisions (Table 1) and support for the Court as an institution (Table 2) (t value = 108.02; 2-tail probability < .000). Part 2a exhibits confidence in and agreement with its judicial powers and its overall judicial policy, i.e., diffuse support. Part 2b demonstrates ideal symbols related to the Court, i.e., mythical support. My empirical tests show that those two types of legitimacy are somewhat different in the public view (t value = 145.69; 2-tail probability < .000).

Approval of the Court as an institution was more pronounced than approval of its specific rulings (mean = 66.20; median = 67.40; standard deviation = 15.25; coefficient of variation = .23). As Table 2 demonstrates, the most popular attitude was the support in principle of a broad judicial review (92.4%). Yet, the Jewish public considered Israeli-Arab-Palestinians as outside the scope of the Court's guardianship. The least popular attitude was granting individual rights for the Palestinians in the occupied territories (34.9%).

Given this high level of specific, diffuse, and mythical legitimacy, the HCJ has enjoyed greater public legitimacy than its American counterpart.[38] In fact, the scope of judicial legitimacy given to the HCJ is broader than the legitimacy conferred to any of the constitutional or supreme courts in Europe and South Africa.[39] Hence, the HCJ can mobilize more social forces and political groups in order to be a hegemonic institution. While the scope of public legitimacy for the HCJ has been broad, measured and analyzed at the collective level, the sources of such a judicial legitimacy should be analyzed at the individual level, and at the historical level of cultural origins. It has been already established that, at the individual level, mythical symbols were the main source of judicial legitimacy. Table 3 presents the results of a rotated factor analysis of individual dispositions based on the data set of 1991. It reveals three main sources of legitimacy.

The first and the most prominent source of judicial legitimacy is myths. It has had two dimensions: Factor A has reflected the perception of the HCJ as an institution significantly "contributing" to the State (factorial grade, fg 84.6). This type of perception indicates mythical support. The HCJ has been publicly categorized as an institution similar to the army (IDF), the State Comptroller, and the police, all of which are perceived as "contributing" a great deal to the State, and as national, a-political, professional, objective, and protectors of the State. Only 10.2 percent hesitated to define the court as "contributing" to the State, and only 2.1 percent have opposed such a definition. Hence, Factor A articulated public myths. The Court was not only perceived as functional to the Israeli

TABLE 1
PUBLIC REACTIONS TO SUPREME COURTS DECISIONS

Question and its number in the questionnaire	Pro	P.C.	Con	N	
(Q. 39) Exclusion of an Arab political party from parliamentary elections, if it strives to change the regime	81.4	8.9	9.8	100.1	[944]
(Q. 41) HCJ should not intervene in executive's decisions to release or not to release Palestinian guerrillas jailed in Israel	75.4	14.3	10.3	100.0	[970]
(Q. 36) Military disobedience is illegal	74.8	12.1	13.2	100.1	[975]
(Q. 35) Right of Standing should be broadened to extreme cases of constitutional grievances even if appellant has not suffered damage	73.4	15.5	11.1	100.0	[959]
(Q. 42) HCJ is authorized to nullify executive decisions which don't include considerations important for the preservation of democracy	68.6	20.6	10.9	100.1	[957]
(Q. 40) HCJ will not adjudicate pure governmental political issues like diplomatic relations with Germany	64.3	23.3	12.6	100.2	[959]
(Q. 43) Palestinians should be equipped with the same protective Gas masks, as Israeli citizens, during the Gulf War	60.1	17.2	22.7	100.0	[972]
(Q. 25) Military censorship on the press is prohibited unless the publication will constitute a proximate danger to national security	59.1	21.1	19.7	99.9	[979]
(Q. 53) HCJ will intervene in governmental decisions regarding activities of economic organizations	55.8	33.4	10.9	100.1	[962]
(Q. 34) HCJ recognizes right of Palestinians in the occupied territories to appeal	54.4	18.6	27.0	100.0	[976]
(Q. 37) Exclusion of a militant right-wing Jewish party from parliamentary elections	50.4	15.9	33.6	99.9	[973]
(Q. 27) Palestinians should enjoy a right to be heard in court, before the security authorities inflict a punishment of house demolition, unless an immediate military need dictates otherwise	50.0	20.1	29.9	100.0	[970]
(Q. 26) HCJ will nullify decisions of the security authorities, which do not attribute a sufficient importance to human rights	46.4	25.9	27.6	99.9	[970]
(Q. 38) Inclusion of radical Arab-Jewish political party in parliamentary elections	36.2	22.4	41.4	100.0	[965]
(Q. 51) HCJ has the authority to nullify decisions to expel Palestinians from the occupied territories	34.8	18.9	46.3	100.0	[974]

Pro: those respondents who replied "support very much" or "support;" Con: those respondents who replied "oppose very much" or "oppose;" P.C.: those respondents who replied that they "partially support and partially oppose." N: valid percentage, and in brackets number of respondents to a specific question.

TABLE 2
PUBLIC DISPOSITIONS TOWARDS THE SUPREME COURT AS AN INSTITUTION

Question and its number in the questionnaire	Pro	P.C.	Con	N	
A. DIFFUSE SUPPORT					
(Q. 7) Broad judicial powers of the HCJ are appropriate	92.4	–	7.6	100.0	[948]
(Q. 56) HCJ contributes to the State	87.6	10.2	2.1	99.9	[974]
(Q. 20) Confidence in HCJ	78.1	17.7	4.1	99.9	[979]
(Q. 21) HCJ contributes to the preservation of the Israeli democracy	72.5	22.6	5.0	100.1	[980]
(Q. 12) HCJ should increase its supervision over the parliament (Knesset)	71.5	20.0	8.6	100.1	[970]
(Q. 14) HCJ is a supreme institution and its rulings should be adhered to regardless of the respondent's attitudes	70.4	16.6	13.0	100.0	[979]
(Q. 47) HCJ should increase its supervision over the government	67.4	18.9	13.8	100.1	[976]
(Q. 54) HCJ should enjoy the authority to review Knesset legislation and nullify non-democratic laws	65.6	18.1	16.2	99.9	[966]
(Q. 50) HCJ should increase its supervision over religious institutions	65.2	19.2	15.6	100.0	[976]
(Q. 49) HCJ should increase its supervision over the police	59.8	21.1	19.1	100.0	[977]
(Q. 52) HCJ should continue its policy of not intervening in the discretion of the security authorities	59.0	24.6	16.4	100.0	[966]
(Q. 11) HCJ should strengthen freedom of religion	58.7	24.2	17.1	100.0	[972]
(Q. 10) HCJ should strengthen freedom of expression and demonstration	56.5	28.2	15.3	100.0	[970]
(Q. 44) HCJ should be involved in state–religion issues	53.4	25.9	20.7	100.0	[970]
(Q. 9) HCJ should grant more civil rights to the Israeli Arabs	39.6	29.9	30.4	99.9	[966]
(Q. 48) HCJ should increase its supervision over the army	36.5	23.6	40.0	100.1	[976]
(Q. 8) HCJ should grant more individual rights for the Palestinians in the occupied territories	34.9	27.1	38.0	100.0	[971]
B. MYTHICAL SUPPORT					
(Q. 13) HCJ is politically neutral	85.5	–	14.4	99.9	[948]
(Q. 33) HCJ is the protector of the citizen vis-à-vis the authorities	79.4	16.3	4.4	100.1	[971]
(Q. 32) HCJ operates in wisdom	79.2	16.6	4.1	99.9	[967]
(Q. 29) HCJ is the public body with the highest morality in the country	71.7	17.6	10.7	100.0	[974]
(Q. 31) HCJ examines every relevant argument without discrimination	70.8	21.1	8.1	100.0	[968]
(Q. 30) HCJ represents the common citizen	66.8	18.8	14.4	100.0	[972]

Note: Categories as in Table 1.

TABLE 3
DIMENSIONS OF PUBLIC DISPOSITIONS TOWARDS THE SUPREME COURT; FACTOR MATRIX*

Specific Legitimacy	Diffuse Legitimacy				Mythical Legitimacy	
Arabs and Palestinian Rights	Judicial Empowerment of Civil Rights	Supervision over other Institutions	State–Religion	Diffuse Dispositions	Judicial Myths	Perceived as 'Non-Political'
Right of appeal (-.71)	Freedom of expression and demonstration (.58)	Police (.68)	Religious affairs (.59)	Confidence (.77)	Fairness (.74)	IDF (army) (.67)
Right to be heard (-.64)	Freedom of religion (.58)	Government (.67)	Religious Institutions (.48)	Satisfaction (.63)	Representation of citizens (.63)	State Comptroller (.52)
Individual rights for Palestinians (.63)		Army (.65)		Contribution of the court to democracy (.43)	Guardianship (.61)	HCJ (.49)
Exclusion of Jewish militant political party (.56)		Religious Institutions (.54)			Wisdom (.60)	Police (.49)**
Inclusion of Arab-Jewish political party (.56)					Highest morality (.56)	
Need that security authorities will respect human rights (.53)						
G(FG 53.8)	F(FG 63.3)	E(FG 63.8)	D(FG 64.3)	C(FG 69.8)	B(FG 71.0)	A(FG 84.6)

* numbers in parentheses indicate a variable's loading on the overall factor
** in addition to this factor, another has been detected which includes institutions defined as political (fg. 59.5): the parliament (.74), the parties (.65) and the government (.63).
a. all computations are based on rotated factor analysis (communalities, eigenvalues, factor loadings) while initial matrix was formed by factor extraction by using the Principal components analysis of the SPSS (V 4.0).
b. the t values between the factors are significant at the level of p<.0001 in two tailed probabilities.

democracy, it was also categorized as a non-political institution in contrast to the Knesset, the political parties, and the government. Those bodies were perceived as somewhat damaging to the State, probably due to their image as partisan, self-interested political institutions.

The second dimension of mythical legitimacy (Factor B) involves expressively articulated myths towards the HCJ (fg 71). The Court was perceived as fair because it "investigates every argument brought before the bench without bias and discrimination" (70.8%). In addition to its procedural justice, the court was conceived as "representative of the ordinary citizen" (66.8%), one which "operates in wisdom" (79.2%), and "takes care that the authorities will not harm the citizen" (79.4%). The public imagined the court as "the institution with the highest moral authority in the country" (71.7%). These images are myths, not because they are wholly fictitious, but because they abstract relative facts into absolute "realities" which have become part of the collective discourse.

Institutional reliability (diffuse support) is the second most important source of judicial legitimacy. It was primarily attributed to institutional faith (Factor C, fg 69.8): confidence in the court, satisfaction with the court's overall functioning, and belief that it contributes to the preservation of the Israeli democracy. Such support was very widespread: only 4.1 percent had no confidence in the court; only 11.4 percent were dissatisfied with the overall institutional functioning of the court; and only 5 percent rejected the belief that it helps to preserve the Israeli democracy. Factors D (fg 64.3), E (fg 63.8), and F (fg 63.3) articulated diffuse support as well. Yet, while Factor C manifested diffuse support for the institution or its overall judicial functioning, Factors D, E, and F expressed diffuse support for the exertion of judicial review in defined public spheres.

Factor D exhibited diffuse support for adjudication of religious affairs. The public tended to encourage secular judicial intervention in national religious issues in order to separate religion from state (53.4%). The public also favored more judicial supervision by the HCJ over religious institutions (65.2%). The fifth dimension (Factor E) showed public support for judicial supervision over the executive and its agencies (primarily government [67.4%] and police [59.8%]); while only a minority supported judicial supervision over the military (36.5%). The sixth dimension (Factor F) reflected public support for judicial review which empowers civil rights, primarily freedom of expression and demonstration (56.5%), and freedom of religion (58.7%). The common characteristic to Factors D, E, F was diffuse support for broad judicial review over public institutions, except for the army.

The third and the least important source of judicial legitimacy was support for specific Court rulings regarding the Palestinians in the occupied territories and Israeli-Arab-Palestinians (Factor G, fg 53.8). Positive responses to several salient rulings were the source of specific legitimacy. Factor G included three types of public reactions: positive, negative, and mixed. Positive reactions indicated approval of granting the Palestinians procedural rights; negative and mixed reactions indicated opposition to granting the Palestinians far reaching procedural or substantive rights.

Positive responses were given regarding the following decisions: the Palestinian procedural right of standing (54.4%); the Palestinian right to be heard prior to the demolition of his/her house by the authorities, so long as there is no contrary "immediate military need" (50%); exclusion of the Jewish, ultra-nationalist party of Rabbi Kahane from the Knesset elections (1988) (50.4%); supplying Palestinians in villages around Jerusalem with gas masks, on the eve of the Gulf War (60.1%). Negative responses were expressed to the following rulings: empowering Palestinians with individual rights (38% opposed, 34.9% agreed); inclusion of the leftist Arab-Palestinian-Jewish "Progressive List" in the 1988 Knesset elections (41.4% opposed, 36.2% agreed); HCJ authority to prevent the expulsion of Palestinians from the territories (46.3% opposed; 34.8% agreed). Mixed reactions were formed regarding the empowerment of Israeli-Palestinian-Arabs with civil rights (only 39.6% approved; 30.4% opposed; 29.9% reserved); prohibiting security forces from acting in ways that do not respect human rights (only 46.4% agreed; 27.6% opposed; 25.9% reserved).

The 1991 data set has explored prevailing public mood among the Jewish population in the end of the 1980s and the beginning of the 1990s. This public was inclined to adopt a more secular and liberal discourse that respected litigation as a source of raising issues to the agenda, mobilizing resources, and resolving disputes. Hence, the large support for tightening the judicial supervision over the religious institutions. This spirit of Americanization, i.e., a respect for a discourse of individual rights, is reflected in this 1991 poll, but it was confined to the Jewish public. The Jewish public was reluctant to include the Arab-Palestinian minority in its liberal discourse of individual rights. The Court was perceived as a Jewish institution that was suppose to grant rights to Jewish litigants. The Court was also perceived as different from other political institutions as the government, the political parties, and the Knesset. While the Court received high levels of popular confidence, the latter institutions were perceived as unreliable. This mirrored the polarization and fragmentation that generated a decline in the faith given to democratic institutions and to democratic practices of election and representation. The HCJ was perceived, on the other hand, as different. Due to the myths referred to it, the Court was considered to be detached from the inefficient and corrupted politics.

HISTORICAL SOURCES OF MYTHICAL AND DIFFUSE SUPPORTS

Jewish sacred law (*halachah*), German democratic law, English common law, and American constitutional law have all affected the Israeli legal system. *Halachah* emphasizes the importance of litigation as a method of conflict resolution. German law underscores the supremacy of state values (*Rechtsstaat*) and obedience to its agencies while preserving democratic procedures. English common law engenders legal formalism as a means to facilitate legal discourse, and American law stresses the supremacy of individual rights. English common law and German law underscore the "rational" and "objective" nature of law and judges. They were very influential among judges of the HCJ until the 1970s. This was due to the legal education of the justices. Until 1970, 13 out of 16 justices who served in the HCJ (1948–1969) studied law in Germany (six) or England (seven). After 1970 (1970–1992), however, 11 out of 20 appointed justices learned law in Israel, while only two judges studied in Germany and one in England.[40] Judges educated in Israel were more exposed to the American rhetoric of individual rights than judges who were educated in Europe. After the 1970s, the American liberal rhetoric has also characterized the legal discourse among the legal community. This was reflected in legal texts, legal arguments, court rulings, and courses in law schools.

Jewish law and English common law have had a special impact on the formation of legal principles that ascribe preferences to judge-made laws, based on a process of interpretations and *stare decisis*. *Halachah* and common law presumed that judges symbolize pure wisdom, pure morality, and objectivity. Despite the frequency of illegal instances in Israeli politics, the legitimacy of the HCJ has not often been questioned.[41] Historical changes in judicial doctrines have had their effects as well.

Before the 1970s, the HCJ was not perceived among other elite as a source of political intimidation. The Court excluded itself from adjudicating issues governed by counter elite: religious issues were primarily submitted to religious tribunals, military issues were often discussed in military courts, parliamentary procedures were formed and altered almost exclusively by the parliament, and partisan procedures were formed and altered by the political parties. The Court was therefore seen as remote and irrelevant to politics. This distance partly resulted from disagreement within the Court on the scope of adjudication. In formal terms, the contention was about the judicial definition of the "right of standing"[42] and the theory and practice of justiciability. In essence, the dispute was over the desired involvement of the Court in the political setting. The predominant position of the Court advocated restraint, and fear of anti-judiciary legislation was a strong motive for this restraint.

The change to more active judicial review since the 1970s was built on public images of the Supreme Court, forged during governmental crises. Frequent instances of government corruption have generated public expectations of "order" and "responsibility." The absence of a written constitution has aggravated public demands for increased judicial involvement. The HCJ has been considered a reliable institution (for many, the only reliable civil institution) for creating and preserving a governable political order. The polarization and severe factionalism within the parliament and the inefficiency of the government have transformed the Supreme Court into a consensual political institution.

The process by which justices are selected and nominated contributes to their reputations as non-political and professional actors. In Israel, justices are nominated by a "professional" and "independent committee." In France, Germany, or the United States, judges in the supreme/constitutional bodies are rarely politically anonymous,[43] while in Israel they have only rarely been politically known. In spite of the prevailing myth, however, two facts have been very clear about justices of the HCJ. First, they often side with government policies, and, second, incumbent justices have only seldom and very reluctantly supported nominations of potential dissenting justices.

ADJUDICATION WITHIN LIMITS

The legitimacy that advanced the HCJ to hegemonic position came with limits. Traditionally, the Court was careful not to intervene in the legislative body in a way that might raise anti-judiciary legislation. For example, in 1995 a draft of a coalition agreement between the ultra-orthodox party of Shas and Labor was signed, whereby the parties consented to alter in legislation any ruling of the Court against the "religious–secular status quo." An appeal was submitted to HCJ against the validity of that agreement. In a split voting of the bench, the appeal was dismissed.[44]

This tradition of respecting the legislative body was relevant even under the leadership of Chief-Justice Aharon Barak, who accelerated the expansion of the Court's judicial review. In 1993 Barak asserted that the HCJ should be able to strike down Knesset laws.[45] He was not the only justice to declare it, but under the influence of the liberal discourse, and facing the polarized fragmentation of the Israeli body politics, his declarations formed a new image of the Supreme Court. Barak's stance became the formal judicial policy of the Supreme Court, which ruled in an *obiter dicta* in 1995 that it held constitutional power to supervise the content of Knesset legislation and nullify a law that cannot be reconciled with the values of Israel as a "democratic and Jewish state."[46]

But the HCJ was careful not to enforce its power, and as of 1997 no Knesset law had been abolished by the Court. On September 24, 1997 the HCJ canceled a clause in a law dealing with vocation of brokers in the stock market. While the general appeal to abolish all legislation in this matter was dismissed, the Court claimed that a specific clause imposed too many restrictions on brokers, contradicting the Basic Law: Freedom of Occupation.[47] The Court may invalidate Knesset laws in the future, but will likely do so only after considering the possible reactions of the elites, public institutions, the government, and the Knesset. In the case of the stock brokers, the HCJ did not involve itself in a sphere that could generate a sociopolitical change and incite significant opposition to the Court.

In addition to institutional caution, the Court has operated under the constraints of two national narratives: Jewishness and national security. In adjudicating controversial issues, the Court has sought to preserve its public image as a majoritarian, Jewish, and security-minded institution. Hence, while the political setting was highly fragmented and polarized, the Court has not challenged any major tenet of the Israeli political regime, it has not altered any fundamentals of the Jewish character of the state, and it has not questioned the military regime in the territories or the dominance of security considerations in Israel's public life. While the HCJ has issued few liberal rulings in the field of freedom of expression *vis-à-vis* national security, it has generally acted more as an agent of political maintenance than as an agent of sociopolitical change.

The pervasiveness of judicial myths has been dominant within the Israeli society, though not at the same intensity. The empirical findings analyzed above point that the Jewish secular public has inclined to grant a high degree of support to the Supreme Court. The findings are from 1991, and since then the drift has probably been stronger. From 1993 until the elections of 1996, the period of the Labor-led peace process, the HCJ experienced its most distinct liberal period. In a series of rulings, the Court ruled in favor of gender equality and homosexual rights, restricted the power of the Chief Rabbi and the orthodox religious establishment, and enhanced its judicial supervision over the military.[48] All those rulings have been favored by the secular Jewish public. The few public opinion polls conducted since 1991 suggest that indeed the Court's popularity has not diminished. For secular Israeli Jews, the Court has been a source of stability.

Israeli-Arab-Palestinians also grant high level of diffuse and mythical support to the Supreme Court. Minority lawyers and political activists see the HCJ as their last resort of hope for a sociopolitical change in Israel, this despite the fact that most of their appeals were dismissed by the HCJ, primarily those dealing with land confiscation. Arab-Palestinian activists generally identify the Court as a Jewish institution, but see its 'professional' facet as rendering more 'objective' judgments than any other public (and Jewish) institution.[49] The fact that courts are controlled by one ethnic group and yet are legitimatized by other groups and classes is a striking global phenomenon.

The HCJ is less acceptable among the orthodox religious public in Israel, especially the ultra-orthodox public, than among the secular public. The orthodox public has inclined to perceive its prime loyalty to the *halachah*, while the virtues of state's law were contingent upon its reconciliation with and inclusion of halachic principles. Judicial rulings that incrementally restrained the social control of orthodox religious institutions decreased the popularity of the HCJ among the Zionist-religious public. Yet, the diffuse and mythical legitimacy have not been completely eroded. Most of the Zionist-religious public has conceived the HCJ as a reliable Jewish institution, and tended to comply with its rulings.[50]

Such perceptions and behavior depend on the Court's rulings. As a reaction to the Court's more liberal rulings in the 1980s and especially in the 1990s, an anti-judiciary coalition accused it of taking an anti-religious stance. Political attempts to stop the Court's judicial activism included suggestions of religious MKs to restrict the HCJ's authority to decide in state-religious issues and a suggestion to limit the position of Aharon Barak as a Chief Justice. These initiatives were raised following the ruling of the Court in favor of equality in benefits to homosexuals and heterosexuals in the working place.[51]

Opposition to the HCJ intensified after the Netanyahu-led Likud rise to power in the 1996 elections, due to its reliance on the support of the religious parties. Reluctant to further sacrifice legitimacy among the religious public and face anti-judiciary measures, the Court also hoped not to lose legitimacy among its main audience – the middle class, secular, and Jewish public. Hence, the HCJ has been more careful in its tendency to impose judicial norms. The Court would intervene, however, if the issue raised clearly necessitated judicial intervention based on the Court's previous rulings, if no severe opposition to the Court was expected, or if the judicial intervention was in accordance to a majoritarian public mood.[52]

CONCLUSIONS

The Israeli case of judicial change is not unique. The ability of courts to translate its sources of judicial legitimacy into a better bargaining position through political fragmentation and polarization has occurred in other countries, including Germany, Italy, and the United States. In addition to the widely noted US case, the fragmented parliament in Italy in the 1980s and 1990s, and the fragmented political structure in Federal Germany, at the level of the Lander (states), have generated a more active judicial review in the political sphere.[53]

The change in the HCJ's public position has been evident, from a more restrained judicial approach prior to the 1970s, to a more active one since, and from a more passive stance of legitimizing the state to a position of articulating and imposing norms. Such a change was possible due to the HCJ's multidimensional legitimacy, chiefly its mythical legitimacy, in a fragmented and polarized fabric. The Americanization of the Israeli setting, the increasing effect of a liberal discourse of individual rights and litigation, has fueled an immense increase in appeals and litigation at the HCJ regarding political issues, and the Court has contributed to this by signaling about its aspiration to become a hegemonic institution. This judicial expansion has led to challenges regarding the Court's legitimacy. In a divided society like Israel, this might result in more serious challenges to the Court and in turn in more initiatives to halt its drive to gather more political power.

The case of the Israeli Supreme Court is comparable, and yet it has, like any other case study, its own uniqueness. The cultural sources of the myths should be traced in the history of the Israeli legal and political culture. The same can be said about the timing of the change from one to another judicial strategy. In this article I have dealt primarily with broader variables of judicial legitimacy which have comparable and theoretical value. This study illuminates the need to further explore changes in public environment of supreme courts, and to evaluate three facets of judicial legitimacy (specific, diffuse, and primarily mythical) which accompany changes in the public position of supreme courts.

ACKNOWLEDGEMENTS

This article benefited from comments made by Robert A. Dahl, Bruce M. Russett, Ian Shapiro, and Rogers M. Smith from the Department of Political Science, Yale University, and Pnina Lahav from the Boston Law School, Boston University. David Levi-Faur, Gabriel Sheffer, and David Vogel have contributed their own useful comments during their editing work on the volume. Helpful comments were also made by the participants of the panel about legitimacy, compliance, and the roots of justice, in the MidWest Political Science Association (1995): Gregory A. Caldeira, James L. Gibson, Allen E. Lind, Albert P. Melone, and Peter D. Russell. Thanks.

NOTES

1. Archibald Cox, *Court and the Constitution*, Boston: Houghton Mifflin, 1987; Harold H. Koh, *The National Security Constitution: Sharing Power After the Iran-Contra Affair*, New Haven, CT: Yale University Press, 1990; Morton J. Horwitz, *The Transformation of American Law 1870–1960: The Crisis of Legal Orthodoxy*, New York and Oxford: Oxford University Press, 1992; Robert J. Mckeever, *Raw Judicial Power? The Supreme Court and American Society*, Manchester and New York: Manchester University Press, 1993.
2. Alexander M. Bickel, *The Least Dangerous Branch*, New York: Bobbs-Merrill, 1962.
3. Martin M. Shapiro, *Law and Politics in the Supreme Court*, New York: The Free Press of Glencoe, 1964, pp.6, 15.
4. Ward E.Y. Elliott, *The Rise of Guardian Democracy: The Supreme Court's Role in Voting Rights Disputes, 1845–1969*, Cambridge: Harvard University Press, 1974.
5. Henry J. Abraham, *The Judicial Process*, 5th ed., Oxford: Oxford University Press, 1986.
6. Hart J. Ely, *Democracy and Distrust*, Cambridge: Harvard University Press, 1980; Bruce A. Ackerman, *We the People: Foundation*, Cambridge: Harvard University Press, 1991; Paul W. Kahn, *Legitimacy and History*, New Haven, CT: Yale University Press, 1992.
7. Charles L. Black, *The People and the Court*, New York: Macmillan, 1960, p.209; Cox (note 1) pp.375–6; Mckeever (note 1) pp.272–9; Rogers M. Smith, *Liberalism and American Constitutional Law*, Cambridge: Harvard University Press, 1985, pp.67–91.
8. See B.M. Cappelletti, *The Judicial Process in Comparative Perspective*, Oxford: Clarendon Press, 1989, pp.40–46.
9. Paul W. Kahn, *Legitimacy and History*, New Haven: Yale University Press, 1992, p.143.
10. Black (note 7); Samuel Krislov, *The Supreme Court in the Political Process*, New York: Macmillan, 1965; Walter F. Murphy, Joseph Tanenhaus, and Daniel Kastner, "Public Evaluations of Constitutional Courts: Alternative Explanations," in Sheldon Goldman

and Austin Sarat (eds), *American Court Systems*, San Francisco: Freeman, 1978.
11. Stephen L. Wasby, *The Impact of the United States Supreme Court*, Illinois: Homewood, 1970; Malcolm M. Feeley, "Power, Impact, and the Supreme Court," in Theodore L. Becker and Malcolm M. Feeley (eds), *The Impact of Supreme Court Decisions*, New York: Oxford University Press, 1973, pp.218–29.
12. Jerome Frank, *Law and the Modern Mind*, New York: Brentano's, 1930; Max Lerner, "Constitution and Court as Symbols," *Yale Law Journal* 46 (1937) pp.1290–1319; Thomas R. Marshall, *Public Opinion and the Supreme Court*, Boston: Unwin Hyman, 1989, pp.132–3.
13. For the general analysis of myths, see H. Tudir, *Political Myth*, New York: Praeger, 1972.
14. Gregory Casey, "The Supreme Court and Myth: An Empirical Investigation," *Law and Society Review* 8 (1974) pp.385–417; Kenneth Dolbeare, "The Public Views the Supreme Court," in Herbert Jacob (ed.), *Law, Politics, and the Federal Courts*, Boston: Little, Brown, 1967; Peter Fitzpatrick, *The Mythology of Modern Law*, London and New York: Routledge, 1992.
15. Bruce Ackerman, *We the People: Foundation*, Cambridge: Harvard University Press, 1991.
16. Pnina Lahav, "A Barrel Without Hoops: The Impact of Counterterrorism on Israel's Legal Culture," *Cardozo Law Review* 10 (1993) pp.529–59; Menachem Mautner, *The Decline of Formalism and the Rise of Values in Israeli Law*, Tel Aviv: Ma'Agalay Da'at, 1993; Gad Barzilai, Ephraim Yuchtman-Yaar, and Zeev Segal, *The Israeli Supreme Court and the Israeli Public*, Tel Aviv: Papyrus, Tel Aviv University Press, 1994 [in Hebrew].
17. Frank (note 12); Peter Fitzpatrick, *The Mythology of Modern Law*, London and New York: Routledge, 1992.
18. Joseph Tanenhaus and Walter F. Murphy, "Patterns of Public Support for the Supreme Court: A Panel Study," *Journal of Politics* 43 (1981) pp.24–39; Gregory A. Caldeira and James L. Gibson, "The Etiology of Public Support for the Supreme Court," *American Journal of Political Science* 36 (1992) pp.635–64.
19. Wasby (note 11) p.237; Greogory A. Caldeira, "Neither the Purse Nor the Sword: Dynamics of Public Confidence in the Supreme Court," *American Political Science Review* 80 (1986) pp.1209–26; Gregory A. Caldeira, "Public Opinion and the American Supreme Court: FDR's Court-Packing Plan," *American Political Science Review* 81 (1987) pp.1139–53.
20. Charles H. Franklin and Liane C. Kosaki, "The Republican Schoolmaster: The Supreme Court, Public Opinion, and Abortion," *American Political Science Review* 83 (1989) pp.751–71; Tom R. Tyler, *Why People Obey the Law*, New Haven and London: Yale University Press, 1990.
21. Franklin and Kosaki (note 20).
22. Tyler (note 20).
23. Mckeever (note 1) p.278.
24. Albert P. Melone and George Mace, *Judicial Review and American Democracy*, Ames: Iowa State University, 1988.
25. Ephraim Yuchtman-Yaar and Yochanan Peres, "Public Opinion and Democracy after Forty-Three Years of Democracy," *Israeli Democracy* 4 (1991) pp.24–7.
26. Mautner (note 16).
27. Barzilai, Yuchtman-Yaar and Segal, *The Israeli Supreme Court and the Israeli Public* (note 16); Martin Edelman, *Courts, Politics, and Culture in Israel*, Charlottesville and London: University Press of Virginia, 1994.
28. Donnald P. Kommers, *The Constitutional Jurisprudence of the Federal Respublic of Germany*, 2nd ed., Durham: Duke University Press, 1997.
29. HCJ 302/72 Hillu V. The Israeli Government P.D. 27 (2) 169.
30. Ronen Shamir, "Landmark Cases and the Reproduction of Legitimacy: The Case of Israel's High Court of Justice," *Law and Society Review* 24 (1990) p.781; E. Eyal Benvenisti, *The International Law of Occupation*, Princeton: Princeton University Press, 1993.
31. Moshe Negbi, *Chains of Justice*, Jerusalem: Kaneh, 1981 [Hebrew]; Pnina Lahav, "Rights and Democracy: The Court's Performance," in Ehud Sprinzak and Larry Diamond (eds), *Israeli Democracy Under Stress*, Boulder and London: Lynne Rienner Publishers, 1993; Barzilai, Yuchtman-Yaar and Segal, *The Israeli Supreme Court and the Israeli Public* (note 16).
32. HCJ 1601/90 Shalit V. Peres P.D. 44(3) 353.
33. E.A. 2,3/84 Neiman and Avneri V. Chairman of the Central Elections Committee P.D.

39(2) 225; E.A. 1/88 Neiman V. Chairman of the Central Elections Committee P.D. 42(4) 177; E.A. 2/88 Ben Shalom V. The Central Elections Committee P.D. 42(4) 749, P.D. 43(4) 221.
34. HCJ 6163/92 Eizenberg V. Minister of Housing P.D. 47 (2) 229.
35. HCJ 5973/92 Israel Association for Human Rights V. Minister of Defense P.D. 47 (1) 267.
36. Yaacov S. Zemach, *Political Questions in the Courts: A Judicial Function in Democracies Israel and the United States*, Detroit: Wayne State University Press, 1976, pp.120–38, 175–240; Barzilai, Yuchtman-Yaar and Segal, *The Israeli Supreme Court and the Israeli Public* (note 16), pp.29–45, 175–90.
37. The questionnaires were disseminated in the framework of another project: Barzilai, Yuchtman-Yaar and Segal, *The Israeli Supreme Court and the Israeli Public* (note 16). I have used the same original data-set, but implemented new procedures and methods in order to investigate the model developed in this article. Personal face-to-face interviews were conducted by a prestigious, private, non-political, and independent research institute ("Dahaf"). Respondents were informed that the questionnaire was designed for pure academic and non-political purposes. Sample size was 1,004 men and women who represented the various sectors and segments of the Israeli society. Israeli-Arab-Palestinians, Jewish settlers in the occupied territories, and soldiers in active duty in military camps were not included in the sample due to methodological difficulties or technical problems involving language differences, translations, special training of interviewers, and accessibility to the potential respondents. All the questions were closed with a choice of five possible answers, from total negation to total consent.
38. Lee Epstein, Jeffrey A. Segal, Harold J. Spaeth and Walker G. Thomas, *The Supreme Court Compendium: Data, Decisions, and Developments*, Washington: Congressional Quarterly Inc, 1994, pp.583–609; Gad Barzilai, Ephraim Yuchtman-Yaar and Zeev Segal, "Supreme Courts and Public Opinion: General Paradigms and the Israeli Case," *Law and Courts* 4/3 (1994) pp.3–6.
39. James L. Gibson and Amanda Gouws, "Support for the Rule of Law in the Emerging South African Democracy," *International Social Science Journal* 152 (June 1997) pp.173–91.
40. Edelman, *Courts, Politics, and Culture in Israel* (note 27) pp.36–7.
41. Ehud Sprinzak, *Every Man Whatsoever Is Right in His Own Mind – Illegalism in Israeli Society*, Tel Aviv: Sifriat Poalim, 1986 [Hebrew]; Barzilai, Yuchtman-Yaar and Segal, *The Israeli Supreme Court and the Israeli Public* (note 16).
42. Zeev Segal, *Standing Before the Supreme Court Sitting as a High Court of Justice*, Tel Aviv: Papyrus Publishing House, 1986 [Hebrew]; Zemach, *Political Questions in the Courts* (note 36).
43. Henry J. Abraham, *Justices and Presidents*, 3rd ed., New York and Oxford: Oxford University Press, 1992.
44. HCJ 5364/94 Velner V. Rabin, Labor Party and Shas P.D. 49 (1) 758.
45. Aharon Barak, "The Constitutional Revolution: Entrenched Basic Rights," *Law and Government* (Mishpat U'Mimshal) 1/2 (April 1993) pp.9–35 [in Hebrew].
46. C. A. 6821/93 United Mizrachi Bank V. Migdal P.D. 49 (4) 221.
47. HCJ 1715/94 The Board of Israeli Investments Managers V. The Ministry of Finance (published 24 Sept. 1997).
48. See, for example, HCJ 153/87 Shakdiel V. The Ministry of Religion P.D. 42 (2) 221; HCJ 953/87 Poraz V. The Mayor of Tel Aviv P.D. 42 (2) 309; HCJ 721/94 EL AL V. Danilovich 48 (5) 749; HCJ 453/94 The Israel Women Organization V. The Israeli Government P.D. 48 (3) 501; HCJ 4541/94 Miller V. The Defence Ministry 49 (3) 94.
49. The data presented here are based on a field research I am conducting among Israeli-Palestinian-Arabs. For some more data, see A. Rattner, "The Margins of Justice: Attitudes Towards the Law and Legal System Among Jews and Arabs in Israel," *International Journal of Public Opinion Research* 6/ 4 (1994) pp.358–70.
50. See Barzilai, Yuchtman-Yaar and Segal, *The Israeli Supreme Court and the Israeli Public* (note 16).
51. HCJ 721/94 EL AL V. Danilovich P.D. 48 (5) 749.
52. For use of such notions also in a game theoretic model, see G. Barzilai and I. Sened, "Why do Courts Accumulate Political Power and Why do they Lose It," Paper presented at the APSA Conference, Washington, DC, 1997.
53. Kommers, *The Constitutional Jurisprudence of the Federal Republic of Germany* (note 28); Alec S. Stone, *The Birth of Judicial Politics in France*, New York: Oxford University Press, 1992.

Israeli Constitutional Politics: The Fragility of Impartiality

MENACHEM HOFNUNG

INTRODUCTION

The power of courts to engage in constitutional politics and to apply judicial review derives, in most countries, from a provision of formal authority and from extension of that authority by the courts. Is it possible, though, that a formal provision of judicial review may lead to a consequent reduction in judicial power to engage in constitutional politics?

Since the late 1940s, western European, eastern European, Asian and Latin American nations have established constitutional courts and equipped them with review powers. These powers of review authorize the courts to assess the constitutionality of laws, regulations or other official actions. The increasing judicial involvement in the political and policy-making processes has been termed "judicialization of politics."[1] This term has two central meanings: (1) The expansion of the province of the courts or the judges, at the expense of politicians and/or administrators, that is, the transfer of decision-making powers from the legislature, the cabinet, or the civil service to the courts; or, at least, (2) the expansion of judicial decision-making methods outside the judicial province proper.[2]

Court powers are used more frequently in the 1990s than before to strike down laws and administrative actions. European, North American and Asian governments, parliaments, and administrators interact differently as a result of this judicial activity.[3] In their comparative study, Shapiro and Stone show how the language, the style, and the outcomes of European policy processes are now different from what they would have been in the absence of constitutional review. Shapiro and Stone

---

Menachem Hofnung is a Senior Lecturer at the Department of Political Science, The Hebrew University of Jerusalem.

identify several main characteristics of the new constitutional politics: (1) Courts may veto legislative initiatives with a crucial, long-term impact on major areas of policy-making; (2) Courts serve as guardians of constitutional rights. The rapidly expanding constitutional politics of rights infects the entire political system because opposition political parties, lawyers, citizen groups, and others realize that rights claims are an effective avenue of social change; (3) Courts affect policy making by applying powers of statutory interpretation and judicial administrative review; (4) By declaring legislative and administrative acts as unconstitutional, courts can force legislators to enter into constitutional dialogue with the courts. They force policy makers to make and seriously consider constitutional arguments, and cast and recast statutory language in light of potential constitutional objections to proposed legislation.[4]

The methods of judicial review described by Shapiro and Stone provide a useful framework for comparative analysis, since they consider both the judicial process and the range of its political implications. In this article, I use the criteria of Shapiro and Stone as a starting point for the study of constitutional politics in Israel and seek to identify the components common to all countries with judicial review in a country (Israel) without formal judicial review. I will then add two other variables, one concerning judicial doctrines employed by courts reviewing political or administrative decisions, and the other dealing with the time required for courts to reach a final decision. I will demonstrate that these two variables add to the understanding of the role which courts play in national politics and in the development and change of the public policy making process.

When speaking of judicial doctrines, I will especially refer to the doctrine of reasonableness. If executive or legislative decisions brought before the court cannot be invalidated by legal criteria, the question remains as to whether the court will still be able to review such decisions on the grounds that they are simply unreasonable. While the grounds for judicial review mentioned by Shapiro and Stone are based on strictly defined legal criteria, intervention on the grounds of reasonableness in political issues touches exactly upon the discretion given to policy makers. When a court applies such flexible criteria to political matters, the scope of its judicial review may be much greater than in a system of merely legal constitutional review, especially if the latter is defined by formal criteria.

The time variable is also crucial when speaking about the political role of the courts. Most scholars who deal with judicial review pay attention to the substantive powers of the courts and especially to those of the supreme or constitutional courts. Not much light has been shed on the speed with which the court can reach a final decision, or the ability of the higher courts to control the timing with which final decisions are delivered. When an applicant brings a constitutional matter to court and has to go through two, three, or four judicial instances, a supreme court frequently renders its decision long after the officials against whom the case was originally brought, have left office, or after the case is no longer as politically important. When courts can hand down final, undisputed decisions within several days after the matter is brought up before the judiciary, they effectively help set the political agenda in real time. This power of immediate intervention can offset some of the weaknesses caused by the lack of substantive powers to review legislative actions.

In Europe and the United States, the courts usually base their constitutional review on an accepted yardstick, namely the constitution (or in the British case, the European Community legislation), when interfering with sensitive political decisions. Judicial review in Israel offers an interesting case. Here, in the absence of a written constitution, the Supreme Court, especially when acting as the High Court of Justice, has been active in national constitutional politics.[5] I will argue that a grant of formal authority in Israel, in 1992, has created a paradoxical situation in which the courts' power to review future legislation and executive policies is jeopardized. This is the case because, to a certain degree, this grant of formal authority has caused the courts to be publicly perceived as partisan actors in the political arena, whereas previously they were viewed as neutral. Furthermore, this shift has induced minority groups to attempt to introduce their own exceptions to the law and thus avoid the implications of judicial review.

THE EVOLUTION OF LIMITED JUDICIAL REVIEW WITHOUT A WRITTEN CONSTITUTION

Upon the founding of the State of Israel on May 14, 1948, the Israeli Declaration of Independence contained an explicit promise to draft a written constitution no later than October 1, 1948. The Declaration issued the powers to draft and enact a constitution to the Constituent Assembly, elected in January 1949. However, both the religious political parties' objection to a constitution referring to the people as the ultimate source of authority, and the secular political parties' subsequent objection to investing ultimate sovereignty in a divine authority, ensured that all efforts to reach a consensus on the language of the constitution failed. In its first legislative act, the Transition Law of 1949, the Constituent Assembly changed its name to the "Knesset" and established itself as "the legislative body of the State of Israel." After debating the matter of the constitution for a year, it became apparent that the Knesset could not draft a constitution without risking the ruling coalition government, which included the religious parties.[6] The Knesset then chose a piecemeal approach and adopted the "Harrari Resolution," which states that:

> The constitution shall be composed of individual chapters, in such a manner that each of them shall constitute a basic law in itself. The

individual chapters shall be brought before the Knesset [...] and all the chapters together will form the State Constitution.[7]

The compromise wording of the Harrari Resolution enabled the Knesset to evade the obligation in the Declaration of Independence to compose a formal written constitution, while preserving its power to enact one. The Knesset would continue to enact new basic laws one by one in the absence of a constitution. Until 1992, nine basic laws were passed, mainly covering the powers invested in the branches of government.[8] Change came incrementally. Then, before the dissolution of the twelfth Knesset in the spring of 1992, three basic laws were passed in two months. These granted the courts new powers of judicial review on primary legislation and on specific political matters. Such powers included the ability to review whether new legislation violates rights protected in the basic laws, such as the rights of human dignity, life, property, freedom of occupation, and others.[9]

Until 1992, the Knesset retained formal legislative powers that only several parliaments in democratic countries (e.g., United Kingdom and New Zealand) held during the same period of time. As a single legislative chamber, the Knesset could change any constitutional principle by a simple majority without fear of possible judicial review. In a legislative process dominated by the executive, this power was reflected in the high flexibility of constitutional principles. Basic laws and constitutional principles were sometimes amended to avoid coalition crises or even to solve personal problems in forming a cabinet government.[10]

Israel's system of judicial review in the early years resembled that of Great Britain in that courts could not review primary legislation. However, by using some of the remedies developed in countries which follow the tradition of the common law, the Israeli Supreme Court was able to expand review powers slowly, especially when acting as the High Court of Justice.

In the Israeli judicial system the Supreme Court operates in two capacities. As the Supreme Court, it serves as the nation's highest court and primarily acts as an appellate court, considering appeals of trial court judgments and appellate decisions of the district courts. As the High Court of Justice (hereafter, the High Court) the Supreme Court acts as a trial court from which there is no appeal. In this capacity, the Court has the authority to issue prerogative writs against branches of government and other authorities operating by virtue of law, in a manner similar to that of the English High Court of Justice.[11] These two judicial capacities complement each other so as to turn the Supreme Court into a powerful actor in national politics. Unlike the division of authority in some European countries, where there is a supreme court for hearing criminal and civil appeals and another constitutional court (such as the Conseil Constitutional in France or the Bundesverfabungsgericht in Germany) to deal with constitutional petitions questioning the enactment or interpretation of primary legislation, the Israeli Supreme Court does not divide its authority. Like the US Supreme Court, the Israeli Supreme Court is the sole supreme judicial instance of the land. However, unlike its American counterpart, the Israeli court does not have to wait for important constitutional cases to rise slowly through the lower tiers of the judicial system. For better or worse, the Israeli Supreme Court, when acting as High Court of Justice, is sometimes asked to make immediate, binding decisions concerning burning political and administrative issues, as they arise.

In the first years after the establishment of the state, the courts exhibited judicial self-restraint when dealing with administrative actions. In those years the Supreme Court (in both judicial capacities but mainly as High Court) had mainly used the powers of administrative review and statutory interpretation.

ADMINISTRATIVE REVIEW AND STATUTORY INTERPRETATION

During Israel's early years, the Court avoided confrontation with the other branches of government. Nevertheless, the Supreme Court did intervene in sensitive political matters by using powers of administrative review and statutory interpretation.[12] By applying strict formal criteria in exercising statutory and administrative review, the High Court of Justice gradually established basic standards of the rule of law, even in security related matters. In the 1970s and 1980s, the High Court began to apply more substantive criteria in reviewing administrative decisions. In one of the most noted judgments of that period, the case of Elon Moreh, the High Court nullified a government land confiscation in the West Bank to build a new settlement. While the Court had previously approved decisions of this nature when convinced that the executive had acted in good faith and within its jurisdiction, this time the Court decided to review the government's decision on its merits.[13] When the Court established that the government had made its decision based on general political grounds and not strictly on national security considerations, as required by international law, the confiscation of land was declared illegal.[14]

Since the late 1970s, the Supreme Court gradually expanded its capacity of intervention through statutory interpretation. It revolutionized the law of standing to such an extent that almost anyone can apply to court on constitutional matters.[15] It extended the doctrine of justiciability, and widened the scope of judicial review to include grounds of reasonableness.[16] The Court held that it has the jurisdiction to examine the decisions of the Knesset and its committees;[17] it established that it will examine every administrative decision on its merits;[18] and it extended the norms of public law to political agreements.[19] In short, even without a constitution, there were very few areas of public life left out of the reach of the Court's review. In the absence of formal judicial review, the courts created and expanded an aggressive tradition of statutory interpretation,[20] which resembled formal judicial review. This pattern of extending judicial procedures into policy making areas not previously characterized by such procedures resembles similar developments in other western countries during the same period, a phenomenon described elsewhere as "Legalization"[21] and "Judicialization II."[22]

Even in the aftermath of the constitutional reform, the Court still uses these powers of administrative review and statutory interpretation to acknowledge rights not prescribed explicitly by law. Thus, for example, in 1994 the High Court voided a ruling of the Grand Rabbinical Court on the grounds that the Rabbinical Court acted outside of its jurisdiction by not applying a law giving equal property rights to women and men in a case of divorce.[23] By returning the case to the Rabbinical Court with instructions, the High Court applied administrative review on a judicial organ (it does not sit as an appellate court on rulings of religious courts), thereby interpreting its previous decisions regarding equal property rights as binding law, affecting all other legal authorities in the country.[24]

THE ACKNOWLEDGMENT OF CONSTITUTIONAL RIGHTS

Over the years, the High Court was able, by judicial interpretation and judicial activism, to establish in the case law several individual and human rights of the kind traditionally entrenched in written constitutions. During Israel's early years, case law, rather than legislation, established and protected rights such as the freedom to engage in any business not prohibited by the law[25] and the freedom of speech.[26] However, in the first three decades, judges generally exhibited judicial restraint and tried to stay away from burning political issues. By applying the doctrines of standing and justifiability,[27] the High Court avoided petitions in which the petitioner was not personally injured by an executive decision. The Court only began to hand down frequent decisions on rights claims, which were in fact class actions, during the 1980s. Part of the change was attributed to the nomination of more active justices. It was also rooted, however, in a new political climate, in which the court was looked upon to intervene and decide on issues traditionally handled by the executive and the legislature.

From 1949 to 1977, in nine electoral campaigns, the elections brought a clear winner. The margin between the winning party and the second largest party was at least 10 percent of the national vote, and in eight of the nine campaigns more than 15 percent. In such a political atmosphere, small parties did not raise excessive demands for joining the ruling coalition, because they could have easily been replaced by other parties willing to join at a more reasonable price. The elections of 1981, however, created a new political balance that would soon affect the Court's role. In the 1981 elections, as well as in the next two campaigns, the governing party was not decided by the elections' outcome, but rather by post elections bargaining. A shift of one small party from Likud to Labor (or vice versa) could have decided the composition of the ruling coalition. Governments were still able to make crucial decisions, such as launching the war in Lebanon in 1982, but only when such decisions were reached by consensus among coalition partners. In many cases, the government found it much more convenient not to decide in controversial matters, thereby keeping peace within the coalition. This situation became even more complicated when the 1984 elections resulted in a virtual tie. In post-election coalition negotiations, each major party secured the support of 60 Knesset members (of 120 Knesset seats).

The 1984 political deadlock was eventually solved with a National Unity Government, with rotation in the post of prime minister between Likud and Labor. In drafting the coalition agreements, the Likud and Labor set up elaborate procedures allowing each party to block the executive and legislative initiatives of the other.[28] This arrangement was extended, with minor modifications, four years later after the elections of 1988. In a parliamentary system, where the legislature is dominated by the executive (leaders of Knesset factions serve as ministers in the government), this meant that the Knesset was not going to make too many independent decisions either. This left the High Court of Justice as the only open channel for deciding matters that were pushed aside, or deliberately left undecided by the executive and the legislature.

The initiative of organized groups to legally challenge the representative institutions' decisions (or nondecisions) was encouraged by the Court's judicial activism and by its willingness to lower the previous high barriers of justiciability and standing, which prevented petitioners from presenting their cases in the past.[29] Over a short period of time, the Court redefined several basic human rights. It allowed two parties, previously banned by the Central Elections Committee to take part in the 1984 elections.[30] It virtually eliminated censorship on theater shows[31] and acknowledged the right of newspaper reporters not to disclose their sources.[32] It limited military censorship[33] and censorship on movies.[34] It ordered the Ministry of the Interior to register as Jewish a woman who was converted to Judaism by a Reform Jewish Rabbi in the United States[35] and ruled against an arrangement forcing women to retire from work five years earlier than men.[36] It forced a Judge at the High Rabbinical Court who became the spiritual leader of a political religious party (Shas) to retire from his judicial post,[37] ordered the inclusion of women in religious councils[38] and in electoral bodies to religious councils,[39] and declared as illegal the Central Rabbinical Council's refusal to grant Kosher certificates to night clubs which offered a program with a performance of a belly dancer.[40] In 1994, without explicitly turning to the new basic laws, the Court upheld a Labor Court decision that a male partner of a homosexual airline steward was entitled to free tickets which were previously given solely to married employees as part of a collective working agreement.[41]

The new basic laws have brought an important change by establishing several explicitly protected rights in the law itself, such as the right to life, body, dignity, property, liberty of the individual, the right to leave and enter the country, and the right to privacy and intimacy and freedom of occupation. The acknowledgment of such rights by the legislature opened the way for the development of broader future court review.

JUDICIAL VETO OF LEGISLATIVE ACTS

In the absence of both a constitution and another legislative chamber, there were very few checks on the power of a parliamentary majority. For many years the Knesset could make and amend any law by simple majority, even a basic law, without court review. The only exception was tied to Section 4 of the Basic Law: The Knesset, which defines the method of Parliamentary elections. This section was entrenched, in that it expressly states that it cannot be amended except by an absolute majority of the Knesset's members. In 1969 the Knesset passed the Party Finance Law providing campaign money only for political parties represented in the outgoing Knesset. This law was challenged before the High Court with the argument that it violated the principle of equality in elections prescribed by the Basic Law: The Knesset, in that it discriminated against new parties. Petitioners further argued that the law, not having been enacted by an absolute majority, was unlawful. The High Court accepted the argument and overturned the law,[42] thereby opening a narrow channel of strictly formal legislative review in cases in which a new law, enacted by a simple majority, violates the principles of an entrenched basic law.[43]

The legislative development that significantly expanded formal powers of judicial review was the enactment of three basic laws in the spring of 1992. The Basic Law: Freedom of Occupation, and the Basic Law: the Government state that they can be amended only by a majority of Knesset members (61 out of 120 members). The Basic Law: Freedom of Occupation even states that it may not be changed "except by a basic law enacted by a majority of Knesset members." The requirement that the change be made not merely by an absolute majority but by a basic law makes this entrenchment stronger than those of previous basic laws.[44]

The third basic law enacted in 1992, the Basic Law: Human Dignity and Liberty, does not contain an expressed entrenchment clause. However, the law sets one balancing test which must be employed in all cases when a right protected by this law is infringed upon. Section 8 of the law states:

> The Rights according to this Basic Law shall not be infringed upon except by a statute that befits the values of the State of Israel and is

directed towards a worthy purpose, and then only to an extent that does not exceed what is necessary, or by regulation enacted by virtue of express authorization in such law.

These new basic laws open to the courts the possibility of overturning any future legislation not conforming with their provisions.[45] They thus mark a clear line between the Knesset acting as a constituent assembly and as a legislature. Although past legislation is protected from judicial review, its interpretation is subject to the provisions and standards of the new basic laws. It is still a narrow constitutional review, limited to legal grounds specified in the basic laws (namely, matters related to human dignity, personal freedom, labor, and free trade or alleged discrimination in these fields). There is no abstract review in the European sense, wherein the court can review *prima facie* the constitutionality of a legislative text, with no connection to concrete litigation involving a statute.[46] Nonetheless, in a decision given in 1995, the Supreme Court, sitting in a rare panel of nine judges, firmly established its power to declare unconstitutional laws which violate the standards set out by the Knesset in the new basic laws.[47] In other cases, the Court used the new powers to give new liberal interpretation to old legislation which placed restrictions on basic human rights. In another landmark case, the Court ordered the army to allow women to take the preliminary exams for entering a combat pilot course (and enlist the ones who pass) on the grounds that previous administrative regulations violate principles of the Basic Law: Human Dignity and Liberty.[48]

The new constitutional legislation proved, however, to be very fragile when faced with a serious political challenge. Several months after the passing of the Basic Law: Freedom of Occupation, the court ordered the Ministry of Commerce to grant a private company permission to import non-kosher meat. In its decision, the Court declared the government's refusal to grant the permit as unconstitutional since it infringed upon the right to engage in any legal economic initiative as established in the new Basic Law.[49] Under the religious parties' pressure, the Basic Law: Freedom of Occupation was amended to allow for future modifications by ordinary laws in the instance of an absolute majority of Knesset members supporting the amendment. Such an amendment, forbidding the import of non-kosher meat, was subsequently enacted. However, as part of the attempts towards securing a parliamentary majority for the amendment, a special reference was made to the Declaration of Independence. This provision, which was added to the law just before the final reading, explicitly acknowledges the principle of religious equality, which may endanger any future preferences granted to Jewish orthodox institutions, thus expanding still further the future of judicial review of primary legislation.[50]

While the new legislation grants the Court new powers, the Court can still turn to its own case law in cases where the new legislation is silent or not clear. One judicial doctrine which played an important role in the expansion of the Court's review was the doctrine of reasonableness.

THE REASONABLENESS DOCTRINE

The doctrine of reasonableness, emanating from English law, holds that an administrative act may be invalidated if it is unreasonable. This doctrine has also been known in the United States, where the courts used the term substantive due process to invalidate popular laws in the early twentieth century.[51] Although the Israeli courts adopted the reasonableness standard in the 1950s, they did not invoke it until the 1980s. In a series of cases in the 1980s, the Supreme Court began to spell out the basis for reasonableness as an independent standard,[52] while only fully applying it in sensitive political cases during the 1990s.

The extensive use of the doctrine of reasonableness in Israeli constitutional law in the 1980s reflects a profound change in the Supreme Court's perception of its role. Traditionally, the Court perceived the legislative and the executive branches as the bodies in charge of reaching political decisions on content of the law, while the judicial function was to apply the law. By the 1980s, the Court began to perceive itself as an organ contributing to the contents of the law and to political decisions, together with the two other branches of government. By employing the doctrine of reasonableness, the Court shifted from ensuring that administrative bodies act within their own jurisdiction to a Court that applies substantive review of the contents of administrative decisions and policies.[53]

In a landmark case,[54] the Labor government ratified the nomination of Yossef Ginossar as the Director General of the Housing Ministry, a decision that was immediately challenged as "unreasonable" by opponents who cited Ginossar's involvement in a state security related cover up. Although Ginossar did not have a criminal record during his duty in the General Security Service, he had been involved in two cover ups. When the first affair became known to the Israeli public, Ginossar and other Shin Bet agents were granted a pardon by the President, after admitting, in writing, of their participation in illegal actions but before charges against them were filed in court.[55] When the government considered Ginossar's nomination, its ministers received full details about the affair and then approved it. Since Ginossar was never convicted in any criminal proceedings, there were no formal legal grounds to invalidate the nomination. Nevertheless, the High Court still found the nomination illegal, on the grounds that such a decision is so unreasonable that it could be regarded as in contravention of the law and therefore null and void.[56] It is hard to imagine a more blatant example of judicial activism than an executive nomination, issued within the limits of legal jurisdiction, with all the related facts considered, struck down because the judiciary saw it as unreasonable.

By using the reasonableness test, the High Court also forced the Attorney General to reconsider his decision not to file charges against top bank managers[57] and the Police Chief Inspector[58] and, in addition, forced a minister and a deputy minister to resign their posts.[59] In a sense, with respect to public nominations, the principle of reasonableness enabled the court to hold public hearings in cases which involved questionable nominations to high positions in the executive branch.

The application of the reasonableness standard, however, raises some serious questions regarding equality before the law. The same court which decided that it is unreasonable for a prime minister to keep a minister who kept the right to remain silent during a criminal investigation in the cabinet, did not find as unreasonable, decisions to demolish hundreds of buildings[60] or to detain, without trial, thousands of people in the Occupied Territories.[61]

THE JUDICIAL PROCESS AND THE POLITICAL AGENDA

One variable which may have been overlooked in the study of constitutional politics is the speed with which courts can bring an end to a constitutional dispute. Research projects on the judicial process have focused more attention in recent years on the process by which judicial agenda choices are made.[62] In some European countries, constitutional courts may act quickly, but these courts do not handle civil, criminal, and other specialized legal disputes, such that judicial power is diffused among several courts.[63] In Anglo American tradition, most cases reach the supreme or high courts as appeals from lower or intermediate appellate levels in the judicial system. In such systems, important constitutional cases are decided years after the initiation of judicial proceedings. Even when a case finally reaches the highest judicial instance, courts can use their prerogative to refrain from hearing an appeal, a power which may significantly reduce the potential political volatility of a case.[64]

In Israel, the Supreme Court hears criminal and civil appeals in an orderly manner that takes years to bring a case to an end. However, when sitting as the High Court of Justice, it has almost complete control over the timing of the proceedings, including the time of decision in constitutional cases. Our sample shows that out of 198 notable constitutional cases, 25 percent were decided within five weeks of a petition's being filed in court and 91 percent (181 out of 198) were decided within one year after the initiation of legal proceedings. This accelerated pace of constitutional proceedings differs substantially from criminal and civil cases where it takes years of court proceedings before a case is finally resolved (the 24 criminal and civil cases in Table 1 represent a small illustrative sample of criminal and civil decisions with constitutional significance).

TABLE 1
LENGTH OF JUDICIAL PROCEEDINGS, HIGH COURT OF JUSTICE VS.
ORDINARY JUDICIAL PROCEEDINGS

	# of cases	25%	50%	75%	100%
H.C. + E.A.	198	1 day – 1.25 months	1.25–3 months	3.6–7.4 months	7.5–31 months
C.A. + Cr.A.	24	12–16 months	17–25 months	26–48 months	49–72 months

H.C= High Court of Justice; E.A.= Election Appeals (appeals on the decisions of the Central Election Commission, conducted in a procedure similar to hearings before the High Court of Justice); C.A. = Civil Appeals at the Supreme Court; Cr.A. = Criminal Appeals.

Those 222 (198 + 24) decisions, represent all the cases which are included in 9 textbooks on Israeli constitutional and administrative law, covering the years 1948–1992.

Sources: K. Klein, *Constitutional Law*, Jerusalem: Academon, 1992 (Vols. 1–5); D. Kretzmer, *Administrative Law*, Jerusalem: Academon, 1992 (Vols. 1–4).

In 1992, the median duration of proceeding in a pecuniary action in an Israeli District Court was 26.9 months.[65] In that same year, the median duration of proceeding in a civil appeal to the Supreme Court (the statistics concerning civil appeals to the Supreme Court are not broken down into pecuniary actions and others) was 22.9 months.[66] This is to say that a typical pecuniary case from its initiation in a district court through to its appeal to and decision by the Supreme Court lasted roughly 50 months. The contrast between civil and constitutional durations of proceeding is clear.

The power of intervening in a political dispute in real time is a double-edged sword. On one hand, it may give the court considerable political power even without its having substantial powers of judicial review. Several examples where the High Court intervened in important decisions without using powers granted under the basic laws of 1992 illustrate this point. A new Likud-led government was inaugurated in mid-June 1996. During the first 60 days of the new government's term, the High Court was called upon to review several of the new regime's policies. In the first case it ruled against the government decision to fire the Head of the Civil Service;[67] then it gave an order against the decision of the Transportation Minister to close off a major road in the city of Jerusalem on Saturdays, approved by the government as a gesture towards religious parties within the ruling coalition.[68] In another petition it upheld Binyamin Netanyahu's decision to appoint Ya'acov Ne'eman as Justice Minister. However, in the proceedings of another petition on the same case, the Attorney General decided, before the submission of an affidavit to the High Court, to initiate an inquiry regarding criminal accusations against Ne'eman, which led the newly appointed Minister of Justice to resign.

On the other hand, such judicial power, when combined with substantial provisions for judicial review, gives the Supreme Court unprecedented political power and have led to subsequent demands for its curtailment.[69] Politicians have noticed the shift of power from the representative bodies to the Supreme Court, and have begun calling for limiting court powers, changing the nomination methods, and taking key issues out of the Court's review. However, the new situation has also fostered a noticeable constitutional dialogue.

THE EVOLUTION OF CONSTITUTIONAL DIALOGUE AND THE COUNTERATTACK ON THE JUDICIARY

Although the term "constitutional dialogue" is referred to, in comparative studies, in the context of judicial review on the constitutionality of laws in view of the constitution,[70] it seems as if this term can be extended to legal systems where there is no single constitutional document with higher normative status. In my opinion, the term "constitutional dialogue" provides a suitable framework for analysis in any given system where primary legislation may be invalidated by the courts because it does not meet the principles or the basic legal documents defining the powers of government branches. When the possibility of invalidating laws by judicial review becomes a recognized constraint which has to be considered in any legislative or administrative proceeding, then the basic condition for the evolution of "constitutional dialogue," with the participation of the three branches of government, is met. Such a dialogue gradually influences the political debate in such a way that the boundaries of political autonomy are no longer defined by the ability to form ad hoc coalitions and secure a simple majority ($n/2 + 1$) for a legislative initiative. When there is a possible conflict between intended legislation and protected basic principles, there is a need for constitutional proceedings to meet the standards of the basic principles/basic laws or, alternatively, for securing the required number of votes within the constituent assembly for amending the basic principles. Political dialogue is no longer confined to the question of desired arrangements and enforcement of the majority's will. Rather, it must also address the question of whether such laws would be approved upon being challenged in court. Such a discussion calls for an understanding of, and for an ability to use, legal texts and constitutional arguments in a political debate.

Some of the effects of the new legislation are felt in the emergence of "constitutional dialogue" in the sense that legislators and executive policy makers begin to debate not only what is good or bad policy, but what has the best chance of surviving the scrutiny of the judicial branch. Until the 1970s, constitutional dialogue involving the courts' input was sporadic and irregular. In fact, there were cases in the early 1950s in which a government blatantly defied court orders.[71] In the late 1970s and early 1980s, especially after the court ruling to remove the Elon Moreh settlement,[72] the possibility of High Court intervention became a noticeable constraint on national policy making. With a strong parliamentary opposition challenging the government's policies in the Occupied Territories, and with more petitions to the High Court, the government could not risk too many legal defeats. Here, the latent power of the Court became evident. We refer not to the ability of the court to set aside wrong decisions made according to the correct procedure, but rather to its ability to prevent harsh decisions based on uncertain legal ground. This is a latent power which is not always possible to gauge since we know more about decisions made and less of options that were considered and dismissed.[73] If it were not for the powers of review of the High Court of Justice, arbitrary administrative decisions would be more common.[74]

The power of review which initially applied only to administrative and judicial acts gradually expanded to legislative matters. It was applied mainly to internal procedures and disciplinary adjudication of the legislature, although in rare cases it touched on substantive legislative matters.[75] However, until 1992 the Knesset kept (with the exclusion of a small number of entrenched clauses in several laws) the powers to amend any law by simple majority, and therefore, a real constitutional dialogue, in which the legislature must consider the possibility of having future legislation invalidated in court, did not evolve fully before the constitutional reform.

A significant effect of the constitutional reform of spring 1992 has been the evolution of constitutional dialogue whereby the courts can affect future legislation and review administrative decisions on new grounds specified in the Basic Laws. Although the Supreme Court has invalidated only one provision in one law since 1992,[76] the new Basic Laws affected judicial interpretation of current laws[77] and have limited the legislature's range of options. Members of the Knesset and government find their own behavior changing in response to the review activities of the judiciary. Legislators now debate not only what is good or bad policy, but what has the best chance of surviving the scrutiny of the judiciary.[78] Technical constitutional arguments are made, debated, and countered by other constitutional arguments on the Knesset floor and in cabinet meetings.[79]

The development of constitutional dialogue was accompanied by other features affecting the status of the judiciary as a neutral, unbiased arbiter in public disputes. The abrupt change in the balance of power between the judiciary and the legislature, although initiated by the latter, increased the formal power of the courts, but damaged considerably the non-partisan image of the judiciary. Although the court system is respected and trusted by a considerable majority of Israeli residents,[80] the role of the courts in the constitutional framework is not yet settled. Influential minority groups, especially the ultra religious parties which for years questioned the authority of courts, realized that political arrangements, attained with parliamentary swing vote tactics, are not immune to court review, even when they are put into primary legislation. The boundaries of political autonomy become much narrower when the courts can declare many ordinary laws as unconstitutional. Suddenly, the justices of the Supreme Court were perceived as pushing their own political agenda.[81] The civil judicial system is viewed by a considerable portion of the Israeli population as an active participant in a political debate, an actor identified with the secular-liberal segment of Israeli society (a segment, which after the elections of 1996, is also identified with the parliamentary opposition).[82]

The political objection to judicial activism of the Court also led to a coalition agreement between an ultra-orthodox religious party, Shas, and the Labor Party, in which an explicit article specified methods of how to limit future intervention of the court in religious matters. Thus the High Court found itself in the delicate position of having to decide on the constitutionality of a coalition agreement, when the decision bore direct consequences for the Court's own powers of review.[83] The High Court decision to turn down the petition may have prevented a political storm and given parties some legal leverage in future coalition agreements, but it also demonstrated the fragile position of the Court. An attempt to decide basic political issues by judicial activism may lead to future political agreements to curb the powers of the Court.

CONCLUSION

The emergence of a strong and active judicial branch is not an isolated, Israeli phenomenon. This development follows a worldwide trend in which courts play greater roles in national politics. Although it was given limited official recognition in Israeli law only in 1992, constitutional review was gradually established without a constitution and without explicitly granting the courts powers to review legislative acts. The Israeli experience shows that such review may be almost as effective as in countries with well defined constitutional review. There are, however, some inherent deficiencies in such an evolutionary model of constitutional review, especially when the courts are called upon to decide sensitive, political questions while there is no national consensus to refer such matters to a non-elected judicial body.

Although the courts can review a sizable portion of new legislation, they can not review old legislation which apparently also defines the courts' powers. The Basic Law: the Judicature, which sets the courts' authority, can still be amended today by a simple majority in the Knesset. The courts are aware of their delicate position in relation to other branches of government. Therefore, the Supreme Court has had to hand down carefully tailored decisions in sensitive political matters.[84] In several cases decided in 1995 and 1996, the Court showed unusual judicial restraint.[85]

The High Court role during the 1980s and early 1990s was crucial in a situation of political stalemate. It helped strengthen democratic tendencies and probably prevented overpoliticization of various spheres of life. In this sense, the Supreme Court's role in public affairs resembles that of a constitutional court in western democracies. However, when the legislature decided to adapt to the new situation and granted the courts powers of limited judicial review, the courts were pushed into the center of political debate. The Israeli judiciary, which enjoyed professional autonomy and which was relatively shielded from political interference, is no longer regarded as a neutral arbiter, but rather, as an active actor in the political arena. As such, professional practices, such as nomination of justices and division of cases between justices,[86] have become the focus of political scrutiny, thereby posing a threat to future impartiality and independence of the judiciary. Unlike other western countries where the courts are gaining power and are portrayed as guardians of democracy, the direction of change in Israel since the mid 1990s finds the Supreme Court faces continuous attack and is labeled by its attackers as an elitist, non-democratic, and unrepresentative institution. There are daily verbal attacks and calls to limit the power of the judiciary and transfer important decisions from the Supreme Court to a proposed new constitutional court with the participation of rabbis and representatives of groups which are not currently proportionally represented in the court system. Accordingly, legal politics are no longer regarded as separate from routine politics. Constitutional politics have become part of routine politics as is the case in most western democracies.

The courts, and especially the Supreme Court, which were able to expand their powers gradually, have found that the new powers may not be fully applicable. In short, the previous "weakness" of not having formally defined review powers made it possible for the Court to incrementally increase its influence without being perceived as threatening the other branches of government. Now, with newly attained formal powers, the added "strength" has proven to be elusive. A considerable number of politicians have discovered the electoral dividends of waging electoral campaigns against the Supreme Court rather than attacking political rivals. Such a situation may induce certain actors in the political arena to support the exclusion of certain groups and certain unegalitarian practices from subjection to judicial review, by amending or enacting new basic laws with various, specific limits on judicial powers.

ACKNOWLEDGEMENTS

Support for this study was provided by the Silbert Institute at the Hebrew University of Jerusalem. It is a pleasure to thank Yoav Dotan, Malcolm Feeley, Danny Breznitz, Uri Resnick, Noam Shapira, Joshua Stayn, and the editors of this book for their extremely valuable comments.

NOTES

1. C. Neal Tate and Torbjorn Vallinder (eds), *The Global Expansion of Judicial Power*, New York: NYU Press, 1995, p.1.
2. Vallinder in Tate and Vallinder (note 1) p.13.
3. Donald P. Kommers, "The Federal Constitutional Court in the German Political System," *Comparative Political Studies* 26 (1994) pp.470–91. Rett R. Ludwikowski, "Constitution Making in the Countries of Former Soviet Dominance: Current Development," *Georgia Journal of International and Comparative Law* 23 (1993) pp.155–267. C. Neal Tate, "The Judicialization of Politics in the Philippines and Southeast Asia," *International Political Science Review* 15/2 (1994) pp.187–97. Torbjorn Vallinder, "The Judicialization of Politics – A World Wide Phenomenon," *International Political Science Review* 15/2 (1994) pp.91–100.
4. Martin Shapiro and Alec Stone, "The New Constitutional Politics of Europe," *Comparative Political Studies* 26/4 (1994) pp.397–420, at pp.416–18.
5. David Kretzmer, "Forty Years of Public Law," *Israel Law Review* 24/3-4 (1990) pp.341–55. Menachem Mautner, "The Reasonableness of Politics," *Theory and Criticism* 5 (1994) pp.25–53. Ronen Shamir, "The Politics of Reasonableness," *Theory and Criticism* 5 (1994) pp.7–23.
6. Emanuel Gutmann, "Israel: Democracy Without Constitution," in Vernon Bogdanor (ed.), *Constitutions in Democratic Politics*, Aldershot: 1988, pp.290–308. Asher Maoz, "The System of Government in Israel," *Tel Aviv University Studies in Law* 8 (1988) pp.9–57, at p.10. Daphna Sharfman, *Living Without a Constitution: Civil Rights in Israel*, New York: 1993.
7. 5 D.K. (Knesset Records) 1743 (1950).
8. For a complete list, see Yitzhak Galnoor and Menachem Hofnung (eds), *Mishtar Medinat Israel: Leket Mekorot (Government of Israel: Selected Readings)*, Jerusalem: 1993 [Hebrew]. For an English translation of the Basic Laws, see Israel's Foriegn Ministry site on the World Wide Web at: http://www.israel.org/gov/laws/.
9. Aharon Barak, "The Constitutional Revolution: Protected Human Rights," *Mishpat Umimshal* 1/1 (1992) pp.9–36. Aharon Barak, "Protected Human Rights: Scope and Limitations," *Mishpat Umimshal* 1/2 (1993) pp.253–74. Daphne Barak-Erez, "From an Unwritten to a Written Constitution: the Israeli Challenge in American Perspective," *Columbia Human Rights Law Review* 26 (1995) pp.309–55. David Kretzmer, "The New Basic Laws on Human Rights: A Mini-Revolution in Israeli Constitutional Law," *Israel Law Review* 26/2 (1992) pp.238–46.
10. For example, the Basic Law: the Government was changed in 1980 to allow the nomination of Simcha Ehrlich as a second Deputy Prime Minister, since this position was already held by Igal Yadin, and the basic law allowed for only one deputy. It was amended again for similar reasons after the formation of national unity government in 1984.
11. Maoz (note 6) pp.49–50.
12. Pnina Lahav, "Foundation of Rights Jurisprudence: Chief Agranat Legacy", *Israel Law Review* 24 (1990) p.229; Shimon Shetreet, "Constitutional Law," *Mishpatim* 19 (1990) pp.573–615, at p.607.
13. Hofnung 1996; Shimon Shetreet, *Justice in Israel: A Study of the Israeli Judiciary*, Dordrecht: 1994, pp.61–78.
14. H.C. 390/79 *Dweikat v. the Government of Israel*, 34(1) P.D. 1.
15. H.C. 217/80 *Segal v. Minister of Interior*, 34(4) P.D. 429; H.C. 428/86 *Barzilai v. Government of Israel*, 40(3) P.D. 505; H.C. 910/86 *Ressler v. Minister of Defense*, 42(2) P.D. 441.
16. Shetreet, *Justice in Israel* (note 13) p.520.
17. H.C. 306/81 *Flatto-Sharon v. Knesset Committee*, 35(4) P.D. 118; H.C. 651/82 *Sarid v. Speaker of Knesset*, 36(2) P.D. 197; H.C. 620/85 *Miari v. Speaker of Knesset*, 41(4) P.D. 169.
18. H.C. 554/81 *Baranse v. Commander of the Central Region*, 36(4) P.D. 247; H.C. 935/89 *Ganor v. Attorney General*, 44(2) P.D. 485.
19. Kretzmer, "Forty Years of Public Law" (note 5); idem, "Political Agreements – A Critical Introduction," *Israel Law Review* 26/4 (1992) pp.407–37; Itzhak Zamir, "Political Contracts," *Israel Law Review* 26/4 (1992) pp.461–98.
20. Amnon Rubinstein and Barak Medinah, *Ha'Mishpat Ha'Constitutioni Shel Medinat*

Israel (Constitutional Law of the State of Israel), 5th ed., Jerusalem: 1996, pp.28–34.
21. Martin Shapiro, "The United States," in Tate and Vallinder (note 1) pp.43–66, at p.62.
22. Tate and Vallinder (note 1) p.516.
23. It should be remembered that the rabbinical courts are empowered by another law to make rulings according to the traditional Jewish law in matters related to marriage and divorce of Jews living in Israel.
24. H.C. 1000/92 Bavli v. the Grand Rabbinical Court, 48(2) P.D. 6. See also C.A. 3077/90 Plonit v. Ploni, 49(2) P.D. 528. In C.A. 3077/90 the Supreme Court overturned decision by a Moslem Religious Court (which is legally entitled to exclusive jurisdiction in Moslem family matters), which exempted an unmarried man from tissue examination for deciding a paternity suit. The man, being sued for child support by an unmarried mother, claimed that Islamic law acknowledges paternity ties only in legal marriage. He contended that the tissue examination could not establish familial relations because he was not married to the plaintiff's mother. The Moslem Court accepted this argument. The Supreme Court ruled that the civil law maintains child support as the ultimate responsibility of the father, and therefore ordered the defendant to pass a tissue examination for establishing responsibility for child support.
25. H.C. 1/49 Bejerano v. Minister of Police, 2 P.D. 80.
26. H.C. 73/53 Kol Ha'am v. Minister of Interior, 7 P.D. 871.
27. H.C. 65/51 Jabotinsky v. Wiezman, 5 P.D. 801; H.C. 40/70 Becker v. Minister of Defense, 24(1) P.D. 238; H.C. 561/75 Ashkenazi v. Minister of Defense, 30(3) P.D. 309; Zeev Segal, Zechut Ha'Amida Be'Bagatz (Standing Before the Supreme Court Sitting as a High Court of Justice) [Hebrew], Tel Aviv: 1986.
28. The ability of the grand coalitions to initiate reforms or new policies was limited by the creation of an inner cabinet of 10 senior ministers, composed of five from each party. The inner cabinet was authorized to make binding decisions on behalf of the entire government on matters of defense, foreign policy, and any other issues presented by either of the parties' leaders. In case of a tie, the status quo would be maintained. Dan Horowitz, "Politics of Mutual Veto: The Israeli National Coalition," in Asher Arian and Michal Shamir (eds), The Election in Israel – 1988, New York: 1990,:p.226.
29. Itzhak Zamir, "Judicial Activism: Deciding to Decide," in Ariel Porat (ed.), Activism Shiputi (Judicial Activism), Tel Aviv: 1993, pp.183–5.
30. E.A. 2/84 Neiman v. Central Elections Committee, 39(2) P.D. 225.
31. H.C. 14/86 Laor v. Council of Reviewing Movies and Plays, 41(1) P.D. 421.
32. H.C. 298/86 Zitrin v. Disciplinary Tribunal of the Israeli Bar, 41 (2) P.D. 337.
33. H.C. 680/88 Schnitzer v. Chief Military Censor, 42(4) P.D. 617.
34. H.C. 806/88 Universal City Studios v. Council of Reviewing Movies and Plays, 43(2) P.D. 22.
35. H.C. 230/86 Miller v. Minister of Interior, 40(3) P.D. 436.
36. H.C. 104/87 Nevo v. High Labor Court, 44(4) P.D. 749.
37. H.C. 732/84 Tsaban v. Minister of Religious Affairs, 40(4) P.D. 141.
38. H.C. 153/88 Shakdiel n v. Minister of Religious Affairs, 42(2) P.D. 221.
39. H.C. 953/87 Poraz v. Mayor of Tel Aviv, 42(2) P.D. 309.
40. H.C. 465/89 Raskin v. Religious Council of Jerusalem, 44(2) P.D. 673.
41. H.C. 721/94 El Al v. Danilovich, 48(5) P.D. 749.
42. H.C. 98/69 Bergman v. Minister of Finance, 27(2) P.D. 785.
43. Itzhak Zamir, "Courts and Politics in Israel," Public Law (1991) pp.523–37, at p.529; Martin Edelman, Courts, Politics, and Culture in Israel, Charlottesville: 1994, pp.13–25. H.C. 246/81 Derech Eretz v. Broadcasting Authority, 35(4) P.D. 1; H.C. 141/82 Rubinstein v. Speaker of Knesset, 37(3) P.D. 141; H.C. 142/89 Laor v. Speaker of Knesset, 44(3) P.D. 529; H.C. 2060/91 Cohen v. Shilanski, 46 (4) P.D. 319.
44. Kretzmer, "The New Basic Laws on Human Rights (note 9) p.241.
45. Section 10 of the Basic Law: Human Dignity and Liberty reads: "This Basic Law shall not affect the validity of any law in force prior to the commencement of the Basic Law." Section 10 of the Basic Law: Freedom of Occupation granted similar protection, for two years, to old legislation.
46. Alec Stone, "The Birth and Development of Abstract Review: Constitutional Courts and Policy Making in Europe," Policy Studies Journal 19 (1990) pp.81–95, at p.81.
47. C.A. 6821/93 Ha'mizrachi Bank v. Migdal, 49(4) P.D. 221.
48. H.C. 4541/94 Miller v. Minister of Defense, 49(4) P.D. 94.
49. H.C. 3872/93 Mitral v. Prime Minister 47(5) P.D. 485.

50. When the implications of this amendment were made clear to the religious parties' representatives (which, ironically, supported the amendment), it caused another political storm. However, no one is willing, at this moment, to propose an omission of the Declaration of Independence from the book of laws.
51. Lawrence M. Friedman, *American Law*, New York: 1984, p.187.
52. H.C. 389/80 *Dapei Zahav v. Broadcasting Authority*, 35(1) P.D. 421; H.C. 910/86 (note 15); H.C. 935/89 (note 18).
53. Mautner (note 5) pp.34–5.
54. H.C. 6163/92 *Eisenberg v. Minister of Housing*, 47(2) P.D. 229.
55. H.C. 428/86 (note 15).
56. H.C. 6163/92 (note 54): 274.
57. H.C. 935/89 (note 18).
58. H.C. 7074/93 *Swissa v. Attorney General*, 48(3) P.D. 749.
59. H.C. 3094/93 *Movement for Government Quality v. Prime Minister* 47(5) P.D. 404; H.C. 4267/93 *Amitai v. Prime Minister*, 47(5) P.D. 441.
60. Shamir (note 5).
61. B'Tselem, *Detained Without a Trial: Administrative Detention in the Occupied Territories Since the Beginning of the Intifada*, Jerusalem: 1992.
62. Burton Atkins, "Data Collection in Comparative Judicial Research: A Note on the Effects of Case Publication Upon Theory Building and Hypothesis Testing," *The Western Political Quarterly* 45/3 (1992) pp.783–92; idem., "Alternative Models of Appeal Mobilization in Judicial Hierarchies," *American Journal of Political Science* 37/3 (1993) pp.780–98; Lee Epstein, Jeffrey Segal, and Timothy Johnson, "The Claim of Issue Creation on the Supreme Court," *American Political Science Review* 90/4 (1996) pp.845–52. Kevin McGuire and Gregory Caldeira, "Lawyers, Organized Interests, and the Law of Obscenity: Agenda Setting in the Supreme Court," *American Political Science Review* 87/3 (1993) pp.717–26; Kevin McGuire and Barbara Palmer, "Issues, Agendas and Decision Making on the Supreme Court," *American Political Science Review* 90/4 (1996) pp.853–66. C. Neal Tate and Panu Sittiwong, "Decision Making in the Canadian Supreme Court: Extending the Personal Attributes Model Across Nations," *Journal of Politics* 51/4 (1989) pp.900–16.
63. Mary L. Volcansek, "Political Power and Judicial Review in Italy," *Comparative Political Studies* 26/4 (1994) pp.492–509; Jan ten Kate and Peter J. Van Koppen, "Judicialization of Politics in the Netherlands: Towards a Form of Judicial Review," *International Political Science Review* 15/2 (1994) pp.143–51.
64. For yearly statistics of the US Supreme Court caseload and voting patterns of the Justices, see the November issues of *Harvard Law Review*.
65. *Judicial Statistics* – Special Series No. 958, Jerusalem: Central Bureau of Statistics, 1994, p.79.
66. Ibid., p.73.
67. H.C.4446/96 *Movement for Government Quality v. Government of Israel*, 50 (3) P.D. 705.
68. H.C. 5016/96 *Horev v. Minister of Transportation*, 51 Dinim Elion 414.
69. For comparative analysis of various methods intended to curtail judicial independence, see Martin Shapiro, *Courts*, Chicago: 1981, pp.32–5.
70. Shapiro and Stone (note 4).
71. Menachem Hofnung, *Law Democracy and National Security in Israel*, Aldershot: 1996, pp.83, 117–18.
72. H.C. 390/79 (note 14).
73. Peter Bachrach and Morton Baratz, "Decisions and Nondecisions: An Analytical Framework," *American Political Science Review* 67 (1963) pp.632–42.
74. Moshe Negbi, *Tzedek Be'Kvalim (Justice Under Occupation)* [Hebrew], Jerusalem: 1981; Hofnung (note 71) pp.273–4. See comments by Minister of Defense Rabin in a Knesset debate on the "Deportation of Intifada Activists from the Territories." *D.K.* Twelfth Knesset, First Session, p.3605 (Aug. 21, 1989). Also, comments by Prime Minister Rabin (*Ha'aretz*, March 31, 1993). In November 1992, Israel allowed 241 spouses of the Occupied Territories residents to remain in their residence two days before a scheduled hearing of 67 different petitions to the High Court of Justice (*Ha'aretz*, Nov. 27, 1992). In December 1996, in answering a petition, the government notified the High Court that it had decided not to implement its decision to nominate Deputy Executive Directors in government ministries, without tenders (*Ha'aretz*, Dec.

29, 1996).
75. Such an example was the case where the Court refused to uphold a political decision to bar a racist party, Kach, from participating in general elections. In this decision (E.A. 2/84, see note 30), the Supreme Court President, Meir Shamgar, set guidelines for future legislation intended to bar such parties. The Knesset, in amending the Basic Law: The Knesset, implemented those guidelines.
76. H.C. 1715/97 *Bureau of Investments' Brokers in Israel v. Finance Minister*, 52 Dinim Elion 709.
77. H.C. 3914/92 *Lev v. the Grand Rabbinical Court*, 48(2) P.D. 457; C.A. 239/92, *Eged v. Mashiah* 48 (2) P.D. 66; H.C. 3299/93 *Vickselbaum v. Minister of Defense*, 49(2) P.D. 195; Cr.A. 6654/93 *Binkin v. State of Israel*, 48(1) P.D. 290; F.H. 2316/95 *Ganimmat v. State of Israel*, 49(4) P.D. 580.
78. See a debate at The Knesset's Law, Constitution and Justice Committee, *Ha'aretz*, June 13, 1995. See also *Ha'aretz*, Oct. 22, 1994, and D.K. (Knesset Records) July 7, 1993, pp.6442–50; March 9, 1994, pp.5358–451; March 14, 1994, pp.5536–53.
79. An example of this phenomenon was given in an interview with Minister of Justice David Libai, in which the Minister explained that a bill setting out the powers of the General Security Service to conduct interrogations of suspects of terrorist activity is delayed because of the need to ensure that the authorizations of the law conform with the provisions of the Basic Law: Human Dignity and Liberty (interview with Minister of Justice, David Libai, *Halishka* 29 (Feb. 1996) pp.3–5). See also on this consitutional dialogue, the protocols of two meetings between the Supreme Court President, Aharon Barak and the Knesset Law, Constitution and Justice Committee, Ibid., pp.14–21; *Halishka* 32 (Nov. 1996) pp.11–16.
80. Gad Barzilai, Ephraim Yuchtman-Ya'ar and Zeev Segal, *Beit Ha'Mishpat Ha'Elion Bein Ha'Hevra Ha'Israelit (The Israeli Supreme Court and the Israeli Public)*, Tel Aviv: 1993. The main findings were also published by the same authors in "Supreme Court and Public Opinion: General Paradigms and the Israeli Case," *Law and Courts* 3 (1994) pp.3–6.
81 Dan Avnon, "'The Enlightened Public': Jewish and Democratic or Liberal and Democratic?," *Mishpat Umimshal* (1996) pp.1–33 [Hebrew].
82. See Knesset debates on that matter, D.K. (Knesset Records) July 7, 1993, p.6443; Aug. 2, 1993, p.7177; Nov. 3, 1993, p.611; Jan. 25, 1994, p.3903; Feb. 1, 1994, p.4153; Feb. 15, 1994, p.4512; Feb. 16, 1994, p.4666; March 9, 1994, p.5358. A preliminary draft of a bill, entrenching a religious "status quo" was passed on the Knesset floor in January 1996 (*Ha'aretz*, Jan. 26, 1996). In April 1996, MK Zevulun Hamer of the National Religious Party (who was nominated after the 1996 elections as Minister of Education) wrote: "In the past 50 years the dominant current of thought in the Supreme Court systematically supported the views of the extreme left wing. The views of Meretz possess influence in the Supreme Court well beyond the proportion of Meretz supporters in Israeli society." MK Hamer wrote this during the election campaign to then prime ministerial candidate Binyamin Netanyahu and the letter was deliberately published during the campaign. (*Ha'aretz*, April 9, 1996, A5); In August 1996, the police introduced stricter security measures for Supreme Court Justices in response to threats issued against them from ultra-orthodox circles, dictating around the clock personal armed guarding of the President of the Supreme Court, Aharon Barak(*Ha'aretz*, Aug. 1, 1996, A5).
83. H.C. 5364/94 *Valner v. Labor Party*, 49(1) P.D. 758.
84. A striking example of the High Court acting under public pressure was in a case were 418 Moslem Hamas activists were expelled from the West Bank and Gaza without a previous hearing. The Court had to deliver its decision while the buses, filled with the deportees, stayed on the Lebanese border, waiting for a final decision. The Court ruled (against its previous case law) that a hearing of each case could be held later, while the petitioners remained outside the country; H.C. 5973/92 *Association of Civil Rights v. Minister of Defense*, 47(1) P.D. 267.
85. In one case, the Court declared the Ministry of Interior's criteria for recognizing conversions to Judaism in Israel as null and void. Realizing the political implications of the case, which touches upon one of the most sensitive internal conflicts in Israeli politics, the court did not order the ministry to register the petitioner as a Jew, referring the matter back to the legislature (H.C. 1031/93 *Pessaru v. Minister of Interior*, 49(4) P.D. 661). In two cases, the Court did not issue an order to stop the use

of "moderate physical force" in the investigation of Islamic fundamentalists (H.C. 7964/95 (VR 336/96) Bilbeisi v. General Security Service [yet unpublished, decision given Jan. 11, 1996]; H.C. 8049/96 Hamdan v. General Security Service [yet unpublished, decision given Nov. 14, 1996]) although this ruling was interpreted as an aquiescence to allow torture during security related interrogations. In other cases, the Court decided not to declare as unconstitutional two new laws, while still recognizing that the provisions of those laws are not compatible with the provisions of entrenched basic laws, and despite the fact that the laws were enacted with less than the required majority. The Court ruled that the extent of the infringements was not substantial enough to warrant judicial intervention (H.C. 7111/95 *Center of Local Government v. Knesset*, 50 (3) P.D. 485; H.C. 3434/96 *Hofnung v. Knesset Speaker*, 50 (3) P.D. 57.
86. H.C. 5771/93 *Zitrin v. Minister of Justice*, 48(1) P.D. 661.

Structural Change and Leadership Transformation

GABRIEL SHEFFER

INTRODUCTION

Due to global and regional trends, which are coupled by internal social and economic developments, the Israeli polity is in a state of flux. This chapter suggests that these extensive external and internal changes have transformed not only the Israeli electoral and party systems, but also the character of the national elites[1] and, more particularly, the nature of national level political leadership.

The purpose of this chapter is to examine the multiple and reciprocal connections between social and regime change, the appearance of a new type of national level leaders and public policymaking.

The underlying assumption here is that, on the one hand, the Israeli polity can be compared with other democratic political systems,[2] and that such a comparison will shed light on the Israeli case, and, on the other hand, that such a comparison can also add to the discussion of the connections between regime transformation and leadership development in general.

The chapter will begin with the theoretical background to the analysis of these questions. It will continue with a discussion of the reciprocal relations between social and regime transformation, leadership development and public policy making. It will then review the main changes that have occurred in these spheres in Israel. The next step will be a comparison between the situation in Israel and other western democracies. The last section will draw some general theoretical conclusions that will demonstrate the potential of the inclusion of the Israeli case for theory development.[3]

Gabriel (Gabi) Sheffer is at the Political Science Department of The Hebrew University of Jerusalem.

THE THEORETICAL BACKGROUND

The general theoretical debate about the nature of political leadership and the reasons for its transformation continues. Thus, it is difficult to envisage the emergence of a widely accepted theoretical approach to a contextual analysis of leadership. It means that most of the divergent approaches will persist.[4] Therefore those who deal with these issues must refer to these approaches. In this vein, this analysis builds from the approach claiming that "leadership is a function of regime, or political culture. [And that] these macro-political regimes constrain the micro-politics of individual encounters."[5] Accordingly, this chapter will not focus on personal traits or on the interactions between elites' members. Rather it will further explore the hypothesis that social needs, structures, and institutions determine the political culture. The political culture influences the nature of the regime and, ultimately, leadership characteristics. It should be noted that the approach adopted here is not strictly functionalist. The approach is cultural-situational, emphasizing the reciprocal nature of society, regime, and leadership development.

Recent developments in various countries provide support for the need to apply this approach. Thus, noticeable leadership transformation has occurred in states undergoing the transition from totalitarianism to authoritarianism and from authoritarianism to democracy. For example, due to such structural changes in totalitarian states like the Soviet Union and China, the nature of leadership in these two polities was transformed too. The leadership qualities and style of Gorbachev and Deng were good examples of this phenomenon. Similarly, when democratic governments replaced authoritarian regimes in Spain and Portugal, leaders like Phelipe Gonzales emerged and contributed to the development of a democratic regime.[6] The same applies to democratization processes in Greece, Chile, and, to an extent, Argentina.

But while it is clear that national level leadership is influenced by such dramatic fundamental regime transformation, especially, of course, during the transition toward a more democratic system, it is less evident what happens to national political leadership when more subtle regime alterations occur in democratic states.

As noted, this article applies the notions concerning the influence of regime type on leadership nature and style in a reexamination of regime changes in an established democracy – Israel. In this it follows the approach suggested by proponents of the Cultural Theory of Leadership.[7] This theory holds that *fatalistic, communitarian, hierarchical and market* regimes respectively create *despotic, charismatic, positional* and *meteoric* leaderships.[8]

REGIME CHANGE IN ISRAEL

Despite what have been termed as structural and behavioral

"imperfections" of Israeli democracy,[9] most analysts have regarded Israel as a stable and well performing polity.[10] Although this democracy faced numerous crises and upheavals and has caused injustice to certain Jewish groups and to the Palestinians, many observers have noted the continuity, regularity, and stability of the regime.

However, a growing number of Israelis and foreign observers now ask tougher questions about the Israeli political system, especially in view of the recent rapid and arduous process of regime change which is accompanied by noticeable difficulties in the system's performance. The most recent change, widely noted for the shift to direct election of the prime minister, is the second major transformation of the Israeli polity since 1948. The first, which occurred gradually during the late 1960s and the early 1970s, was a shift from a consociational[11] to a neo-corporatist regime.[12] The present transition is from neo-corporatism toward an individualistic semi-liberal democracy. In order to understand the current transition, a brief review of that earlier transformation is necessary.

From Consociationalism to Neo-Corporatism

Israel inherited its main political features from the Yishuv and through it from the Zionist movement.[13] While there is an ongoing debate about the scope of Israeli consociationalism after the establishment of the Jewish state in 1948, that new polity clearly demonstrated a number of consociational features inherited from the Yishuv.[14] Thus from the late 1940s until the mid-1960s, the Israeli polity resembled in essential aspects consociational arrangements that had been implemented during various periods in the history of countries such as Holland, Belgium, Austria, and Switzerland.

Like these consociational states, the Israeli society and polity were deeply segmented. Foremost among these cleavages was the Jewish–Arab divide, but the Jewish sector itself was also deeply divided. Hence the application of the consociational principles to both ethnic sectors, though less generously toward the Israeli-Palestinians, was intended to deal with a host of problems, which are created in such societies, and to satisfy the needs of each of the two communities and of their main subgroups. Like in other similar cases, this arrangement was also essential in any effort to avoid vehement intra- and inter-bloc clashes within the Jewish sector.

While maintaining the social structures of the Yishuv, after 1948 the Jewish sector in Israel revealed a number of ideological, social, and economic cleavages. These, rather than ethnic factors, created the complex patterns of segmentation in this sector. Although the Labor bloc and its elite, which dominated all political coalitions and their governments until the late 1970s, tried to foster integration and promote an *etatist* approach (*mamlachtiut*), the pre-state segmentation patterns persisted. The result was the endurance of three superficially united camps – the Labor, the Religious, and what was known as the Civic Bloc.

The *raison d'être* of these three blocs was their divergent ideologies. The mainstream in the Labor bloc followed relatively moderate foreign and defense strategies and social-democratic ideology, which was responsible for an elaborate welfare system that led in turn to a highly centralized state. The main groups in the loosely organized Civic Bloc adopted a liberal economic and social platform and a nationalist ideology on the Arab–Jewish conflict. The third bloc was religiously based, comprised of those determined to maintain the orthodox tradition. On these diverse ideologies there were superimposed cultural, social, economic, and occupational schisms.

None of these camps gained enough electoral support to form governments on their own. Since grand coalitions could not be established, there was a continuous need for power sharing through the establishment of changing smaller coalitions. The partners in these coalitions held mutual veto power to guarantee that none of them would be outvoted when its vital interests were at stake. The system included arrangements intended to allocate national resources according to a strictly proportional yardstick, to avoid uncontrolled conflicts, to manage conflicts that erupted nevertheless, and to maintain the autonomy of the camps.

Each of these camps was relatively well organized and catered to the needs of the members of its constituent parties and factions. In return for benefits that members received through their blocs and constituent parties, they were expected to show loyalty. Firm loyalty and discipline were required for two reasons: to prevent defection, since maximal membership guaranteed a maximal proportional share of national resources. The second reason was that this arrangement was designed to prevent spontaneous clashes between members of the camps, which could wreck the entire boat. Indeed, usually the members of these camps showed loyalty to the camps and their leaders. These leaders gained considerable respect, prestige, and power. Taken together, all these arrangements explain the remarkable systemic stability, reflected in the electoral results throughout the Yishuv period and during the first two decades after 1948.

Since it met many of the blocs and their constituent parties' basic needs, the Israeli *proporzdemokratie*[15] preserved the pure proportional (PR) electoral system that had been practiced by the Zionist movement and the Yishuv that it created. Consequently, ministries were allocated to coalition partners in accordance with their relative strength in the Knesset (the Israeli Parliament). Other government jobs were also proportionally granted to coalition partners, and most economic resources and benefits were allocated according to the same proportional yardsticks.

To avoid any spark that might have caused undesired public clashes between the blocs, the Israeli parliament was designed as a junior partner in national policy making. The entire system was firmly controlled by a strong elite-cartel through the highly centralized government. Power sharing among elites dictated most of the internal developments.[16] To further maintain stability, the elite promoted a symbolic structure intended to ensure national solidarity, acceptance of the state's predominance, and compliance with the national leadership. They emphasized national myths, fostered respect to the national anthem and flag, encouraged "authentic" Israeli food, and sponsored "Israeli folklore." At the same time, the elite augmented control mechanisms over the entire society and the members of the various camps, while implementing policies intended to minimize friction. Thus, for example, the system allocated considerable resources to parties of the Civic Bloc that were traditionally excluded from the governing coalitions (though less than their strict proportional share in accordance to their weight in the entire electorate). By the same token, the system opted for maintaining the religious Status Quo Agreement, that prevented state and religion separation and guaranteed religious practices, such as kosher food in state agencies, religious holidays, religious burials, marriages and divorces. As part of this arrangement it was agreed that all religious services would be controlled by the orthodox and ultra-orthodox religious parties, and provided by agencies that they headed.

This consociational arrangement influenced most political developments during the first two decades after the establishment of Israel.[17] Yet the system was not completely frozen. The consociational arrangements also resulted in "dynamic conservatism," which meant gradual political development through adaptation within a rigid political structure.[18] Among other things this arrangement allowed successive Labor governments to alternate between hard-line and moderate policies regarding the Arab–Israeli conflict and the Israeli Palestinians, to pursue a non-selective immigration policy that increased more than threefold the Israeli population, to implement a state sponsored social integrationist policy for the incoming immigrants, to promote the gradual emergence of state capitalism, and to simultaneously implement expansionist economic policy and generous universal welfare services.

As in other consociational democracies such as the Netherlands and Austria, the very success of this arrangement in the Jewish sector narrowed the gap between the blocs and thus ultimately made these arrangements obsolete.[19] Gradually, the integrative policies that successive Israeli governments had pursued, coupled with the etatist ethos, contributed to the erosion of the traditional political blocs and, later, to the erosion of their constituent parties. As larger groups, especially of immigrants that had arrived in the late 1940s and the early 1950s, became better acquainted with the Israeli social and economic systems, and accustomed to the political arrangements prevailing in the Jewish state, they replaced their dependence on the camps and parties with reliance on the government. Consequently they began to defect from the blocs and parties that had facilitated their immigration and initial integration. In the long run it turned out that the main loser in this gradual process was the Labor bloc. These processes enhanced popular support for the rightist, nationalist and religious parties.

The late 1960s and 1970s also saw an equally gradual process of economic liberalization. This resulted from the rapid economic development in the wake of the 1967 War, from attempts by successive Israeli governments to participate in various international economic organizations and arrangements, such as GATT and the emerging European Union. Israeli economic and political elites, who had intended to benefit from the support of the World Bank and IMF, accepted the demands of these IGOs for gradual liberalization of the Israeli economy.

These developments also affected the Israeli Palestinian sector. In the mid-1960s, the Israeli government launched an initiative to alleviate the severe limitations imposed on that sector. A major step in this direction was eliminating the oppressive military government that had controlled all aspects of life in the Israeli Palestinian community. While until then, consociationalism had only a limited effect in this sector, from the late 1960s onward the Israeli Palestinian community began its long and arduous road toward political and economic, but not social integration.

Neo-Corporatism in Israel

As noted, it is not surprising that in Israel too the consociational arrangement was replaced by neo-corporatism. There were several reasons for this shift. First, rank and file began to rely on social and political interest groups to promote their interests, rather than on the traditional social-political blocs, the old parties, or state agencies. Second, society and politics were freed from the firm control of the traditional ideological blocs. Other factors included the reduced power of the parties, the relaxation of the centralized power structure, and the consequent decentralization of policy making, accompanied by more elaborate consultation between elites.

As a result of these changes, the polity turned to the logical alternative to the consociational power-sharing model. As was the case in other consociational small states, especially such as the Netherlands and Austria, the closest arrangement that could satisfy all actors was neo-corporatism.[20] In view of further political and economic liberalization that began in the late 1960s and the further weakening of the camps and parties, Israelis turned to a variety of established and emerging interest groups. They joined these groups with hope that they would promote their well-being and protect their interests. Indeed, single-issue and multi-purpose interest groups have substantially increased in number and significance.[21]

The deterioration of the traditional political blocs and parties, the rapid expansion of interest groups, and the continuation of consultative public policy making all led to a growing role not only for grassroots interest groups but also for "peak organizations," such as those of the industrialists, bankers, large commercial firms, organized labor, and professionals. By the same token, the volume, scope, and intensity of regional and local interest group activity, at what is known as the mezzo-corporatist level, has also increased. Again as in other neo-corporatist democracies, these peak, regional, local, and grassroots interest groups became indispensable partners in public policy making. For a while the government remained the senior partner, but its power began to dwindle.

The further weakening of the grip of the state and especially of the executive branch, combined with economic liberalization, enhanced the political power of the private sector by the 1970s. Consequently, the Israeli political system gradually acquired new features: members of the traditional interests formed hierarchically ordered and functionally differentiated powerful entities. By then some of these corporatist associations were either formally or informally recognized by state agencies as worthy participants in public policymaking. Each of these corporations acquired representational monopolies within its sphere. The heads of the large banks, for example, formed an informal "cartel" that enjoyed an unproportional influence in policy making. The industrial, commercial, and professional associations, however, were only loosely organized, and the peak organizations of these groups maintained federal structures. While these groups recognized the "first among equals" position of the central government in the public policy making process, they succeeded in limiting its veto power and its ability to mediate between the capitalists and labor. Moreover, each of these organizations learned to formulate policies on their own, without prior consultation with other corporations.[22] Under the emerging Israeli neo-corporatist arrangement, national policymaking reflected the relative strength of those corporations.

Since the late 1960s, Israeli political arrangements reflect an early description of the main traits of neo-corporatism. According to this portrait, this arrangement is

> more than a peculiar pattern of articulation of interests. Rather it [is] an institutionalized pattern of policy-formation in which large interest organizations cooperate with each other and with public authorities not only in the articulation (or even 'intermediation' of interests), but – in its developed forms – in the 'authoritative allocation of values' and in the implementation of such policies. It is precisely because of the intimate mutual penetration of state bureaucracies and large interest organizations [that] we are dealing with an integrated system of 'societal guidance'.[23]

Like the previous consociational arrangement, the neo-corporatist arrangement sought political stability, social integration, and efficient economic and political performance in a potentially unstable polity. In national level public policy making, the goal was to build a pluralist consensus on pressing social and economic policies. As in the previous arrangement, neo-corporatist consensus building was attempted mainly at the elite level, but this time among the leaders of the peak associations. The decision making pattern was that of bargaining leading to compromise, especially in the economic sphere. These policymaking patterns were not limited to spheres such as wages and employment, these had spill-over effects in welfare policies, municipal matters, and even in the military industries.

The changes that began by moving from a consociational to a neo-corporatist arrangement have continued to reverberate, and it now seems that neo-corporatism in Israel was but an intermediary step. In retrospect, the great contribution of neo-corporatism was to facilitate further change. It has affected many aspects of social action (especially the tremendous increase in the number and activities of promotional and protective single-issue interest groups), leadership formation, leadership style and performance, the style of national level policy making, and the reforms in the electoral system.

The Current Transformation

As noted, Israel is now in the midst of its second social and political transitional period. In the late 1990s there are three deep social-ideological cleavages: those between religious and secular Jews, those between Jews and Israeli Palestinians, and those between veterans and immigrants, especially from the former Soviet Union and Ethiopia. Also, but to a lesser degree, the ideological cleavage concerning the future of the occupied territories is a source of disagreement and friction. Although other previously deep cleavages, such as the class and Ashkenazi–Sephardi schisms, have lost much of their severity, they linger and may cause unexpected eruptions.[24]

In the non-religious segment, the slow amelioration of the old ideological and "ethnic" (that is, the cleavage along the lines of country of origin) differences has been accompanied by a gradual weakening of collective identities and loyalties. This weakening process accelerated since the mid-1980s and, with the notable exception of the religious segment, it still continues. The coveted for "Israeli personality," which involved identification with overarching national values, symbols, and goals, has been diluted and blurred. Few Israelis seriously believe in notions such as "one integrated society," "homogeneous culture," "pioneering," "mutual responsibility," or "Israel is a model society and state." If it exists at all, the "Israeli Personality" is a strange mix of nationalist, religious, xenophobic, selfish, and individualistic attributes. Not surprisingly, the popularity of the old ideological camps, parties, and the kibbutz and Moshav movements has waned. Loyalty is shifting to smaller particularistic, local, "clannish," familial, and occupational entities. Israelis increasingly join specialized voluntary associations and primarily identify with them.

This waning of collective identities has caused a marked decline of ideological political commitments, religious and ultra-religious Jews being the exception. In any event, none of the emerging "new ideologies," such as Milton Freedman style economic liberalism, libertarianism, dedicated "dark-green environmentalism," and feminism, has become a significant rallying point for popular mobilization. In other words, as yet the Israelis have not developed clear liberal post-materialist views.

The dwindling of old ideological commitments and communal loyalties has contributed to a growing fragmentation of Israeli society. Instead of traditional social camps, new "normal" single-issue interest groups, such as parents', ecological, occupational, and religious associations proliferate. The result is an unstructured, almost chaotic, pluralism, with growing islands of individualism.

A considerable degree of fragmentation and regrouping is generated at grassroots level. Yet new elites influence cultural, social, and political development. Thus, prominent members of these elites gain attention in the mass media, attract followers, and gain power. On the other hand, the traditional elites are loosing their clout over Israeli society and politics. Judging from the current ongoing processes in this sphere, some traditional elites are bound to disappear almost altogether. This is the fate of the old Histadrut (the Israeli trade union movement) elite that has been replaced by powerful chairpersons of the various large trade unions. This is also the case with the old parties' elites, and to an extent of the academic elite too. Newer and younger elites replace other veteran elites. Thus, for example, very young pacesetters have appeared in the cultural sphere, in the electronic and written media, and in industry.[25]

At the other end of the social ladder, at the grassroots level, more Israelis are becoming aware of their new social freedom and autonomy. Not surprisingly, these persons are groping for additional empowerment. Regardless of "ethnic" or class background, the trend among young Israelis is toward individualism and personal fulfillment. It is difficult to determine the exact size of this group of Israelis, but by any yardstick it is rapidly growing. The cumulative result of these trends is that the social and political culture of the non-orthodox sector is gradually losing its previous "parochial" and "servile" characteristics, and it is acquiring new western style liberal features.

A particularly striking transition is occurring in the economy, which is in the midst of rapid liberalization. Although after the 1996 elections liberalization and external investment have clearly slowed down, mainly due to uncertainty about the peace process and domestic economic stability, there is a widespread consensus that state intervention in the economy must be further reduced and that privatization should be carried out. The fact that the Histadrut has been in a continuous crisis – and its present leadership shares the consensus on liberalization and even a degree of privatization – has enhanced the political role of the private sector. While during earlier periods, Labor governments and the Histadrut were senior partners in public policy making, policy-packages, not only concerning economic but also security and foreign policy matters, are now discussed mainly between government and the chiefs of the private sector. An example of this trend is the participation by economic elites in the peace talks with Jordan and in the convoluted negotiations with the Palestinians. Partly through personal acquaintances and partly on the basis of their contributions to political candidates and parties, industrialists, brokers, and bankers have established close relations with senior politicians. The late Yitzhak Rabin, as well as Shimon Peres, Ehud Barak, Arie Derei, and Binyamin Netanyahu, have been known for their close contacts with wealthy Jews in Israel and the Diaspora, and with other less prominent members of the economic, commercial, and financial elites.

The unavoidable cumulative result of these processes is a weakening of the state. Yet not all state institutions are losing power at the same pace or to the same degree, and some are even gaining. With the decline of the parties and the Knesset and the weakening of the executive branch, the courts' centrality is increasing. In the final analysis, however, political power is shifting to the intermediate levels of the political system – to smaller, mostly local, promoting and protecting interest groups, to trade unions of workers in large and strategic industries, and to other small powerful voluntary associations. Meanwhile, veteran power brokers, such as the parties' aparatchikis and members of Knesset, fight hard to maintain the vestiges of their prestige. As will later be argued, these developments significantly influence the leadership phenomenon.

These developments both feed and are influenced by trends at the grassroots level, where there is a growing feeling that the "man in the street" can affect political outcomes. For instance, many that had voted for Netanyahu's Likud Party in the 1996 elections emphasized that their vote was conditional, and indeed in the 1999 elections they gave their votes to Ehud Barak, the leader of the Labor Party. Moreover, Israelis are increasingly willing to confront the government, especially through the courts, but also through interest groups and the media. Judges, especially of the Supreme Court, are showing a healthy appetite for political clout. Chief Justice Aharon Barak, for instance, stipulated that his court can pass judgment on almost all political issues and has been active in gaining full administrative and financial control over the judicial system.

Although it might sound paradoxical, the recent reform in the Israeli electoral system, which introduced direct elections of the prime minister, has further diminished the government's control. The reason is that growing pragmatic political attitudes, reduced loyalty to parties, and the enhanced power to select between individual leaders leads Israelis to shift their support from one leader and party to another. This complements the social and political transformation mentioned above. Power further shifts to single issue as well as special interest groups and to individuals who in turn support the formal candidates. Yet it should be emphasized that large segments in the Jewish sector still adhere to their old communal, clannish and sectorial loyalties. It means that in Israel there are large enclaves of conservatism.

Despite the current leaning toward nationalist and religious-fundamentalist loyalties, nevertheless the present chaotic situation and transitional period may result in a more "normal" polity, that is, one more resembling other western nations, with legitimate multiculturalism, social pluralism, economic liberalism, and a reasonable degree of privatization. Thus Israel will continue to move toward a "private-liberal democracy," based on a stronger civil society. Against this backdrop, now it is possible to consider developments in Israeli leadership over the last fifty years.

LEADERSHIP CHANGE IN ISRAEL

The *scope* (that is, "whether leaders in each regime will be obeyed over a wider or narrower spectrum of affairs") and *duration* of leadership power and influence are significant aspects of the phenomenon at hand.[26] Yet these are not sufficient elements in the analysis of regime and leadership change. A proper way to enrich such an analysis is to follow James MacGregor Burns' well known categorization of leaders.[27] Thus the following analysis of changes in Israeli leadership patterns will utilize the distinction between *transforming*[28] and *transactional* leaderships. The main reason for using Burns' typology here is that it focuses on the intensive interactions between leaders and followers. Therefore it will facilitate a contextual reexamination of the Israeli leadership. Following Burns' scheme, the analysis here will deal with leaders' *aspirations, motivations, goals, power bases, policymaking, decision taking, and reciprocal relations with followers,* including the *mutual assessment of capabilities.*[29]

Israeli Leadership during the Consociational Period

David Ben-Gurion, Yitzhak Ben-Zvi, Yitzhak Tabenkin, Meir Yaari, Yosef Sprinzak, and Rabbi Yehuda Leib Maimon were among the founding fathers of Israel. In 1948, when the Jewish State was established, all these were far from political novices. Each was an established leader, and some were internationally known. In fact, these men constituted the third generation of Zionist and Yishuv leadership, having climbed to national leadership within the institutions of the Zionist movement and the Yishuv.[30] Although they had not founded these political systems and institutions, they helped fortify them. Their promotion was not particularly quick, and they moved up in the political hierarchy mainly due to their dedication, loyalty to their respective political blocs and parties, and sheer stamina. The nature of this generation of leaders and the practices that they used help explain both the continuity and relative stability of the political arrangements of the Jewish community.[31]

These leaders, however, were not merely in the shadows of their great predecessors, like Theodore Herzl, Chaim Weizmann, Leo Motzkin, and David Wolfsohn. They were outstanding leaders in their own right. Having guided the Yishuv in the diplomatic, political, and military struggles leading to 1948, they influenced the political development in Israel during the two decades after its establishment.[32] In this they had the invaluable assistance of the fourth generation of Zionist and Yishuv leaders that included figures such as Moshe Sharett, David Remez, Eliezer Kaplan, Pinchas Rosen, Moshe Shapira, and Levi Eshkol. This close intergenerational cooperation ensured systemic continuity.

Most of these leaders were *charismatic and innovative*, but they also knew how to use the institutional, especially executive, powers that they had accumulated. Most of them were from middle class families, and the values of their parents and peers strongly influenced them. Nonetheless, later some of them adopted various shades of socialist ideology and became members of the labor movement. Taken as a whole, this generation of leaders functioned as a *transforming* leadership. Some of what I have called the "third generation of Zionist and Yishuv leaders," especially Ben-Gurion, Tabenkin, and Yaari, should be regarded, according to Burns' sub-categorization, as *transforming ideologues*.

The more senior members of the next generation of Zionist and Yishuv leaders, like Sharett and Eshkol of the Labor bloc, Pinchas Rosen and Peretz Berenstein of the Civic bloc, and Moshe Shapira and Yosef Burg of the religious bloc, still belonged to the transforming leadership category, but more specifically they should be characterized as *reformist*, or rather *reforming*, leaders, since many of them implemented reforms in each of the spheres in which they were active. Despite their divergent bloc and party affiliation, all these leaders worked within the existing consociational framework, elaborating on it and making it more responsive to their constituencies' needs.

Israeli Leadership during the Neo-Corporatist Period
During the transition from the consociational to neo-corporatist regime, a new type of national leadership emerged. Most in this group, like Golda Meir, Pinchas Lavon, Zalman Aranne, and Israel Galili, obtained almost their entire political education and socialization in Palestine. They were strongly influenced by their elders in the various blocs and parties and were selected, trained, and promoted by leaders of the two former generations. In short, they were the products of an existing political system. They owed their political careers to their parties and to the established leadership thereof. Slowly and mainly through promotion in their parties this group rose to power on the national level.

None in this group was a heroic, revolutionary, ideological, or even a reforming leader, to list the most significant sub-types of Burns' transforming leaders category. In fact their leadership qualities became apparent, if at all, only after assuming party or executive tasks. This was the case with both Levi Eshkol and Golda Meir. By the same token, none was particularly innovative or contributed to any major ideological breakthrough or to premeditated practical change, other trademarks of transforming leaders. On the contrary, because of their ingrained conservatism and staunch belief in the status quo, some of them, like Meir and Galili, were held partly responsible for major national debacles such as the Israeli Black Panthers eruption in the 1960s, or the 1973 War.

According to the then prevailing political tradition, these leaders belonged to the existing "elite-cartel." They accepted the norms of power sharing, the principles of proportionality, and most of the other fundamental elements of the consociational arrangement. This third generation of Israeli leaders was, taken as a whole, a *transactional* leadership. And within this category, they best fit the sub-types of *party* and *parliamentary leaders.*

And yet, their main contribution was paradoxically to relax the parties' and blocs' control over society, politics, and economy. They have done so because they sensed subterranean trends pushing in this direction. In doing so, they paved the way to the next stage of regime and leadership transfiguration. Their leadership style befitted the relaxation of the bloc system and the transition from an elitist to a pluralist system.

When neo-corporatism fully emerged in Israel in the late 1960s, the next generation of leaders was positioned to take over. This group included figures like Yitzhak Rabin, Shimon Peres, Abba Eban of the Labor bloc, and Ezer Weizmann, Ariel Sharon, and Yitzhak Shamir of the Likud Party. Most were educated and socialized on the eve of the establishment of the state, and were involved in defense and gained their executive training in state hierarchical organizations – the IDF, the Defense establishment, the secret services, or the Ministry of Foreign Affairs. They were neither rebels nor innovators. They showed loyalty to the "system," which rewarded them with inducements, legitimacy, and authority. The "system" became their main power-base. Thus they were promoted within their organizations, and from there their respective parties catapulted them to senior political positions. Rather than being elected, they were selected and placed in leadership positions. In fact, most showed distrust for liberal democratic patterns. None was charismatic or particularly innovative, with the exception of Peres at a much later stage in his career.

For these leaders, policymaking was a hierarchical organizational affair, well suited to the prevailing neo-corporatist regime. Hence they had no difficulty operating in harmony with the hierarchical system of interest representation that was at the heart of the neo-corporatist regime. Thus, for example, Rabin and Peres joined in a national unity government headed by the then formal leader of the Likud, Shamir, who was supported by new rightist and religious parties and interest groups.

The most appropriate characterization of this group's leadership style is *transactional executive and bargaining leadership.*

Current Trends in Israeli Leadership

Within the current transformation of the social structure and political regime, a new generation of leaders has gained prominence. Binyamin Netanyahu of the Likud; Yitzhak Mordechai of the Center Party; Natan Sharansky of Israel Be'aliah; Arie Derei and Eli Yishai of SHAS; Meir Parush of Degel Hatorah; Ehud Barak, Chaim Ramon, and Shlomo Ben-Ami of the Labor Party, as well as the Chancellor of the Bank of Israel, Yaacov Frankel, all belong to this generation of leaders.

Although these political figures come from all corners of the political spectrum with differing personal and organizational backgrounds, all of them have much in common. Their shared traits reflect a changing Israeli society that, as noted, is on the one hand more individualistic, materialistic, and aggressive, and on the other hand more conservative and traditional. Except for the religious and ultra-religious leaders, this group of leaders pays little heed to ideology, and they demonstrate little respect or loyalty to their parties. The former Likud leader and Israel's prime minister, Netanyahu, and the Labor leader, Barak, have been inclined to reduce their parties' power and influence. They are pragmatic and materialistic, and their own careers are of paramount importance in their eyes. They are almost obsessed with power. They are fully aware of the tremendous significance of the media, and they know how to handle it, if not how to manipulate it. They have developed close and useful relations with the wealthy and the economic elite both in Israel and in the Jewish Diaspora. Most were promoted to their senior positions through primaries, and, compared to earlier generations, they are much less dependent on their parties. They are staunch supporters of market economy, all of them support economic liberalization and privatization.

These clearly fit the description of *meteoric leaders,* since they are both beneficiaries and proponents of Israel's rapid transformation into that mix of private-liberal and nationalist-religious regime. At the same time they are also consummate *bargainers* of the *transactional* types of leadership.

THE COMPARATIVE PERSPECTIVE

In most western democracies, as well as in former communist countries, regime transformation has been accompanied by marked changes in national level leaderships. Both regime and leadership change have been noticeable in the USA, Britain, Denmark, Sweden, Spain, and Portugal, as well as in Holland, Belgium, and Austria. In the former authoritarian Russia and Poland, processes of change have also been in full swing.

All these countries have been characterized by political and economic liberalization, which has in most cases been accompanied by an intended weakening of the state. US President Clinton and Vice President Gore; Britain's Prime Minister Blair and the Conservative Party leader, Hague; Norway's Prime Minister Jagland and many in his cabinet; Sweden's Prime Minister Persson; Denmark's Prime Minister Rasmussen; Spain's Prime Minister Aznar and Portugal's Prime Minister Guterres; Russia's deputy prime ministers, Chubais and Nemtsov and opposition leader Lebed; and Poland's Prime Minister Kwasniewski, belonged to a new breed of leaders. All are relatively young – most of them are in their forties or early fifties. They have young and attractive wives and children – reliable assets during election campaigns – and they rose to political prominence rapidly. They have close friends and supporters in the business and economic community, and compared to their predecessors are much less ideological. They are highly pragmatic, and are cautious and flexible reformers. They are masters of dealing with the mass media. They favor weaker states, liberalization, careful privatization, reduction of welfare services by the state, tax reduction, smaller government, and as far as possible they try to avoid internal conflicts and clashes.

Yet, the most relevant comparison of the regime and leadership development in Israel is with some of the smaller European democracies that underwent similar transformations. The most apt comparisons are with Holland, Belgium, and Austria. For during this century, these three small European democracies experienced transitions from consociationalism to neo-corporatism, and then from neo-corporatism to private liberal democratic patterns.[33] With respect to the transition from neo-corporatism to a private-liberal model, Israel can also be compared to some of the Scandinavian countries.

An examination of all these cases shows that the changes in the nature of their political regimes also caused or were accompanied by leadership change. In former consociational democracies, the post-World War II powerful, visionary, and in certain cases also charismatic leaders, such as Henri Spaak and W. Martens in Belgium, W. Drees and Joseph Luns in the Netherlands, Karl Renner, Otto Bauer, Theo Lefevre, and Bruno Kreisky in Austria, who had many of the attributes of the ideological *transforming* leadership, were replaced by *transactional* leaders of the *executive, parliamentary and party* types. Jean-Luc Dehaene of Belgium, Wim Kok of the Netherlands, and Franz Vranitzky of Austria all fit this pattern. In sum, in all these countries now moving toward the private-liberal model, there is also a clear tendency toward *transactional, meteoric* and *public opinion* leadership.

CONCLUSIONS

Since the upsurge in leadership studies in the 1970s, which *inter alia* enhanced the comparative approach to the research of leadership and elaborated the methodological aspects involved,[34] there has not been much progress in this sphere. Therefore, in addition to examining the nexus between structural and leadership development in Israel, this article has sought to contribute to the largely neglected comparative study of leadership in democratic and democratizing states.

The Israeli case is pertinent for two main reasons. The first reason is the *scope* and *intensity* of Israel's current transformation: it has, in a short period, undergone two regime transformations. The second reason is the remarkable parallel changes that have occurred in Israel's national level leadership. Israel has moved from a collectivist and elitist, to a pluralist, and more recently to a democratic regime in which individuals are more assertive. From the comparative perspective this is a relevant transformation, because, as has been noted, some of the smaller European states have undergone similar processes.

This article has suggested that certain aspects of Aaron Wildavsky's assumptions about the connections between regime and leadership change are valid. This model stipulates that a combination of charismatic and positional leadership appears in what Wildavsky calls "social democracy." He further stipulates that a hierarchical regime facilitates positional leadership, and that a market regime encourages *meteoric* leadership. This categorization closely fits Israel and some of the small European states that have undergone similar transformations.

Yet since Wildavsky's categorization is mainly based on two attributes of leadership – *scope* and *duration* – there is a need for a category that deals with other significant leadership characteristics. This article has added the distinction between *transforming* and *transactional* leadership and their various sub-categories. It is suggested that these categories help describe leadership in the three regime types that emerged in Israel since its establishment.

On the basis of these observations, it can be expected that a transition from a neo-corporatist to liberal-private market regime in other democratic states will likely be accompanied and influenced by the emergence of transactional, meteoric, and bargaining leaders, whose particular strength is in their pragmatism, cautious and flexible reformism, and especially clever and skillful use of the media.

NOTES

1. E. Etzioni-Halevy, *A Place at the Top. Elites and Elitism in Israel*, Tel Aviv: Tcherikover, 1997 (Hebrew).
2. For a similar view about Israel's comparability see M. Barnett (ed.), *Israel in Comparative Perspective: Challenging the Conventional Wisdom*, Albany, NY: SUNY Press, 1996.
3. Ibid.
4. B. Bass, *Bass and Stodgdill Handbook of Leadership,* New York: The Free Press, 1990.
5. A. Wildavsky, "A Cultural Theory of Leadership," in B. Jones (ed.), *Leadership and Politics*, Lawrence, KS: University Press of Kansas, 1989, p.98; for a more reserved

view on this issue see J. Blondel, *Political Leadership*, London: Sage Publications, 1986.
6. J. Linz, "Innovative Leaders in the Transition to Democracy and a New Democracy: The Case of Spain," in G. Sheffer (ed.), *Innovative Leaders in International Politics*, Albany, NY: SUNY Press, 1993.
7. M. Douglas and A. Wildavsky, *Risk and Culture*, Berkeley: California University Press, 1982.
8. Wildavsky (note 5) p.98; for a more reserved view on this issue see Blondel (note 5) pp.100–4.
9. A. Yaniv (ed.), *National Security and Democracy in Israel*, Boulder, CO: Lynne Rienner, 1993, pp.227–30.
10. E. Sprinzak and L. Diamond (eds), *Israeli Democracy Under Stress*, Boulder, CO: Lynne Rienner, 1993.
11. A. Lijphart, *The Politics of Accommodation*, Berkeley: University of California Press, 1968; Lijphart, "Consociational Democracy," *World Politics* 21/2, 1969; Lijphart, "Majority Rule versus Consociationalism in Deeply Segmented Societies," *Politikon* no.4, 1977; Lijphart, *Democracies: Patterns of Majoritarian and Consensus in Twenty One Countries*, New Haven, Yale University Press, 1984; Lijphart, "Israeli Democracy and Democratic Reform in Comparative Perspective," in Sprinzak and Diamond (note 10); K. McRae (ed.), *Consociational Democracy: Political Accommodation in Segmented Societies*, Toronto: McLelland and Stewart, 1974.
12. P. Schmitter, "Still the Century of Corporatism," *Review of Politics* 36, 1974; Schmitter, "Modes of Interest Intermediation and Models of Societal Change in Western Europe," *Comparative Political Studies* 10/1, April 1977; P. Schmitter and G. Lehmbruch (eds), *Trends Towards Corporatist Intermediation*, California: Sage, 1979; Lehmbruch, *Proporzdemokratie: Politiches System und Politische Kultur in der Schweiz und in Osterich*, Tubingen: J.C.B. Mohr, 1967; Lehmbruch, "Consociational Democracy, Class Conflict, and the New Corporatism," Paper presented to IPSA Round Table on "Political Integration," 1974; Lehmbruch, "Liberal Corporatism and Party Government," *Comparative Political Studies* 10/1, April 1977; A. Cawson (ed.), *Organized Interests and the State: Studies in Meso-Corporatism*, London: Sage, 1985; Cawson, *Corporatism and Political Theory*, New York: Basil Blackwell, 1986.
13. S. Eisenstadt, *Israeli Society*, Jerusalem: Magnes, 1967 (Hebrew); M. Lissak and D. Horowitz, *The Origins of the Israeli Polity*, Tel Aviv: Am Oved, 1977 (Hebrew); A. Dowty, "Israel's First Decade: Building a Civic State," in I. Troen and N. Lucas (eds), *Israel: The First Decade of Independence*, Albany, NY: SUNY Press, 1995.
14. On the debate about the applicability of the consociational model to the Israeli case, see E. Gutmann, "Parties and Camps – Stability and Change," in M. Lissak and E. Gutmann (eds), *The Israeli Political System*, Tel Aviv: Am Oved, 1997 (Hebrew); G. Sheffer, "Elite Cartel, Vertical Domination and Grassroots Discontent in Israel," in S. Tarrow et al. (eds), *Territorial Politics in Industrial Nations*, New York: Praeger, 1978; M. Lissak and D. Horowitz, *Trouble in Utopia*, Tel Aviv: Am Oved, 1990 (Hebrew); P. Medding, *The Founding of Israeli Democracy 1948-1967*, New York: Oxford University Press, 1990; Lijphart, "Israeli Democracy and Democratic Reform" (note 11); Dowty, "Israel's First Decade" (note 13).
15. Lehmbruch, *Proporzdemokratie* (note 12).
16. E. Nordlinger, *Conflict Regulation in Divided Societies*, Cambridge, MA: Center of International Affairs, Harvard University, 1972; and on its application to the Israeli case, see Sheffer, "Elite Cartel, Vertical Domination and Grassroots Discontent" (note 14).
17. Troen and Lucas, *Israel. The First Decade of Independence* (note 13).
18. S. Eisenstadt, *The Transformation of Israeli Society*, London: Weidenfeld and Nicolson, 1985.
19. Lehmbruch, "Liberal Corporatism and Party Government" (note 12) pp.112–13.
20. Ibid.
21. Y. Yishai, *Interest Groups in Israel*, Tel Aviv: Am Oved, 1987 (Hebrew).
22. M. Shalev, *Labor and the Political Economy in Israel*, New York: Oxford University Press, 1992.
23. Lehmbruch, "Liberal Corporatism and Party Government" (note 12) p.94.
24. Lissak and Horowitz, *Trouble in Utopia* (note 14).
25. Etzioni-Halevy (note 1).
26. Wildavsky (note 5) pp.100–1.

27. M. Burns, *Leadership*, New York: Harper, 1979; Bass (note 4); B. Bass and B. Avolio, "Transformational Leadership: A Response to Critiques,", in M. Chemers and B. Ayamn (eds), *Leadership Theory and Research*, San Diego: Academic Press, 1993.
28. P. Gronn, "Greatness Re-visited: The Current Obsession with Transformational Leadership," *Leading and Managing* 1/1, 1995.
29. Burns (note 27) p.434.
30. On the concept of leadership generations and its applicability to the Yishuv and Israeli case see, for example, Y. Shapiro, *An Elite Without Successors, Generations of Political Leaders in Israel*, Tel Aviv: Sifriat Poalim, 1984, pp.54–6 (Hebrew).
31. Eisenstadt, *Transformation of Israeli Society* (note 18).
32. Troen and Lucas, *Israel. The First Decade of Independence* (note 13).
33. L. Edinger, "The Comparative Analysis of Political Leadership," *Comparative Politics*, January 1975.
34. Bass (note 4).

Interest Politics in a Comparative Perspective: The (Ir)regularity of the Israeli Case

YAEL YISHAI

Interest groups have long been central to understanding political structure and political process. The study of associational politics may provide a clue to one of the most intriguing questions addressed by political scientists: Who governs? Who, in other words, controls power and influence? The state or social actors? Organized interests or public authorities? The literature on interest groups in developed countries is voluminous, and there are also excellent studies on interest politics in less developed countries.[1] Yet relatively few attempts have been made to tie together the study of interest groups in various economic and political systems. Thus, in studying interest groups comparatively, Gabriel Almond and Henry Ehrmann were pioneers in this respect,[2] but their work has not stimulated a larger volume of literature.[3] This article uses Israel as a focal point for such an undertaking, probing the nature of Israeli interest politics in an effort to grasp both the uniqueness of Israel and the changes it is undergoing. Does Israel fit into models describing interest politics in other democracies? What is the scope and direction of change in interest politics? What are its determinants? These are the central questions addressed below.

ISRAELI INTEREST GROUPS IN A COMPARATIVE PERSPECTIVE

The major goal of this article is to review, through comparative lenses, how government and the major interests in society connect. This is part of the general attempt made by political scientists to understand the relationship between state and society. Three answers have been given to the question of who has the power to influence policy decisions: the pluralist, the corporatist, and the partyist (elitist). In the first, the state responds to the will of interest groups; in the second, it shares power

Yael Yishai is at the Department of Political Science, University of Haifa.

with organized public groups, incorporating them into decision making; and in the third, the state "governs," that is imposes its will on voluntary associations using political parties as a major instrument of control. More specifically, pluralism is associated with a strong society where interest groups form the core of politics, a civil society comprised of diverse, fluctuating, competing goups of individuals with shared interests.[4] Liberal corporatism, while not clearly defined[5] constitutes a system of "integrated participation," where formal rights are granted by the state to major interest groups.[6] In the elitist configuration, the state is colonized by political parties, also tending to penetrate social organizations.[7] While these three configurations of power are ideal types, they provide useful tools to explore relationships between state and society in democratic regimes.

Elitism

Elitism has been identified in states undergoing a process of nation-building where political parties are pervasive. These states tend to suffer from three disadvantages: economic want, unsettled legitimacy, and external threat. To overcome these challenges the state takes upon itself to mobilize the voluntary sector to extract resources and maintain control over society.[8] Mobilization is sustained through a national "vision," a feature prevalent among countries undergoing structural and political changes.[9]

Strong parties also breed elitism. As a general rule, parties offer policy alternatives and attempt to secure control of government. In such "party states" parties are not content with their formal "political" role but also penetrate society, attempting to pervade social institutions, including voluntary associations.

Corporatism

Corporatism is characterized by a powerful state machinery and centralized interest arena. A strong state enjoys autonomy, attains cohesion among its sub-units, and enlists the support of important social sectors.[10] The application of a host of laws, rules, regulations, and administrative decrees that govern society and the economy through the state bureaucracy constitutes a manifestation of power by state organs.

Furthermore, corporatist society is characterized by a limited number of interest groups, each monopolizing its own domain of interest. The interest group map is plotted by their functional contribution to society. Competition among groups is infrequent. Rather, continuing attempts are made to forge mutual accommodation and collaboration among major economic interests.

Pluralism

Pluralism (or polyarchy) is by definition a product of diversity and, moreover, a normative acknowledgment that this diversity is essential for

Interest Politics 75

the maintenance of society. The proponents of pluralism posit that civil society is made up of a plethora of fluctuating, competing groups of individuals with shared interests. Consequently, politics is perceived as competitive and contentious. Assorted groups co-exist under a thin roof of consensus. The intricate social web is made up of a variety of threads that mesh into a colorful and kaleidoscopic fabric.

Another underlying feature of pluralism is the access available to policy contenders. All means of access to the authorities are acceptable so long as they remain within legal bounds. According to Dahl, under pluralism there is a high probability than any active and legitimate group in the population can make itself heard effectively at some crucial stage in the process of decision.[11]

The application of these characteristics to interest politics in Israel reveals both its compatibility with and departure from the three models of interest group politics. Israel, as pictured through the lens of interest group politics, does not fit neatly into any of the models, yet it reveals characteristics of all three.

THE IMPERATIVES OF NATION-BUILDING

Israel was established by Zionists who were determined to revolutionize the Jewish people by resettling them in their historic homeland. The founders coped with external hostility, domestic turbulence, physical hardships, and cultural challenges. The copious flow of immigrants, many requiring retraining to fit into a modern economy, placed another burden on the state. Consequently, there was vital need for a strong central power capable of mobilizing the population and enlisting its energy for national goals. One manifestation of this need was a sweeping regulation of interest groups.

The Associations' Law, adopted in 1980, regulated interest groups by imposing the duty to register and by issuing directives for internal organization. The law specifies that an association can become fully established only upon registration by the Registrar, an appointed state official. Although freedom of association is upheld by the law, request for registration may be denied if the objectives of the association are contrary to law or public morale, and if they endanger the security of the state or public order. These vague but sweeping conditions for registering interest groups vest enormous powers in the state official, at whose discretion interest groups rise and fall. An interest group can appeal, though, to a District Court to challenge the Registrar's decision.

Once an association is registered it enjoys all vested rights, such as the right to hold property and the right to appear in court. Yet the association's internal affairs remain supervised by the state, specifying in great detail what must and must not be done in associational life. For example, the group must convene an annual general meeting and elect a central committee and an audit committee. It is free to issue its own regulations, but these must comply with those specified by the law. The state can, without much difficulty, dismantle an association under one of five conditions specified by the law, including violation of the Associations' Law. Likewise, if the association aims at undermining the existence of the State of Israel or its democratic nature it may be abolished.

This regulation of interest groups, almost unmatched by other democracies, was provoked by the exigencies of nation-building. Faced with the need to mobilize the population on the one hand and to safeguard the state against domestic insurgency on the other, the state could not allow wide leeway for associational activity. The formal political space available to interest activity was thus highly supervised by the state.

A PARTY STATE

Political parties played a crucial role in the formation of the state and in managing its political affairs. Israel has been called a party democracy because political parties provided social services, including welfare and health. They also mobilized the electorate by penetrating different sectors of the population and offering them services in exchange for political support.[12] Parties controlled nomination to political offices, and they colonized the state by securing patronage positions in the bureaucracy and in the major public and quasi-public corporations. In short, they established a network of relationships, based on the allocation of benefits and state assistance in exchange for votes and political activism. To perform these functions Israeli parties established a disciplined organizational structure and penetrated the bureaucracy. Needless to say, in a party state political parties fulfill an essential role in the policy process.

One of the products of the party-state was the establishment of close relationships with interest groups, with the parties integrating them into their ranks. A good example is the kinship between the Labor Party and settlement associations. Most parties established women's associations, sports clubs, sick funds, and other associations providing welfare and benefits for their membership. Public interest groups were also linked to political parties. Gush Emunim, for example, maintained a close relationship with the National Religious Party and Hatehiya, a small right-wing party. Its adversary Peace Now was affiliated with Mapam (Meretz) and the Labor Party. Most immigrant associations were directed by political parties. Party penetration into the interest arena was thus deep and ample.

THE POWERFUL BUREAUCRACY

By any standard, the Israeli state has long been one of the more pervasive political organizations in the democratic world. This includes the proportion of government spending, influence on the labor market, taxation, domination of the credit market, ownership of natural resources, and control of infrastructure. The state was also the largest employer in the country, with a large civil service.[13] The state is big and powerful, and the extent of economic regulation has been enormous. State hegemony is embedded in the political culture. Israel was founded by people who were brought up in countries where a "statist" political culture prevailed. As noted by Elazar, the expectations of Israelis were that "a proper state must be a reified one, that is, one standing outside of and above its citizens and existing independently of them. Such a state...was viewed as a major instrument for social change and, accordingly, was expected to...intervene in every aspect of life in order to bring about the necessary changes."[14] A collectivist economic philosophy assigned great significance to the achievement of national economic goals through the public sector owned by the state. The state, in short, was the institution responsible for the fulfillment of a primordial Jewish right to sovereignty.[15]

State supremacy was also manifested in bureaucratic control over decision making, be it in economic, social, or defense arenas. Who would gain and who would lose was to a large extent an administrative decision, giving enormous power to those occupying senior positions in the civil service, particularly on the national level but also in local government. For decades the state qualified as "strong" because it was sufficiently autonomous to make important decisions, was not threatened by deep internal friction, and was not seriously challenged by contending groups and associations.

GROUP CONCENTRATION AND MONOPOLIZATION

Israeli interest groups are notable for their concentration. The business community is organized in a peak association known as the Coordinating Bureau of Economic Organizations, which claims to represent the sector as a whole. The Bureau is "comprehensive" because it draws its membership from most business sectors and addresses the general problems facing business in Israel.[16] The Histadrut, an umbrella organization of trade unions, also concentrates authority in this sector of the society. Concentration is evident on the meso-level as well. There is only one manufacturers' association; only one Chamber of Commerce; a single association of Contractors and Builders; and a single association of Hotel Owners. There is only a single medical association, and one organization of the student body in the country.

High membership density – that is, the proportion of actual members out of those eligible for membership – one of the major determinants of organizational monopolization, is also apparent in Israel. A wide range of rules and arrangements exists, both to bind members to "their" association and to prevent the emergence of competing groups. Data reveal that the majority of interest groups reported a membership density of 85 percent or more.[17] These include the major economic and professional associations. This concentration and monopolization of the interest arena is a major factor in the corporatist arrangements prevalent in Israeli society.

THE MELTING POT

Israel is a relatively small, highly centralized country with a unified system of government imbued with ideology, a "vision" that steers its political life. Yet it has also been described as a melting pot, having taken in an assortment of immigrants from all corners of the world. After 50 years of existence, many Israelis are still first-generation immigrants. In 1995, only 60 percent of the country's Jewish population were native born, and less than a quarter (24.7 percent) were second-generation Israelis.[18] Out of this diversity a nation has been forged. Genuine efforts were made to erase previous loyalties and redirect them to the nation as a whole. But remnants of the past have survived these efforts. Diversity is evident in other aspects of social life as well. Israeli society constitutes a zigzag of secular and orthodox, Jews and Arabs, affluent and underprivileged.

The interest group universe in Israel is growing daily. Between 1982 and 1996, 28,229 new associations were registered (including non-profit organizations),[19] for an annual average growth of 1,882. These cover all types, sizes, and shapes of organizations from the giant business associations to tiny groups of individuals organized to influence government to reduce the price of their medications. Despite the restrictions placed on group formation, the state has refrained from barring the formation of new interest groups.

Interest groups outside the economic sector have mushroomed. For example, the Ethiopian immigrants created some ten associations to represent their interests. The tendency to splinter is even more evident among the immigrants from the former Soviet Union. The new so-called "Russian" immigrants formed no fewer than thirty associations and groups. There are associations based on geographic location, such as Georgia, Caucasia, and Buchara, and others formed on the basis of profession, religiosity, and ideological orientation. This diversity, legitimized (albeit half-heartedly) by the authorities, provides a fertile soil for the emergence of pluralism.

GROUP ACCESS

Data collected in the late 1980s[20] reveal the high access enjoyed by associations to the centers of power. Robert Dahl's condition for pluralism, namely that each and every one will have an opportunity to raise a voice during the policy process, has been realized in Israel. The intensity of interaction between group activists and the formal organs of the state (including the bureaucracy and the legislature) reveals the extent of their access. Interest groups were offered ample opportunity to exert influence and make themselves heard in all corridors of power.

Access was obtained through political parties, as in the case of the Histadrut and the settlement movements, or through personal relations, as in the case of the professional and business community. While Israel has grown in population size, it still carries the intimacy of a close-knit and intimate society where personal acquaintance opens many doors. The elite connection, noted by scholars to be particularly extensive,[21] has enabled many segments of society to integrate into the core of power. This does not mean that every single group in society enjoys a privileged status. In fact, a clear distinction between "insiders" and "outsiders" was apparent in the first two decades of statehood. But even those not at the center of power could approach the authorities by exerting pressure. Studies of Israeli society reveal high incidence of pluralistic strategies, namely, the application of pressure on government authorities. Israel has abounded with demonstrations and strikes.[22] Some demonstrations, such as those following the massacre in Sabra and Shatila, actually made history, forcing the government to change its course.

As the foregoing has demonstrated, Israel fits into each of the three models of interest politics: it was deeply immersed in the process of nation-building, and controlled by powerful political parties (elitism); it displayed a strong state apparatus and a concentrated system of interest groups (liberal corporatism); and has a multitude of interest groups with wide access to decision making (pluralism). Yet the combination of the characteristics deriving from the three models places Israel in a unique "irregular" position, compared with the democracies on whose features these models were based.

WHITHER ISRAEL?

The underlying question is whether contemporary Israel portrays the same syndrome of interest politics as it did in the past. Have the political and economic changes sweeping the country left their imprint on interest group politics? If change is noticeable, as might be expected, is it revolutionary or radical? The answer to these questions is ambiguous. The associational arena is undergoing a discernible change, but some of the changes are frail and precarious. In each of the characteristics enumerated above change can be traced, and in each of them the picture is equivocal. Change has not been abrupt but has gradually evolved with the progress of Israeli society. Six changes are discernible on the interest group arena.

First, Israel now is a far less mobilized society than in the past. Decrease of mobilization has had various manifestations. To begin with, young people are much less inclined to rally around the flag. The military reported (in 1996) a decline in motivation among young army recruits to volunteer for combat units, and committees of investigation were formed to look into the causes of this phenomenon. Reduced mobilization is evident also in public behavior. Adamant challenge to the authorities is no longer as rare as it was in the heyday of state power. Challenge has turned into a daily matter, turning interest groups into more competitive and combative actors.

The second change is evident on the party scene. Parties have declined in terms of legitimacy, organizational assets, and control of power. Political parties enjoy the least trust (only 14 percent) accorded to public institutions by the Israeli public.[23] They are respected even less than the business community, generally a target of public discontent. Party membership has also declined, as membership stood at 19.4 percent for men and 14.9 percent for women in 1973 but by 1992 had declined to 11.9 percent and 6.3 percent.[24] Furthermore, the major parties (Labor and Likud) have lost control over the nomination of candidates for political office. The introduction of primaries has shifted the core of power from the party's elite to the mass membership, whose ties with the party may be tenuous. Finally, parties in Israel no longer play a socializing and mobilizing role as they did in the past. The party no longer provides health, education, jobs, or social security. The party press has collapsed, and social services have been bureaucratized. The electoral campaign is no longer conducted in smoke-filled home gatherings (*hugei bait*) but is administered by media experts. The upshot of these processes is an attenuation of the linkage between political parties and interest groups. Data indicate that only 20 percent of the groups in Israel contact political parties often or occasionally.[25] Since kinship no longer marks the Israeli associational arena, interest groups enjoy more autonomy in their choice of influence targets. Integration with a political party is no longer a necessary condition for political success, although it may still be useful. Change is nevertheless equivocal, because Israeli parties, while losing some of their previous power, still wield considerable influence. It would be an exaggeration to describe Israel as a US-style interest group democracy.

Third, while contemporary Israel is committed to economic decentralization and the downsizing of state power, only a small portion of government companies have been transferred to private ownership. The reasons for the delay lie both in the state's double language (stating its intention to privatize but not taking actual measures) on the one hand, and in the strong union resistance to the sale of public companies to private entrepreneurs on the other. Despite the slow pace of privatization, it appears that the power of the state is on the decline. The new Likud government has expressed a firm commitment to reduce the government's involvement in the economy. Global economic trends have also contributed to the reduction of state's control of the economy. As a result, some economic interest groups are more reluctant to maintain corporatist arrangements in alliance with the state. This may be the reason for the near collapse of the Agricultural Councils, responsible for planning and executing farm policy. However, despite the visible tendency toward economic downsizing public authorities still hold the reins of interest groups. In fact, regulation of interest groups has become more strict. A series of amendments to the Associations' Law was recently adopted, increasing the state's meddling in interest groups' affairs. In its attitude toward interest groups the state still adheres to the rule laid down by an ancient Jewish proverb: respect them and suspect them.

Fourth, interest groups have generally maintained their organizational concentration and monopolization. A remarkable change is noticeable, however, in the power of the Histadrut, a major example of monopolistic representation. The Histadrut has undergone a triple crisis: organizational, financial, and ideological. Separation of its sick fund from the Labour Federation itself has substantially diminished its numbers. The skyrocketing debts of the Histadrut enterprises, together with the decrease in membership fees, have generated a severe financial crisis. In addition, the Histadrut no longer perceives itself as a spearhead of nation-building but as a trade union fighting for the privileges of *some* salaried workers. Admittedly, the Histadrut still maintains a key position in wage negotiations, but its power has much dwindled. There has been a marked increase in so-called "private contracts" in the Israeli economy, particularly in the fast-growing high-tech industry, in which many workers are not represented by the Histadrut. The proportion of self-employed persons also doubled within two decades from 6.7 percent in 1974 to 12.7 percent in 1994.[26] Thus, although the Histadrut still signs collective agreements on behalf of salaried employees, it no longer serves as the only, and omnipotent, spokesperson for the workers in Israel.

The picture of change is equivocal, however, because efforts to decentralize the business sector have not been very successful. In 1972–73, 2 percent of all industrial establishments employed 100 or more workers. Some two decades later the proportion of "big" establishments had increased by more than 50 percent to 3.2 percent, with nearly half (49 percent) of industry workers.[27] These data reveal that the Israeli economy is highly concentrated, with giant corporations dominating many markets. The attempt to break the monopoly of the Coordinating Committee was only partly successful. An association representing the self-employed (Lahav) strove to join the economic triangle of state–workers–employers. But Lahav remained on the fringes of the economic arena, commanded by the big manufacturers, contractors, and importers, who continue to play a leading role in forging Israel's economic policy.

Fifth, the question is whether Israel is moving toward more diversity. Here no significant change has been identified but only the continuation of an ongoing process. Groups and movements continue to mushroom, giving vent to all interests and shades of opinion. The electoral campaign provides a good example this. Some three dozen groups published ads in the daily press urging the voters to prefer one candidate for premiership over the other. These movements, some of which are highly organized (such as the Committee of the Golan Settlers) and some less structured (such as The People with Peres), clustered along the ideological positions dividing Israeli society. Civic activity has become rampant on the local scene as well. There are daily reports of disgruntled citizens organizing to pressure their local authority to address a grievance. Israel is now a more participatory society than in the past.

Finally, the basic tenet of pluralism, that any voice should be heard at some stage of the policy process, has also become more valid. Very few voices have retained the status of permanent outsiders. Religious zealots (such as the Hassidic movement Habad) eagerly campaigned on behalf of a secular contender for premiership; ardent nationalists (Zu Artzenu) operated under the auspices of the right-wing political camp; Muslim extremists (the Islamic Movement) openly preached their advocacy and gained legislative representation; homosexuals were cordially hosted in the Knesset, and Ethiopians, violently protesting against alleged discrimination, were guests of honor in the President's residence. Not one single group appears to have remained excluded. The wide access available to groups is, however, not immutable. The ascendancy of the national-religious camp may limit the access of those speaking with a different voice. It will, for instance, temper the access of gays, castigated by religious precepts, or reform Jews, who are unacceptable to rabbinical institutions.

In sum, changes are noticeable in every aspect of interest group politics: groups are no longer mobilized to the national cause. They have torn the umbilical cord that attached them to political parties, and state power is gradually shrinking. Organizational concentration of interest groups has somewhat dissipated, while the associational arena has become more diverse and access has widened. Nonetheless, these changes are equivocal, and the paradoxes characterizing Israeli society are still clearly visible.

DETERMINANTS OF CHANGE

The changes in interest politics result from economic, cultural, and political developments. Economic changes have turned Israel into an affluent society with an average annual growth of nearly 6 percent throughout its existence. The personal income of the Israeli was nearly $16,000 in 1996, not far from the European level. The standard of living, as measured by the diffusion of durable goods, has risen dramatically. Some 60 percent of Israelis own their own home; some half the population possess a car. Air tickets must be reserved months ahead because of the massive exodus of the Israeli travelers during summer vacation. Inflation, at least double that of the western levels, is a reminder that there are flaws in the economic heaven. But economic prosperity is highly conspicuous. The heading of a letter printed in a daily paper declared: "We are tired of raising the banner. We want to enjoy life."[28] In contemporary Israel, consumerism is the good life, not draining swamps or making the desert bloom.

The most important cultural factor contributing to the change in interest politics is the shift from collectivism to individualism. Emphasis on the private realm is evident in art, music, poetry, and literature. Israel's intellectual and cultural elite have challenged the collectivist mores of Israeli society, mores that mobilized the citizenry to fulfill national missions. Young Israelis, like their US counterparts, are turning into a "me generation," centered upon the self rather than upon the future of the Jewish people. These changes have evolved gradually. Already in the 1970s they were grasped by Amos Elon, who pinpointed the generation gap in Israeli society. He said: "The old pioneers pursued essence; the younger generation's approach is existential....The former were oriented to a future perfect; the latter are living intensely in the here and now."[29] Surveys comparing needs in 1970 and 1990 reveal a decline in all collective-oriented items. Fewer people are "proud we have a state," and fewer are interested in "what the world thinks of us." A striking decline of 13 percent (from 1970 to 1990) is evident in the feeling of a need to trust our leaders. At the same time individual-oriented items, such as "having a good time," "relaxing," or "getting to know myself," rose substantially.[30] This mood was captured by a senior military commander, who lamented the fact that "gratification of personal wishes is the absolute guiding principle evident during the military service."[31] Despite these clear indications of change nationalism, ethnocentrism, and fundamentalism are very much apparent among large sectors of the Israeli society, as manifested by the electoral results. Labor was defeated, so it was alleged, because it was associated with the "Sheinkin culture" identified with western non-Jewish values and remained oblivious to the widespread quest for tradition among Israelis.

Political changes have both resulted from and precipitated the shift in interest group politics. Macro-level changes were triggered by the inception of the peace process, but more relevant to interest politics are micro-level changes, particularly the primaries as a chief method of candidate selection by political parties, and the direct election of the prime minister. The political implications of these two practices on the polity are beyond the scope of this paper. Here, it is sufficient to note their impact on the associational arena. These two structural changes have made groups, associations, and movements extremely important in the political process for three reasons. First, interest groups constitute effective vote mobilizers. Although financial contributions of associations and corporations are strictly forbidden by law, groups can enlist support and muster resources other than money. This is, for example, what the Women's Network did for all women candidates. Second, associations can act on behalf of candidates by disseminating the message advocated by aspiring politicians, as the peace/territories movements did in the 1996 elections. Third, interest groups can rival parties by running a list by themselves. The split of vote between party and premier animates such rivalry. This was the case with the association of Russian immigrants who challenged the veteran parties with its own electoral bid. It remains an open question whether the structural changes in the Israeli polity killed its political parties. It is clear, however, that groups and movements have gained from the alteration in the rules of the political game.

To sum up, whether the changes evinced in Israel will turn it into a more democratic and/or efficient polity remains to be seen. The impact of these changes on the interest group arena, however, are likely to be significant.

CONCLUSIONS

Interest groups politics have been a central focus of this paper, offering a comparison between Israel and other democracies both on synchronic and diachronic levels. The three models of interest group politics – colonization of groups by the state (partyism), cooperation between state and groups (corporatism), and separation between state and groups (pluralism) – served as a basis for a synchronic comparison. Israel reflects none of these models yet all of them at one and the same time. It featured elitism because of the formidable tasks of nation-building, and because of the overwhelming power of political parties penetrating many aspects of social life. It also manifested strong corporatist attributes, owing to its capacious bureaucracy and the concentration of the economic sector. As an exuberant and vibrant democracy, it featured many elements of the pluralist society.

The underlying question is whether this particular combination is stable or dynamic. The foregoing analysis seems to point to discernible changes. Israel is no longer the immature state struggling with problems typifying new nations. The initiation of the peace process as well as the degree of economic development mitigate the effect of hardships characterizing the formative era. Political parties have encountered losses of power and influence; the state bureaucracy, while still holding many reins, is yielding at least some of its power to the private market. The Histadrut, the citadel of corporatism, is struggling to catch its breath, with the new circumstances wreaking havoc with its organization. The business community, while still concentrated, is gradually becoming diffused. Individualism and pluralism are ascending, the state and its establishment are descending.

Despite these noticeable changes, evoked by alteration in the economy, in society, and in the polity, the more things change the more the scene appears to be stable. While Israel of 1998 has little resemblance to Israel of 1948, the equivocation elaborated in each of the changes noted above reveals an evolutionary pattern, full of internal contradictions. Some of these contradictions are highly relevant to interest politics. If political parties have declined, why do so many associations (e.g., the association of ex-Soviet immigrants, the Golan settlers) choose to run an electoral list? If state power is becoming diffused, why does it enhance its penetration into the organizational life of voluntary associations? If individualism is on the rise, why did the people vote for coalitions of parties that emphasize collective needs? The answer to these questions may lie in one of the propositions suggested at the outset of this volume, namely that predicting that Israel will follow a slow and gradual pace of institutional change.

NOTES

1. Robert Bianchi, *Interest Groups and Political Development in Turkey*, Princeton, NJ: Princeton University Press, 1984.
2. For example, Gabriel A. Almond, "A Comparative Study of Interest Groups and the Political Process," *American Political Science Review* 52 (1958) pp.270–82, Henry W. Ehrmann (ed.), *Interest Groups in Four Continents*, Pittsburgh: Pittsburgh University Press, 1958.
3. For an exception see Clive Thomas (ed.), *First World Interest Groups: A Comparative Perspective*, Westport, CT: Greenwood, 1993.
4. Robert A Dahl, *Who Governs? Democracy and Power in an American City*, New Haven, CT: Yale University Press, 1961.
5. See, among others, Grant A. Jordan, "Pluralist Corporatism and Corporate Pluralism," *Scandinavian Political Studies* 7 (1984) pp.137–51; Peter J. Williamson, *Corporatism in Perspective. An Introductory Guide to Corporatist Theory*, London: Sage, 1989.
6. Johan P. Olsen, "Integrated Organizational Participation in Government," in P.G. Nystrom and W.H. Starbuck (eds), *Handbook of Organizational Design*, Vol.2, New York: Oxford University Press, 1984.
7. Alan Ware, *Citizens, Parties and the State. A Reappraisal*, Cambridge: Polity Press, 1987.
8. Joel S. Migdal, *Strong Societies and Weak States, State-Society Relations and State Capabilities in the Third World*, Princeton, NJ: Princeton University Press, 1988.
9. David Apter, *The Politics of Modernization*, Chicago: University of Chicago Press, 1965, p.25.
10. A.E. Nordlinger, *On the Autonomy of the Democratic State*. Cambridge: Harvard University Press, 1981.
11. Robert A. Dahl, *A Preface to Democratic Theory*, Chicago: University of Chicago Press, 1965, p.154.
12. Peter Y. Medding, *Mapai in Israel*, Cambridge: CUP, 1972; Nathan Yanai, *Party Leadership in Israel. Maintenance and Change*, Ramat Gan: Turtledove, 1981; Asher Arian, *Politics in Israel. The Second Generation*, Chatham, NJ: Chatham House, 1989.
13. Ira Sharkansky, *The Political Economy of Israel*, New Brunswick, NJ: Transaction, 1987; Yakir Plesner, *The Political Economy of Israel*, Albany, NY: State University of New York Press, 1994.
14. Daniel Elazar, *Israel. Building a New Society*. Bloomington, IN: Indiana University Press, 1986, p.186.
15. Yoav Peled, "Ethnic Democracy and the Legal Construction of Citizenship: Arab Citizens of the Jewish State," *American Political Science Review* 86 (1992) pp.432–43.
16. William Coleman and Wyn Grant, "The Organization, Cohesion and Political Access of Business: A Study of Comprehensive Associations," *European Journal of Political Research* 16 (1985) p.468.

17. Yael Yishai, *Land of Paradoxes, Interest Politics in Israel*, Albany, NY: State University of New York Press 1991, p.180.
18. *Statistical Abstracts of Israel*, Jerusalem: Central Bureau of Statistics, 1996, p.86.
19. State Comptroller, *Annual Report 1996*, Jerusalem, 1997, p.608.
20. Data published by Yishai, *Land of Paradoxes* (note 17).
21. Eva Etzioni-Halevi, *Kesher Haelitot Vehademocratia BYisrael* (The Elite Connection and Democracy in Israel), Tel Aviv: Sifriat Poalim, 1993.
22. Sam Lehman-Wilzig, *Stiff-Necked People, Bottle-Necked System*, Bloomington: Indiana University Press, 1990.
23. Yohanan Peres and Ephraim Yuchtman-Yaar, *Trends in Israeli Democracy. The Public's View*, Boulder, CO: Reinner, 1992, p.20.
24. Yael Yishai, "Equal But Different? The Gender Gap in Israel's 1992 Elections," in Asher Arian and Michal Shamir (eds), *The Elections in Israel 1992*, Albany, NY: State University of New York Press, 1995, p.117.
25. Yishai, *Land of Paradoxes* (note 17) p.129.
26. *Statistical Abstracts* 1975, p.289; 1995, p.379.
27. *Statistical Abstracts* 1975, p.404; 1996, p.357.
28. *Haaretz*, 22 June 1996.
29. Amos Elon, *The Israelis, Founders and Sons*, London: Weidenfeld, p.260.
30. Elihu Katz *et al.*, *Leisure in Israel. Changes in the Forms of Cultural Activity 1970–1990*, Jerusalem: Israel Institute for Applied Social Research, 1992.
31. Ran Goren, "Parents for Easy and Pleasant Military Service," *Maariv*, 23 December 1994.

The Social Organization of the Israeli Economy: A Comparative Analysis

DANIEL MAMAN

While most scholars and public commentators still view the Israeli economy as organized along sectorial lines, this classification became less relevant in the mid-1960s as a consequence of the centralization and polarization of the economy. Instead of this sectorial classification, the Israeli economy might be viewed as a dual structure in which big business coexists with small firms. A central place in big business is held by several business groups, a feature shared with many societies in both developed and developing nations.

This article examines the factors contributing to the formation and dominance of business groups in Israel. To study these factors, I will draw upon studies of other societies where these groups prevail, especially studies on Japan, South Korea, and Taiwan. This is, therefore, a comparative analysis on two different levels: *within Israel*, I examine changes over time, while *between Israel and other societies* I highlight and contrast the structural characteristics of business groups. This article consists of three parts. First, the theoretical frame focuses on the central role of business groups and considers different explanations for their emergence. The second part centers on the Israeli business groups and compares the Israeli structure with that of the east Asian societies. The third focuses on political and economic factors contributing to the emergence of business groups in Israel.

BUSINESS GROUPS AND THE EXPLANATION FOR THEIR EMERGENCE

Business groups are a widespread phenomenon in modern capitalism and are found in many countries under various names, such as the *keiretsu* in

---

Daniel Maman is a Lecturer at the Department of Sociology and Anthropology at The Hebrew University of Jerusalem.

Japan, the *chaebol* in Korea, and the *grupos econ'omicos* in Latin America. Such groups play dominant roles in the economic and political realms in a variety of politically and economically different societies.[1]

Granovetter[2] defines a business group as "a collection of firms bound together in some formal and/or informal ways." Business groups can be seen as characterized by an "intermediate" level of binding. This definition excludes firms bound merely by short-term strategic alliances, as well as those groups of firms legally consolidated into a single entity. Thus, holding companies, trusts, stable cartels, and stable and loose coalitions such as some of the Latin American groups and Japanese intermarket groups are included, whereas trade associations are excluded. In the case of conglomerates, those that are stable, such as the Korean *chaebol*, and those which maintain personal and operational ties among sister firms, thus enabling resources to be shifted between firms in the group, are included. In contrast, the instability of American conglomerates excludes them, as owners acquire them on financial grounds and when the financial situation changes they are quick to sell.

Studies on the emergence and dominance of business groups center on three theories: market imperfections, cultural heritage, and political economy. Economists suggest several explanations for the emergence of business groups.[3] Some of these explanations center around the notion that business groups are responses to economic problems. Leff, for example, argues that they are a microeconomic response to market failure in less developed countries.[4] Granovetter criticizes these arguments and notes that if they were correct, it would be difficult to explain the persistence of business groups in advanced capitalist economies such as those of Japan, Korea, and western Europe.[5]

Other economic explanations suggest that business groups arise in situations where they can provide some type of economic advantage. Goto[6] suggests that business groups offer a more efficient alternative for the transaction of intermediate goods than that of the market mechanism or internal organization. Biggart[7] criticizes the efficiency argument and asks how we can know that all existing structures are the most efficient if only the fittest survive.

Cultural explanations do not deal directly with the emergence of business groups. However, scholars have tried to establish some connection between the importance of the family, the inheritance system, and the emergence of business groups. Such a link is suggested in their explanation for the emergence of the Taiwanese family-oriented business groups. The Taiwanese business groups, in a similar way to those in South Korea, are based on family ties, except that they express the interests of an extended family rather than the will of a single patriarch.[8] In addition, the Chinese system of equal inheritance for all sons favors the fragmentation of family holdings from generation to generation. In spite of this, the Confucian belief system encourages trust among the extended family members. A Chinese businessman can with some assurance trust that people in his family network will respect the Confucian obligation to act with honor toward relatives whenever possible. Therefore, business is primarily conducted with members of one's kinship.[9]

The major weakness of the cultural explanation is that "culture pervades everything and therefore explains nothing."[10] For example, the importance of the family is common to Japan, South Korea, and Taiwan since they are part of eastern civilization. Nonetheless, the structure of business groups differs in these societies. Thus, Hamilton and Biggart argue that cultural explanations are not able "to distinguish the many differences that exist among these societies, including the organizational structure of business enterprises."[11]

Political economy explanations suggest that the emergence and dominance of business groups relate to the nature of the relationship between state and society. In each of the east Asian countries, for example, the state has pursued similar policies to promote industrialization.[12] However, the types of relationships between state and society differ markedly. In South Korea, the state actively participates in the public and private spheres of the economy. By controlling access to foreign exchange, offering bank credit at low interest rates and tax concessions, imposing price controls, and threatening tax investigations, the South Korean state has directed the strategic choices of major firms, especially the business groups, the *chaebol*.[13]

In Japan, in contrast to South Korea, the state policy toward business creates and promotes strong intermediate powers with considerable autonomy. The state coordinates activity and mediates between conflicting interests. The business groups and member firms are independent of direct state control, although they may acquiesce to the state's administrative guidance. Thus, the state–business groups relationship is one of cooperative partnership.[14]

Clearly, no single perspective can provide a full explanation for the emergence of business groups in every society. However, the political economy explanation seems relatively efficient when compared to other perspectives. As Feenstra *et al.* assert with regard to Japan, South Korea, and Taiwan, "the link between political and business power is unquestionably an important factor in the development of the business groups."[15] Still, such an analysis must take into account the specific historical context of the society examined.

This article therefore argues that a combination of political and economic factors has led to the emergence of business groups in Israel, with relationships between the state and society playing an important role. Moreover, the combined consequences of several economic developments have contributed greatly to the emergence and dominance of these groups.

BUSINESS GROUPS IN THE ISRAELI POLITICAL-ECONOMIC STRUCTURE

The history of the social organization of the Israeli economy can be divided into two periods: the sectorial and the dual. The sectorial period of the Israeli economy extended from the pre-state period to the second half of the 1960s. The roots of the sectorial economy are in the pre-state period, the Yishuv, during which several economic sectors existed. In addition to the important role played by the British Mandate in the economy, there were several economic sectors within the Jewish community itself, aligned to a political group: the private, the Histadrut, and the public or national sectors.[16] The establishment of the Israeli state brought significant changes to many areas, not least to the economy. The most notable change in the economy was the emergence of the state organizations as the central actor. However, the sectorial organization of the economy persisted, and in addition to the private and Histadrut sectors, a new sector was established, the state sector.[17]

The sectorial structure of the economy of Israel had, by the late 1960s, shifted to a dual structure, in which a multitude of small firms and self-employed proprietors coexisted with big business.[18] The transformation of the social organization of the economy resulted from the processes of concentration which occurred primarily as a consequence of the business collapse in the recession of the 1960s, the 1967 and 1973 wars, the hyperinflation of the late 1970s, and the income derived from the weapons industries.

Since the early 1970s, Israel's core economy has been composed largely of a few firms that produce a significant proportion of the gross national product, employ a major share of the labor force, and control most of the capital in the system.[19] For example, in 1993 the total sales of the top 100 industrial firms made up 30 percent of the GNP. In this year, 133 industrial firms, which form less than 1 percent of all industrial firms, employed 31 percent of the entire industrial labor force; and the total exports of the top 100 industrial firms comprised 63 percent of all Israeli exports. Moreover, out of 54,000 corporations, the top one percent – the 540 largest firms in the economy – generated 67 percent of the corporate tax payments.[20]

At the top of Israel's core economy are six business groups. These groups and member firms are well known to the public and are frequently discussed in the popular press, where they are termed "concerns," but these groups have not been the subject of scholarly attention. The six key groups are: (a) the Koor group; (b) Bank Hapoalim; (c) Bank Leumi; (d) the I.D.B. group, owned by the Recanati family; (e) the Clal group (a partnership between Bank Hapoalim and the I.D.B. group); and (f) the Eizenberg group, owned by the Eizenberg family, which as of 1995 also owns the Israel Chemical group (ICL), previously owned by the State of Israel.[21]

There are three types of business groups in Israel: industry-centered groups (Koor); bank-based groups (Hapoalim and Leumi); and cross-sector groups (I.D.B., Clal, and Eizenberg), which own firms in different sectors of the economy. The I.D.B. group, for example, owns financial institutions, industrial firms, transportation firms, and energy and infrastructure firms. The Hapoalim and Leumi groups are mainly financial institutions; however, they also own a large number of stocks in industrial, construction, insurance, transportation, and energy and infrastructure firms. In contrast, industrial business groups own firms only in the industrial sector.

The centrality of business groups in the Israeli economy is evident on a variety of dimensions. For example, the total sales of the Koor group made up 9.2 percent of the Israeli GNP in 1985; this group employed 11 percent of the total industrial labor force and was responsible for 6 percent of Israeli exports. The total sales of Clal Industries, the parent company of industrial firms in the Clal group, made up 3 percent of the Israeli GNP in 1988, and Clal employed 4.1 percent of the total industrial labor force. The Hapoalim group controlled 31–36 percent of all activities of the banking industry in 1993.[22]

Each business group in Israel consists of many firms. In 1986, the Koor group, for example, wholly or partly owned 300 companies, while the Clal group owned more than 100 firms. Each firm in the group has an independent legal existence and separate management and boards of directors. The firms in each group are owned directly by holding companies, and the parent firm in each group owns all the holding companies. For instance, the Clal group is organized around several sectors: industry, insurance, finance, building and construction, and trade. In each division, the holding company owns the firms in that branch. Thus, Clal Industries owns many industrial firms; Clal Israel, the parent firm in the group, owns all the holding companies, which in turn own the firms in specific industries. This structured pattern of vertical authority characterizes all Israeli business groups.

The dominance of business groups in the Israeli economy is strengthened by intergroup ties. The groups are tied together through business relations and share many joint venture firms. Some are co-partnerships between groups (e.g., Clal group, Delek, Nesher), others between business groups and other firms from big business (Teva), and still others are joint ventures between state organizations and business groups, which are politically and economically the most important (Zim, Industrial Bank).

The business groups in Israel, as in other societies, are tied together not only through business relations but also via social relations. Managers from one business group sit on boards of firms from other groups, while the boards of joint venture firms shared by many business groups serve as institutional linkages among managers of different business groups.[23] Similarly, policy forums, which are institutional settings for encounters between state and non-state organizations, allow divergent interests to influence decision-making, linking managers of different business groups, along with other elite members.[24]

A Comparative Analysis of the Structure of Business Groups

A comparative analysis suggests that the social organization of the Israeli economy is not unique, and that it shares several structural features with other societies where business groups prevail. There are many differences in the social organization of the economies of Japan, South Korea, and Taiwan. However, the significant actor in the economy of these societies, as in Israel, is not the firm *per se* but rather collections of firms. In each society there are distinct organizational sets. In Japan there are six intermarket groups *(Kigyo Shudan)* and ten large independent industrial and financial groups *(kerietsu)*; in South Korea scholars identify 50 large groups, the *chaebol*; in Taiwan 96 business groups *(jituanqiye)*; and in Israel six business groups, which are termed the "concerns." Thus, Israel has the fewest business groups (Table 1), and its business groups differ markedly in several other dimensions, namely: the number and size of affiliated firms, authority structure, relationship between the groups, and the economic impact of the groups.[25]

Israel's business groups are most similar to those of Japan with regard to number of affiliated firms. In Israel tens and even hundreds of firms are owned fully or partly by each group. Similarly, in Japan the six intermarket groups average 112 firms each and the ten independent *kerietzu* have approximately 33 firms each. By contrast, in South Korea each group has few affiliated firms, an average of 11, and in Taiwan the number of affiliated firms is the smallest, typically fewer than 8 each.[26]

The vertical authority structure of the Israeli business groups, however, more resembles the South Korean *chaebol* than it does the Japanese and Taiwanese business groups. In both Israel and South Korea, member firms are closely controlled by central holding companies. In Japan, by way of contrast, two authority structures exist: horizontal in the inter-groups and vertical in the independent groups. Unlike either Japan or South Korea, Taiwan has a relatively low level of vertical and horizontal integration and a relative absence of oligarchic concentration.[27] However, in spite of the similarities between Israel and South Korea, the holdings companies in South Korea are owned by an individual or a family,[28] whereas in Israel two of the groups are owned by family owners (Recanati and Eizenberg), two more by other business groups (Hapoalim and I.D.B.), and another two used to be owned until the mid-1980s by public organizations (Histadrut and World Zionist Organization) and in 1996 were owned *de jure* by the State of Israel and *de facto* by their managers.

The relationships among the business groups in Israel resemble those of Japan more than South Korea. In both Israel and Japan, cooperation characterizes business group relations, whereas in South Korea intense

TABLE 1
COMPARISON OF BUSINESS GROUPS FEATURES

	Israel	South Korea	Japan	Taiwan
The Unit of Analysis	Six groups: 1 industrial 2 bank 3 cross sectors	50 largest groups the *chaebol*	Six intermarket (*Kigyo Shudan*) and the 10 largest independent industrial and financial groups (*keneitsu*)	96 business groups (*jituanqiye*)
Number	Few	Many	Few	Many
Number of Affiliated Firms	Large – tens and even hundreds of firms owned fully or partly by each group	Few – an average of 11 firms	The Largest – an average of over 112 firms to each of the six intermarket groups; and about 33 firms for each of the ten independent *keritezu*	The smallest – typically fewer than 8 affiliated firms each
Number of Workers of Affiliated Firms	Large - the number of workers ranges from hundreds to thousands	Not as large as Japan – averaging less than 1500 workers	Large - with an average of more than 2800 workers	Small companies with only few hundred workers
Authority Structure	Vertical	Vertical	Two different modes: horizontal in the intergroups; vertical in independent groups	Relatively low levels of vertical and horizontal integration and oligarchic relative absence of concentration
Relationships between the Groups	cooperation – many joint ventures; direct and indirect interlocking ties	competition – member of the groups will not buy from firms in others group	cooperation – firms participate in more than one group; reciprocal inter-group stockholdings; inter-group financing; inter-group exchange of goods by trading companies; many joint enterprises; membership in many business associations	
Position in the Economy	Central	Central	Central	Not central

competition exists between the groups. However, in Japan there are more social and organizational mechanisms fostering inter-group cohesiveness that are not found in Israel. In Japan, firms participate in more than one group and economic activity and are characterized by reciprocal inter-group stockholdings, inter-group financing and inter-group exchange of goods by trading companies. There are many joint enterprises, and membership of many business associations is commonplace. In Israel, the cooperation between the groups takes the form of numerous joint ventures and direct and indirect interlocking ties between boards of directors.[29]

In addition, Israeli, Japanese and South Korean business groups are at the center of their respective economies. In Israel, for example, the contribution in 1994 of the Hapoalim group to the Israeli GNP was 8.2 percent.[30] In contrast, in Taiwan, business groups are not such a central feature in the economy.[31]

To summarize, the social organization of Israeli big business resembles that of other societies where business groups prevail. Analysis of structural features, in addition, indicates that the Israeli groups are similar in some respects to those in Japan, and in others to those in South Korea. This comparative analysis facilitates deeper understanding of the social organization of Israeli big business. The rest of this article considers factors that have contributed to the emergence and dominance of business groups.

EXPLANATIONS FOR THE EMERGENCE OF BUSINESS GROUPS IN ISRAEL

The emergence of business groups in Israel is the result of a combination of political and economic factors. These factors are interwoven, but for analytical purposes I will treat them separately. In any case, a crucial factor in the emergence and dominance of business groups has been the intended policies and actions of state organizations and the unintended consequences of these policies. The Israeli state itself, as in other newly industrializing countries, directed economic development. The state was responsible for the industrialization from the 1950s onward, for the emergence of the military-industrial complex in the mid-1960s, and for the privatization policy in the 1980s. Economic developments also have heightened the extent of economic concentration trend, including the business collapse after the recession of the 1960s, the hyperinflation of the late 1970s, the economic crisis in the mid-1980s, and the rapid growth from the early 1990s.

Political Factors: The Israeli State and the Business Groups

State organizations, together with business groups, are the main actors in the political-economic structure of Israel. The state, which is the most important actor, is composed of many organizations, some of them political networks, others bureaucratic institutions, and still others economic enterprises. Three factors have led to the centrality of the state in the Israeli economy. First, state organizations have been involved, directly and indirectly, in the management of the economy to a greater degree than normally occurs in other western industrial democracies. Second, unlike these democracies, the Israeli state possesses a vast array of capital resources, some derived from foreign aid. Finally, the burden of maintaining a democratic society in the face of continuous military conflict and periodic waves of immigration has led to an unusual concentration of power in the hands of the state. The dominance of state organizations means that political considerations often dictate economic activity.[32] One consequence of the deep involvement of state organizations in the economy is the emergence of business groups. In this respect, Israel is closer to South Korea than it is to Japan and Taiwan.[33]

The economic boom from the mid-1950s to the mid-1960s stemmed from the development policy of state apparatus, the mobilization of capital from foreign sources, such as German reparations, and the population's continuous expansion as a result of huge waves of immigration.[34] One important consequence of the economic boom was the capital accumulation by some of the largest firms, which used this capital to purchase other firms.

Consolidation in the financial sector was already underway by the 1950s. For example, the number of cooperative credit associations shrank from 95 in 1954 to 29 in 1960. Most of the cooperative credit associations were merged into the commercial banks and in particular to the three largest banks (Leumi, Discount, and Hapoalim). As a consequence of this wave of mergers, by 1961 the three largest banks together controlled two-thirds of the finance sector.[35] For example, between 1956 and 1957, the balance of Bank Hapoalim grew by 48 percent, the equity grew by 200 percent, and the number of branches grew from 19 to 82.[36]

While origin of the business groups resulted from the state developmental policy in the 1950s and early 1960s, the prosperity of the military industry from the late 1960s onwards led to the polarization of the economy and dominance of business groups. The 1967 War was the turning point for the weapon industry in Israel. After that war, the arms race in the Middle East led to a sharp increase in the Israeli defense budget. In addition, the French embargo on military equipment after the 1967 War strengthened the self-sufficiency doctrine, which encouraged the development of the weapon industry. According to this doctrine, local producers should supply most of the needs of the Israel Defense Forces.[37]

Since 1967, the defense industry developed into the country's central industry. In the early 1980s defense manufacturing accounted for over 25 percent of the entire industrial labor force (compared to 3.7% in 1955); 28 percent of Israeli exports were derived from this industry (compared to 13% in 1972). In 1984, more than 65 percent of the research and development in Israel was carried out in the defense industry (compared to 13% in civilian industry); more than 50 percent of all scientists and engineers were employed in this sector; and between one-quarter and one-third of them were engaged in research and development.[38]

Most defense firms are large corporations with central positions in big business. In addition, most defense firms are either state-owned corporations or members of one of the business groups. For example, the State of Israel owns the Israel Aircraft Industries, the Israeli Military Industry (Taas), and the Armament Development Authority (Rafael); the Koor group owns firms such as Tadiran, Soltam, and Telrad; the I.D.B. group owns firms such as Elbit and Iscar Ballads; and the Clal group owns firm such as Urdan Industries and Voulkan Industries.

The central position of the defense industry in the economy of business groups is exemplified in the activities of Koor group. Mintz[39] shows how defense production accounts for a significant share of Koor's industrial activity. For example, in 1982 over 50 percent of Koor group employees (out of a total 34,500 employees) were employed in defense-oriented firms; about 17 percent of Koor's local sales were directed towards the defense sphere; and about 20 percent of all Koor's exports originated in industries directly connected with defense manufacture.

Since the mid-1960s and especially after the 1973 War, the defense industry was the engine of the growth of the Israeli economy. However, corporations in the defense industry are highly dependent upon the state, through the defense budget. This dependency was particularly manifest in the economy of business groups. Actually, the defense budget was one of the important factors behind the prosperity and dominance of business groups in Israel. However, the enormous reliance on these budgets was one of the sources of crisis for the business groups in the 1980s. This dependence was most clearly manifested after the implementation of the "Stabilization Plan" in 1985. The aim of this government plan was to reduce inflation and to return the economy to more "normal" functioning. One of the measures adopted by the National Unity Government was a drastic cut in the state budget.[40] The sharp reduction of the defense budget, together with the crisis in the international weapons market, sparked a severe economic crisis in the defense industry, and consequently in some of the business groups. The most serious crisis took place in the Koor group (in firms such as Soltam, Tadiran, and Koor Metal).

The privatization policy in the 1980s, as with the industrialization of the 1950s, and the militarization of Israeli industry, is another state policy which affected the prospects and dominance of business groups in the Israeli economy. The Israeli state, with the support of most political parties, has since the early 1980s adopted this policy in order to privatize state industries. In at least two of the most important privatization acts in the Israeli economy in the 1990s the state sold its share to business groups. In the case of the Israel Chemical group (ICL) which controls all the mineral resources of Israel, the State of Israel sold 41 percent of its shares to the Eizenberg group, giving it control of ICL. In addition the state sold Shikun Vepituach, the largest building firm in the country to the Clal group (50%), the Eizenberg group (25.1%), and the Renaissance fund (24.9%), which is a joint firm of the Hapoalim group and other private investors. Thus, privatization policies have strengthened the central role of business groups in the economy.

Moreover, the state of Israel's ownership of the major banks, since the bank shares collapse in 1983, has opened the way for a state policy to restrict their non-financial activity. The government decided in 1995 that the banks should sell their shares in non-financial corporations, and by the end of 1996 they could not own more than 25 percent of the shares of non-financial corporations, and by the end of 1999 not more than 20 percent. Consequently, Bank Hapoalim, one of the largest business groups, sold 12 percent of its shares in Clal group. Most of these shares where sold to the I.D.B. group.

Thus, the privatization policy and the actions of state apparatus in selling state corporations have strengthened the centralization and polarization of the Israeli economy. This, together with other intended policies and actions of state organizations and the unintended consequences of these policies, has played a central role in the emergence and dominance of business groups.

Economic Developments and the Business Groups

The intended policies and actions of state organizations and the unintended consequences of these policies together with the consequences of a series of economic developments have strengthened the concentration trend and the central role of business groups. These economic developments include the business collapse after the recession of the 1960s, the hyperinflation of the late 1970s and early 1980s, the economic crisis in the mid-1980s, and the rapid growth from the early 1990s.

In the early 1960s, before the recession, the banks expanded their non-financial activities. Heth[41] asserts that this resulted from two developments: the profits from common banking activity shrunk due to a monetary constraint policy by the central bank, while the commercial banks invested in non-financial sectors as a result of the economic boom of the mid-1950s, and the prosperity of the stock exchange after the devaluation of 1962. This prosperity gave the banks a new opportunity to raise capital.

The recession in the 1960s, an intentional state policy,[42] was a turning point, and it deepened the processes of concentration and polarization, which Bichler[43] suggests were very intense during the period from 1967 to 1973. For example, the number of industrial firms with more than 300 employees grew from 72 in 1964–1965 to 164 in 1983–1984. The share of bank credit apportioned to large industrial firms also grew from 82 percent in 1960 to 91 percent in 1972, and the contribution of the largest industrial firms to the industrial output grew from 73 percent in 1969 to 81 percent in 1972.

Moreover, in the recovery from the recession there was a rash of mergers and takeovers. As a consequence of the process of concentration and of mergers and takeovers, business groups began to emerge. Heth, for example, reported on the wave of mergers in banking,[44] while Aharoni reported on the takeover of industrial and non-financial firms by the emerging business groups.[45]

The central position of business groups in Israel was strengthened even in the inflation era. Economists characterize the decade 1974–1984 as the "lost decade of the Israeli economy."[46] From the perspective of business groups, however, it was a golden era. In the hyperinflation period the only two economic sectors which continued to expand were the defense industry and the financial sector.[47] These two were the major source of growth of business groups in the inflation era. Bichler and Nitzan suggest that in the mid-1970s there was a sharp increase in the net profits of business groups, as a result of "military bias."[48] In other words, business groups benefited from the reliance on defense budgets and the militarization of big business.

In addition to the contribution of the military-industrial complex, high inflation helped business groups strengthen their dominance in the economy. Bruno and Meridor, for example, suggest that high inflation enables firms to achieve high profits through successful financial manipulation.[49] Shalev, in addition, asserts that banks were the most spectacular winners from the unleashing of inflation. By 1980 their share of Israel's barely growing GNP was close to double the level it had been five years earlier, and the same period also saw the collective net profits of the big three banks increase nearly fourfold in real terms.[50]

The mass immigration of Jews from the former Soviet Union in the 1990s is an additional factor strengthening the dominance of business groups. From mid-1987 until the mass immigration at the beginning of the 1990s the Israeli economy was characterized by recession.[51] From the end of 1989 until mid-1996 more than 750,000 immigrants from the former Soviet Union immigrated to Israel. This wave of immigration was one of the major causes of Israeli economic growth. The Israeli state, as in the past, adopted a developmental policy, in particularly in the building and infrastructure sectors.

One of the major firms which has reaped the benefits of the building sector boom since the beginning of the 1990s has been Nesher, which is a joint company owned by the Koor and Clal groups. Nesher has a monopoly in producing cement. The net profit of Nesher from 1989 to 1996 was one billion shekels (more than 300 million dollars). Tadiran and Telrad, two of the most important firms in the Koor group, benefited more than any other firm from the investment in the communication infrastructure by Bezek, a state-owned firm. For example, Telrad was responsible for more than 25 percent of the net profit of the Koor group in the years 1991–1996 (more than 460 million shekels).

To conclude, continuous concentration has occured in the Israeli economy, at least in part resulting from economic development. The effects of these economic processes cannot be separated from political factors, as the emergence and dominance of business groups are also the result of intended policies and actions of state organizations and the unintended consequences of these policies.

CONCLUSIONS

This article has, using comparative analysis, examined the factors which contributed to the emergence and dominance of business groups in the Israeli economy. The comparative analysis is organized along two axes of comparison: temporal changes in the structure of the Israeli economy and comparisons between structural features of the Israeli business groups and those of Japan, South Korea, and Taiwan.

The social organization of the Israeli economy had, by the mid- to end of the 1960s, changed from a sectorial to a dual structure, in which many small firms coexist with big business. A central place within that structure is held by several business groups. The shift in the economic structure has been an evolutionary process, a gradual and incremental process of change which continues today.

These organizational arrangements are not unique to the Israeli economy, and a comparative analysis indicates that with regards to their structural features, the Israeli business groups are similar in some respects to those in Japan, and in others to those in South Korea. In both Israel and Japan a central position in the economy is held by only a small number of business groups, there are many affiliated firms in each group and cooperation characterizes the relationships among the groups. Israeli and South Korean business groups share the vertical authority structure, and more importantly, in both countries state organizations play a crucial role in the economy.

The dual economic structure in which several business groups play a decisive role within big business was not the preferred structural arrangement of the state elites. Both the political leaders and heads of state bureaucracy favored a dispersed structure and have even taken action to advance it.[52] Given political and bureaucratic leaders' preference for a pluralist structure, it is ironic that their actions contributed to the emergence of the dual structure. This article has suggested that both political and economic factors led to the shift in the organization of the Israeli economy and to the emergence of dominant business groups. The intended policies and actions of state organizations and the unintended consequences of these policies, together with a series of economic developments, strengthened the concentration trend and placed the newly emerging business groups at the center of the Israeli economy.

ACKNOWLEDGEMENTS

The research on this paper has been supported by ISEF – The International Sephardic Education Foundation. A previous version was presented at the conference *Israel in Comparative Perspective: The Dynamics of Change*, Berkeley, CA, September 1996. I would like to thank Eyal Ben-Ari and Zeev Rosenek for their helpful comments and suggestions on earlier drafts. Special thanks are due to Daniel Salem for editorial assistance.

NOTES

1. See Encaoua David and Alexis Jacquemin, "Organizational Efficiency and Monopoly Power: The Case of French Industrial Groups," *European Economic Review* 19 (1982) pp.25–51; Michael L. Gerlach, *Alliance Capitalism: The Social Organization of Japanese Business*, Berkeley: University of California Press, 1992; Akira Goto, "Business Groups in a Market Economy," *European Economic Review* 19 (1982) pp.53–70; Gary G. Hamilton, William Zelie and Wan-Jin Kim, "The Network Structures of the East Asian Economies," in S.R. Clegg and S. Redding (eds), *Capitalism in Contrasting Cultures*, Berlin and New York: Walter de Gruyter, 1990, pp.105–29; Nathaniel H. Leff, "Industrial Organization and Entrepreneurship in the Developing Countries: The Economic Groups," *Economic Development and Cultural Change* 26 (1978) pp.661–75; Marco Orru', "Particle and Theoretical Aspects of Japanese Business Networks," in G. Hamilton (ed.), *Business Networks and Economic Development in East and Southeast Asia*, Hong Kong: Center of Asian Studies, University of Hong Kong, 1991, pp.244–71.
2. Mark Granovetter, "Business Groups," in J.N. Smelser and R. Swedberg (eds), *The Handbook of Economic Sociology*, Princeton, NJ: Princeton University Press, 1994, p.454.
3. Goto, "Business Groups in a Market Economy" (note 1); Hamilton *et al.*, "The Network Structures of the East Asian Economies" (note 1).
4. Leff, "Industrial Organization and Entrepreneurship" (note 1).
5. Granovetter (note 2) p.457.
6. Goto (note 1) p.64.
7. Nicole W. Biggart, "Explaining Asian Economic Organization: Toward a Weberian Institutional Perspective," in M. Orru', N.W. Biggart and G.G. Hamilton (eds), *The Economic Organization of East Asian Capitalism*, Thousand Oaks: Sage, 1996, p.16.
8. Marco Orru', Nicole Woolsey Biggart and Gary G. Hamilton, "Organizational Isomorphism in East Asia," in W.W. Powell and P.J. DiMaggio (eds), *The New Institutionalism in Organizational Analysis*, Chicago, The University of Chicago Press, 1991, pp.387–8.
9. Gary G. Hamilton and Nicole Woolsey Biggart, "Market, Culture, and Authority: A Comparative Analysis of Management and Organization in the Far East," *American Journal of Sociology* 94 (1988) p.S73.
10. Ibid., p.S87.
11. Ibid., p.S74.
12. Hamilton *et al.* (note 1).
13. Jones and Sakong, 1980, pp.100–40, cited in Richard D. Whitley, 1991, "The Social Construction of Business System in East Asia," *Organization Studies* 12/1 (1991) p.17.
14. Whitley, "The Social Construction."
15. Robert C. Feenstra, Tzu-Han Yang and Gary G. Hamilton, *Market Structure and International Trade: Business Groups in East Asia*, National Bureau of Economic Research, Working Paper No.4536, 1993, p.9.
16. Jacob Reuveny, *The Administration of Palestine under the British Mandate, 1920–1948: An Institutional Analysis*, Ramat Gan: Bar-Ilan University, 1993.
17. Yair Aharoni, *The Israeli Economy: Dreams and Realities*, London and New York, Routledge, 1991; Dan Horowitz and Moshe Lissak, *Trouble in Utopia: The Overburdened Polity of Israel*, Albany, NY: SUNY Press, 1989.
18. The classification of the Israeli economy as a sectorial structure may still have political and symbolic significance, but it lacks any practical significance.
19. Aharoni, *The Israeli Economy* (note 17); Shimshon Bichler, "The Political Economy of Military Spending in Israel," unpublished doctoral dissertation, The Hebrew

University of Jerusalem, 1991; Michael Shalev, *Labour and the Political Economy in Israel*, Oxford: Oxford University Press, 1992.
20. Dun and Bradstreet (Israel), *Dun's 100, Israel's Leading Enterprises*, Tel Aviv: Dun & Bradstreet, 1994; *Statistical Abstracts of Israel*, Central Bureau of Statistics, 1994; *State Revenue Administration*, Economic Research Development, Annual Report, No.44, 1994.
21. From the mid 1980s' changes began to occur in the ownership structure of several business groups as a consequence of the collapse of the bank share, privatizations of state corporations, and the reorganization of the Histadrut (Labour Federation). Until 1983 the Histadrut owned Bank Hapoalim and Koor, and the World Zionist Organization owned Bank Leumi. As a result of the banks' share collapse in 1983 the State of Israel in 1996 de jure owned Bank Hapoalim (with the Histadrut), Bank Leumi (with the World Zionist Organization), and Bank Discount (with the Recanati family). The Israel Chemical group, which until 1995 used to be owned by the State of Israel, was privatized and now is owned by the Eizenberg group. The Koor group, as a result of the reorganization of the Histadrut in the early 1990s and the economic crisis of the 1980s, in 1996 was owned by Bank Hapoalim and a group of international corporations (Shamrock group). The changes in ownership did not affect the dominance of business groups in the Israeli economy but rather strengthened it.
22. Dun and Bradstreet (Israel), *Dun's 100*, 1986, 1989; The State of Israel, *The Committee to Investigate Bank Investment in Commercial Companies*, 1995.
23. Daniel Maman, "Business Groups and Networks in Israel; A Study of Interelite and Intercorportae Relations," 1996 (unpublished manuscript).
24. Daniel Maman, "The Power Lies in the Structure: Economic Policy Forum Networks in Israel," *British Journal of Sociology* 48 (1997) pp.269–85.
25. Hamilton and Biggart, "Market, Culture and Authority" (note 9); Hamilton et al. (note 1); Gary G. Hamilton and Cheng-Shu Kao, "The Institutional Foundations of Chinese Business: The Family Firm in Taiwan," *Comparative Social Research* 12 (1990) pp.135–51; Orru' et al., "Organizational Isomorphism in East Asia" (note 8); Richard D. Whitley, "Eastern Asian Enterprise Structures and the Comparative Analysis of Forms of Business Organization," *Organization Studies* 11/1 (1990) pp.47–74.
26. Orru' et al., "Organizational Isomorphism in East Asia" (note 8) p.368.
27. Hamilton and Biggart, "Market, Culture and Authority" (note 9) p.S57–60.
28. Ibid., p.S59.
29. Maman, "Business Groups and Networks in Israel" (note 23).
30. *The Committee to Investigate Bank Investment in Commercial Companies* (note 22) p.45.
31. Hamilton and Kao, "The Institutional Foundations of Chinese Business" (note 25) pp.140–2.
32. Aharoni, *The Israeli Economy* (note 17); Samuel Hadar, "The Blurring of the Public and the Private in the Relationship of Government and Industry," unpublished doctoral dissertation, The Hebrew University of Jerusalem, 1988; Shalev, *Labour and the Political Economy in Israel* (note 19); Daniel Shimshoni, *Israel Democracy: The Middle of the Journey*, New York: The Free Press, 1982.
33. Nicole W. Biggart, "Institutionalized Patrimonialism in Korean Business," in Orru' et al. (eds), *The Economic Organization of East Asian Capitalism* (note 7) pp.215–36; Hamilton and Biggart, "Market, Culture, and Authority" (note 9); Whitley, "The Social Construction" (note 13).
34. Y. Ben-Porath, "Introduction," in Y. Ben-Porath (ed.), *The Economy of Israel: Maturing through Crisis*, Cambridge, MA: Harvard University Press, 1986.
35. Meir Heth, *Banking in Israel, Part One: Historical Survey*, Jerusalem: The Jerusalem Institute for Israel Studies, 1994, p.52.
36. Nachum Gross and Yitzhak Greenberg, *Bank Ha'poalim: The First 50 Years 1921–1971*, Tel Aviv: Bank Ha'poalim and Am Oved, 1994, pp.389–93.
37. Haim Barkai, "The Defence at a Crossroads," *Monthly Survey*, I.D.F. Chief Education Officer 34/9 (1987) pp.35–48; Eitan Berglas, *Defence and the Economy: The Israeli Economy*, Discussion Paper 83:01, The Maurice Falk Institute of Economic Research, Jerusalem, 1983; Aharon Klieman, *Double-Edged Sword: Israel Defence Exports as an Instrument of Foreign Policy*, Tel Aviv: Am Oved, 1992.
38. Haim Barkai, "The Defence at a Crossroads" (note 37); Alex Mintz, "An Empirical Study of Military Industrial Linkages in Israel," *Armed Forces and Society* (1985) pp.9–28.

39. Mintz, "An Empirical Study" (note 38).
40. Shalev, *Labour and the Political Economy in Israel* (note 19); Michael Bruno, *Crisis, Stabilization and Economic Reform: Therapy by Consensus,* New York: Oxford University Press; 1993; Paul Rivlin, *The Israeli Economy,* Boulder, CO: Westview Press, 1992.
41. Meir Heth, *Banking in Israel, Part Two: Structure, Activities and Crisis,* Jerusalem: The Jerusalem Institute for Israel Studies, 1994, pp.151–5.
42. Shalev, *Labour and the Political Economy in Israel* (note 19), suggests that during the first half of the 1960s the state's external resources of revenue contracted and, as a result, its dependence on foreign loans and overseas investors to finance the import surplus grew sharply. To counter its inability to maintain past levels of subsidy to business, during the 1966–1967 recession (*mitun*) the state attempted to cut capital's dependence on it; see also Lev L. Grinberg, *The Histadrut Above All,* Jerusalem, 1993.
43. Bichler, "The Political Economy of Military Spending in Israel" (note 19) p.179.
44. Heth, *Banking in Israel, Part One: Historical Survey* (note 35). For example, in 1971 the largest cooperative credit association, Halva Vehisacon, merged with Bank Hapoalim. The same credit association had previously merged with Zurbavel Bank in 1968, and with Bank Haroshet and Mischar in 1969.
45. Yair Aharoni, *Structure and Behavior in the Israeli Market,* Tel Aviv: Shericover, 1976. For example, in 1972 Bank Leumi took over Africa Israel, which is one of the largest building firms, and which owns the largest insurance corporation, Migdal; Clal group, which was set up by the State of Israel in 1962 to draw investment of Jews from South America, in 1972 took over the Havera Haisraelit Hamercizit, which was one of the largest investment firms and through this corporation it today owns many industrial firms; the Recanti family, which owns the Discount Bank, started in the early 1960s to invest in non-financial firms through Discount Investing Corporation, and gradually became one of the major business groups. In 1966, for example, it took over PEC, a firm owned by American Jews which invested in many industrial firms in Israel.
46. Ben-Porath, "Introduction" (note 34).
47. Jacob Kondor, *The Israeli Economy,* Jerusalem: Shocken, 1984; Arie Marom, "The Contribution of Inflation to the Growth of Israel's Banking Industry," *Seker Bank Israel* 62/33–44 (1987).
48. Shimshon Bichler and Jonathan Nitzan, "Military Spending and Differential Accumulation: A New Approach to the Political Economy of Armament – The Case of Israel," *Review of Radical Political Economics* 28/1 (1996) pp.56–7 and Figure 2.
49. Michael Bruno and Leora Meridor (Rubin), "The Costly Transition from Stabilization to Sustainable Growth: Israel's Case," *Bank of Israel: Research Department,* Discussion Paper 90:01, 1990; See also Marom, "The Contribution of Inflation" (note 47).
50. Shalev, *Labour and the Political Economy in Israel* (note 19).
51. Bruno and Meridor (note 49).
52. For example, in the late 1950s the political state elite and the Mapai leader in the Histadrut split the Solel Boneh conglomerate; in the early 1970, Pinhas Sapir, the finance minister, initiated the establishment of a new bank, the First International Bank, in order to increase the competition in the banking industry and reduce the centralization trend; in the mid-1990s the Israeli government decided that Bank Hapoalim and Bank Leumi should sell thier shares in non-financial corporations.

Business in Politics: Globalization and the Search for Peace in South Africa and Israel/Palestine

GERSHON SHAFIR

THE REDEFINITION OF THE CONFLICTS

Time chose as its "Men of the Year" for 1993 two pairs of peacemakers: F. W. de Klerk and Nelson Mandela, and Yitzhak Rabin and Yasser Arafat.[1] Earlier that year, the *New York Times* offered the direct Israeli–PLO talks as the model for Great Britain *vis-à-vis* Sinn Fein in Northern Ireland.[2] Indeed the coincidence in the breakthroughs in South Africa and Israel/Palestine, and the potential for such development in Northern Ireland, have been noted by many an observer but usually seen as fortuitous, due, as *Time* asserts, to the common genius and independent decisions of the four leaders. This perspective conveniently ignores the fact that of the four, only Mandela held to his non-racialist principles throughout, while de Klerk, hailing from the conservative wing of the National Party, was a latecomer to ideas of non-racialism and democracy. Arafat, for his part, sought to dismantle Israel through armed struggle for decades. Only in November 1988 did he accept the principle of a two state solution and Israel's right to exist. Finally, Rabin declined to respond to President Sadat's peace overtures during his first tenure as Prime Minister in 1977. If de Klerk, Arafat, and Rabin were destined to be peacemakers, it is a fate they embraced reluctantly and only in response to changing circumstances. In both cases, the turn toward peacemaking came after a long escalation period and the sudden softening shows signs of global influences. My question, therefore, is what were these global changes and how did they lead to amelioration in each case?

My purpose is not to provide a comprehensive explanation for the electoral transfer of power in South Africa or for the Israel–PLO agreements. I will not, therefore, undertake a detailed analysis of

---

Gershon Shafir is at the Department of Sociology, University of California, San Diego.

changes in the international environment, such as the breakup of the Soviet Union or the effects of the Gulf War on Arab solidarity, though these played a crucial role, limiting military options and creating auspicious circumstances for the peace process. I will also not examine security concerns, although this does not mean that they were insignificant. Without the massive civil disobedience campaign in South Africa or the six-year old Palestinian *intifada* and the failure of both security regimes to overcome the challenge, the moderation would never have occurred. The across-the-board mobilization disabused both white South African and Israeli Jews of whatever illusions they harbored concerning the passivity or the inability of blacks and Palestinians to undertake sustained national liberation struggles. There is little doubt that, in both cases, what William I. Zartman called the "hurting stalemate" swayed the security apparatus and their intelligence branches toward accommodation.

But if military security considerations in both South Africa and Israel began leaning toward accommodation, concerns for *economic* security took an equally prominent role. It is this latter that is the focus of this paper. The link between the festering conflicts and economic conditions became increasingly unavoidable after the post-1948 economic expansion, which provided a growing standard of living for whites and Jews for about a generation, was replaced by an extended period of economic stagnation. In South Africa, the downturn lasted throughout the 1980s, while in Israel most of the 1970s and the 1980s were marked by economic malaise directly or indirectly resulting from escalating conflict. In both countries, outward-looking business sectors, civil service elites, and intellectuals outside the state apparatus began questioning the institutions and practices that had provoked economic boycotts and sanctions preventing full participation in the world economy. Both conflicts remained at an impasse as long as they were viewed as racial or national confrontations or territorial and security problems, but both became "solvable" when reconceptualized as obstacles to the modernization of the economy. The new framework linked the imperative of economic growth to existing territorial, economic, and power redistribution questions, thus replacing a zero-sum game with one in which compromise could be mutually beneficial. In both South Africa and Israel, the accommodationist positions of business leaders and their allies helped redefine the conflict as an obstacle to economic modernization. This occurred at a moment of acute consciousness concerning the difference between "winning" and "losing" countries and belonged to a broader process extending the boundaries of the "economic" at the expense of the "political."

There are many differences between the South African and Israeli business communities. The former is over a century old and predates the South African state, while the latter is relatively new. Israel does not have the mineral riches and large labor force of South Africa, but South Africa largely lacks the high-tech industries that increasingly characterize the Israeli economy. Despite these and other differences, they share some remarkable similarities that led significant segments of the business community in both countries to mobilize for peacemaking. These factors include (a) the escalation and tenaciousness of non-white and Palestinian opposition; (b) the crumbling of both country's state-centered economic institutions, which, while designed to subsidize Afrikaner and Jewish workers, had become counterproductive for their business communities; (c) a powerful, society-wide impulse to move beyond the "wasted years" of sanctions, embargo, and conflict, an impulse reflected in a growing pro-business consensus strengthened by (d) the globalization of trade and finances and the intervention of allies who sought to integrate of South Africa and Israel into the world economy, and (e) the autonomy of business elites (long-established in South Africa and of recent vintage in Israel) which allowed them to take advantage of these factors. In this short article I can only touch on some aspects of the first four topics, which I will do in the next section, while devoting the bulk of the paper to the fifth factor in the third section. A detailed treatment of the earlier topics will take place in longer essays.

THE WASTED YEARS AND THE CRISIS

South African economists repeatedly told the story of the wasted 1980s. Economic growth declined from 5.5 percent annual rate in the 1960s to 2.9 percent in the 1970s, and "in the decade 1981–1990, economic growth collapsed to 0.6 percent per annum." The real output of manufacturing, mining, and construction in the 1981–1991 years showed negative annual growth rates between 0.8 and 2.3 percent. Fixed investments declined by 30 percent. The growth of black unions by over 300 percent and their willingness to strike led, despite negative real growth in per capita income, to a narrowing of racial inequalities from 8.9:1 to 8.4:1, and the white minority's share of total personal income fell from 58.1 to 52.6 per cent.[3] Though racial inequality remained vast, the decline of the privileged share seemed a portent of things to come. A talk presented by businessman Christo Nel to IDASA in April 1988 summed up the ailments of South Africa as "declining productivity, increased cost of living, declining standards of living, large-scale poverty, unemployment and widespread social unrest and conflict."[4] A confidential report of the President's Economic Advisory Council from August 1986 reached similar conclusions, stating that the current "course cannot be pursued much longer" and calling for "certain fundamental adjustments."[5]

International economic sanctions resulted in 350 foreign corporations disposing of their South African investments by the late 1980s. The most damaging sanction was the decision of a number of international banks in 1985 not to renew short-term credits to South

Africa, leading to a severe debt crisis and massive capital flight. While the sanctions did not cripple the economy, and in some cases led to import substitution, they did create an environment in which lack of investment reduced growth and caused South Africa to suffer from "absence of technological renewal," denying it the benefits of globalization. This prospect weighed heavily on the South African business community.[6]

In Israel, the policy of accelerated economic growth through inflows of unilateral capital transfers and immigration worked remarkably well, with some interruptions, from the 1920s until 1973. Economists report that "the period which started with the Yom Kippur War and lasted until...1990 is known as the 'lost years'."[7] A factor analysis by Arie Shachar and Maya Choshen measuring the change in Israel's relative position in the world between 1965 and 1989 demonstrated that Israel had remained lodged in the gap between the upper layer of the developing and the bottom layer of developed countries. Not only has it failed to make it into the ranks of the developed countries, but "the disparities between Israel and the countries of the developed world are growing, while the disparities with the upper section of the developing countries are decreasing." The prolonged continuation of this trend was likely, therefore, to move Israel from its "intermediate position...into the large group of developing countries."[8] Michael Barnett argued that "if Israel resembles many East Asian states prior to the 1970s, since then it favors the Latin American states."[9]

This widespread sense of crisis was evident at a conference held at a 1989 conference at The Hebrew University of Jerusalem on "Trends in the Transformation of Israeli Society." A political scientist, Yechezkel Dror, expressed the conference's consensus that Israel suffers from "stalemate and blockage" because of the Palestinian issue, the demographic threat of high Arab birthrates, and a possible chain of wars with Arab states. Israel's creation involved massive intervention in history, Dror added, which leaves a legacy of long-term problems that are far from being solved. On the contrary, Israel has not yet created a critical mass of accomplishments which will guarantee its survival.

Even as these indications of deep structural crisis were identified, alternatives were emerging in both South Africa and Israel. Historically, mining was the engine of South African growth, but starting in the 1970s, the commercial and industrial sector began to provide real growth and higher incomes. As Robert Price and others have argued, the eclipse of mining and agriculture by manufacturing in the 1970s exposed the limits placed by apartheid on South Africa's economic development. Manufacturing requires a stable, literate, technically skilled, and relatively permanent urban labor force. By the late 1960s there was a shortage of skilled whites, and the large black population began filling the jobs created by the maturing industrial sector.[10] Meanwhile, the erosion of black labor control and the failure of the "homelands" to slow black urbanization removed the *raison d'être* of apartheid.

In Israel, meanwhile, a military-industrial complex developed in response to a French weapons embargo. The military industries became the engine of growth, the focus of knowledge for high-tech industries, and the primary force for modernizing large segments of the economy. The defense industries trained and recruited technological and managerial manpower, part of which subsequently, moved to private industry. Military production led to spin-offs of civilian uses, and at the end of the 1970s, high-tech civilian companies began expanding rapidly, and the complex of military industries also became the main source of growth for exports. Not only did military production produce relatively high added value but it also helped pry open doors for Israeli civilian products. Even with the crisis of the military industrial production since the mid-1980s, civilian production and exports continued to grow on their own. South African manufacturing and Israeli high technology provided tangible alternatives to the older economic models since they were more modern, less dependent on state regulation, and more export-oriented.

I now turn to an exploration of how attitudes within South African and Israeli business communities changed and how these changes translated into political influence.

THE BUSINESS–POLITICS NEXUS

One of the major axes around which the relations between business and political elites revolved in both South Africa and Israel was the employment of Afrikaner or Jewish workers. Since large pools of low-paid unskilled workers threatened the employment of Afrikaner and Jewish workers, these sought protection in nationalist movements. The defense of a "European standard of living" and the struggle for "Hebrew labor" became key demands of the Afrikaner and Zionist nationalist movements, as is typical in colonial situations when two groups of workers from different regions of the world economy and with different standards of living and organizational skills are brought together.

These movements forged an economic caste system in South Africa, while in Palestine an exclusivist Jewish economic sector became entrenched. Starting in 1924 the South African "Pact government" adopted a series of acts to protect white workers through non-market mechanisms such as the color bar which reserved skilled jobs for them. In Palestine, the two institutional pillars of Zionist colonization, the World Zionist Organization's Jewish National Fund and the Histadrut (the labor federation), joined to monopolize a section of the land and labor markets and create a large, horizontally and vertically integrated co-operative Jewish sector of the economy. Nationalists thus created non-market mechanisms and shaped markets in favor of the Afrikaner and Jewish workers. The continuing threat for these political arrangements came from English and Jewish business interests, especially employers, who were not inclined to subsidize the Afrikaner and Jewish workers. But business also learned to live with these interferences, and by allying themselves with the nationalist movements and the states they controlled, received access to cheap, and frequently forced, labor in South Africa and to low interest capital in the Yishuv and Israel. The business–politics nexus in South Africa and Israel thus reflects the tensions and accommodations in regard to the issue of white and Jewish employment.

In the 1970s and 1980s the two business communities gained confidence in their opposition to the massive, but inefficient and costly, extra-market institutions that provided Afrikaner and Jewish settler-immigrants and their descendants, but in South Africa also English mining capital, with conditions favorable for settlement and prosperity. As institutions of the colonial era were losing their value and their political defenders began abandoning them and the world economy and its institutions – the World Bank, IMF, and the World Economic Forum – demanded greater openness to the world, new opportunities opened up for the business communities in both societies. To take advantage of these, and end the crippling economic crises, would require peaceful resolution to the conflict. Thus, the central figures in the business elites of both societies became vocal supporters of such a course of action.

Business and Politics in South Africa

The South African gold and diamond mining industries became dependent on the "the migrant labor and compound system, low wages, pass laws and the refusal to grant black miners union rights."[11] Manufacturers, whose labor needs required a stable urban and semi-skilled or skilled labor force, and merchants, who wished for a larger and more thriving market, were taken aback by the victory of the forces of apartheid under the National Party in 1948 and on occasion objected to it. In their own manufacturing and commercial enterprises, however, the same racial hierarchy was not altered. The period after 1948 saw partial accommodation between the National Party governments and organized business groups: the FCI (Federated Chamber of Industries) and the ASSOCOM (Association of Chambers of Commerce of South Africa), which were joined in the 1970s by the AHI (Afrikaanse Handelsinstituut), the organization of small-scale Afrikaner manufacturing and commerce. In David Walsh's judicious evaluation, penned in 1988,

> industrial capitalism originated in South Africa at a time when the premise of racial inequality was already firmly established. It adapted itself to the available structure, utilized what was useful to its interests, objected to what was not (such as job ratios and job reservation), but until fairly recent times substantially acquiesced in the racial ordering of society. South Africa's business elites were whites before they were entrepreneurs.[12]

The resources of the South African English-speaking business community and its legendary levels of concentration – the top four conglomerations controlled as late as January 1995 76.3 percent of the Johannesburg Stock Exchange's capitalization, and the top company, Anglo-American, controlled over 40 percent[13] – made it into a state within the state. The pro-Afrikaner South African state could ignore the English-speaking business community only at its own risk. Nevertheless, the English speaking businessmen tended to keep away from subjects that had been construed by the apartheid regime as political and express themselves in regard to issues narrowly defined as economic. Of course, "mental apartheid" between economics and politics was but a smoke screen, since apartheid was just as much an economic as a political system. This convenient division, however, gradually unraveled.

The business community's political involvement correlated with two cycles: the cycle of resistance and oppression and the business cycle. After each wave of resistance, an expanding sector of South African business realized that it could not "do good business in a rotten society"[14] and was propelled to demand reform and act in ways which increased the rift between it and the government. As long as economic growth was not seriously affected by political protest the business community returned to its quiescent ways. For example, after the 1960 Sharpeville crisis, "for the first time organized business voiced unambiguous, even scathing criticism of government's economic policies" but the coincidence of repression with a consistent yearly growth of the GDP led again to business passivity.[15] The slowness of South African business's responses was also due to its multiple divisions by sectoral distinctions, the size of enterprises, language, color, and political ideology.

The first significant permanent change in the attitude of the business community occurred after the massive strike wave in 1973, when primary producers (agriculture and mining), until then the most the hostile employer group to black unions, reversed their attitude.[16] Their position was adopted by the Wiehan Commission which recognized that the right to unionize already possessed by their white counterparts could not be withheld from black workers any more. Subsequently, the 1976 Soweto confrontation led the business community to set up its own reform organization, the Urban Foundation. The UF's success in knocking down two major props of apartheid – influx control and the pass laws – helped remove interference with its member's direct business interests, but its success in lifting prohibitions on urban property rights for blacks also helped consolidate a small urban black middle class.

The African and Indian resistance to the 1984 tri-cameral parliamentary elections had even more far reaching consequences because it led to the linkage of the cycle of violence with the business cycle. The refusal of international banks to renew South Africa's short term credits led to a devastating credit crisis and massive outflow of capital and made very clear that further economic growth was contingent on far-reaching political reform. Organized business put on the table its own initiatives and plans which reached openly into political issues, and some businessmen opened communication with the ANC.

In June 1985, ASSOCOM published a paper written by Afrikaner establishment economists Jan Lombard and Andre du Pisanie, entitled *Removal of Discrimination Against Blacks in the Political Economy of South Africa*. The proposal contained an awkward combination of basic principles that could underlie reform negotiations, inspired in equal parts by Friedrich von Hayek, monetarism, and federalism. In January 1986, the FCI published its *South African Business Charter of Social, Economic, and Political Rights*. The charter went much further and called for a liberal-democratic form of government based on non-discrimination, civil rights, the rule of law, and "every citizen's...right to take part in public affairs, directly or through freely chosen representatives."[17] Continuing to recognize the leading role of the government, the FCI document called for cooperation between the business community and government in facilitating negotiations. These documents, however, were ignored by the government and probably represented only the views of part of their organizations' memberships.

In September 1985, in a dramatic move and in defiance of the government, a high-powered delegation of businessmen, led by Gavin Relly, the Chairman of Anglo-American Corporation, met with ANC representatives in Zambia. The results were mixed. Important areas of agreement were reached but suspicion concerning the ANC's socialist leanings remained, in part because of its links with the SA Communist Party.[18] In 1987, the government initiated the "parliamentary pillorying" of Barclays Bank Director Chris Ball, for advocating contact with the ANC, and very few of his business colleagues came to his defense.[19]

The periodically radicalized position of business and, significantly, its slow redefinition of its proper area of competence and the lowering of the division between the political and economic spheres was, on a deeper level, motivated by the transformation of the South African economy. Greenberg, Adam, Price, and others argue that the eclipse of mining and agriculture by manufacturing in the 1970s exposed the limits placed by apartheid on South Africa's economic development.

The changing socioeconomic character of the National Party's Afrikaner constituency also subverted many of the arguments in favor of apartheid. In 1948, the National Party's political base, the Afrikaner community, was almost entirely rural, but agricultural consolidation reduced the number of white farmers. Just as significantly, apartheid redistributed wealth and employment to large cross-sections of the Afrikaner community, and the new Afrikaner professional and middle class forged alliances with its English speaking counterpart. The gap between the FCI, ASSOCOM, and the AHI gradually disappeared and the representatives of white-owned business spoke with one voice regardless of the language in which they spoke.

In the 1980s, two major and sustained initiatives with long term consequences for the politicization of South African business had begun. The first was "scenario planning." Adopting a forecasting method developed by Shell, Anglo-American under Clem Sunter's leadership developed a set of simplified scenarios for South Africa's future. It concluded that either civil war or the co-optation of the opposition would lead South Africa down the "low road" of "losing nations." In contrast, negotiations, compromise, and commitment of resources to development would allow the country to take the "high road" of industrial export-oriented countries.[20] This scenario was completed in 1985 and informed the Anglo-American decision to participate in the Lusaka meeting with the ANC.[21] It was further presented to 230 audiences comprising some 25,000 people and was even shown to Mandela in jail.[22]

The second major initiative was the Consultative Business Movement. In August 1988, after some 200 preparatory meetings between the representatives of business, professionals and the African and Indian Mass Democratic Movement, the "Consultative Business Movement" was set up "to mobilize business as a major change agent and communication mechanism."[23] The CBM declared itself to be "an objective and even-handed organization trying to promote the national interest," and gained substantial credibility in the black community.[24] As a consequence, the CBM became the facilitator of all the major consultative processes, political, constitutional, and economic, that shaped post-apartheid South Africa.[25] Throughout this process, CBM mobilized the business community by convening workshops with the representatives of virtually all the major corporations.[26] CBM took pride in placing economic issues at the center of the transitional dialogue:

> societies in transition are commonly dominated by political and constitutional issues, with economic issues...relegated to the back burner. By contrast, the fact that economic issues do feature on South Africa's transitional agenda is a distinctive positive feature.[27]

Within the framework of the negotiations, the ANC position on economic issues had shifted as the USSR's economic model faded with the collapse of the USSR. The ANC's Harare Program, for example, which proposed to dismantle the huge South African conglomerates, was forgotten. "It appears," argued the CBM, "that the economic reality is beginning to dawn on the players and there is a growing convergence of views on economic priorities."[28] In the debate of redistribution through growth versus growth through redistribution, a compromise position was struck in the ANC's *Reconstruction and Development Programme* (RDP), one much closer to the free market position.[29]

The first budget submitted by the new ANC government was hailed by the business community. By scrapping non-resident shareholders tax and remaining import surcharges, this budget "made a strong case for improving foreign investor sentiment toward South Africa."[30] The budget "did not introduce any measures which would be unpopular with local or foreign business." In general, it was concluded that

> the focus of the Budget is the deficit before borrowing rather than a wealth tax, or some other unspeakable horror, speaks volumes about the newfound conservatism of the ANC members of the government of national unity.[31]

"Fifteen years ago many in the ANC regarded business as part of the 'enemy,'" wrote David Welsh in 1994. "Today leading ANC figures speak of 'partnership' between government and the private sector, and President Nelson Mandela emphasizes the private sector's 'central role' in promoting the sustained growth that must be attained if the *Reconstruction and Development Programme* is to succeed."[32] Though apartheid fell and its opponents assumed political power, the preparation of the transition process and the close involvement of business in it contributed to the safeguarding of the business community's interests, indeed to its transformation into the representative general interest. According to this economic view, greater social and economic equality are expected to be, insofar as they occur, merely the by-product of economic growth.

Israeli Business and Politics

National interests, defined in terms of employment and working conditions of Jewish workers, played an even stronger role in the Yishuv than in South Africa, largely due to the absence of a significant business community. The struggle for "Hebrew labor" assumed a central and symbolic role in the national struggle, especially in the agricultural sector. In 1932–36, for example, the Histadrut, threatened by the rising political strength of the Revisionists and citrus growers, conducted "a demonstrative and often violent 'principled' struggle...against the employment of Arab labor by Jewish employers," despite economic prosperity and the shortage of Jewish agricultural workers.[33]

There was less conflict with small and medium-scale urban manufacturers because their settings were more segregated, either in Jewish cities and towns or Jewish neighborhoods of mixed cities. At the same time, there remained a clear and unbridgeable cultural gap between the Labor Movement and the middle-classes as they "shared neither a joint framework of activity, nor a similar world view, nor did they have common interests."[34] The Manufacturers Association of Israel, founded in 1921, remained for many decades a weak and apolitical body, even at the height of early industrialization in the late 1950s.[35] Furthermore, this group was fragmented as there was no leading sector strong enough to impose a direction on manufacturing.[36] Another source of the MAI's weakness was the sectoral separation. State and Histadrut-owned industries were not part of the association which, consequently, could not speak on behalf of the industry as a whole.[37] The Chamber of Commerce, originating in 1919, represented a traditional Jewish occupation and was held in even less esteem by the Labor Movement.[38]

Larger entrepreneurs, however, have been caught between the rock an the hard place. In seeking the support of the Zionist movement they sought to describe their undertakings as part of the "pioneering" project. But they were also less able and willing to accept the principle of a 100 percent "Hebrew labor" because of their ties with the British mandatory authorities and the Palestinian and Middle Eastern economy. With the outbreak of the Arab Revolt in 1936, the directors of three of the largest Jewish-owned enterprises joined two key civic leaders in opening negotiations with moderate Palestinian leaders. "The Five," as they came to be known, offered limits on Jewish immigration and land purchases, a political regime based on parity, and the partial integration of the private Jewish and Palestinian economic sectors (but not the Zionist one) to quiet the Revolt. The "Five" were viewed with suspicion by the Jewish Agency which rejected their plan, and there are doubts whether the Palestinian national leadership would have adopted it either.[39]

Jewish businessmen in Palestine were few and were unwilling to challenge the political leadership for the protection of their economic interests except at the moment of supreme crisis – and even then they were capable of only a short-lived effort. They were much weaker than their English-speaking South African counterpart, because they did not possess the autonomy that export-generated revenues brought. Consequently, in the Yishuv even the fiction of the division between economic and political factors was harder to maintain. If the autonomy of the South African business community from the government was based on large measure on their integration into a global market through the export of gold and diamonds, in Palestine Jewish businesses by and large remained dependent on Zionist sources of capital.

State-driven, or *dirigiste*, economic growth, typical to "developmentalist states" acquired unparalleled financial dependence on unilateral transfer of foreign capital, in fact on subsidy. Developmentalism and unilateral capital imports became interconnected even more strongly after the establishment of Israel in 1948, when the state became the main conduit of capital influx and, consequently, maintained and enhanced its control, conjointly with the Histadrut, over the economy. In Efraim Kleiman's calculation, "approximately three-quarters of all capital imports were received by the public sector, which, in turn, financed nearly two-thirds of all capital formation."[40]

Domestic capital formation in Israel became a circular affair. The Histadrut's provident funds were made available to the government to finance public and private investments approved by the government itself. This arrangement in effect expressed and ensured the identity of the political and economic elites in Israel.[41] But the same logic operated within the private sector as well. The economy's chief source of investment credit remained under effective government control, regardless of whether the investment was made in the public, Histadrut, or the private sector. As long as the private sector remained dependent on government-allocated credit, no autonomous business sector could emerge and business decisions were made in response to or as part of political decisions.

Though the autonomy the business community in Israel came late, it was attained rapidly. It was prepared by some of the reforms that began with the July 1985 "Emergency Economic Stabilization Plan" (EESP) undertaken by Shimon Peres' National Unity Government to reduce the 466 percent annual inflation. The EESP program aimed only at stabilizing the economy by bringing down the triple digit inflation, but it went much farther in recasting the Israeli economic structure from its protectionist and state-centered origins into a more open ended neoliberal economy.[42] Actions in subsequent years pared back the government role in the capital market, eased foreign currency regulation, reduced import quotas, and initiated a slow privatization process. All of these tilted the balance from public to private interests and from workers organizations to capital and employers' bodies.

Reduced government intervention in the disposition of private sector savings led private enterprises, for the first time, to raise capital by issuing securities through the stock exchange free from government control. An even more important role in liberating the capital markets was the relaxation in borrowing foreign capital. Israeli corporations began floating their securities on the New York Stock Exchange and these added up to 36 percent of the total market value of publicly held Israeli nonfinancial corporations as of January 1992. Firms received permission to invest up to 40 percent of their equity abroad. Consequently, between 1985 and 1990 the share of government securities held by the public fell from 83 to 65 percent of the stock of financial assets. Similarly, the share of direct or indirect government loans to the private sector fell from 57.6 to 29.7 percent in just three years, from 1987 to 1990.[43] The autonomy of the Israeli business community dates from this newly acquired ability to finance itself through the Tel Aviv or New York Stock Exchanges, independent of the government.

This autonomy was expressed in the Israeli business community's unprecedented role in the peace process. The redefinition of the conflict as having an important economic dimension and, consequently, as an obstacle to modernizing the Israeli economy was articulated differently in Israel than was in South Africa. In South Africa, several institutions formed specifically to oppose apartheid and offer blueprints for reform, while in Israel the leaders of all the main economic institutions spoke out, but only as individuals. Whereas South African business leaders regularly met with the ANC leadership in exile, their Israeli counterparts met only with the Palestinian business elite and not with the PLO. Nor did Israeli business serve as a mediator or provide the institutional umbrella for the talks. Independent business voices were more timid in the Israeli case, and the line between economic and politics remained more distinct, but the move from lobbying to public campaign in Israel was, nevertheless, unprecedented. It was the first time Israeli business leaders openly tackled an issue until then defined strictly as political.

This independence was first tested in regard to the safer question of the absorption of the masses of Jewish immigrants who began arriving in 1989 from the ex-USSR. This was an issue well within the national consensus but linked by businessmen to the peace process. In his survey article of 4 December 1989, John Rossant of the *Business Week* found that:

> To make Israel more attractive to the immigrants, many Israeli businessmen insist that peace is needed. The pragmatic Israeli business community is putting behind-the-scene pressure on the Shamir government to negotiate with the Palestinians.[44]

"Israeli businessmen know that without peace with the Arabs," Rossant found, "there is little chance of the country building a stable civilian economy." It is this conviction, which led "many Israeli businessmen 'to join' the Bush Administration in leaning on Prime Minister Yitzhak Shamir to become more flexible in his approach to negotiations." Eli Hurwitz, the Director of Teva Pharmaceuticals, Israel's largest drug company, and former president of the MAI, stated that from this economic perspective "the future is problematic without peace."[45]

In the Jerusalem Business Conference, held one week before the crucial 1992 national elections, Dov Lautman, President of the Israeli Manufacturer's Association, issued his first statement linking the then deadlocked Madrid peace talks to economic issues. In his words, the major obstacle to foreign investment in the Israeli economy was regional instability, and only a combination of an appropriate economic policy and progress in the peace talks could make Israel attractive to foreign investors.[46] In November, Lautman added the Arab boycott to his list of conditions that hurt Israel, and in this context argued that the business community made a mistake in the past decade by not placing at the top of the list of its priorities the creation of a close linkage between peace and growth.[47] He was seconded by Danny Gilerman, the President of the Israeli Chambers of Commerce, who alleged that Israel lost $44 billion as a result of the Arab boycott. Gilerman called on Rabin to view the abolition of the boycott as a top priority.[48] Finally, in January 1993, Lautman promised that a breakthrough in the peace talks in 1993 would serve as a tremendous turning point in the fortunes of the Israeli economy in general and of industry in particular.[49] During this period, Lautman asked Peres to discuss the role of the business community in the political process and in the negotiation of bilateral and multilateral trade accords with the leadership of the Manufacturers Association.[50] Benny

Gaon, CEO of Koor, the largest Israeli conglomerate, began seeking potential Palestinian and Arab partners already in 1992.[51] In early 1993, Gaon set up a $100 million investment firm "Salaam 2000" as part of Koor's "Peace Enterprises" (*mifalot shalom*), to seek out joint ventures with Palestinian and Moroccan entrepreneurs.[52]

The same explicit support for combining peacemaking and the liberalization of the economy within moderate social-democratic limits was adopted in the political arena by the Meretz Party and within the Labor Party, at the time in opposition, by the Chug Mashov (Feedback Circle) faction. Chug Mashov was established in 1982 by the younger generation in the party leadership and led by Yossi Beilin, one of the most original minds in Israeli politics. In Chug Mashov's May 1991 Congress, about a year before the Labor Party replaced the Likud at the helm of the government, Beilin, in his keynote address on Society and the Economy, surveyed the failings of the planned socialist economy and after decorously praising the Histadrut for its illustrious past he proceeded to offer a list of concrete reforms to privatize its enterprises and make its sick fund part of a National Health Program, thus making the Histadrut a typical trade union.[53] Beilin's plan was carried out with great gusto by a fellow young leader of the Labor Party, Haim Ramon, who not only did away with the power and independent economic bases of the Histadrut but also changed its symbol, restructured and renamed its socialist sounding bodies, and called the new body the New Histadrut. The planned tinkering with the Histadrut turned into a veritable revolution.

The most innovative aspects of the 1991 program are found in the linkage of the economic and political dimensions of peacemaking. The platform of the Meretz Party clearly and dramatically posed the relationship between Israel's economic growth and its commitment to the peace process and serves as a clear example of the redefinition of the Israeli–Palestinian conflict.

> Peace agreement with our neighbors and a policy consistent with the values and interests of the democratic world will enable Israel to integrate into the world economy and into a stronger and expanding European Community, to become the recipient of investments and credit and to possess a progressive and exporting economy.[54]

Reaching peace is described by Meretz as imperative not only for gaining security but also for realizing a larger socioeconomic vision: the attainment by Israel of the European Community's standard of living by the year 2000.

Shimon Peres was even more sanguine about reversing the historical process of separation of the Israeli and Arab economies by knitting Israel, the Palestinians, and Jordan into a common market. Peres' outlook, according to his biographer, was geared toward the technocratic and professional stratum in Israeli society, and consequently placed major emphasis on "industrialization, modernization, economic productivity, national planning, encouragement of higher education and extended use of science as technology" which he views as antidotes to the populism of both Israel's right wing and Middle Eastern fundamentalism.[55] Peres' book, *The New Middle East*, which appeared a few months after the signing of the Oslo DOP, presented a complex three-tiered program of regional cooperation. Atop binational or multinational projects geared toward specific topics such as water desalination or desert management, he expected international consortia to undertake projects that require massive capital investment, such as the Red Sea–Dead Sea Canal, to be capped by regional cooperation, leading to the evolution of official regional institutions. In Keren's summary the main features of this plan are "the precedence of economics over politics, and the formation of partnerships which can be instituted before borders are drawn and peace treaties signed." In short, in Peres' new Middle East "business precedes politics and hence allows cooperation between peoples set apart by political differences."[56]

Parallel with the public opinion campaign launched by Lautman and others, the Manufacturers' Association and the Israel Management Center under Uri Manashe sought to commence talks with Palestinian businessmen with the intention of facilitating economic cooperation and through it advance the political talks. Uri Menashe expected that the changing economic reality could marginalize political problems or have politicians follow the lead of economic cooperation. "Palestinian industrialists," argued the General Director of the Manufacturers' Association, Yoram Blizovsky, "view us, industrialists, as a more credible partner than the government, since we are perceived as a more neutral factor," a sentiment that is shared by other Israeli business leaders.[57] The eventual talks between the two economic elites, however, remained sporadic and inconclusive, due to the inability of the Palestinian side, still under Israeli military occupation, to separate its economic concerns from its political demands or due to restrictions imposed by their political leadership.[58] In addition, Palestinian businessmen still remembered the customary opposition of Israeli industrialists to the establishment of industrial enterprises in the West Bank and were less than keen on an open border policy. Under these conditions two separate decisions to establish a permanent joint forum for the two elites did not take effect.[59]

While the Israeli business leaders represent different economic sectors, they all support export-oriented growth and trade liberalization. The success of the peace process strengthened their hand in limiting the influence of the inward-looking industrialists, farmers and merchants, who expect to suffer the adverse economic effects of open trade that would result from Israel's accommodation with the Arab world. Israeli political leaders "sold" the peace accords not only by promising an end to the *intifada* and security for Israel, but even more by presenting peace as a key to prosperity.[60] The separation of businessmen and politicians typical of the Yishuv period is but a distant memory. The bonds of the industrialists are particularly strong with the Labor Party's elite which they view as more business-oriented than the right-wing Likud which is perceived as catering more to populist desires.[61] During the 1996 elections, full page pro-Peres declarations signed by the captains of industry were placed in Israeli dailies.[62]

CONCLUSION

There are obvious differences between the white–black and the Jewish–Palestinian conflict. The solution to the former was domestic, though not for lack of effort by the government to make it look like a foreign conflict, while the Israeli–Palestinian confrontation was accepted as a "foreign conflict," though only after the Palestinian *intifada* foiled attempts to erase the "green line." Though both South Africa and Israel suffered from boycotts and sanctions, the economic dimensions of the apartheid played a more central role in the South African economy then the Israeli–Palestinian conflict did in Israel. Despite these differences, both Israeli and South African business emerged as major players in resolving these conflicts. Both lobbied, mobilized public opinion, and met with the representatives of the other side. Above all, by linking South Africa's and Israel's economic growth to their commitment to find peaceful solutions, they helped redefine the conflicts as barriers to economic development during a period of intense economic globalization.

The authority the Israeli and South African business communities' views commanded reflect what may be viewed as a global shift in the relative weight of social resources from political (and related cultural legitimations) to economic ones. This is not to contend that politics have become irrelevant or that political aspirations and concerns cannot override economic interests. But in the current stage of global economic influences it is becoming more costly to assert the primacy of political, and attendant legitimational, concerns and the effort of putting together a coalition to oppose global economic and cultural forces becomes more difficult. It becomes, therefore, ever more important to examine simultaneously global, national, and local forces in their multifarious interactions. Here, I focus on the growing importance of the global forces, institutions, and those groups or elites most able to take advantage of the shift in this amalgam.

The authority wielded by globally-oriented elites and their autonomy usually stems from their privileged access to global resources and allies: export revenues, access to international credit, assistance by international organizations, and so on. The business elites examined, in spite of many other differences between them, have access to all these. In South Africa, the mining houses were always closely integrated with the international market. In Israel, the ties with international stock exchanges and banks that freed large companies from dependence on the government controlled capital market developed only in the late 1980s and early 1990s. The South African and Israeli business communities, though their large cross-sections had been the beneficiaries of apartheid and military-industrial production for years, used their ties to the world economy to enhance their autonomy and become major supporters of the peace process. Ironically, these business communities were among the main beneficiaries from the liberation struggles of the oppressed in South Africa and Palestinians in the occupied territories of the West Bank and Gaza.

ACKNOWLEDGEMENTS

I would like to thank Rogers Brubaker, David Lake, David Levi-Faur, and Gay Seidman for their helpful suggestions on earlier versions of this paper and the Social Science Research Council, the American Council of Learned Societies, the Institute on Global Conflict and Cooperation, and the University of California, San Diego, for funding various parts of the research that led to this paper.

NOTES

1. *Time*, 3 Jan. 1994.
2. *NYT*, 22 Nov. 1993.
3. Mike McGrath and Merle Holden, "Economic Outlook 1981–1992," *Indicator SA* 9/4 (Spring 1992) p.35.
4. Christo Nel, "The Viability of a Mixed Economy in Post-Apartheid South Africa," paper presented to the IDASA seminar, "A View of the Economy Beyond Apartheid," 22 April 1988.
5. Economic Advisory Council of the State President, "Proposed Long-Term Economic Strategy," 7 Sept. 1990, p.1.
6. Interviews with Michael Spicer, Advisor to the President of Anglo-American, 28 July 1994; Mick Bernhart, Former Chief Economist AHI, 26 July 1994; Gavin Keeton, Anglo-American, 25 July 1994; Adam Jacobs, Senior Economist, Amalgamated Bank of South Africa, 27 July 1994. J.C. Van Zyl, "Sanctions Against South Africa," press release by FCI, 7 Aug. 1986.
7. Assaf Razin and Efraim Sadka, *The Economy of Israel: Malaise and Promise*, Chicago, 1993, p.16.
8. Aryeh Shahar and Maya Chosen, "Israel Among the Nations: A Comparative Study of the Israel's Place Between the Developed World and the Developing World," *Mechkarim Begeographia shel Eretz-Yisrael* [Studies in the Geography of Palestine] 14 (1993) p.324 (Hebrew).
9. Michael Barnett, "Israel in the World Economy: Israel as an East Asian State?" in his *Israel in Comparative Perspective*, Albany, NY: SUNY Press, 1996, p.134.
10. Robert M. Price, *The Apartheid State in Crisis*, NY, 1991.
11. David Welsh, "Politics and Business in South Africa," *Optima* 36/3 (Sept. 1988) p.162.
12. Ibid., p.162; Stanley B. Greenberg, *Race and State in Capitalist Development*, New Haven, 1980, p.178.
13. Robin McGregor and Anne McGregor, *McGregor's Who Owns Whom*, 15th edition, Rustenburg, 1995.
14. Welsh (note 11) p.164.
15. Ibid., p.163.
16. Heribert Adam and Kogila Moodley, *The Opening of the Apartheid Mind*, Berkeley, 1993.
17. Federated Chamber of Industries (FCI), *Charter of Economic, Social and Political Rights*, 1986.
18. Welsh (note 11) p.166.
19. Welsh (note 11) p.167.

20. Clem Sunter, *The World and South Africa in the 1990s*, Tafelberg, 1987.
21. Interview with Spicer (note 6).
22. Ibid.
23. Nel, "Viability" (note 4).
24. *Consultative Business Movement – CBM*, March 1989; CBM, *Managing Change: A Guide to the Role of Business in Transition*, Johannesburg, 1993, p.xiii.
25. CBM, 1993, p.xiv.
26. CBM, 1993.
27. CBM, 1993, p.20.
28. CBM, 1993, p.20.
29. Graham Larcombe, "Economic Policy Debates in South Africa," unpublished paper, Oct. 1994, p.11.
30. Jacques Magliolo, "Liebenberg Eases Tax for Foreign Investors," *Business Mail*, 17–23 March 1995.
31. Reg Rumney, "Howzat? Kepler Liebenberg," *Business Mail*, 17–23 March 1995.
32. David Welsh, "Liberals and the Future of the New Democracy in South Africa," *Optima* 40/2 (Nov. 1994) p.44; idem, "Maintaining Peace in South Africa: An Analysis of the Transition," paper delivered at the conference on "The Resolution of Intractable Conflicts: The Israeli-Palestinian and the South African Experience," The Tami Steinmetz Center for Peace Research, Tel Aviv, 19–21 March 1995.
33. Anita Shapira, *Futile Struggle: The Jewish Labor Controversy, 1929–1939*, Tel Aviv, 1977, pp.252–7 (Hebrew); Michael Shalev, "The Political Economy of Labor Party Dominance and Decline in Israel," in T.J. Pempel (ed.), *Uncommon Democracies: The One-Party Dominant Regimes*, Ithaca, 1990, pp.83–127.
34. Yossi Beilin, *Israel: A Concise Political History*, NY, 1992, p.211; David Levi-Faur, "Nationalism and the Power of Business: The Manufacturers' Association of Israel," *Environment and Planning C: Government and Policy* 14 (1996) p.16.
35. Levi-Faur (note 34) pp.193–209; Beilin, *Israel* (note 34) p.211.
36. Shalev, *Labor and the Political Economy in Israel*, Oxford, 1992, p.92.
37. Levi-Faur (note 34).
38. Yael Yishai, *Land of Paradoxes: Interest Politics in Israel*, NY, 1991, p.70.
39. Shmuel Dotan, *The Struggle for Eretz-Yisrael*, Tel Aviv, 1981, pp.114–18 (Hebrew).
40. Ephraim Kleiman, "The Place of Manufacturing in the Growth of the Israeli Economy," *Journal of Development Studies* 3/3 (April 1967) p.233.
41. Interview with Efraim Reiner, past-Chairman of Hevrat Haovdim, 25 June 1995.
42. Nicholas Kochan, "Israel: Bidding to Be the Next 'Economic Dragon,'" *Multinational Business* (Spring 1992).
43. Razin and Sadka, *The Economy of Israel* (note 7) pp.191–5.
44. John Rossant, "Israel Has Everything It Needs – Except Peace," *Business Week*, 9 Dec. 1989, p.58.
45. Ibid., p.54.
46. *Ha'aretz*, 17 June 1992.
47. *Ha'aretz*, 17 Nov. 1992.
48. *Ha'aretz*, 7 Aug. 1992.
49. *Ha'aretz*, 1 Jan. 1993.
50. *Ha'aretz*, 28 May 1993.
51. *Business Week*, 14 Dec. 1992.
52. Interview with Benny Gaon, CEO Koor, 7 July 1995.
53. Chug Mashov in the Labor Party, *Mashov's Fifth Congress: Proposed Resolutions*, Efal, 4 May 1991, pp.2–4 (Hebrew).
54. Meretz, Platform for the 1992 Elections, Chapter on "Economy and Society" (Hebrew).
55. Michael Keren, "Israeli Professionals and the Peace Process," *Israel Affairs* 1/1 (Autumn 1994) pp.152, 156.
56. Ibid., p.157.
57. Interview with Yoram Blizovsky, General Director of Manufacturers' Association, 19 Jan. 1995.
58. Interview with Uri Menashe, COE Kargal, 29 March 1995; *Ha'aretz*, 18 Dec. 1992.
59. *Ha'aretz*, 17 Feb. 1993.
60. See *Globes*, Nov. 1993.
61. Interview with Dov Lautman, COE Delta Textiles, Former President of the Manufacturers' Association of Israel, 16 Feb. 1995.
62. *Business Week*, 17 June 1996.

Have Globalization and Liberalization "Normalized" Israel's Political Economy?

MICHAEL SHALEV

In his 1960 study *The Israel Economy: The First Decade*, the distinguished economist Don Patinkin complained bitterly that Israel's political leaders acted as if they could defy the laws of economics.[1] The government consistently spent far more than it raised in taxes, just as the economy as a whole consumed more, especially in imports, than it could ever pay for. Patinkin believed that policymakers would be forced to adopt more market-conforming policies, but he was mistaken. So long as the leaders of the country could exploit Jewishness and geopolitics to mobilize loans and gifts from abroad, they did not need to heed the dictates of the market. Rationalized by its goals of building and defending the precarious new state and attracting and retaining Jewish immigrants, the government's "profligacy" had a remarkably long life.

During roughly the first four decades of Israel's existence there was a durable and almost wall-to-wall policy consensus among policymakers in Israel regarding the indispensability of open, organized, and subsidized Jewish immigration; the need for the state to underwrite the economic security of all Jewish citizens and to "close gaps" between different Jewish ethnic groups; the necessity to meet Israel's defense "imperatives" irrespective of economic considerations; and the desirability of the state playing an active developmental role in the economy. Over the past 10–15 years these four consensual pillars, especially the last, have for the first time been confronted by a comprehensive and vigorously articulated alternative: the (neo) liberal view which glorifies individual acquisitiveness and views the state as an impediment to the workings of the market economy, a conviction hitherto voiced only by economists or by disaffected businessmen lacking the right connections. Both of Israel's two major political parties are now committed to reducing the economic

---

Michael Shalev is at the Department of Political Science at The Hebrew University of Jerusalem.

role of government, making the economy more attractive to foreign investors and other shibboleths of contemporary economic liberalism. Has the long-standing "exceptionalism" of Israel's political economy come to an end?

This paper reviews and weighs empirical evidence on the contemporary evolution of Israel's political economy which is drawn mainly from published data and documentary sources. For two reasons, this is not an easy task. First, liberalization is an ongoing drama, one in which the actors often have good reasons to engage in misinformation and camouflage. Second, we are dealing here with politically charged issues that many writers find it hard to be dispassionate about. Under these circumstances, *theory* and *comparison* (both historical and cross-national) are crucial aids to interpretation of the evidence.

The theoretical underpinnings of this paper are drawn from my book *Labour and the Political Economy in Israel*, in which the political economy was conceived as "a dynamic and potentially contradictory *gestalt* that encompasses a broad range of institutional spheres."[2] This perspective assumes that "state" and "economy" are always interdependent, but that the terms of this interdependence are contingent on struggles and alliances among economic classes and sectors on the one hand and the political and bureaucratic managers of the state on the other. When a lasting pattern of policy priorities becomes buttressed by institutions, coalitions, and discourses it is helpful to speak of a "policy regime." Extending the notion of policy regimes to incorporate the structure of the economy and its principal engines of growth conveys the broader notion of a political-economic regime.[3] In order to understand why Israel has taken the path of liberalization, and what this might mean, the next section of the paper will attend to both the stable and the dynamic elements of its political-economic history: the inner logic characterizing the country's past and present regimes, and the tensions and conditionality built into them.

The paper also draws inspiration from a growing literature in the comparative study of political economy on the consequences of globalization for domestic policy. Scholars disagree sharply on this issue. Some have issued doomsday proclamations of the end of national sovereignty, but it is also reasonable to reverse the apparent relationship of global to domestic processes, recognizing that globalization is filtered and in part even constructed by the intentional policies of national governments.[4] Recent comparative research vigorously asserts the relative autonomy of nation-state, finding little or no evidence for the claim that economic and social policies are bound to converge in the wake of rising openness to international trade and capital mobility. National policy distinctiveness persists, and in some critical areas retrenchment of the state's role is problematic and may even be followed by further expansion. The progress of liberalization and structural change has not been wholesale, mechanical, or uniform. The pressures posed by globalization vary both in their objective dimensions and in the manner that they are politically constructed. Politics still appear to matter: conflicts of interest and ideology between political parties have persisting (although weakened) effects on policy, and the political costs of liberalization policies are sometimes prohibitive.[5]

Case research has an indispensable analytical role to play in clarifying the universality of the thrust to liberalize. Careful study of individual countries typically reveals that the structural features of political economies – especially those defining characteristics which are likely to enhance or impede liberalization processes – are quite distinctive, even within clusters of countries that appear to share the same political-economic regime.[6] Accordingly, it is reasonable to assume that the particular barriers to liberalization in Israel must be sought in those features of the Israeli political economy that most distinguish it from other economically advanced capitalist democracies.

THE POLITICAL ECONOMY OF ISRAELI EXCEPTIONALISM

Any observer of Israeli society over the last decade cannot fail to be struck by the rise of the market and market culture in contemporary Israel. Adapting John G. Ruggie's well-known phrase, I find it helpful to think of Israel's previous political-economic regimes as having shared an "embedded illiberalism" with roots in the pre-state experience of colonization by Jewish settlers and their conflict with the Palestinians and the Arab world.[7] Briefly, the conditions of Jewish settlement required that the political institutions of the Zionist movement and the Jewish community in Palestine dominate the mobilization of capital and the purchase of land. Because of their common interest in neutralizing an unfavorable labor market, the labor and Zionist movements cooperated intensely. Organized Zionism supported the workers' movement, which shielded Jewish workers from Arab competition by providing subsidized employment and social services. A wide consensus developed around the view that economic collectivism was indispensable to the success of Jewish colonization but that it could and should coexist with a capitalist market economy.[8]

The labor movement so dominated Zionist politics over so long a period, that it was tempting to identify this collectivism with socialist ideology. In fact, the world-view of labor Zionism was only secondarily socialist; its central theme was Jewish nationalism.[9] The arrival of sovereignty reinforced the collectivist consensus. The ruling Labor Party adopted a highly interventionist economic stance but embraced neither of the innovations associated with western parliamentary socialism after the war – nationalization and the welfare state. The government was committed to assisting the private sector along with state and Histadrut-owned enterprises; in any case, the local bourgeoisie was neither able nor willing to bear principal responsibility for economic development, and private industrialists were the first to demand a controlled (protected and subsidized) economy. In the domain of social policy, attempts to introduce a modern system of social insurance along the lines of postwar British reforms were stillborn.[10]

In the event, state intervention was rationalized by specifically Israeli constructions: the challenges of arming and defending the country, settling huge waves of new immigrants, bringing territory where Arabs lived or which bordered Arab countries under the control of the state, and developing an economic infrastructure that would permit immigrant absorption and eventually eliminate Israel's dependence on charity and loans. This constituted what may be thought of as the "demand side" of the interventionist state in Israel. The "supply side" was no less compelling. It rested on Israel's singular capacity to attract gift capital from foreign donors stemming partly from its active alignment with the West in the East–West struggle, but even more importantly from the Jewish character of the state which enabled it to make claims on Jewish communities abroad and obtain substantial financial compensation from Germany on behalf of world Jewry.[11] These "unilateral transfers," as well as a relatively favorable borrowing capacity for a struggling new entity, provided the Israeli state with the means to steer economic development and play a very active role in distributional processes. Economic growth was powered by the state's ability to mobilize money and people from abroad. Tellingly, both before and since sovereignty business cycles have been driven by waves of immigration and periodic eruptions of violence and war.[12] Under these conditions, it is not surprising that liberal arguments in favor of "free" markets and self-interested private investment enjoyed limited appeal among policymakers.

CONTINUITY AND CHANGE

Perhaps the clearest indication of the structural underpinnings of the role of the state in the Israeli economy was the continuity that became evident after the 1977 elections, when Labor's long period of uninterrupted rule was abruptly brought to a close. Despite the new Likud government's claims to be embarking on a radical program of liberalization (complete with a cameo appearance by Milton Friedman), widespread expectations of a fundamental shift in economic policy priorities proved to be premature.[13] The enduring parameters of economic policy proved to include the following:[14]

1. High levels of government expenditure and employment (biased by commitments to defense and immigrant absorption), relative to the economy's level of development.

2. Extensive state control of savings, investment, and foreign currency.

3. Modest public ownership alongside a high degree of public subsidy of private and Histadrut-owned business.

4. Corporatist delegation of state functions to the Histadrut, with the state trading subsidies for policy cooperation and legitimation.

This is not to suggest that Israel's political economy has been immutable to change. Rather, changes have not necessarily been coupled with policy proclamations and they must be understood more broadly than exclusive concentration on policy allows. This is why it is more useful to think in terms of political-economic regimes, an analytical construct which abstracts the underlying "model" of political economy in a given epoch from the broad ensemble of economic, political, and institutional variables which supports it.

For an understanding of the background to contemporary economic liberalization in Israel, two such regimes are noteworthy. The first, characterizing the period of rapid growth from the mid-1950s to the mid-1960s, rested on the synergy created by the meeting of two imported influences: German reparations and other foreign gifts, and the arrival of masses of propertyless immigrants who (among other things) expanded the markets for housing and consumer essentials and simultaneously provided a cheap labor force for their production.[15] The state was positioned strategically, as the factor that directed immigration and settlement, the disposal of foreign gifts, and housing and industrial policy. It created a highly politicized and closely regulated economy with partially competing blocs of public, private, and Histadrut capital, and a high degree of labor market segmentation parallel to ethnic and national divisions in the working class. These arrangements, which I have described elsewhere as "the system of 1948," awarded both the state and the party that dominated it considerable autonomy – that is, the capacity to steer business interests and civil society rather than be steered by them.[16]

After a decade of rapid growth, this regime was exhausted. The shift to full employment upset power relations by reducing the dependence of ordinary workers on the state and the ruling parties. The winding down of immigration and German aid persuaded the state to cut back both the scope of its presence in the economy, and the extent of its subsidizing role. It was thought necessary to discipline both labor and capital. The instrument for exercising this discipline was a recessionary economic policy – the *mitun* or slowdown of 1966–67.[17]

This cooling-off period proved to be short-lived. In the aftermath of the Six Day War a new "system of 1967" came into being that fundamentally altered key elements of Israel's political-economic regime. Although senior politicians and bureaucrats developed a sudden fondness for laissez-faire rhetoric, and some elements of economic regulation did become less direct, there was no undermining of the state's role as the central pivot of the economy. Instead, this pivot found a new axis in the "military-industrial complex."[18] The basis for this development was a potent combination of government-subsidized local military procurement, the burgeoning world market for arms, and (from 1970) US government financing of Israel's foreign arms purchases. The occupation of the West Bank and Gaza also played an important part in reviving growth along new lines, both by extending the scope of Israel's "domestic" product market, and by providing a source of cheap labor to replace increasingly scarce Israeli manual workers, especially in construction.

During the 1970s the structure of the Israeli economy, and its labor market, became increasingly dualistic. "Big business" developed in the bureaucratic sector, nominally controlled by the state or the Histadrut, frequently linked to military requirements, and employing exclusively Jewish labor under the favorable conditions of a sheltered or "primary" labor market. The more competitive economic periphery, smaller-scale and privately owned, operated a "secondary" labor market employing a mixed (Jewish and Arab) workforce.[19]

As in the prewar period, the coherence of the post-1967 growth model rested on state subsidy of both capital and labor. The most compelling claims to subsidy were made by the bureaucratic sector. The key actors in this respect were the big banks and the big conglomerates under their control; the "strong" Workers' Committees in the bureaucratic sector; and the Histadrut (simultaneously representing big business and "big labor"). The state found itself increasingly indebted to these powerful interests, and unable to assert its will and extract benefits in return for the rising tide of subsidies. Under the conditions prevailing in the world economy of the post-1973 period, and given the earmarked nature of US aid, economic policy became strikingly "undisciplined." Symptomatic of this was the public sector's excessive deficit spending, frequent recourse to corrective devaluations, and government lending policies that favored borrowers at the state's expense. The result of these policies was to exacerbate Israel's immanent condition of stagflation after 1973, while paradoxically enriching its big banks and conglomerates.[20]

This is the background to the Emergency Stabilization Plan of June 1985.[21] In hindsight, the astonishing success of the plan in bringing the Israeli economy back from the brink of hyperinflation is of lesser importance than the structural change that it inaugurated – the contemporary liberalizing shift in Israel's political-economic regime. The most compelling interpretation of the stabilization plan is that, just like the *mitun*, it was a radical attempt by the state – led by senior economic policy mandarins and sages – to regain autonomy by strengthening market discipline.[22] The plan and the structural reforms temporarily hidden in its shadow constituted a frontal attack on mechanisms that had previously protected societal interests, directly or indirectly at the expense of the state: devaluations, protectionism, wage indexation, unlinked public lending, and diffuse investment incentives.

Why had it taken the state so long to develop a coherent policy response to the problems of economic stagnation and hyperinflation? While most observers have emphasized the role of public opinion and the leadership finally shown by the government, the state's drive to reinstate its autonomy accounts more effectively for the timing of its stabilization initiative. By 1985 the economic crisis posed tangible threats to the state itself – its fundamental legitimacy and, no less importantly, its economic viability. While critics cast doubt on the plan's macro-economic effectiveness,[23] its consequences for the viability and autonomy of the state were very substantial indeed. Talk of the need for a "strong leader" (an ominous threat to the political regime) disappeared; state extraction of economic resources through taxation was restored to effectiveness; it was possible to set in motion a long-overdue flattening of military expenditure; and a worrying hole in Israel's foreign reserves was filled, in large part by virtue of enlarged United States aid.

This is not to argue that the acute crisis which economic instability posed to core state interests was the only relevant factor. As is often the case when history turns at a major crossroads, multiple causal forces converged in mid-1985. First, many of Israel's largest corporations and investors began to believe that there were limits to the profitability of military-based demand and inflationary subsidies, and that the time was ripe for a new and more outward-looking economic strategy.[24] Second, the political conjuncture in mid-1985 was especially favorable to radical policy initiatives.[25] There was little scope for profiting from party rivalry under the National Unity government which was then in its early stages. And the leadership of the Histadrut, the most vocal potential opposition to the stabilization plan given that it was expected to slash real wages, was politically indebted to the government for its aid in a recent election. All of these circumstances together offered exceptional leeway to the professional economists in state agencies and university economics departments who prepared and lobbied for the stabilization plan. The architects of the plan cannily grasped the opportunity to go beyond crisis management and engineer a strategic reorientation of economic policy.[26] Have they succeeded in liberalizing the Israeli economy?

INDICATORS OF LIBERALIZATION

The term liberalization is typically applied to reforms of countries' trade policies (removing barriers to imports and ending preferential treatment of exports) and their foreign currency regimes (eliminating restrictions on inward and outward flows of foreign currency and letting exchange rates float more freely). From a broader perspective, the principal goal of liberalizing economic reforms in Israel and elsewhere has been state contraction, a fundamental alteration of the division of labor between markets and the state by means that include privatization, expenditure, and tax cuts, sectoral "deregulation," etc. To the extent that this aim is achieved, the state's ownership, regulatory, and distributional roles are diminished in favor of the market and the private sector. The conventional wisdom assumes that combining state contraction with increased exposure to international competition causes markets to become both more important and more competitive.

Internationalization

In 1996 Israel's "internationalization" was ranked 18 out of 46 countries – including all of the OECD and the rapidly growing NICs – by the *World Competitiveness Yearbook*.[27] Liberalization in the sense of opening up to the global economy should be evidenced at the macro level by buying more from the outside world and selling more to it, and at the micro level by the elimination of import restrictions and export incentives. The scope and regulation of trade can only tell part of the story, however, especially in Israel where politicization has been the most salient feature of external economic relations. In the Israeli context liberalization would also imply a change in the character of capital inflow, from state to market-sponsored and from gifts to loans or investments.

Has the economy become more involved in trade? Since its establishment as a state and in fact well before that, Israel has been chronically dependent on imported goods and services yet unable to pay for them from export revenues alone. The total value of trade (imports + exports) relative to national product has always been exceptionally high compared to other countries, three-quarters or more of GNP. Setting aside fluctuations, it is evident that this ratio experienced a *declining trend* between the late 1970s and the early 1990s. The seeming absence of a tendency toward increasing openness is again unusual from a comparative perspective.[28]

Part of the puzzle is resolved by recognizing that Israel's relatively strong growth rates in the 1990s hide a major increase in the absolute volume of trade. Since stabilization the dollar value of both imports and exports has surged upwards, even taking account of rapid population growth. In addition, two elements of Israel's trade that arguably warrant separate consideration – the diamond-processing industry and arms imports – have been contracting. The Bank of Israel estimates that setting these elements aside, during the 1990s the scope of trade increased from roughly 50 percent to 70 percent of national product.[29] No less significant than the quantitative trend, foreign sales have altered qualitatively – more high-tech yet less military-centered; less dependent on the European market and more on "emerging" markets in eastern Europe and, especially, Asia.[30] Nevertheless, during the present decade exports have failed to keep pace with rapidly rising imports as trade barriers came down and cheap imports became a *de facto* mainstay of Israel's anti-inflationary policy. Consequently, the civilian "import surplus" (excess of imports over exports, again net of diamonds) has risen to a staggering 15 percent of national product – far above OECD standards.[31]

Theoretically, opening up to trade should have important microeconomic effects, obliging domestic producers to feel the whip of foreign competition and encouraging exports to be driven by comparative advantage in world markets. The first of these variables, exposure to competition from import substitutes, has increased significantly since stabilization. Between 1985 and 1990 there was a 30 percent increase in the penetration of domestic markets for manufactured goods.[32] Still, the impact of greater openness to imports on competition has been weakened by monopolistic tendencies among importers. Moreover, while after much foot-dragging Israel honored its free trade agreements with the EU (1975) and the United States (1985), defenses against competing imports from other countries (mostly NICs) were actually fortified for a time. However, during the 1990s these barriers have gradually come down.[33] On the other side of the trade ledger, export subsidies –at least those for which statistics are available – have been phased out (see *State Expenditure*, below, and Figure 2). At their peak in the period 1970-84 these subsidies averaged 3 percent of GNP, but by 1990 they had been virtually eliminated.[34]

FIGURE 1
MILITARY SPENDING AND FOREIGN AID

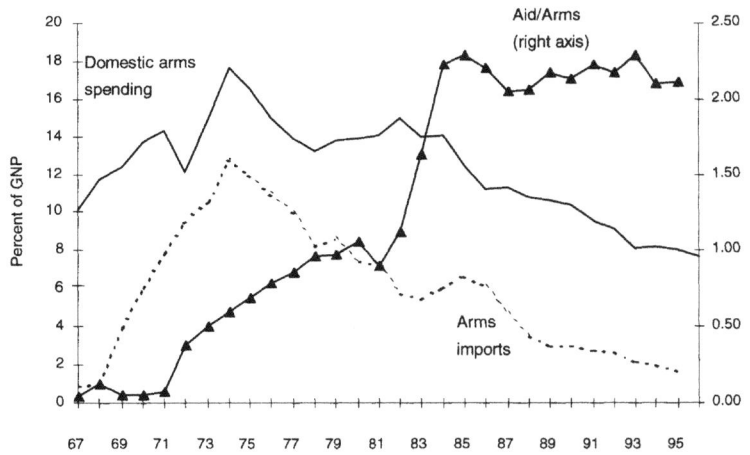

Note: Military spending as a percent of GNP, using the SNA system from 1980 (old series linked to new at 1980). "Domestic" is net domestic defense consumption; "imports" is direct defense imports, including advance payments. The "aid to arms" ratio is intergovernmental transfers divided by defense imports. To dampen their volatility, imports and aid are three-year moving averages (BOI-96, Appendix Table Hay-1a,1b).

FIGURE 2
THE STATE AND BUSINESS

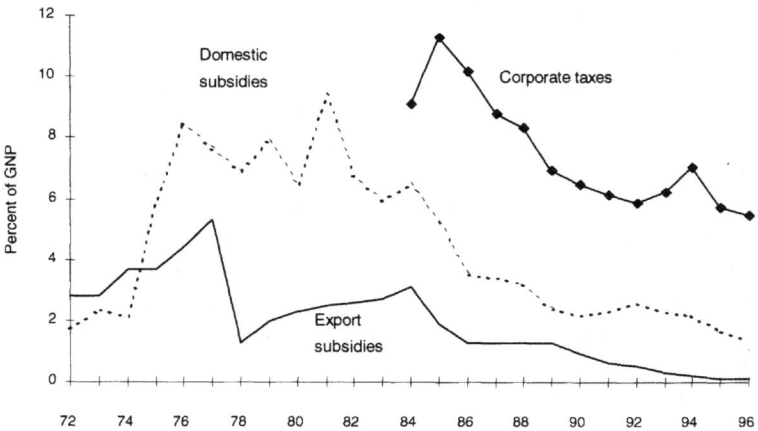

Note: Subsidies on exports and domestic production combine direct supports and credit subsidies. (BOI-96, Appendix Table *Hay*-7). Revenues from corporate taxes combine two series. First, corporate income tax data published by the State Revenues Administration (annual report for 1996, Table *Chet*-1 and parallel data from earlier reports). Second, CBS data on social security contributions and payroll taxes (Abstract-97, Table 6.13 and earlier years).

Has the nature of capital inflow changed? "Unilateral transfers" from foreign sympathizers and governments have always been crucial both for meeting Israel's external obligations and for financing the role of the state in the economy. One variety of gift capital, that which emanates from Diaspora Jewry, has gradually declined in importance.[35] Since the beginning of the 1970s the United States government has become the pre-eminent source. By the late 1970s the import of American arms had plateaued at around 8 percent of GNP, and American aid was effectively paying for them in full (Figure 1). In 1984 and 1985 Israel's foreign economic relations took a dramatic new turn. A wide gap emerged in Israel's favor between what it receives from the US government and its purchases of US arms. In the first half of the 1990s net US aid averaged over 3 billion dollars a year, up by a billion dollars from a decade before. At the same time Israel's purchases of imported arms were declining, especially in relation to the rapidly growing national product. As the combined result of these two trends, for more than a decade the ratio of aid to arms has been at least 2:1.

Not only has the pure gift element in US aid increased substantially since the mid-1980s, but following the transition to a Labor government after the 1992 elections Israel was able to obtain official US guarantees for $10 billion worth of future commercial loans. Like the peace process which was also inaugurated following the 1992 elections, the loan guarantees have helped raise Israel's commercial credit-worthiness abroad.[36] So far, in most years of the 1990s this has helped give the state the resources and flexibility to maintain or increase non-defense spending while actually reducing the budget deficit and the public debt and accumulating very high levels of foreign reserves.

The political-economic implication of these changes is multi-dimensional. The increase in the gift component of US aid and the addition of the loan guarantees has enhanced the scope and autonomy of the state in the economic arena. At the same time, by helping relieve the budget deficit and the shortage of hard currency that reached crisis proportions prior to stabilization, American aid created necessary (although not of course sufficient) conditions for liberalization of the capital market and the foreign exchange regime, which in turn opened up new possibilities for capital inflows and outflows through the market.

Foreign direct investment (FDI) has been the most novel and noticed element of Israel's contemporary integration into the world economy.[37] Net FDI was insignificant until the early 1990s and only at mid-decade did it reach substantial levels (1.5–2.0 billion dollars a year).[38] In the past the Israeli economy was too small and resource-poor to interest most foreign investors, and many big financial and corporate interests also stayed away because of the chronic state of war or their fear of losing Arab markets. The little FDI that did enter Israel typically involved Jewish businessmen with connections to Zionist philanthropy and the Israeli political establishment, who were induced to invest by a combination of generous subsidies and patriotic appeals.[39] Investments in Israel by Volkswagen, Nestles, Macdonalds, and numerous other well-known transnational enterprises indicate a substantial departure from this tradition, although not its elimination. The recent acquisitions, led by Charles Bronfman and Ted Arison respectively, of controlling interests in Koor and Bank Hapoalim – arguably the two most important corporate entities in Israel – are eloquent testimony to the continuing role of well-connected Jewish magnates.[40]

There are additional reasons why the features of the new foreign investment warrant careful scrutiny. The effective scope of the capital inflow accompanying FDI is far more modest than the imagery conveyed by government and business discourse suggests. The largest deals (including those just mentioned) have been financed almost entirely by Israeli banks.[41] The mushrooming of franchise operations in consumer markets also takes place, by definition, with a minimal financial commitment on the part of the foreign investor. Another significant limitation of FDI is that the state continues to generously subsidize showcase foreign investments. Intel's decision to open a major production facility in Israel was conditional on a government subsidy so large ($600 million) that the Investment Incentive Law had to be amended to make it legally possible.[42]

FDI is not, of course, the only means by which overseas investors channel capital to Israel. Indeed, it has been complemented by an equal or larger stream of foreign purchases of shares issued by Israeli firms. Both, in turn, are overshadowed by the liquid capital (much of it "hot money" originating in Israeli companies) which has been attracted simply by high interest rates and convenient opportunities for "laundering."[43]

It is still too early to assess the scope or durability of Israel's new status as a target for foreign investment, but there is no gainsaying the growing international orientation of Israeli business (mainly big business, but also smaller hi-tech firms), which in the last few years have become much more committed to raising capital via foreign banks and stock markets, undertaking joint ventures with foreign firms, and in some cases even setting up branch plants abroad. Reports of such activities fill the business-oriented media in Israel, although it is hard to gauge their scope with any precision. Aggregate data confirm, however, that like incoming FDI, outward direct investment has risen far above previous levels. For instance, in the period 1994–96 alone, industrial firms in Israel purchased one billion dollars worth of equity in foreign concerns.[44]

State Expenditure

The decline since the mid-1980s in the share of national resources distributed by the state is quite remarkable. Total public expenditure had been equivalent to at least three-quarters of the national product since the "Yom Kippur War" in 1973. But two years after stabilization the figure fell to 62 percent and by 1994 it had troughed at only 54 percent. Almost all of the decline in government spending since the early eighties can be traced to defense (a drop of over 10 points of GNP), capital subsidies (down 8 points) and debt service (down nearly 5 points).[45]

The welfare state for business.[46] The decline in capital subsidies is especially significant, given that much of the increase in transfer payments during the 1970s – which was the major factor behind the fiscal crisis of the early 1980s – consisted of payments and benefits to business.[47] One element in the cutback, already noted, has been the termination of subsidies specifically targeted to exporters. Subsidies on production for the domestic market have also been sharply reduced. As shown in Figure 2, during Israel's initial inflationary spurt in the mid-1970s, the burden of these subsidies jumped fourfold to 8 percent of GNP, remaining at this level through the early 1980s. Phased reductions over the next decade brought their share back down to 2 percent.[48]

Because of their indirect effects on the business sector, the implications of the other principal budget cuts – in debt service and defense – have been no less portentous. Servicing the government's debt became a major source of profitability for Israel's biggest banks, especially during the 1983–88 period when it preempted an average of nearly a fifth of GDP.[49] Reductions since stabilization in the domestic defense budget, which had showered lucrative cost-plus contracts on large-scale local suppliers,[50] may also be assumed to have indirectly eroded the profitability of big business. From 1985 the domestic military procurement budget failed to increase in real terms, so that its share of Israel's growing GNP fell substantially (Figure 1).[51]

All of the data reviewed thus far appear to signify massive retrenchment of the "welfare state for business." But a fuller assessment of this issue also requires us to consider whether the apparent harshness of post-1985 policy toward business has not been mitigated by two developments that would not necessarily show up in these data: compensatory "tax expenditures," or the replacement of old subsidies by new ones.

Regarding taxation, as Swank has recently noted in a comparative study of OECD economies, despite the pressures exerted by mobile global capital on state managers, they continue to "defend the treasury." Accordingly, while governments have found it necessary to cut taxes on business the primacy of markets has also been invoked to justify the withdrawal of investment incentives.[52] The same is true in Israel, where the other side of the equation is also evident: in aggregate, as can be seen in Figure 2, massive cuts in subsidies have been offset by tax cuts of similar magnitude. One of the immediate effects of stabilization was to revive the state's capacity to extract revenues from the business sector – a capacity which had been badly undermined by rapid inflation. Revenues from corporate income and payroll taxes rose sharply relative to national product immediately following stabilization, but since then taxes and subsidies have been declining more or less in tandem. A major reform in the mid-1980s and gradual additional cuts since then have brought the tax rate on undistributed profits down from an internationally high level of 61 percent in 1984 to the rich-country norm (only 36 percent) in 1996.[53] In addition, employer contributions to the social security system and other payroll taxes have been either reduced or taken over by the Treasury in order to help employers lower their labor costs.[54]

Finally, while automatic and indirect capital subsidies have been dramatically cut, targeted incentives are more generous than ever. This has already been noted with respect to foreign investment, in the specific case of Intel's enlarged presence in Israel. It is also true of direct investment grants issued by the Ministry of Industry and Commerce, especially assistance to startup companies in high technology fields which was three times higher in real terms in 1992–94 than in 1985–87.[55]

The welfare state for households. There is no evidence that aggregate social spending in Israel has fallen during the contemporary era of liberalization – an irony that holds for other countries as well.[56] Following a period of budget cutting in the 1980s, in the first half of the 1990s spending on the major categories of social services – health and education – rose, returning to approximately the same share of GNP as a decade earlier.[57] Expenditure on housing and immigrant absorption (important components of Israel's generosity toward Jewish newcomers) increased by well over 3 points of GNP, in response to the wave of immigration from the former Soviet Union. Transfer payments to households also grew, by about one and a half points of GNP.

The record of annual fluctuations in real social expenditure over the last 15 years shows that in addition to immigrant absorption, increased commitments have come about for a variety of reasons. The cost of the key income maintenance branches has grown mainly because of automatic benefit adjustments and demographic shifts (a larger and older population). In other instances, specific programs have experienced innovations that caused sudden steps in expenditure. The most notable example is the national health insurance law adopted in 1994 (see *The Labor Market*, below). There have also been a few cases where spending rose when liberal demands for equality coincided with increased political clout, leading to a broadening of the universal basis of social security.[58] Finally, one of the social services – a very expensive one, education – actually expanded during the 1990s. The Labor government elected in 1992 restored per capita spending to the level that prevailed before cuts were instituted in the 1980s.[59] This momentum has, however, stalled in several recent years.

None of this necessarily means that there has been no rollback of the welfare state, broadly-conceived. At least one significant form of social protection has been all but eliminated since the stabilization plan – consumer subsidies on food and public transportation, which at their peak in 1984 amounted to $1.4 billion.[60] The Treasury has also sought and sometimes succeeded to erode entitlements (child allowances have been a favorite) or stymie the implementation of costly political promises (such as extension of the school day). As in most other countries, eligibility rules for unemployment insurance have become more restrictive, although this has not prevented rising take-up.[61]

In addition, it has been widely observed in Israel that private expenditure on social services has increased in the last decade to compensate for inadequate public provision.[62] The public school system both requires and encourages parents to pay a range of fees and subsidies in public education. In the health field supplementary insurance schemes have recently proliferated, and the Treasury is expected to try to cut the cost of national health insurance by creating additional membership fees and service charges.

Critics see these signs of privatization of welfare as part of a broader project of undermining the generosity and universality of the welfare state.[63] No less important but less noticed so far are the implications of the ascendancy of market-oriented criteria in relation to public sector employment and government policy toward outlying Jewish areas. So long as the "bureaucratic sector" sheltered key parts of the defense industries and other key industrial sectors that exclusively employed Jewish citizens, it was a haven for government-subsidized occupational welfare.[64] The retrenchment of both the scope and conditions of blue-collar employment that tends to follow privatization seriously threatens this system of welfare. Regional development incentives constituted a second element of the state's traditional role in supporting the living standards of Jewish citizens. The claim that these incentives are inefficient and no longer justified by security considerations has generated ongoing policy changes that threaten to substantially erode direct and indirect subsidies to housing, employment and public services in peripheral "development towns."

Competition and the Structure of Capital

The industrialization of Israel was both directed and financed by the state, working through the managers of the private, public and Histadrut sectors.[65] This *dirigisme* was practiced in a fashion which strongly encouraged the monopolistic tendencies that characterize capitalism in general, and small-country capitalism in particular.[66] Since the late 1960s a very substantial and quite integrated sector of big business has emerged in Israel. At the apex are only a handful of "business groups" constituted by very large conglomerates and banks. These two wings – the financial and non-financial – are moreover closely connected by virtue of bank ownership or simply as a result of the banks' multiple roles as investors, creditors and stockbrokers. The two biggest banks account for a majority of the country's highly diversified banking business, while conglomerates and other large firms have typically dominated the branches in which they operate.[67]

The period between the Yom Kippur War and the stabilization plan furnished hothouse conditions for growth in the profitability and power of the big business groups.[68] Direct incentives and capital subsidies, cost-plus procurement contracts, and windfall profits from the government's practice of lending unlinked money and borrowing linked money all contributed to an impressive increase in capital accumulation at the apex of the business sector, despite the dampening effect of economic stagnation on profitability as a whole. The changing profile of state expenditure since stabilization which has already been discussed undoubtedly hurt the profitability of the large banks and conglomerates.[69]

No less important, the government's nominal ownership of the largest banks – the result of the bailout which followed the stock market collapse of 1983 – offered the reformers an opportunity to force the big banks to divest their controlling interests in industrial and service enterprises. This demand is part of a wider recent tendency for Treasury officials to place the issues of monopoly power and ownership concentration on the public policy agenda and to advocate tighter regulatory inhibitions on big business.[70] Together with the inflow of competing imports discussed in an earlier section, the result has been a decline in the monopolistic character of the market for manufactured goods.[71]

The recent "trust-busting" activities of the state, so alien to its traditional role of fostering concentration, should not, however, be overdramatized. The Treasury's attempts to limit bank ownership of non-financial firms are only the latest round in a long-running battle, and some seasoned observers remain unconvinced that this battle will ever be won.[72] There are a number of indications that the status quo is highly resistant to reform. First, by offering the banks postponements, special exceptions, tax incentives, and compensatory approved rises in bank fees and rate spreads, the state has gone to considerable lengths to sweeten the bitter pill of divestiture.[73] Second, even though new local and foreign private investors have acquired controlling interests in segments of big business, the existing groups were also strengthened in the 1990s by opportunities for expansion furnished by some major privatizations and by boom conditions in construction and infrastructure.[74] Third, the top executives who formerly ran firms in the public and Histadrut sectors continue to be major players in big business.

While the personal wealth of members of the former managerial oligarchy and their potential role as capitalists in their own right have grown substantially, their struggles for control have not always been crowned with success.[75] But internationalization need not threaten the interests of the local business elite, whether owners or managers. They are equally likely to utilize it as a resource in struggles for personal and institutional wealth and power.[76] Koor, which came close to bankruptcy in the 1980s, illustrates the renewed vitality of big business in the era of globalization. Like other big manufacturing interests, Koor has evidently benefited from economic trends of the nineties – diversification away from arms production, penetration of new overseas markets, increased financial ties with overseas capital, and booming local and global stock markets.[77]

Privatization and Deregulation[78]

The changes that liberalizers seek to effect in the structure of the economy are, of course, directed not only at stimulating competition but also at reducing the scope of state ownership of firms and organizations producing marketable goods and services. Summing up developments in Israel prior to the mid-1980s, one survey concluded that in this period "no serious effort was made to privatize public corporations."[79] The first major initiative occurred in 1988, when the cabinet embraced an ambitious privatization program drawn up by an international consulting firm. Yet as in other countries, privatization has been hampered by the problem of finding a method of sale that would be at once feasible, politically acceptable, and make a worthwhile addition to the state treasury, as well as the need to overcome opposition from employees, executives, and responsible cabinet ministers in corporations targeted for privatization.

Beginning in 1990 the government budget has included sizable projected revenues from privatization, but until recently only 15–20 percent of the targeted revenues were actually raised.[80] The first few major sales, based on hastily-concluded deals with local and foreign investors, netted disappointingly low revenues. Several subsequent public offerings on the Tel Aviv Stock Exchange were more successful but this outlet was closed off when the market collapsed in 1994. The Likud-led government that assumed office following the May 1996 elections has carried the process much further, most notably by the sale in September 1997 of the government's controlling stake in the country's largest bank (Bank Hapoalim) to a consortium of foreign and local investors. A number of other major privatizations in banking, arms production, and transportation appear imminent, but could yet run into obstacles of various kinds.

Deregulation, a second catchword of neoliberal reform programs, has been carried out at least partially in several areas, notably by the dismantling of producer boards in agriculture.[81] As part of their recent "trust-busting" frenzy, the authorities have launched specific measures designed to eliminate monopoly "rents" created by licensing and rationing mechanisms that were operated by or with the consent of the state. Current examples include the markets for insurance, pay TV, overseas and cellular telephony, and taxis. However, insofar as barriers to entry other than licenses are high (as in most of these examples), the result is typically an expanded market capable of supporting a few more large-scale players, rather than the substitution of many small players for one big one.

By far the most important locus of deregulation in Israel has been the attempt to roll back the state's domination of what in the past could only euphemistically be called the "capital market." It will be recalled that prior to 1985 the state was the dominant source of investment capital; both reinvestment of undistributed profits and unregulated bank credit played very limited roles. The disposal of long-term savings (in bonds, pension funds, and bank savings plans) was heavily regulated in ways that funneled the lion's share of these assets to the state, with the result that the stock market played virtually no role in the mobilization of investment capital for the business sector.

Two different factors account for the state's historic domination of capital flows. Its ability to acquire extensive foreign gifts, part of which took the form of donated capital goods or raw materials, naturally encouraged the state and its political masters to prefer institutional and political modes of allocation. Both the state bureaucracy and the governing party benefited greatly from their resultant ability to directly steer the course of economic and indeed societal development right down to the micro level. However, once erected this interventionist bias proved highly durable even when the state's ability to cover the costs by foreign gifts and the political profits to be reaped from intervention both diminished. The 1967 and 1973 wars were turning points after which the state's commitments grew far beyond its extractive capacities, with the result that budget deficits and the cost of servicing accumulated public debt greatly increased.

This fiscal crisis reinforced the state's long-standing preference for meeting its commitments by pre-empting private savings through regulations requiring banks, pension funds, and other institutional investors to automatically convert the bulk of their accumulations into government securities.[82] Under these circumstances the state's relationship with the big banks became characterized by competition to attract private savings, as well as by collaboration (the banks were charged with the profitable tasks of mobilizing funds for the state and distributing credit on its behalf). The authorities' seeming inattention to the banks' extensive manipulation of their own share prices in the early 1980s was one of the ways by which the state's economic managers attempted to handle this mix of competition and collaboration.[83]

In addition, to protect the state's autonomy in fixing domestic credit and interest rates, international currency flows and the holding of foreign currency inside Israel were limited or banned outright. While most foreign currency controls were removed by the first Likud government in 1977, it was still necessary to finance a growing deficit and as a result controls were gradually reinstated.[84]

As this example demonstrates, lowering fiscal indebtedness was a necessary condition for capital market deregulation. With the abrupt ending of hyper-inflation by the stabilization plan in 1985, public sector costs were reduced and state revenues enhanced. Along with other elements of the plan (such as large cuts in price subsidies and the partial de-indexation of wages), these developments virtually wiped out the domestic budget deficit. Since then, Treasury and Bank of Israel officials and the responsible cabinet ministers have been committed to ending the various forms of government regulation of savings and credit and to easing the local capital market into the international market. The measures already implemented or decided upon include eliminating "directed credit" and encouraging businesses to turn instead to banks and the stock market; and cutting the state's claims on (and obligations to) pension funds, provident funds, and insurance companies. In addition, foreign currency flows and holdings have been partially deregulated, so that while the Israeli shekel is still not fully convertible, foreign interest rates now exert a stronger influence over local ones.

That the state today makes a diminished claim on domestic savings, and that it has devolved the setting of important financial parameters onto the market, cannot be in doubt. Yet it remains uncertain whether the still ongoing process of capital market reform will be fully completed.[85] As I have emphasized, the competitiveness of the enlarged capital market is significantly bounded, especially given the obstacles facing attempts to limit the role and power of the big banks. On the other hand, both sides have reason to be satisfied by the partially liberalized status quo. The Treasury and the Bank of Israel have been at least partly freed of the necessity of propping up financial institutions and bidding up the cost of attracting private savings, and are themselves among the potential beneficiaries of the accessibility of foreign capital markets.

At the same time, the new avenues for raising capital (especially the stock market) which have been opened up by the state's withdrawal and deregulation measures have widened the scope for at least the very largest concerns to lessen their traditional dependency on both the government and the banks. Yet this enhanced flexibility need not promote a radical break with past patterns of ownership and control of business. Companies that "went public" during the stock market boom of 1992–3 by and large continued to be dominated by the same individual owners or holders of controlling blocks of shares. Similarly, the increased role of stock markets – domestic and overseas – in the 1990s has not eliminated either government subsidies or bank credit as mainstays of investment finance. Reliance on the New York exchanges is realistic only for big or "hot" enterprises, while the local market is operated largely by, and to an important extent for the benefit of, the large banks. It is a testimony to this continued domination that independent brokers, nonbank financial institutions, and foreign commercial banks have all made very limited inroads into the market for financial services, despite facilitating changes in the rules of the game.[86]

The Labor Market

Liberalization of the labor market merits separate treatment because, as I emphasized in the historical introduction, the labor market was the stimulus and original site of many of the most distinctive features of Israel's political economy. The problem of creating jobs for propertyless Jewish settlers and insulating them from Arab competition led to the creation in 1920 of the Histadrut as a unitary, multifunctional, politicized national labor organization that for more than half a century played a dominant role in politics, the economy, and social protection. The problem of generating work for settlers also stimulated the public and Histadrut economies, where Israel's "bureaucratic sector" took root. The drive to provide immigrants with jobs and prevent emigration encouraged a political consensus on the desirability of full employment, as well as the readiness of successive governments to subsidize an inefficient business sector provided that jobs were created.

Given this background, the labor market sphere has generated what must be judged as perhaps the three most remarkable signs of contemporary change in Israel's political economy. First, revolutionary transformations of the structure and rationale of the Histadrut have led some observers to cast doubt on its continued viability. In the last few years the labor organization has experienced an internal political upheaval, massive membership losses, and the paring down of its mandate to trade union representation. Second, the government has violated an enduring nationalist taboo by admitting large numbers of foreign *gastarbeiter* who have replenished and enlarged Israel's stock of cheap non-citizen labor. Third, privatization of public and Histadrut-owned business enterprises accompanied by reduction or "casualization" of employment, together with diminished activity by the public sector (including the military) in creating new jobs, have retrenched the "bureaucratic sector."

It is hard to exaggerate the importance of the Histadrut, prior to the 1990s, in diverse spheres of Israel's political economy: power-brokering in the Labor Party; shaping the formation of economic and social policy; monopolizing the national-level representation of labor and centralized collective bargaining; nominally directing the country's main health fund and several of its largest financial and industrial enterprises; and leading an irresistible "distributional coalition" by coordinating the demands of private and Histadrut business and siding with privileged public sector workers.[87] The decomposition of the Histadrut's complex role-set had multiple sources, but the most salient (and mutually reinforcing) developments may be summarized as follows.

1. In 1979, after failing to gain the vital cooperation of the Histadrut for restrictive wage and economic policies, the Likud government's Minister of Finance revoked a long-standing arrangement whereby the Treasury authorized and subsidized the Histadrut's use of its pension fund accumulations to finance investment by its corporate affiliates. This act eliminated the principal source of Bank Hapoalim's leverage over its largest client, the Histadrut economy. Then in 1983 following the bank share collapse Bank Hapoalim suffered major losses and was effectively nationalized pending privatization. Along with contraction of military-related demand in Israel and worldwide, and the effects of deflation, the loss of favorable pension fund financing also precipitated an acute crisis in Koor, the Histadrut's flagship conglomerate.

2. In the labor relations sphere, determined employers – including Koor – embarked on the same road to decentralization and flexibilization of labor relations followed by their counterparts in other countries. Preoccupied with rearguard struggles to defend its affiliated pension funds, health service, and business enterprises, as well as its position inside the Labor Party, and sensitive primarily to pressures from

powerful groups of workers who could threaten its representational monopoly, the Histadrut leadership did little to counter layoffs and clawbacks in crisis-stricken firms, or the growth of individual employment contracts, subcontracting, and temporary employment. Then, partly for conjunctural political reasons and partly with an eye to obtaining aid for Koor's ailing enterprises, the Histadrut cooperated with a key element of the 1985 stabilization plan – the dismantling (albeit incomplete) of wage indexation. This removed the most significant aspect of its role in countrywide wage negotiations. In addition, the "framework agreements" hitherto negotiated for the whole of the business sector between the Histadrut and the Manufacturers Association were scrapped.[88] The combined result of the twin crises in the Histadrut's economic and labor-representation roles was that it lost not only economic assets and trade union legitimacy, but also the ability to pivot an alliance of big labor and big business against the state.

3. Finally, a long-brewing political crisis inside the labor complex came to a head in the runup to the 1994 Histadrut elections. Because of its unpopularity and the pressure on Labor cabinet ministers to prioritize aid to Histadrut enterprises and services over other policy goals, the labor organization had become a political liability. A group of younger liberals who had risen within the Labor Party independently of (and in conflict with) the old Histadrut-based "machine" openly articulated this tension. They succeeded in ousting the party-appointed Histadrut oligarchy, and given the labor organization's desperate fiscal crisis and the government's unwillingness to bail it out the result was not only a severing of the traditional political ties between the Histadrut and the party, but also the selling off of the Histadrut's business assets, the cessation of its responsibilities for health care, and consequently its loss of hundreds of thousands of captive members.[89]

Current attempts to reformulate a role for the Histadrut as a trade union and to add roots from below to its corporate and centralized traditions are best understood as a belated adaptation, almost half a century after the event itself, to the challenge which statehood presented to the Histadrut's pre-state mode of operation. In contrast, the presence of some 200,000 foreign "guest workers" – perhaps one eighth of business sector employment – poses a stark contradiction to a core feature of Israel's state tradition, its hostility to the entry of non-Jews other than for tourist purposes. Following the occupation of the West Bank and Gaza, in an effort to prevent unrest in the territories and meet unmet demand for construction and agricultural labor, the government sanctioned the entry of Palestinian day laborers on a commuter basis. In the late 1980s and early 1990s, when this flow was disrupted by Palestinian strikes, Israeli retaliations, and security closures during the

Intifada, the number of Palestinians employed in Israel remained high (around 100,000, down by only 20%). But in 1993 security-related prohibitions were tightened considerably. Over the next two years the escalating scarcity of Palestinian labor was compensated almost precisely by increased quotas for "temporary" imported laborers, the largest contingents originating in Thailand and Romania.[90]

The scope of the guest worker phenomenon has rapidly outgrown the problem of substituting for Palestinians, however, and observers agree that today there are probably as many illegal as legal immigrant laborers in Israel. Not only is this an indication of internationalization affecting yet another of Israel's markets, but in consenting to labor importation and delegating responsibility for its operation to private manpower companies, the state has yielded capacities that include but go well beyond its role in regulating the economy. Yet in contrast to other reforms, Israel's opening to the global market in cheap labor does not reflect a strategic embrace of liberalization by state elites. The decision to open the floodgates to foreign labor is the consequence of the state's contradictory interests. The political economy of Palestinian pacification – whether under conditions of reconciliation and self-rule, or continuing Israeli occupation – requires that the Palestinian proletariat be able to earn a living inside Israel, but the real and perceived threat of terrorism leads policy in the direction of shutting the Palestinians out.

The third dimension of liberalization of Israel's labor market is the diminished (although by no means exhausted) role of the state in furnishing employment. Privatization and deregulation, although incomplete, have putatively lowered both the scope and the sheltered quality of employment in public corporations, military industries, infrastructural monopolies, and the former Histadrut enterprises. Employment in the public services (health, education, government administration, etc.) has declined somewhat during the 1990s, and there has been a pronounced growth of new jobs in the business sector.[91] In particular, industry has responded to the low cost of employing experienced skilled labor and highly specialized scientists and engineers from the former Soviet Union.[92] The third component of the public sector is the military, which like public corporations and services has played a significant role in the past in absorbing excess (Jewish) labor. In 1983 the regular army (including conscripts) and reserve duty together accounted for over 12 percent of the total (civilian + military) labor force. By 1995 this proportion had fallen to 8 percent.[93]

CONCLUSIONS

Israel's political-economic regime is without question in the advanced throes of policy reforms, institutional shifts, and structural changes that are at odds with its long record of embedded illiberalism. Although much of the traditional exceptionalism of the political economy in Israel is disappearing before our eyes, three important reservations must be noted. First, like any rapid major transformation liberalization has not occurred evenly, consistently, or completely. Second, despite dramatic reductions in the role of the state, "normalization" of the Histadrut and the cultural ascendancy of the market, the legacy of Zionist collectivism persists in many of the practices – and even more, the discourses – that surround the political economy. Third, the process of liberalization is indeterminate because of its inherently political nature: it is an occasion for struggle between winners and losers. The winners seek to exploit the rhetoric and the institutional tools of liberalization in order to protect and strengthen their favorable position in the status quo ante, thus changing both everything and nothing. Backlash from the losers may retard, limit, or even reverse changes.

These are the reasons why many of our findings have seemed contradictory. State expenditure is down, but some branches of public spending persist and even grow. The state has reduced or eliminated its control of the capital and foreign exchange markets, yet its role in wooing big multinational corporations, marketing Israeli-made weapons technology, and subsidizing hi-tech startups has if anything increased. Big business is still the core of the political economy, but it has been forced to accept huge cuts in state subsidies and budget-derived profit opportunities. However, the state has also greatly lowered corporate taxation and has opened up new opportunities for private mobilization of capital and entry into foreign markets. While Israel's business elite has become much more internationally oriented, at least part of this process seems to reflect its interest in preserving the hyper-concentrated structure bequeathed by the long era of state patronage.

The literature of political economy teaches us that transitions between policy regimes are propelled by a combination of endogenous and exogenous pressures for change: unintended and undesired consequences of existing policies and institutions accumulate, while changing external conditions add new opportunities and constraints. A long-term perspective on contemporary trends reveals that in both the mid-1960s and the mid-1980s the Israeli state found itself unable to revive a failing growth model that imposed heavy burdens on the state itself. In both cases it was no longer possible to resolve the contradictions by taking advantage of windfalls of imported financial and human capital. Given a political conjuncture that made it possible to ignore or even attack entrenched interests, the state responded with radical breaks from past habits. Its new policies were aimed at shedding economic obligations to powerful interests and defending its capacities to manage both the public economy and the wider national economy.

Theoretically, this dialectic fits well with a view of public policy as grounded in the state's interest in autonomy. When the pendulum swings and the state becomes burdened by commitments that no longer empower it *vis-à-vis* social groups and economic sectors, it may cast off these fetters by devolving responsibilities to the market arena. The apparent paradox of willful liberalization – that *states willingly shed power in order to regain it* – makes sense analytically if we recognize the difference between *power as resources* and *power as autonomy*. Forfeiting resources may be the price which has to be paid for regaining lost autonomy.[94]

This perspective sheds light on the *origins* of radically liberalizing policy initiatives like Israel's *mitun* and its current liberalization drive. It is less helpful in dealing with the question of how *durable* such policy realignments are likely to be. After little more than a year, even before the June 1967 War and its consequences propelled Israel toward a new political economic regime, the liberalizers of the time encountered serious difficulties in sustaining recessionary discipline and reaping the expected harvest of export-led growth.[95] However, in the dozen years that have elapsed since 1985 the structural reforms which were the subtext of the stabilization plan have been partially and sometimes haltingly implemented, but incontrovertibly so. Israel's political economy has changed, in ways that did not seem possible in the past.

To understand how a new regime becomes viable, we need to focus on the formation of mutually profitable coalitions that link (sectors of) the state with (sectors of) society.[96] Established patterns are unlikely to be broken for long unless the state's interest in initiating change connects with compatible interests (or at the very least, encounters a low probability of resistance) in important power centers outside of the state. This survey has identified trends during the 1980s and early 1990s that furnished precisely this condition.

1. The multifaceted political exchange between the Histadrut and the state – key to the persistence of the collectivist/interventionist bias in economic policy – was undermined by the Histadrut's decomposition, which also wore away the common political destiny which had bound the labor organization and the Labor Party.

2. Several key centers of the "big economy" – the major banks and the Koor conglomerate – were weakened by serious crises.

3. Globalization offered new opportunities to market, produce, and finance business activity – opportunities that were greatly enhanced by free trade agreements on the one hand and the "peace process" on the other.[97]

The first two of these developments weakened the capacity of the most powerful beneficiaries of "excessive state intervention" to resist retrenchment; the third trend is indicative of a new global strategy for big business no less profitable than the previous regime. Indeed, the new turn in state/economy relations opened the way to transforming what had been vicious circles into virtuous circles. From the state's viewpoint, its new profile in the economy not only greatly eased fiscal strains,[98] but also contributed to the new 1990s formula for rapid economic growth led by the export-oriented hi-tech sector. For big business a slimmer state meant fewer capital subsidies but also turned out to offer significant advantages. Privatization offered opportunities for private takeover of public enterprises and weakened the pressure from the bureaucratic sector on private sector wages. A smaller state budget led to lower taxes and a far more open capital market. But the budget has remained big enough to sustain vigorous state intervention helpful to business, including absorption of masses of cheap and productive immigrants, and educational and industrial policies that enhance Israel's edge in technology and expertise.

The role of the state thus remains crucial even though it is less obvious. In particular, it remains true that the state's management of the national conflict continues to impact on the political economy. The state plays a decisive trail-blazing role for Israel's arms industry, which remains the world's fifth largest exporter.[99] Perhaps most important of all, if the state were to turn its back on the peace process then internationally-oriented business strategies would be hampered and the military burden on the budget would rise again. Not only the conflict but another traditional extra-economic state function – its "demographic interest" – continues to be invested with major economic implications. I am referring of course to the immigration wave of the early 1990s, on which liberalization impacted not by ruling out state intervention but by transforming its instruments. Most of the privileges earmarked for immigrants have been dispensed as entitlements to financial aid rather than (as in the past) by bureaucratic allocation of state-provided goods, services, and exemptions. Similarly, the shift in industrial policy from blanket subsidies to "picking winners" in hi-tech fields is testimony to the renewed (albeit "market-conforming") steering capacities of the state.

The virtuous circles metaphor for the current thrust of relations between the state and business should not be pushed too far. There is still ample room for tension between the two sides. In this connection it is important to recognize that the Treasury performs a dual role, both orchestrating diminution of the state and attempting to appropriate some of the benefits of liberalization for the state. In the specific cases of taxing capital gains on stock-market profits and diminishing the holdings of the big banks in industrial and service corporations, this "clawback" dynamic has resulted in sometimes acrimonious and still unsettled conflicts with big business.[100]

It is not difficult to imagine other potential threats to the institutionalization of liberalization. The decline of hitherto protected industries, shrinkage of the bureaucratic labor market, and the mass importation of non-Jewish guest workers could all give rise to politically potent reactions.[101] The 1996 elections have already demonstrated that the losers from liberalization can crystallize into a substantial political force, although so far this force has been focused on issues relating to peace/borders and identity politics. The evident contradiction between the present government's activist impulses in relation to settlement and defense and its proclivity for shrinking the economic presence of the state could end up forcing it to backtrack on liberalization.

In any event, it is by no means obvious that the new growth model is sustainable, or even that it is entirely new. The developing economic downturn during 1997 raises the possibility that in the future Israel's strong economic performance in the 1990s may come to be seen as only a conjunctural success, a latter-day version of the old-fashioned growth machine powered by inflows of human and financial capital. Even if the market-driven and globally anchored growth model envisioned by the champions of economic liberalization really has taken root, it remains vulnerable should the collapse of the "peace process" and tension between the US and Israel cause foreign investors and financial institutions to revise their favorable view of Israel's economic potential. In sum, liberalization is real, entails far-reaching changes, and is supported by a genuine mutuality that bridges the state and business. But it is still too early to predict how complete and how durable the transformation of the Israeli political economy will turn out to be.

From the comparative standpoint espoused by this volume, the Israeli story is similar in essence to trends discernible elsewhere. The state has inaugurated a series of reforms very much in line with the "Washington consensus." Major barriers to national integration into international capital markets have been removed, stimulating cross-border capital flows and foreign trade. Some large government-owned banks and businesses have been sold to private owners. Public expenditure, taxes, and the state's indebtedness have all been markedly reduced. Deregulation has eliminated important forms of economic guidance and control by the state, and has eroded the preeminence of some significant public and private monopolies.

As in other countries, there are also contradictions. To a greater or lesser extent specific processes of liberalization have been incomplete or only skin-deep, a testament to the continuing ability of states to retain nationally distinctive institutions and policy paradigms (albeit within limits set by global pressures). Israel is also no exception to the rule that at the ideological level, liberalization has become the sole economic program favored by all major political parties, yet the employees and beneficiaries of the welfare state oppose its retrenchment and the mass public remains much more positive towards state expenditure than the politicians and their economic advisors. In short, the politics of liberalization, like the politics of economic policy generally, is rooted in the conflicting interests of winners and losers; furthermore, these interests are just as likely to be camouflaged as revealed by the contenders' ideological positions.

A comparative perspective on liberalization is handicapped by the

Is Israel's Political Economy "Normalized"? 147

absence of reliable cross-national data against which the relative progress of state contraction in Israel could be assessed.[102] An educated guess is that, relative to trends in other countries, Israel has gone particularly far in cutting (non-social) public expenditure and in deregulating the state's role in capital markets; is around the average with respect to trade and foreign-currency reforms and privatization; and ranks below the average in terms of welfare state retrenchment.

A comparative perspective on the dependent variable (how much liberalization?) is important for defining the puzzle: like other countries, over the last decade or so Israel has fundamentally altered long-standing patterns of state/economy relations; but as elsewhere, some elements of state contraction have been much more marked than others. Immigrant absorption, settlement over the pre-1967 borders, and aid to outlying areas within those borders continue to make significant claims on national resources, as do military commitments that continue to preempt close to one quarter of government budgets.[103] A comparative perspective on the independent variables (what are the forces that advance or retard liberalization?) requires that we pay attention to the continuing distinctiveness of Israel as a settler society with contested borders and legitimacy. The collectivist economy that was the historical legacy of Jewish settlement and Arab–Jewish conflict in the pre-state period is difficult to dismantle precisely because conflict and settlement continue to shape state commitments.

These issues are of course hotly contested in Israel's political discourse and practices. Ironically, while both the left and right wings of the political spectrum favor liberalization, they hold opposed positions on how to resolve long-standing boundary disputes. The "expansionist" position requires considerable state activism and funneling of economic resources to consolidate and defend territory, a requirement patently at odds with state contraction.[104] The right in Israel is also political home to Jewish social groups whose precarious economic standing would be deeply threatened by a rollback of Israel's settler-society welfare state and the triumph of meritocratic individualism.

The left, which in Israel means the "peace camp," holds out the prospect of further reducing military spending and altogether eliminating the costs of occupying and settling Palestine, as well as profitable exploitation of the regional and international economies formerly blocked by the Arab–Israeli conflict. Yet except for Arab-backed parties, the left remains committed to continued military strength and Jewish territorial, demographic, and cultural predominance. It is thus both unable and unwilling to contemplate an alternative to the active settler-society state.

The logical option for the left – a "post-Zionist" vision of Israel as a politically liberal state in the service of (all of) its citizens – is fundamentally at odds with almost the entire spectrum of Jewish opinion, both at the elite and the mass levels. It is especially at odds with the religious-nationalist ethos of the right, on which the socio-political standing of the economic losers from liberalization is so dependent. But both right and left share a commitment to the Zionist consensus. The triumph of economic liberalization may eventually overpower this hegemony, unintentionally and perhaps even unconsciously.[105] Whatever the outcome, it is precisely the high and unique stakes involved – for Israel's identity as well as its political economy – which a comparative view of liberalization so effectively clarifies.

ACKNOWLEDGMENTS

This paper was completed at the beginning of 1998. An earlier version, which includes a more extensive selection of data, was published as "Zionism and Liberalization: Change and Continuity in Israel's Political Economy," *Humboldt Journal of Social Relations* 23/1-2 (1998) pp.219–59. Research for this project began while I was a guest at the Swedish Institute for Social Research, where I benefited from the hospitality and stimulation provided by Walter Korpi and Joakim Palme and generous assistance from afar by Daniel Maman and Meir Shabat. Welcome financial support has been provided by the Israeli Science Foundation, founded by the Israel Academy of Sciences and Humanities. I am indebted to Gershon Shafir, Meir Shabat, and Dani Filc for exceptionally thoughtful comments.

NOTES

1. D. Patinkin, *The Israel Economy: The First Decade*, Jerusalem: Falk Project for Economic Research in Israel, 1960.
2. M. Shalev, *Labour and the Political Economy in Israel*, Oxford: Oxford University Press, 1992.
3. On the notion of policy regimes, see G. Esping-Andersen, *The Three Worlds of Welfare Capitalism*, Cambridge: Polity Press, 1990. The concept of "political-economic regimes" is an alternative to the more grandiose "social structures of accumulation" used in my book. For discussion of these and related conceptualizations, see B. Jessop, "Regulation Theories in Retrospect and Prospect," *Economy and Society* 19/2 (May 1990) pp.153–216; L. Mjøset, "Nordic Economic Policies in the 1970s and 1980s," *International Organization* 41/3 (Summer 1987) p.403.
4. For a concise survey, see B. Cohen, "Phoenix Arisen: The Resurrection of Global Finance (Review Article)," *World Politics* 48/2 (Jan. 1996) pp.268–96. Economist Paul Krugman has argued vigorously that politicians and other interested parties exploit "pop internationalism" to their own end; P. Krugman, *Pop Internationalism*, Cambridge, MA: MIT Press, 1996. The political construction of "global imperatives" has been insightfully discussed in the Latin American context by B. Geddes, "How Politicians Decide Who Bears the Costs of Liberalization," in Ivan T. Berend (ed.), *Transition to a Market Economy at the End of the 20th Century*, Munich: Sudosteuropa Gesellschaft, 1995, pp.203–28; K. Weyland, "Neo-Populism and Neo-Liberalism in Latin America: Unexpected Affinities," *Studies in Comparative International Development* 32/3 (Fall 1997) pp.3–31.
5. For evidence of cross-national divergence, see S. Berger and R. Dore (eds), *National Diversity and Global Capitalism*, Ithaca, NY: Cornell University Press, 1996; R.O. Keohane and H.V. Milner (eds), *Internationalization and Domestic Politics*, Cambridge: Cambridge University Press, 1996. On the limits and paradoxes of retrenchment, see P. Pierson, "The New Politics of the Welfare State," *World Politics* 48/2 (1996) p.143; S.K. Vogel, *Freer Markets, More Rules: Regulatory Reform in Advanced Industrial Countries*, Ithaca, NY: Cornell University Press, 1996. On the role of partisan differences and party dynamics, see T.R. Cusack, "Partisan Politics and Public Finance: Changes in Public Spending in the Industrialized Democracies,

1955–1989," *Public Choice* 91/3-4 (1997) pp.375–95.
6. L. Mjøset, "The Nordic Model Never Existed, But Does It Have a Future," *Scandinavian Studies* 64/4 (1992) pp.652–71; F.G. Castles, *Families of Nations: Patterns of Public Policy in Western Democracies*, Brookfield, VT: Dartmouth, 1993.
7. J.G. Ruggie, "International Regimes, Transactions, and Change: Embedded Liberalism in the Postwar Economic Order," *International Organization* 36/2 (Spring 1982) pp.379–415.
8. B. Kimmerling, *Zionism and Territory: The Socio-Territorial Dimensions of Zionist Politics*, Berkeley: Institute of International Studies, University of California, 1983; G. Shafir, *Land, Labor and the Origins of the Israeli–Palestinian Conflict 1882–1914*, Cambridge: Cambridge University Press, 1989; M. Shalev, *Labour and the Political Economy* (note 2).
9. Z. Sternhell, *Nation-Building or Social Reform? Nationalism and Socialism in the Israeli Labor Movement 1904–1940*, Tel Aviv: Am Oved, 1995 (Hebrew); M. Shalev, "Time for Theory: Critical Notes on Lissak and Sternhell," *Israel Studies* 1/2 (1996) pp.170–88.
10. On economic policy see H. Barkai, "The Public, Histadrut, and Private Sectors in the Israeli Economy," in *The Falk Project for Economic Research in Israel: Sixth Report, 1961–1963*, Jerusalem: The Falk Project for Economic Research in Israel, 1964, pp.15–77; Y. Plessner, *The Political Economy of Israel: From Ideology to Stagnation*, Albany, NY: State University of New York Press, 1994. The failure of early welfare state initiatives is discussed by A. Doron and R. Kramer, *The Welfare State in Israel – the Evolution of Social Security Policy and Practice*, Boulder, CO: Westview, 1991.
11. U. Bialer, *Between East and West: Israel's Foreign Policy Orientation, 1948–1956*, Cambridge: Cambridge University Press, 1989; G. Yago, "Whatever Happened to the Promised Land? Capital Flows and the Israeli State," *Berkeley Journal of Sociology* 21 (1977) pp.117–46.
12. N. Halevi, "Economic Growth and Economic Cycles in the Jewish Economy of Mandatory Palestine," *Iyunim Bekalkala 1981*, 1983, pp.313–21 (Hebrew); M. Beenstock, J. Metzer and S. Ziv, *Immigration and the Jewish Economy in Mandatory Palestine: An Econometric Explanation*, Falk Institute Discussion Paper No. 93.02, Jan. 1993.
13. I. Sharkansky and A. Radian, "Changing Domestic Policy 1977–1981," in Robert O. Freedman (ed.), *Israel in the Begin Era*, New York: Praeger, 1982, pp.56–75; Y. Ben-Porath, "The Conservative Turnabout that Never Was," *Jerusalem Quarterly* 29 (Fall 1983) pp.3–10.
14. N. Halevi and R. Klinov-Malul, *The Economic Development of Israel*, New York: Praeger, 1968; Y. Ben-Porath, "Introduction," in Yoram Ben-Porath (ed.), *The Economy of Israel: Maturing through Crisis*, Cambridge, MA: Harvard University Press, 1986, pp.1–23; Y. Aharoni, *The Israeli Economy: Dreams and Reality*, New York: Routledge, 1991.
15. D. Bernstein and S. Swirski, "The Rapid Economic Development of Israel and the Emergence of the Ethnic Division of Labour," *British Journal of Sociology* 33/1 (March 1982) pp.64–85.
16. Shalev, *Labour and the Political Economy* (note 2); P. Evans, D. Rueschemeyer and T. Skocpol (eds), *Bringing the State Back In*, Cambridge: Cambridge University Press, 1985.
17. M. Shalev, "Labor, State and Crisis: An Israeli Case Study," *Industrial Relations* 23/3 (1984) pp.362–86.
18. A. Mintz, "The Military-Industrial Complex: The Israeli Case," *Journal of Strategic Studies* 6/3 (Sept. 1983) pp.103–28; H. Barkai, *The Defense Industries at a Crossroads*, Research Paper No.197, Falk Institute for Economic Research in Israel, Jerusalem, 1987 (Hebrew).
19. E. Farjoun, "Class Divisions in Israeli Society," *Khamsin (London)* 10 (1983) pp.29–39; Y. Aharoni, *Structure and Performance in the Israeli Economy*, Tel Aviv: Tcherikover, 1976 (Hebrew); M. Semyonov and N. Lewin-Epstein, *Hewers of Wood and Drawers of Water: Noncitizen Arabs in the Israeli Labor Market*, Ithaca, NY: ILR Press, 1987.
20. L.L. Grinberg, *Split Corporatism in Israel*, Albany, NY: State University of New York Press, 1991; M. Shalev, "Israel's Domestic Policy Regime: Zionism, Dualism, and the Rise of Capital," in Francis G. Castles (ed.), *The Comparative History of Public*

Policy, Cambridge: Polity Press, 1989, pp.100–48; S. Bichler, *The Political Economy of Military Spending in Israel*, unpublished PhD dissertation, Department of Political Science, Hebrew University of Jerusalem, 1991 (Hebrew).
21. M. Bruno, *Crisis, Stabilization, and Economic Reform: Therapy by Consensus*, Oxford: Clarendon Press, 1993.
22. M. Shalev and L. Grinberg, *Histadrut-Government Relations and the Transition from a Likud to a National Unity Government: Continuity and Change in Israel's Economic Crisis*, Discussion Paper 19-89, Pinhas Sapir Center for Development, Tel Aviv University, Oct. 1989; H.J. Barkey, "When Politics Matter: Economic Stabilization in Argentina and Israel," *Studies in Comparative International Development* 29/4 (Winter 1994) pp.41–67.
23. A. Razin and E. Sadka, *The Economy of Modern Israel: Malaise and Promise*, Chicago: University of Chicago Press, 1993.
24. S. Bichler and J. Nitzan, "Military Spending and Differential Accumulation: A New Approach to the Political Economy of Armament – The Case of Israel," *Review of Radical Political Economics* 28/1 (March 1996) pp.51–95. The shift in opinion among key figures in the business elite has been retrospectively confirmed by a series of interviews carried out by Yehezkel Lein and myself during the summer of 1997.
25. L.L. Grinberg, *Split Corporatism in Israel* (note 20).
26. M. Keren, "Economists and Economic Policy Making in Israel: The Politics of Expertise in the Stabilization Program," *Policy Sciences* 26/4 (1993) pp.331–46.
27. The *World Competitiveness Yearbook* is an expensive annual compendium published privately in Switzerland and targeted at governments and well-heeled investors. The cited ranking summarizes a battery of quantitative and qualitative indicators, including the results of a survey of executives in all the countries studied.
28. For the sake of comparability I cite data from The Penn World Table (Mark 5.6), as made available at http://datacentre.epas.utoronto.ca:5680/pwt/pwt.html. Bank of Israel data covering the same period (1975–92) exhibit almost identical trends but have much higher absolute values. The idiosyncratic nature of the Israeli trend is emphasized by the fact that during the 25 year period ending in 1990, in the average OECD member-state the ratio of trade to GNP rose by 10 points. G. Garrett and D. Mitchell, "Globalization and the Welfare State: Income Transfers in the Industrialized Democracies, 1966–1990," paper presented at the Annual Meeting of the American Political Science Association, San Francisco, 1996. The Penn Tables cover 40 countries in Europe, the Americas and East Asia, excluding East Germany and Puerto Rico. Israel's rank on openness declined from 6 in 1975–84 to 7 in 1985–89 to 10 in 1990–92.
29. BOI-96, Diagram *Vav*-1. Throughout this article, annual reports of the Bank of Israel in Hebrew are cited in the form "BOI-96" (for the 1996 edition).
30. For detailed data on manufacturing exports, see the annual *HaTa'asiya Beyisrael* published by the Ministry of Industry and Commerce's Planning Administration.
31. The comparison with 19 OECD members is drawn from the OECD's *Main Economic Indicators*, which indicates that Austria and Switzerland have the highest import surpluses – at only around three percent of GDP.
32. H. Regev and S. Bar-Eliezer, *Control over the Domestic Market and Economic Performance in Israeli Industry*, Falk Institute Discussion Paper No. 94.05, 1994 (in Hebrew). Significantly, the overall rise between the low of 1980/81 and the peak reached in 1990 was quite widely diffused. Increases were posted in this period for 20 of the 22 disaggregated branches investigated by Regev and Bar-Eliezer, although in 3 cases the change was only negligible.
33. N. Halevi (ed.) *Import Policy and Exposure of Israeli Industry*, Jerusalem: Falk Institute, 1994 (Hebrew). On import duties, see the annual reports of the State Revenues Administration.
34. Both the figure cited here and the presentation in Figure 2 are based on data published in BOI-95, Appendix Table 12 which include both explicit supports and implicit credit subsidies. However, many other traditional elements in government aid to exporters, such as the provision of subsidized land, infrastructure, and labor, are not included in the figures.
35. A high estimate of philanthropic aid, based on the category "foreign transfers to the national institutions and non-profits" in Appendix Table 11 of BOI-95, put it at under 2% of GNP throughout the last decade. In an article in *Yediot Acharonot* on

20 Aug. 1996, former Deputy Foreign Minister Yossi Beilin wrote that Israel's receipts from the United Jewish Appeal had declined to less than $300 million a year, and that the Israel Bonds had become a more expensive way of raising money than free market loans.
36. BOI-95, p.238.
37. For an optimistic survey of foreign investment, which dates the breakthrough to the Madrid peace conference of 1991, see H. Sher, "After the Revolution," *The Jerusalem Report*, 17 Oct. 1996, pp.37–41. I have also benefited from conversations on this topic with two Israeli bankers, Yair Saroussi and Nir Oliver.
38. BOI-96, Appendix Table *Vav*-13.
39. D. Levi-Faur, *Pinhas Sapir and the Industrial Development of Israel*, Tel Aviv: Sapir Center for Development, Tel Aviv University, 1993 (Hebrew).
40. *Yediot Acharonot (Mamon)*, 1 Oct. 1997.
41. Natan Lipson and Sami Peretz, *Ha'aretz*, 28 Oct. 1997.
42. The dubious economic benefits to Israel of the gigantic Intel subsidy have been noted in many media commentaries (e.g. Oded Lipschitz in *Davar Hashavua*, 29 March 1994). Another noteworthy case is the 38% subsidy promised to Volkswagen (the government paid for $133 of its nominal $350 million investment) for a joint magnesium production venture with the Dead Sea Works (*Jerusalem Report*, 27 June 1996).
43. In a communiqué dated 6 Nov. 1996, the Economics Desk of the Government Press Office reported that investment in Israeli shares by foreign citizens had reached $5.5 billion, while other financial assets held by foreigners amounted to $14 billion.
44. Manufacturers' Association of Israel, *Globalization in Israeli Industry: Report of the Committee for Strategic Thinking*, Tel Aviv: Economic Division, MAI, 1997 (Hebrew); BOI-96, Appendix Table *Vav*-13.
45. Comparison is between the five years preceding stabilization (1980–84) and the most recent five-year period for which data are available (1992–96). BOI-96, Appendix Table *Hay*-1a.
46. This terminology is borrowed from R. Friedland and J. Sanders, "The Public Economy and Economic Growth in Western Market Economies," *American Sociological Review* 50 (Aug. 1985) pp.421–37.
47. M. Shalev, *Labour and the Political Economy* (note 2) pp.266–7.
48. In addition to subsidies granted under the Investment Incentive Law, the main formal means of capital subsidy – since abolished – was "directed credit" channeled through the commercial banks. Already by 1990 the cost to the government of directed credit was less than a quarter of its 1984 level in real terms.
49. Data are based on budgetary allocations and are derived from Tables 1 and 2 of the statistical appendix to Y. Kop (ed.) *Allocation of Resources to Social Services 1996*, Jerusalem: The Center for Social Policy Studies in Israel, 1997 (Hebrew). According to the same source, in the 1990s the ratio of debt service to GDP fell by about 6 points. The Bank of Israel's estimates of the ratio of debt service to GNP (BOI-96, Appendix Table *Hay*-2b) are much more conservative, but they also indicate a major drop in the burden of both domestic and foreign interest payments.
50. S. Hadar, *Blurring of the Boundaries between Public and Private in Relations between State and Industry*, Unpublished doctoral dissertation, Department of Political Science, Hebrew University of Jerusalem, 1990 (Hebrew); Bichler and Nitzan, "Military Spending and Differential Accumulation" (note 24).
51. The data on domestic military expenditure in Figure 1 combine procurement expenses (including construction costs) with wage costs. The latter have hardly declined, while between 1985 and 1995 the share of the former in national product fell from 7.5% to 3.5% (calculated from BOI-95, Table *Hay*-7.)
52. D. Swank, "Funding the Welfare State, Part I: Global Capital and the Taxation of Business in the Advanced Market Economies," Paper presented at Annual Meeting of the American Political Science Association, San Francisco, 1996.
53. See the annual report of the State Revenues Administration for 1996, Table *Kaf*-12.
54. Z. Schuldiner, *A Look at the 1996 Budget*, Tel Aviv: Adva Center, 1996 (Hebrew). Schuldiner estimated that relief of employer contributions to social security and health insurance, along with a wage subsidy paid to employers for the first two years of new hires, accounted for 12.5% of the government's "social expenditure" budget for 1996.
55. O. Yosha and Y. Yafeh, "The Capital Market Reform 1985–95 and Modes of Finance

in Israeli Manufacturing," *Rivon Lekalkala* 43 (1996) Table 3 (Hebrew).
56. For comparative discussions, see J.D. Stephens, E. Huber, and L. Ray, "The Welfare State in Hard Times," Paper presented at Conference on the Politics and Political Economy of Contemporary Capitalism, Humboldt University and the WZB, Berlin, 1995; P. Pierson, "New Politics of the Welfare State" (note 5). This section relies on data presented in the annual report of the Center for Social Policy Studies in Israel; Y. Kop, *Allocation of Resources* (note 49). The estimates from this source, which are based on substantive definitions of expenditure categories and refer to budget allocations, are more conservative (especially regarding income maintenance) than the national accounts data published by the Bank of Israel and referred to earlier.
57. See also Schuldiner, *A Look at the 1996 Budget* (note 54).
58. Retired women who did not work outside the home are now entitled to pensions, and an economically significant form of discrimination against Palestinian citizens has been ended with the decoupling of child allowances from military service.
59. Schuldiner, *A Look at the 1996 Budget* (note 54).
60. H.J. Karger and M. Monnickendam, "The Radical Right and Social Welfare in Israel," in James Midgley and Howard Glennerster (eds), *The Radical Right and the Welfare State: An International Assessment*, Savage, MD: Barnes & Noble, 1991, pp.124–40.
61. While rules for the receipt of unemployment benefit were toughened with a view to making refusal of job offers more difficult, this failed to reduce the number of unfilled vacancies during the period of high unemployment in the early 1990s. S. Amir, *Unemployment in Israel 1964–1989: An Analysis based on the Beveridge-Curve Model*, Discussion paper No. 96.04, Falk Institute for Economic Research, Jerusalem, March 1996.
62. For a general discussion, see A. Doron and H.J. Karger, "The Privatization of Social Services in Israel and its Effects on Israeli Society," *Scandinavian Journal of Social Welfare* 2 (1993) pp.88–95. It is hard to find reliable indicators of expenditure on "gray" health and education services. One analysis of the Household Expenditure Survey has shown little change in expenditure on private health services between 1986/7 and 1992/3, but this conclusion is probably already outdated. See A. Berg, B. Rosen, and G. Ofer, *Changes in Household Expenditure on Health*, Research Report No. RR-246-96, Brookdale Institute of Gerontology, Jerusalem 1996.
63. A. Doron, *In Defense of Universalism: The Challenges Facing Social Policy in Israel*, Jerusalem: Magnes Press, 1995 (Hebrew); A. Doron, "The Contradicting Trends in the Israeli Welfare State: Poverty, Retrenchment and Marginalization," Paper presented at 19th Meeting of the ISA Research Committee on Poverty and Social Policy, Copenhagen, 1997; Z. Schuldiner, *A Look at the 1996 Budget* (note 54).
64. E. Farjoun, "Class Divisions in Israeli Society" (note 19). A. Doron, "The Histadrut, Social Policy and Equality," *Jerusalem Quarterly* 47 (Summer 1988) pp.131–44.
65. E. Kleiman, *The Structure of Israel Manufacturing Industries 1952–1962*, Unpublished paper for the Falk Project for Economic Research in Israel, Jerusalem, Dec. 1964; A. Bregman, "Government Intervention in Industry: The Case of Israel," *Journal of Development Economics* 25 (1987) pp.353–67; D. Levi-Faur, *Pinhas Sapir* (note 39); Y. Aharoni, *The Israeli Economy* (note 14).
66. F.L. Pryor, *Property and Industrial Organization in Communist and Capitalist Nations*, Bloomington, IN: Indiana University Press, 1973.
67. On the theory and the Israeli experience of business groups, see respectively M. Granovetter, "Business Groups," in N.J. Smelser and R. Swedberg (eds), *The Handbook of Economic Sociology*, Princeton: Princeton University Press, 1994, pp.453–75 and Daniel Maman's contribution to this volume. Until recently the striking role of big business in Israel and of banking within it was rarely mentioned by mainstream economists and never studied by them. Yair Aharoni and Shimshon Bichler were the first scholars to definitively establish the dualist character of Israeli capitalism. Y. Aharoni, *Structure and Performance* (note 19); R. Rowley, S. Bichler and J. Nitzan, *Some Aspects of Aggregate Concentration in the Israeli Economy 1964–1986*, Working paper No. 7/88, Department of Economics, McGill University (1988). More recently, hyper-concentration in banking and the big banks' multiple roles as owners, financiers and investors have been explored by A.L. Bebchuk, L. Kaplow and J.M. Fried, *Concentration in the Israeli Economy and Bank Investment in Commercial Companies*, Unpublished typescript, 1995; and by Yosha and Yafeh,

"Capital Market Reform" (note 55). Indirect indications of the market domination of big business are furnished by Regev and Bar-Eliezer, *Control over the Domestic Market* (note 32).
68. S. Bichler, *The Political Economy of National Security in Israel: Some Aspects of the Activities of the Dominant Blocs of Capital*, Unpublished MA Thesis, The Hebrew University of Jerusalem, 1986 (Hebrew); M. Shalev, *Labour and the Political Economy* (note 2).
69. The most up to date source of data on big business profits is S. Bichler and J. Nitzan, "The Great U-Turn: Restructuring in Israel and South Africa," *News from Within* 11/9 (Sept. 1995) pp.29–32, but these figures are not entirely consistent with earlier publications by Bichler cited in previous notes. According to Bichler and Nitzan, big business profits declined precipitously after 1984 and experienced only a very modest recovery through 1993 (the latest date of the series).
70. The "Brodet Committee" on bank ownership of non-financial corporations was a milestone in this respect. D. Brodet, *Report of the Committee to Examine Structural Changes in the Capital Market*, Jerusalem: Israel Ministry of Finance, 1995 (Hebrew). The unprecedented activism of the current directors of two units of the Treasury – the Supervisor of the Capital Market and the Antitrust Commission – also constitute a sharp break with past practice. See for example *Ha'aretz* weekend supplement, 28 Nov. 1997.
71. Between 1982/3 and 1990 the three-firm concentration ratio fell from 43% to 34% of total domestic sales. Regev and Bar-Eliezer, *Control over the Domestic Market* (note 32), Appendix Table 1.
72. On the skepticism of well-placed observers, see the articles in *Globes* by Haim Barkai on 20 Dec. 1995 and by Orna Raviv on 4 Dec. 1995. As long ago as 1981 the Banking Law tried unsuccessfully to prohibit banks from holding more than 25% of the equity of any non-financial corporation. See O. Yosha, "Privatising Multi-Product Banks," *Economic Journal* 105/433 (1995) pp.1435–53. The recommendations of the Brodet Committee, endorsed by the government at the end of 1995, postponed the deadline for implementation of the Banking Law to the end of 1996, although the ownership ratio is supposed to be further reduced (to 20%) by the end of the century.
73. See two articles by Sami Peretz in *Ha'aretz*, 29 March 1996.
74. See the article by Daniel Maman in this volume.
75. Privatization of the Histadrut-linked Koor conglomerate is a case in point. The June 1995 sale of the Hevrat Ovdim's 22.5% stake in the Koor group to Shamrock Partnerships, an American investment company, was immediately followed by the distribution of options to Koor's management with a theoretical value of close to $30 million. Shamrock later sold out, for a considerable profit, to a consortium led by the Bronfman family. Benny Gaon, the aggressive CEO of Koor, initially kept his position under the new regime but was subsequently unseated by one of the new owners. See *Globes*, 5 and 27 Feb. 1996 and 24 July 1997. For a perceptive commentary on the changing position of the managerial elite, see Ephraim Reiner in *Ha'aretz*, 20 Nov. 1997.
76. As Benny Gaon has candidly pointed out, one of the uses of internationalization has been the possibility of countering dependence on traditional bank partners (in Koor's case, Bank Hapoalim) by exploiting new opportunities to raise capital abroad. B. Gaon, *He Who Dares Wins*, Tel Aviv: Yediot Acharonot, 1997 (Hebrew).
77. *Ha'aretz*, 26 July 1996.
78. For a description of developments through 1992, see E. Murphy, "Structural Inhibitions to Economic Liberalization In Israel," *Middle East Journal* 48/1 (1994) pp.65–88.
79. S. Eckstein, B.-T. Zilberfarb, and S. Rosowitz, "The Process of Privatizing Public Corporations in Israel: Survey and Evaluations for the Future," *Rivon Lekalkala* (May 1993) pp.31–47 (Hebrew). A recent study suggests that in the 1968–88 period, Labor and Likud governments were equally inactive in privatization. M. Harris, Y. Katz, and G. Doron, "Ideology and Privatization Policy in Israel," *Environment and Planning C: Government and Policy* 15/3 (August 1997) pp.363–72. Additional sources on privatization are Y. Katz, "Privatization in Israel: 1962–1987," *Medina, Memshal Veyachasim Benleumim* 35 (1991) pp.133–45 (Hebrew); M. Hasson, *The Privatization Policy of the Government of Israel: Declarations versus Action in Practice*, Unpublished MA thesis, Dept. of Political Science, Hebrew University,

Jerusalem, 1995 (Hebrew).
80. M. Hasson, *Privatization Policy* (note 79).
81. M. Schwartz, *Unlimited Guarantees: History, Political Economy, and the Crisis of Cooperative Agriculture in Israel*, Beersheba: Ben-Gurion University Press, 1995 (Hebrew).
82. L. Leiderman and G. Bufman, *Financial Reform in Israel: A Case of Gradualism*, Tel Aviv: Pinhas Sapir Center for Development, 1994.
83. Despite the judicial discourse of individual culpability in which it was framed, the report of the commission of inquiry into the bank shares collapse made this abundantly clear. See Commission of Inquiry into the Regulation of Bank Shares, *Final Report*, Jerusalem: Ministry of Justice, 1986 (Hebrew).
84. Leiderman and Bufman, *Financial Reform in Israel* (note 82); I. Tov, "The Economic Upheaval of 1977 – Implementation of Operational Goals," *Rivon Lekalkala* 135-6 (April 1988) pp.33–47 (Hebrew).
85. See the conclusions reached by O. Yosha and Y. Yafeh, *The Capital Market Reform and its Influence: An Analysis from the Angle of "Industrial Structure"*, Jerusalem: Bank of Israel Research Department, 1995 (Hebrew); and by Leiderman and Bufman, *Financial Reform in Israel* (note 82).
86. These assertions are empirically supported by a recent wave of research sponsored by the Bank of Israel. See especially Yosha and Yafeh, "Capital Market Reform" (note 55); H. Ber, Y. Yafeh, and O. Yosha, *Conflicts of Interest in Universal Banking: Evidence from the Post-Issue Performance of IPO Firms*, Jerusalem: Bank of Israel Research Department, 1997, Discussion Paper 97.05.
87. L.L. Grinberg, *Split Corporatism in Israel* (note 20); L.L. Grinberg, *The Histadrut Above All Else*, Jerusalem: Nevo, 1993 (Hebrew); Shalev, *Labour and the Political Economy* (note 2).
88. Between 1980–84 and 1992–93 the role of cost of living adjustments in business sector wage increments was reduced by almost half (69% to 37%) and national-level wage increases (formerly 13.5% of the total increment) were eliminated altogether. D. Sharon, "Wage Policy and its Implementation," *Kalkala Veavoda* 9 (Oct. 1994) pp.97–115 (Hebrew); see also Z. Sussman and D. Zakai, *The Decentralization of Collective Bargaining and Changes in the Compensation Structure in Israel's Public Sector*, Jerusalem: Bank of Israel Research Department, 1996.
89. The decline of the Histadrut has hardly been investigated systematically. See, however, the symposium in *Rivon Lekalkala*, April 1995. For earlier developments (through the late 1980s) see L.L. Grinberg, *Split Corporatism in Israel* (note 20). On the traditional political functions of the Histadrut health fund and its ultimate loss, see respectively A. Arian, "Health Care in Israel: Political and Administrative Aspects," *International Political Science Review* 2/1 (1981) pp.43–56; and D. Chinitz, "Israel's Health Policy Breakthrough: The Politics of Reform and the Reform of Politics," *Journal of Health Politics, Policy and Law* 20/4 (Winter 1995) pp.909–32.
90. On the factors accounting for the entry of Palestinian labor to Israel and its implications, see Grinberg, *The Histadrut Above All Else* (note 87) Ch.6; Semyonov and Lewin-Epstein, *Hewers of Wood* (note 19). For an overview of the foreign worker phenomenon see D.V. Bartram, "Foreign Workers in Israel: History and Theory," *International Migration Review* 32/2 (1998) pp.303–25. Further documentation may be found in *Ha'aretz*, 22 March 1996; *Skira Kalkalit* (Bank Hapoalim Economic Department), 29 Aug. 1996; and the *Kav LaOved* website, a source of current information on the employment of Palestinian as well as foreign labor (http://www.aic.org/org/kav-oved).
91. BOI-96, Appendix Table *Dalet*-8.
92. Annual surveys of immigrant employment in industry conducted by the Manufacturers' Association have revealed the scope of immigrant employment in industry. Indirect evidence from the surveys, as well as media reports, point to the role of downgrading (such as the employment of qualified engineers as technicians, and technicians as skilled manual workers), low pay, and government wage subsidies in rendering immigrants attractive to employers.
93. My calculations are based on estimates of the number of conscript and career soldiers published in *The Military Balance* (London: International Institute for Strategic Studies) and the extent of absence due to reserve duty as estimated by official labor force surveys.

94. I recognize, but have not investigated, a parallel (and complementary) dialectic located *inside* the state apparatus: the economic-policy bureaucracies favor a slimmer public economy with fewer commitments, because this enhances their autonomy by trimming the sails of other departments of state.
95. These difficulties derived from the resistance of the business sector to operating without state subsidies, and challenges posed to the legitimacy of the recession by popular unrest and individual out-migration. M. Shalev, "The Mid-Sixties Recession: A Political-Economic Analysis of Unemployment in Israel," *Machbarot Lemechkar Ulebikoret* 9 (Feb. 1984) pp.3–54 (Hebrew).
96. P. Gourevitch, *Politics in Hard Times: Comparative Responses to International Economic Crises*, Ithaca, NY: Cornell University Press, 1986; P. Swenson, "Bringing Capital Back in, or Social Democracy Reconsidered – Employer Power, Cross-Class Alliances, and Centralization of Industrial Relations in Denmark and Sweden," *World Politics* 43/4 (1991) pp.513–44.
97. The links between economic liberalization and globalization and the peace process have been emphasized by Y. Peled and G. Shafir, "The Roots of Peacemaking – the Dynamics of Citizenship in Israel, 1948–93," *International Journal of Middle East Studies* 28/3 (1996) pp.391–413. For other discussions of the "peace dividend," see J. Lederman, "Economics of the Arab–Israeli Peace Process," *Orbis – a Journal of World Affairs* 39/4 (1995) pp.549–66; A. Retzky, "Peace In the Middle East – What Does It Really Mean For Israeli Business," *Columbia Journal Of World Business* 30/3 (1995) pp.26–32; B.-Z. Zilberfarb, "The Effects of the Peace Process on the Israeli Economy," *Israel Affairs* 1/1 (1994) pp.84–95; E.C. Murphy, "The Arab–Israeli Peace Process: Responding to the Economics of Globalization," *Critique* (Fall 1996) pp.67–91.
98. Comparison of experience in the 1990s with a decade earlier shows that the state not only reduced its claims on the national product but also changed the profile of public finance: capacities of tax extraction were enhanced and reliance on debt and gifts reduced (BOI-96, Appendix Table *Hay*-1b).
99. Israel's rank in arms exports as reported by Israel Radio on 14 Oct. 1997, based on International Institute of Strategic Studies data. A good example of the state's role in facilitating military exports is an agreement reached between the Israeli and Polish governments for refurbishing helicopters in Israel (*Yediot Acharonot*, 15 Oct. 1997), a $600 million deal that pressure from another trail-blazing state – the US – might ultimately force Israel to yield.
100. The Finance Minister of the 1992–96 Labor government was forced by business pressure to reverse the government's decision to tax stock market gains. The saga is documented and analyzed by Yehezkel Lein in a forthcoming MA thesis in the Department of Political Science at the Hebrew University.
101. As this article was being completed (Dec. 1997) a major confrontation developed between the Histadrut and the Ministry of Finance. While a dispute over pension reform was the central issue nominally at stake, the deeper source of tension was the attempt by the country's strongest groups of organized labor in the public sector to preempt state attacks on their privileged position by allying themselves firmly with the Histadrut.
102. One area in which data are readily available – openness to international trade – is the exception which proves the rule. I pointed out earlier that evaluation of trends in Israel's trade ratio is complicated by the role of arms and fuel imports and the diamond-processing industry. Truly comparable data which take account of these elements would be difficult to assemble.
103. According to the 1997 annual report of the Center for Social Policy Studies in Israel, defense accounted for 23.9% of 1997 budgets.
104. While "expansionism" requires an interventionist state, some of the means of this intervention can and have been effectively "liberalized", i.e. delegated to the market. In the heyday of Jewish settlement in the occupied territories, the state used massive subsidies to attract private contractors and home buyers on the basis of financial self-interest.
105. Compare the similar argument made by Lustick on the implications of competition between the main Zionist parties for their de facto orientation towards Israel's Palestinian-Arab minority. I. Lustick, "The Political Road to Binationalism: Arabs in Jewish Politics," in Ilan Peleg and Ofira Seliktar (eds), *The Emergence of a Binational Israel – The Second Republic in the Making*, Boulder, CO: Westview, 1989, pp.97–123.

Warfare, Polity-Formation and the Israeli National Policy Patterns

DAVID LEVI-FAUR

We live in an era in which global processes affect more and more spheres of human life, national cultures converge, economies are increasingly interdependent, and political institutions face substantial transformation. These global processes, combined with intense internal conflicts, have led to widespread changes in the Israeli polity. But while change seems to be everywhere, one must be careful interpreting its impact. Without denying either the extent or the scope of change, this article points to "national policy patterns" as one set of constraints on the scope of change.[1] National patterns of policy making reflect cultural codes of behavior as well as the distribution of power among dominant societal and state actors.

Three national patterns are often suggested as characterizing the common framework by which different countries shape policy: pluralism (e.g. the USA), corporatism (e.g. the Netherlands), and etatism (e.g. France). Pluralism is associated with weak autonomy of the state and strong societal actors; corporatism with a strong state and strong societal actors; and etatism with a strong autonomous state and weak societal actors.[2] These three policy patterns are generally considered to result from the formative periods in which a trajectory of state formation was followed and specific state–society relations were formed. State formation on the one hand and class formation on the other are the central processes which shape a specific national policy pattern of the post-war state. In the Israeli case, warfare, late-industrialization, and a combination of nationalism and socialism affected both state and society formation, and thus are also critical for understanding the Israeli pattern of policy making.

In this article, I will present a comparative account of the formation of national policy patterns in Israel and the constraints that they impose

---

David Levi-Faur is at the Department of Political Science, University of Haifa.

on change. Specifically, I discuss the effects of warfare on the formation of the Israeli polity, including both the institutionalization of sovereign political authority, the rise of the labor movement, and the decline in the power of the Zionist middle class (*ezrahim*).

WARFARE AND POLITY FORMATION – A COMPARATIVE EXAMINATION

There is substantial agreement among social scientists and historians regarding to the importance of war in the formation of states in general and of the modern state in particular. "All state organization was originally military organization, organization for war," wrote the German historian, Otto Hintze.[3] In one of the most oft-cited sentences in the literature of state formation, Charles Tilly asserts that, "War made the state, and the state made war."[4] Indeed, central features of the modern state such as bureaucratic centralization, taxation, conscription, and nationalism, as well as entitlement to social services and education, all seem to have been formed in response to the challenges of warfare.[5]

The early modern state grew out of the feudal system of governance and its particular management of warfare. Three striking features characterized that system: fragmentated political power, privatized political power, the chivalrous method of warfare.[6] These characteristics underwent change during the fifteenth century, when shock combat between mounted, heavily armored, and highly skilled warriors on horseback was replaced by a new system of warfare characterized by battles of siege, infantry, and firearms.[7] The changes were gradual, cumulative, and geographically dispersed, but in the sixteenth century they gave birth to the military revolution that changed the political map of Europe and eventually of the world. The most important change was the marked growth in the size of the armies. After about 1500, the size of armies maintained in the field relative to the supporting population was several times larger than during the previous ten centuries.[8] These armies were engaged in almost perpetual warfare, and between 1560 and 1660 proportionately more Europeans were under arms than ever before.[9]

These developments stimulated the bureaucratic growth of the modern European state. The chain of causation linking the military revolution to the centralization of political authority included (1) escalating intensity and technology of warfare, (2) innovations in the means and extent of resource mobilization, including taxation, (3) new bureaucracies and administrative innovations, (4) resistance by nobility, burghers, and peasants to the new burdens of war and administration, (5) renewed coercion and/or generation of national identity, (6) an increase in the extractivensss of the state, (7) mercantilist economic policies, and finally (8) the etatization of the economy.[10]

Although centralization as an outcome of war is common to many countries, significant differences in both and intensity have resulted in contrasting structures and styles of governance.[11] Two extreme cases are often contrasted. The first is the Continental model, the product of intensive warfare in the heart of Europe. The "patterns cases" are usually those of Habsburg Spain under Philip II (1555–1598), of France under Mazarin, Louis XIV, and Colbert, as well as Prussia under the Great Elector (1640–1680).[12] The usefulness of a strong interventionist state in the context of warfare is said to have led to etatist polities on most of the Continent. This is often contrasted with the British[13] and American pluralism, and the differences are then explained in terms of intensity and scope of warfare.[14] Already in 1835 Alexis de Tocqueville observed that Americans have no strong neighbors, and that consequently they also have no fear of great wars, financial crises, inroads, or conquests. "They require neither great taxes, nor large armies, nor great generals...."[15] Following the end of the War of Independence and the signing of the Treaty of Paris, the American army shrank to only 700 men. Only two garrisons were kept, one of 55 men, the other of 25. In 1796 a French visitor was stunned to find the American war office staffed by only two clerks.[16]

Yet while warfare makes the centralized state a rational option, there is still some space for political choice. Perhaps the most prominent example is the Dutch Republic (1579–1806), which avoided the forces of centralization and bureaucratization that characterized other European states. This is especially remarkable when one considers the intense warfare that accompanied the Dutch state formation, one of the most violent periods in European history. The Dutch Revolt lasted longer than any in modern European history, and the war of independence against the Spanish Habsburgs, called the Eighty Years War (1568–1648, with a 12-year truce between 1609 and 1621) involved more continuous fighting than any other war in modern times.[17] Against this background, it would only be natural to expect the development of a strong, authoritative state. But this did not happen.[18] The challenges of warfare, even in their most extreme forms, as encountered by the Dutch, did *not* render the Dutch polity a strong state.

In contrast to the Dutch case, the Israeli case seems to confirm the general assumption that war and war preparations will result in a strong centralized state. Long before the establishment of Israel, conflict between Jews and Palestinians led to a strong Jewish political center as well as a central military organization (the Hagana), which later was the basis for the Israel Defense Forces. This centralization of political and military authority within the context of an intense conflict seems to confirm the common view of the effects of war on state formation and, more specifically, on the creation of a centralized bureaucracy, an interventionist economic policy, and etatist policy patterns.

War has a critical effect not only on the structure of the state but also on the power of dominant societal groups. Yet, the effects of war on society formation in France were remarkably different from the United States and the Netherlands. In the French case, which is probably typical, warfare consolidated a dominant position for the aristocratic class, with legitimacy derived from war service. The Dutch and American cases differ, corresponding to Tilly's capital-intensive trajectory of state formation.[19] In those cases, the forces of centralization that accompanied the war were defeated by a strong business class. The interests of the Dutch and American capitalists in a weak state strongly affected their polity formation.[20] Israel represents a third type. While society formation in France elevated the influence of a strong aristocratic class of warriors, and in the United States and the Netherlands a strong business-oriented class, in Israel the Arab–Israeli conflict contributed to the consolidation of the labor movement hegemony.

It is often asserted, and rightly so, that it was the dominance of the labor movement that led to the formation of a strong state. But the dominance of the labor movement and the strong state institutions are themselves two outcomes of the conflict. The conflict in Palestine made the collective institutions of the Zionist movement vital for the success of the project. Those institutions were critical for managing the conflict, mobilizing resources to secure Jewish control over the land, and protecting Jewish labor. Even if there had been no strong labor movement, strong state institutions to subsidize Jewish labor and to control land were necessary. With the rise of the labor leadership to a position of national leadership they made a critical decision to ground their authority in the state and not in the movement's major institution, the Histadrut. This political strategy, formulated by David Ben-Gurion and named *mamlachtiut* [etatism], contributed to the institutionalization and expansion of state power, this time by strengthening the power of labor.

WARFARE AND ETATIST PATTERNS OF POLICY MAKING IN ISRAEL

War and war preparations shaped both the institutions of the Israeli strong state and the power of competing classes. Wide-scale armed conflict came to Palestine only with the Arab Revolt of 1936–1939, but the first manifestations of the conflict between Jews and Arab were evident in the labor and land markets from the beginning of the twentieth century. The conflict for land and labor markets had critical effects on both the organization of the Zionist movement and the dominance of the labor movement within it.[21] The high costs of Jewish labor led Jewish employers to turn almost exclusively to cheap Arab labor. This exclusion was severe, not only for newly-arrived Jewish laborers, but also from the Zionist viewpoint as a whole because it threatened to dampen Jewish immigration and thereby undermine the Zionist project. The Jewish bourgeoisie were in an inferior position in the conflict between their economic interest in employing cheap Arab labor and the Zionist interest of encouraging Jewish immigration.

This was not the first time that economic logic and Zionist logic clashed, and it certainly was not the last, but this case was especially significant. The struggle in the labor market, known as the "conquest of labor," created conditions under which the labor movement could mobilize its members against the Jewish employers, demoralize its political competitors, and press its demands for national financial support. A second conflict, this one over land ownership, also made the labor movement important for the Zionists. Important, too, was the labor movement's ability to organize itself in collectives that populated the country on "national land," or land bought and owned by Zionist institutions. In the context of conflict over land, the ability of the labor movement settlements, from the Kibbutz to the Moshav, to better serve Zionist aims (better than private forms of economic and social organization) made it a privileged candidate for a position of dominance in the Jewish community in Palestine.

This identity of interest led to an alliance between the Jewish labor movement and the Zionists in the early years of the twentieth century. This coalition reacted to the economic exclusion of Jews from the labor market with the political exclusion of Arab labor, intensively promoting Jewish interests in controlling and settling the country. In the 1930s this alliance resulted in the hegemonic rule of the labor movement in the Yishuv[22] and later in Israeli politics.

The conflict over land and labor not only determined the power of labor and the bourgeoisie but also shaped state power. The national conflict in Palestine made the collective institutions of the Zionist movement vital for the success of the Zionist project. Those institutions helped manage the conflict, mobilize resources to secure Jewish control over the land, protect Jewish labor, and coordinate defensive efforts in the Yishuv. Their function in manageing the conflict accounts for much the dominant and interventionist nature of the strong Israeli state. Against this background of a highly developed political center that functioned as a "state-in-the-making," it is not surprising that the entry of the Arab states into direct military involvement further consolidated and strengthened the strong state.

The invasion of the Arab armies in May 1948 reinforced the need for a strong state that could mobilize all resources for war. The intervention of the Arab states turned the conflict into a grave problem of survival for Israel. And in contrast to the past, it was now possible to use Jewish sovereignty to build an effective military machine with few constraints. Furthermore, international recognition allowed the new state not only to buy weapons, but also to raise new resources and obtain international aid. To finance a costly and large military machine, a large budget and a comprehensive tax system were required. The ability of David Ben-Gurion to quickly construct and finance a citizens' army was one of the main indications of the high degree of stateness of the Israeli polity-in-creation.[23] Israel is thus a rare case among both the post-colonial states and the settlers societies, which were rarely able to enforce mass conscription.

Before, during, and after the 1948 crisis, the strong state developed a piecemeal process in response to the Arab–Israeli conflict. During the first fifty years of the Yishuv period, the level of violence was largely restrained, and hence the organization of Jewish military forces progressed slowly. But following the Arab revolt, the former paramilitary organizations, which were oriented mostly toward local self-defense and were only loosely coordinated, changed their course of development. A more centrally directed armed force was secretly built up, with central systems of recruitment, training, strategic planning, and budgeting.[24] The national conflict, which had previously placed the responsibility for land purchasing, management, and allocation on the national institutions, now necessitated a strong military machine as well. A successful, voluntary effort of tax-mobilization, called *Kofer Hayishuv*, launched by the national institutions, paved the way to even more extensive resource mobilization later.

A noteworthy event in the development of the future Israeli military force was the enlistment of over 25,000 men and women (out of a Jewish population of 500,000) in the British army during the Second World War. These volunteers, largely responding to the call of the Yishuv leadership, later made a crucial contribution to the Israeli War of Independence and to the creation of a strong army within the newly created strong state. According to Gross and Metzer, the Second World War had significant effects on the Israeli economy, including the expansion of government involvement in economic life. This expansion included control over capital movement and foreign exchange as well as price intervention in the form of subsidized goods and price controls. In addition, certain other primary instruments of economic policy making, such as inflation control and wage indexation schemes, also originated in the Second World War.[25]

There were five direct effects of the Arab–Israeli conflict on the creation of the strong Israeli state.

1. The conflict allowed the state to mobilize resources for its own uses. The conflict not only made taxation possible, but also made fund-raising in the Jewish Diaspora easier and more successful. Both domestic taxation and international resource mobilization of resources greatly strengthened the state *vis-à-vis* societal actors. These resources gave the state leverage in enforcing policy preferences in wide spheres of action, not just security.

2. The emergence of a strong military machine consumed a considerable chunk of the Israeli GNP. While the average range of military expenditures of western countries for the postwar period was about

5 percent of GNP, those of Israel exceeded 10 percent since 1962, and 20 percent since 1969.[26] Military consumption created military-dependent sectors in the fields of armaments, food supply, clothing, and even entertainment, turning the government into the biggest consumer in the Israeli economy and the most influential force in setting patterns of demand.

3. Through a system of comprehensive compulsory conscription and the creation of large reserve forces, the Israeli army became a ubiquitous presence in everyday Israeli life. As a national mass army it served as a major socialization agent and took an active role in educating the Israelis for "good citizenship" and for "love of the country." The army also established a position in the media industry through a popular radio station, and in the culture industry through ownership of magazines and a publishing house.

4. The Arab–Israeli conflict led to the creation of a state-owned military-industrial complex, whose excessive share of the Israeli economy makes it not only a tool for preserving physical security, but also a key national economic factor; it has considerable influence on the level of employment, is a major foreign exchange earner (through exports), and is a supplier of health and welfare services and an agent of socialization.[27]

5. The conflict made the developmental role of the government more attractive and attainable, since the Arab boycott limited the amount of direct foreign investment, as well as the entry of multinationals into the Israeli economy.[28]

Thus, the Arab–Israeli conflict helped shape the statist patterns of policy making in Israel. Foreign exchange had to be managed, taxes increased, inflation monitored, production of certain goods maximized, supplies rationed, and the dangers of the black market controlled. Thus, war gave Israeli state officials the opportunity to gain autonomy, to maximize their strength, and to create a strong interventionist state.

Modern Israel was founded about three centuries after the consolidation of the strong European states. The literature on postcolonial states tells us that the conditions in which state makers in the twentieth century operate are radically different from those encountered by the European state makers in the sixteenth and seventeenth centuries.[29] Some question whether new states can be considered strong. Stein Rokkan argued that, "The European sequence simply cannot be repeated in the newest nations."[30] That Israel's status as a strong state is exceptional among the postcolonial states is widely acknowledged in the literature. Rokkan himself mentioned this, and it was later confirmed by the comparative studies of Gabriel Ben-Dor and Joel Migdal.[31] An important reason for this exceptional circumstance seems to be the intensity of conflict in all respects of Israel's war preparations and its penetration into all spheres of life, including the economy. This intensity and range consolidated institutions of a strong-new-state, and thus Rokkan's assertion that strong state patterns should be expected only in "old states" needs to be qualified.

Rather than contradicting warfare-driven theories of state-building, the Israeli experience confirms them. Between the extremes of the strong continental state and the weak American state, Israel's state formation under conditions of intensive warfare matches the Continental pattern far better than the American. The history of Israel, like that of Europe, is to a large extent one of conflict and war. The duration of the Arab–Israeli conflict, its high intensity, and its effect on every domain of communal and international relations all reflect European standards of conflict and state formation.

NATIONAL POLICY PATTERNS: THE CONSTRAINTS ON POLICY CHANGE

While national policy patterns do not prevent change they certainly constrain it. Three illustrations of state and society formation – the United States, France, and the Netherlands – are offered here. In a study of the roots of the current American political order, Huntington went as far back as the late medieval and Tudor political ideas of the English colonists.[32] By pointing to the specific trajectory of state formation in America, Huntington offered explanation to current political choice which are constrained by tradition and continuity of a period of about 400 years.

A brief example illustrates this effect. The framers of the American Constitution paid heed to the interests and autonomy of the states in the Constitution, not least because the states had to ratify it. Thus, the Constitution divided power between the federal government and states in a way that gave considerable authority to the states. This political arrangement was framed more than two centuries ago, but it still has a major impact on American policy, constraining the role of the federal government and causing fragmentation in American policy. Changes in these relationships are hard to achieve, and thus historical circumstances constrain present policy choices.[33] Comparativists who studied smoking regulations in the United States, Canada, and France have demonstrated how different government structures and political traditions, products of different trajectories of state formation, can explain differences in national strategies of regulation.[34]

In the French case, etatism is usually explained as a product of centuries of history: "From Hugues Capet to Louis XIV, from the French Revolution to Napoleon III and to the Gaullist regime, the state has constantly tightened its grip on civil society, has increased its own autonomy in order to form a closed center, an immense administrative machine able to dominate all the peripheries."[35] Industrial policy, protectionism, large projects, strong bureaucracy – all features that characterize current French policy – have roots in the past. Continuity in both the French and the American case suggests that while countries often face common challenges, they react (and in the course of reaction also change) in different ways. Thus, one significant set of constraints on the form of change is derived from existing national policy patterns.

Of course, even national policy patterns are not change-proof. Such changes are quite rare, however, and as the Dutch example shows, change does not always mean transformation. From the establishment of the Dutch Republic in the end of the sixteenth century and during 216 years of the Republic's existence, only relatively minor changes were apparent in the organization of the weak Dutch state and strong bourgeoisie.[36] It was only after 1795, following the French occupation, that a change in Dutch policy patterns became apparent. This change involved the centralization of authority and to a much lesser extent the bureaucratization of public functions.[37] This was manifested in the areas of taxation, education, the military, the police, legislation, judiciary, as well as in the relationship between central and local governments. These changes granted the executive much more power than it ever had, and the stateless Dutch polity, with its federal structure and extreme decentralization, became significantly more statist.

The radical change that followed the collapse of the Republic and the French occupation led a strong state, which consolidated its power alongside a strong civil society.[38] This change in the Dutch national policy patterns had its impact well after the retreat of the French and is evident even in today's Dutch policy making. Rudy Andeweg put it thus: "the Emperor [Napoleon] can be proud of himself: through its institutions the Dutch nation still feels his influence."[39] The relatively balanced relationship between the state and civil society that was shaped during the French period is important for the understanding of the later formation of Dutch corporatist institutions. They also had some impact on the consociational elements of the Dutch policy-making system.[40]

Despite the impact of Napoleon and the centralization of authority and the nationalization of politics since the early nineteenth century, current Dutch policy patterns are still embedded in critical features of the sixteenth century Dutch Republic. When bureaucratization was finally adopted by the Dutch, it was structured in a fragmented form: "There are *no* general competitive examinations.... There is *no* real central recruitment of higher civil servants. There is *hardly* anything like conscious career planning within, let alone across departments. There is *no* rotation of posts.... In short there is *no* national civil service."[41] The fragmentation of the bureaucracy is responsible for the "functional decentralization and sectorization of the Dutch policy making."[42]

This comparative perspective on the origins and perseverence of national patterns of policy patterns points to the need for a careful consideration of the case for change in the Israeli national policy patterns. While Israel is becoming more open to the outside and experiencing domestic pressures for change, we still may expect continuity in the high autonomy of the Israeli state. What may have appeared to be a transformation following the crisis of governability of the late 1970s and the first half of the 1980s seems instead to have resulted in the stabilization of state autonomy rather than its transformation.[43]

The Israeli polity is only 100 years old, yet this does not mean that it is necessarily more prone to change than old polities. National policy patterns are created and consolidated in a specific "formative period" which imprints a birthmark on state and society interaction. Because countries do not simply move from pluralism to corporatism or etatism, it seems that Israel may be "stuck" with a self-perpetuating strong state, as well as with its own distinctive policy pattern.[44] The policy implications of this observation are that the past experience of state-led public policy making, with relatively minor input by interest groups and other societal interests, may prevail over the normative tendency of dominant social groups to adopt a more "American" type of pluralism in Israeli policy making and may constrain the converging effects of globalization over the Israeli political economy.

CONCLUSIONS

War and war preparations resulted in the formation of a strong and centralized military machine and an autonomous and strong Israeli state. They also contributed to the consolidation the Jewish labor movement and the political decline of the Jewish middle class. Under the hegemony of the labor movement, the state was perceived as a problem-solving institution for dealing with external threats, national reconstruction, rapid modernization, and social inequality. This, in turn, helped to solidify a tradition in which the state enjoyed a privileged position in the economic sphere. The centrality of the economic sphere guaranteed that the effects of etatism would have strong impact on other spheres as well and thus contribute to the consolidation and preservation of an etatist national policy pattern.

The comparative study of polity formation in general, and of state formation in particular, brings history back into public policy analysis, a discipline that often tends to neglect history. In the opening remarks of his classic volume *The Formation of National States in Western Europe*, Tilly compares the relationship between political analysis and historical experience to that of a dog tied to a long leash. "The dog can roam in almost any direction. He can even have the illusion of rushing off on his own. But let him rush too far, too fast, and his collar will jerk him back; it may even knock the wind out of him." Some political analysts may wish to cut the leash by ignoring history. But, as Tilly rightly warns us, "any theory which claims to encompass general processes of political transformation must be consistent with past experience and ought to be checked carefully against that experience before gaining wide acceptance."[45]

Etatist national patterns in Israel make it important for students of public policy not to neglect the strong Israeli state in policy analysis and not to put too much emphasis on parties, classes, interest groups, business power, or any other societal actor. To stress continuity is not to deny change, just as to stress the divergent effects of change is not to deny its convergent effects. Rather, the emphasis on continuity means an analysis of change needs to be applied with caution grounded in in national policy patterns and state traditions. When attention is paid to how basic societal and political institutions constrain human choices and to the fact that today's and tomorrow's policy choices are shaped by the constraints of past policy decisions, the rarity of changes in national policy patterns becomes understandable. Thus, we have good reason to expect that national policy patterns are self-perpetuating and that the Israeli etatism is here to stay.

ACKNOWLEDGEMENTS

This research has been supported by ISEF and was written during my stay as a visiting scholar at the center for Management and Policy at the University of Utrecht. I would like to thank Prof. Frans van Waarden who sponsored my stay. An extended version of this paper was presented at the conference *Israel in Comparative Perspective: The Dynamics of Change*, Berkeley, California, September 1996. For helpful comments on an earlier draft my thanks to Michael Shalev. The responsibility is, however, all mine.

NOTES

1. Jeremy Richardson, *Policy Styles in Western Europe*, London and Boston: Allen & Unwin, 1982.
2. Although the distinction between "strong" and "weak" states has been criticized as too vague to allow its users to do justice to the complexities of state–society relations, for our purposes it remains the best distinction currently available in the literature of comparative policy making. For an excellent clarification of the distinctions between strong and weak states from a comparative point of view, see Linda Weiss and John Hobson, *States and Economic Development: A Comparative Historical Analysis*, Cambridge: Polity Press, 1995. For a theoretical account, see Eric Nordlinger, "Taking the State Seriously," in Myron Weiner and Samuel Huntington (eds), *Understanding Political Development*, Boston: Little, Brown, 1987, pp.353–90. Our general characterization of national patterns of policy making does not imply, however, that there are some spheres of action (meso or micro) in which "pluralist" patterns cannot occur within corporatist or etatist polities, and vice versa. The notion of national policy patterns demands a high degree of generalization and therefore can be characterized as top-to-bottom approach; it mirrors the forest rather than the trees and is much better at portraying the general characteristics of Israeli policy making than its complexities (for a bottom-up analysis of Israeli policy making, one that emphasizes the complexities of the system, see Yael Yishai, *Land of Paradoxes; Interest Politics in Israel*, Albany, NY: State University of New York Press, 1991.
3. Otto Hintze, selection edited by F. Gilbert, *The Historical Essays of Otto Hintze*, New York: Oxford University Press, 1975, p.181.
4. Charles Tilly (ed.), *The Formation of National States in Western Europe*, Princeton, NJ: Princeton University Press, 1975, p.42.

5. M.D. Feld, "Military Professionalism and the Mass Army," *Armed Forces and Society* 1 (1975) pp.191–214; R.B. Posen, "Nationalism, the Mass Army, and Military Power," *International Security* 18 (1993) pp.80–124.
6. R.J. Strayer, *Feudalism*, New Jersey: Van Nostrand Company, 1965, pp.12–13.
7. M. Roberts, *The Military Revolution; 1560–1660*, An Inaugural Lecture delivered before the Queen's University of Belfast, Marjory Boyd, 1956.
8. R. Bean, "War and the Birth of the Nation State," *The Journal of Economic History* 33 (1973) p.211.
9. A. Corvisier, *Armies and Societies in Europe 1494–1789*, Ann Arbor, MI: Indiana University Press, 1968, p.8.
10. Cf. Tilly, *The Formation of National States* (note 4) pp.73–4.
11. Samuel Finer, "State- and Nation-Building in Europe: The Role of the Military," in Tilly (note 4) pp.84–163.
12. E. Barker, *The Development of Public Services in Western Europe: 1660–1930*, CT: Archon Books, 1966; Hintze (note 3).
13. This is true of the British Isles as well. Much like America, it has rendered resistance to a strong, interventionist, government quite feasible, and thus played a crucial role in the formation of a weak British state (and a stateless society).
14. Samuel Huntington, *Political Order in Changing Societies*, New Haven and London: Yale University Press, 1968, p.123.
15. Alex de Tocqueville, *Democracy in America*, New York: Alfred A. Knopf, 1835, 1963 edition, pp.288–9.
16. D.B. Porter, "The Warfare State," *American Heritage* 45 (1994) p.58.
17. Geoffrey Parker, *Spain and The Netherlands, 1559–1659*, London: Collins, 1979, p.45.
18. Cf. C.M. Hart, *The Making of a Bourgeois State: War, Politics and Finance During the Dutch Revolt*, Manchester and New York: Manchester University Press, 1993, p.4; D.B. Porter, *War and the Rise of the State; the Military Foundation of Modern Politics*, New York: Free Press, 1994, p.94.
19. Charles Tilly, *Coercion, Capital, and European States, AD 990–1990*, Cambridge and New York: Blackwell, 1990.
20. Frans van Waarden, "The Historical Institutionalization of Typical National Patterns in Policy Networks between State and Industry: A Comparison of the USA and the Netherlands," *European Journal of Political Research* 21 (1992) pp.131–62.
21. These aspects were illuminated by excellent accounts of Shalev and Shafir. See, Michael Shalev, *Labour and the Political Economy in Israel*, Oxford: Oxford University Press, 1992; Gershon Shafir, *Land, Labor and the Origins of the Israeli–Palestinian Conflict 1882–1914*, Cambridge: Cambridge University Press, 1989.
22. The Jewish polity before sovereignty.
23. Michael Barnett, *Confronting the Costs of War*, Princeton: Princeton University Press, 1992, pp.251–2.
24. Dan Horowitz and Moshe Lissak, *Origins of the Israeli Polity; Palestine under the Mandate*, Chicago and London: University of Chicago Press, 1978, p.50.
25. Nachum T. Gross and Jacob Metzer, "Palestine in World War II: Some Economic Aspects," in T.M. Geoffrey and H. Rockoff (eds), *The Sinews of War*, Ames: Indiana University Press, 1993, p.80.
26. Eithan Berglas, "Defense and the Economy," in Yoram Ben-Porath (ed.), *The Israeli Economy: Maturing through Crisis*, Cambridge, MA and London: Harvard University Press, 1985, p.173.
27. Alex Mintz, "The Military-Industrial Complex: The Israeli Case," in Moshe Lissak (ed.), *Israeli Society and Its Defense Establishment*, London: Frank Cass, 1984, p.124.
28. The net flow of US-based multinationals to Israel between 1951 and 1971 was 20 – a rather limited number. Of the 67 countries included in the Harvard Business School study, Israel is the 62nd, almost closing the list. See Joan P. Curhan, William H. Davidson and Rajan Suri, *Tracing the Multinationals*, Cambridge, MA: Harvard University Press, 1977, pp.22–3.
29. Cf. Gabriel Ben-Dor, *State and Conflict in the Middle East; Emergence of the Post Colonial State*, New York: Praeger, 1983, pp.1–34.
30. Stein Rokkan, "Dimensions of State Formation and Nation-Building: A Possible Paradigm for Research on Variations within Europe," in Tilly (note 4) p.600.
31. Ibid., p.598; Ben-Dor, *State and Conflict in the Middle East* (note 29); Joel Migdal,

Strong Societies and Weak States, Princeton: Princeton University Press, 1988.
32. Huntington, Political Order in Changing Societies (note 14).
33. Thus, the question of sovereignty (or the right to secede) was resolved in the United States only through a civil war.
34. Robert Kagan and David Vogel, "The Politics of Smoking Regulation: Canada, France, the United States," In L.R. Rabin and D.S. Sugarman (eds), *Smoking Policy: Law, Politics, and Culture*, New York and Oxford: Oxford University Press, 1993, pp.22–48.
35. Pier Birnbaum, "State, Center, and Bureaucracy," *Government and Opposition* 16 (1981) pp.59.
36. Waarden, "The Historical Institutionalization" (note 20).
37. Hans Daalder, "Consociationalism, Center and Periphery in the Netherlands," in P. Torsvik (ed.), *Mobilization Center–Periphery Structures and Nation-Building. A Volume in Commemoration of Stein Rokkan,* Bergen, Oslo: Universitatsforlaget, 1981, pp.181–240; Frans van Waarden, *State and Civil Society in the Netherlands*, SFB 221, Project C-4, Research Report, University of Konstanz, 1990, Chapter 3 and Chapter 5.
38. Waarden, "The Historical Institutionalization" (note 20).
39. Rudy B. Andeweg, "Institutional Conservatism in the Netherlands: Proposals for and Resistance to Change," *West European Politics* 12 (1989) p.42.
40. For instance, on the broker role of the Dutch bureaucracy, see Hans Daalder, "On Building Consociational Nations: the Cases of the Netherlands and Switzerland," *International Social Science Journal* 23 (1971) pp.355–70; Rudy Andeweg, "Institutional Conservatism in the Netherlands" (note 39).
41. Hans Daalder, "The Mold of Dutch Politics: Themes for Comparative Inquiry," *West European Politics* 12 (1989) p.8.
42. Rudy Andeweg and Galen Irwin, *Dutch Government and Politics*, London: Macmillan, 1993, p.18.
43. Henry Barkey, "When Politics Matter: Economic Stabilization in Argentina and Israel," *Studies in Comparative International Development* 29 (1994) pp.41–67.
44. Cf. Ira Sharkansky, "The Overloaded State," *Public Administration Review* (1993) p.203.
45. Tilly, *The Formation of National States* (note 4) p.3.

Consociationalism and Ethnic Democracy: Israeli Arabs in Comparative Perspective

ALAN DOWTY

Israel is one of the major cases of democracy in a deeply-divided society. Ethnic and religious cleavages clearly make the achievement of democracy more difficult. Only a handful of states with deep and numerically significant ethnic divisions have maintained stable democracies: Switzerland, Belgium, Canada, arguably India – and Israel. The Israeli case is thus not unique, and pressures for convergence are further reducing this uniqueness.

From a comparative perspective, what can be said about Israel's record in extending democracy to include a 19 percent Arab minority ethnically identified with external enemies? In answering this question, it is important to understand just what *kind* of democracy Israel has managed to maintain, and where the strength of its democratic habits lie. It is useful to begin with the distinction that Arend Lijphart makes between *majoritarian* democracy, on one hand, and *consensus* democracy, or *consociationalism*, on the other.

Majoritarian democracy, or the "Westminster model," presupposes that majority rule is the essence of democracy and should not be diluted (by a minority veto, for example). The British style of parliamentarism with unicameralism, bare-majority governments, and fused executive and legislative power is an expression of the majoritarian ideal. It may also be characterized by a unidimensional two-party system with one-party governments, by non-proportional electoral systems, by centralized as opposed to federalized government, and by unentrenched (or even unwritten) constitutions that can be altered by ordinary acts of parliament. All of these arrangements help to guarantee that the untrammeled will of the majority will prevail.[1]

Consociational (or "consensus") democracy assumes that excluding losing groups or minorities from all decision-making is undemocratic.

Alan Dowty is at the University of Notre Dame.

This model holds as an ideal diffused and shared power according to some principle of proportionality. Arend Lijphart identifies eight elements of consociational democracy that stand in contrast to the majoritarian model: executive power-sharing among parties, checks and balances between the executive and legislative branches, a multiparty system, political divisions along many dimensions (socioeconomic, ethnic, religious, etc.), proportional representation, federalism/decentralization, two legislative houses to check each other, and a written constitution that cannot be changed by a simple majority.[2]

By some of these measures, including the multi-party system and proportional representation, Israel clearly ranks among the more consociational regimes. On others, including centralization, unicameralism, an unwritten constitution, Israel is "majoritarian."[3] But this mixed picture exists primarily on the level of formal institutions. When viewed in terms of the broader concept of consociationalism, informal power-sharing is much more evident. *Thus, a focus on the formal structure and powers of Israeli institutions is misleading.* The Knesset may at first glance invite comparison to the Westminster model, but its most important policy decisions result from bargaining involving not only various branches of government, but also important quasi-governmental bodies and major social groups. In practice, then, Israeli democracy has important power-sharing consociational features: grand coalitions, autonomy, proportionality, mutual veto, pluralism, and social bargaining.

TRADITIONAL JEWISH POLITICS

Power-sharing in Israeli politics is rooted, in part, in the Jewish historical experience, especially in eastern Europe but also elsewhere. The main elements of this experience were: (a) struggle for survival on both community and individual levels in a hostile environment; (b) self-regulation through well-developed legal and judicial institutions and the development of legislative mechanisms; (c) processes for selecting the community's own leadership, with at least some input from the larger public; (d) provision of a broad range of community services without reliance on the outside; (e) a resulting tendency to a collectivist or cooperative model of social organization; (f) enforcement without recourse, in most cases, to the most direct forms of force; and (g) a gap between the formal structure of power and the actual influence patterns within the community.[4]

Though not "democratic" by modern standards, these governing practices did provide a foundation for the growth of democratic institutions. They did this by providing modes of participation that reflected the essentially voluntary nature of community membership, by fostering (before the appearance of modern liberal political theory) an attitude of skepticism toward all authority, and by developing a body of law that *de facto* mandated important basic human rights. These traditions also strongly inclined toward consociational rather than majoritarian democracy. Competition between different centers of authority, the lack of defined hierarchy, proliferation and influence of organized groups, and the reality of bargaining and power-sharing marked Jewish political experience. By the late nineteenth century, moreover, the eastern European Jewish community was divided into a multidimensional political and social system, with splits along socio-economic, religious, and ideological lines as well as among traditional elites. Long before theorists had identified the essence of "consensus" or "consociational" democracy, Jewish communities exemplified many of its characteristic patterns.

A crucial feature of traditional Jewish politics, however, was that Jewish law and Jewish politics within the community applied only to Jews. Relations between Jews and non-Jews were under the jurisdiction of the state and governed by non-Jewish law, but within the community Jewish law prevailed. Furthermore, this Jewish law was in many respects highly particularistic. Jacob Katz notes how surprised many Jews were to be reminded by the "scientific" antisemites, in the 1880s, of the discriminatory elements in Jewish tradition: "Even learned Jews sincerely maintained that Judaism had always taught universalistic ethics only."[5]

Jewish law clearly distinguished Jewish rights from general human rights because rights in Jewish law are inferred from obligations. Non-Jews have fewer obligations than Jews, basically the seven commandments of Noah, and thus they also have correspondingly fewer rights, essentially the rights to life and property, and security from injustice, lawlessness, and bloodshed.[6] There were, to be sure, numerous Biblical injunctions regarding the humane treatment of foreigners: "Thou shalt neither vex a stranger, or oppress him: for you were strangers in the land of Egypt" (Exodus 22:20); "One law and one code shall there be for you, and for the stranger that sojourns with you" (Numbers 15:16). Injunctions in the Talmud also invoke the principles of "the interests of peace" and "avoidance of ill feelings" as grounds for kindness toward non-Jews, even if this involved a breaking of Jewish laws.[7] But Talmudic law, by distinguishing among resident aliens between the *ger tsedek* (who has converted to Judaism) and the *ger toshav* (who has not), limits the demands of strict equality to the former. The *ger toshav*, on the other hand, is subject to a number of disabilities: he may not act as agent for a Jew, is generally disqualified as a witness in civil matters, and even his right of refuge is circumscribed. According to Maimonides, no non-Jew (a category he extends to include converts "even after many generations") may be put in any position of power (*serara*) within the Jewish community.[8]

The essence of Jewish law toward "strangers" was, therefore, humanity. Civic equality of Jews and non-Jews in a Jewish society was as unthinkable as the idea of equal status for Jews in non-Jewish society was at that time. Furthermore, the injunction of humane treatment was geared to the *individual*, and not to non-Jewish groups who might claim recognition of their collective identity. While recognizing the rights of individual aliens to humane treatment did not provide for any collective legal or political expression of non-Jewish identity, the matter was never seriously tested under Diaspora conditions. There the Jewish law of the *ger toshav* was adequate to deal with those non-Jews who chose to live as individuals in a Jewish community. Jewish communities never had under their jurisdiction large non-Jewish populations seeking to maintain their own collective identity, and thus Jewish political traditions were singularly unequipped to deal with such a situation. These traditions were not racist in the modern sense: they simply had nothing to say about minorities as such.

Arabs in Israel

The Arab minority in Israel – 19 percent of the population in May 1948, and still 19 percent in 1997 – posed a challenge to Jewish consociational politics. Power-sharing techniques were widely used in the Zionist movement, in the pre-state Jewish Yishuv within the British Mandate of Palestine, and in Israel after its founding. But while Israeli Arabs enjoy the formal rights of citizenship, including voting and access to the political system, they stood outside the sphere of traditional Jewish politics. There was no meaningful power-sharing with the Arab community, and despite the progress made by Israeli Arabs since 1948, no proportionate distribution of benefits. Until very recently, there was no independent nation-wide Arab political party or organization, dedicated to the vigorous pursuit of Arab rights within the Israeli political system and speaking credibly for the Arab community or a large part of it. Nor have there been truly independent Arab newspapers of significance or Arab leaders of national stature.

In the bargaining process that characterizes Israel politics, there has been, in short, no Arab negotiating partner. As Ian Lustick summarizes the situation, "There simply does not exist an elite cartel within which leaders of the Jewish and Arab communal groups engage in quiet ethnic bargaining and careful apportionment of social, political, and economic resources."[9]

Critics on both ends of the spectrum argue *ipso facto* that Israel cannot be both Jewish and democratic if it has a large Arab minority: either it must shed its Jewishness to remain democratic (the position of Arab oppositionists), or it must exclude or expel Arabs in order to remain Jewish (as Israeli ultra-nationalists urge). Posing this as a stark "either–or" choice, however, ignores the reality that all nation-states, democratic or not, must in some fashion balance the demands of cultural, ethnic, and historical particularity against universalistic precepts of governance and justice. Israel must, in Kretzmer's words, manage the tension between two conceptions of nationhood: "As a democratic state Israel must serve the needs of all its citizens; as the state of the Jewish people its function is to pursue particularistic goals."[10] This tension helps explain the contradiction between formal equality, where laws reflect universal standards, and informal discrimination where Jewishness serves as the *de facto* point of reference. But Israel is hardly the only state facing this dilemma.

Sammy Smooha has suggested that Israel belongs to a category of "ethnic democracies" that combine a dominant ethnic character with democratic rights for all. He posits this category as a third democratic alternative for deeply divided societies, in addition to majoritarianism and consociationalism. Smooha defines ethnic democracy as "the extension of political and civil rights to individuals and certain collective rights to minorities with institutionalized dominance over the state by one of the ethnic groups," or as "a system that combines a genuine democracy for all with institutionalized dominance for one of its constituent groups."[11] Yoav Peled has developed the idea of ethnic democracy, in the Israeli case, as a confluence of two types of citizenship: "republican" citizenship with communal dimensions for Jews, and "liberal" citizenship with civil and political rights, but no share of communality, for Arabs.[12]

However, ethnic democracy by this definition does not represent a third type on the majoritarian–consociational axis. The distinction between majoritarian and consociational democracies is in the broadest sense a question of undiluted majority rule against a broader diffusion of power. Ethnic democracy as defined does not measure the mechanics of majority rule, but addresses the relationship of nations to states. In this role it is an extremely useful concept in discussion of minority rights. The basic idea – dominance of one ethnic group in a democratic framework – in fact approaches the basic definition of a nation-state. Since ethnic borders seldom correspond perfectly to political borders, the "national" majority in any given state constitutes a dominant ethnic group with respect to minorities not identified with that nationhood, no matter how democratic the procedures. All nationalisms have a potential problem with minority rights, since a hostile majority can suppress a minority by democratic as well as non-democratic means. The critical question is the degree to which ethnonational identity is intertwined with the very definition of the state.

In theory, liberal democracy is indifferent to distinctions among citizens. But no political system exists in a social, cultural, linguistic, and historical vacuum; even the most liberal regime is shaped by its context. This imprint will be lighter where the prevailing model of nationality is assimilative and where it corresponds to the concept of citizenship. In this "New World" model, state forms nation: there is a territorial focus, citizenship is extended to those born within its borders (*jus solis*), and naturalization is not tied to ethnicity, culture, or descent. This sense of particularity is stronger in the "Old World" model where nation forms state. Here, there is an ethnic focus, and while citizenship is distinguished from nationality, it is often extended on grounds of descent (*jus sanguinis*), while naturalization is more difficult since it is tied to ethnicity, culture, or language. As a product of the nation-state idea at its most intense, Israel lies toward the more ethnic end of this continuum. It is not, however, in a category by itself. There are other states in which ethnicity is likewise closely intertwined with the definition of the state ("nation forms state"). Many states, for example, confer citizenship by descent and/or ethnicity to those who can establish an ancestral link.[13]

Israel's link to ethnicity is not unique. But the Law of Return and its other explicitly Jewish features do place it among the more ethnic nation-states, and thus among the more problematic in terms of ethnic minorities. How does it compare in this regard to other ethnic democracies? In 1995 there were approximately 71 states in the world with a dominant ethnic group, defined by language, of over 50 percent but less than 95 percent (less than 50 percent would indicate a multiethnic society, while states with less than 5 percent linguistic minorities can be considered homogeneous).[14] Of these 71 states with a dominant ethnic group but a significant minority or minorities, 26 were ranked as "free" on political rights and civil liberties in the annual Freedom House survey of 1994–1995.[15]

From Israel's perspective, an important question is how many of these 26 states (which include Israel) practice some form of ethnic power-sharing and how many do not, and whether this is related to the size of the minorities. Arend Lijphart's four basic characteristics of power-sharing are (1) participation in the governing coalition or executive, (2) a high degree of group autonomy, (3) proportionality in representation and allocation, and (4) a formal or informal minority veto on matters of fundamental importance. *Addressing only ethnic divisions*, 11 of the 26 states meet at least three of these four conditions (Table 1).

TABLE 1
ETHNIC DEMOCRACIES WITH MINORITIES

No Ethnic Power-Sharing		Ethnic Power-Sharing	
Bahamas	85-15	Belgium	58-39
Belize	60-25-8-7	Benin	66-14-13-5
Bulgaria	85-8	Botswana	75-12-6
Cape Verde	70-30	Canada	62-25
Ecuador	93-7	Finland	94-6
Estonia	65-32	Guyana	78-21
France	87-7	Malawi	59-15-14
Israel	81-19	Mauritius	54-39
Latvia	54-33	South Africa	55-20-16-9
Lithuania	80-11-6	Spain	70-21-7
Mongolia	90-7	Switzerland	65-19-12
New Zealand	81-9		
Panama	81-14		
Slovakia	87-11		
US	89-6		

Nations ranked by Freedom House as "free" that have a dominant ethno-national group, defined by language, of 50–95 percent. The numbers following each state indicate the percentage of the linguistic majority, followed by minorities above 5 percent.

In the 15 ethnic democracies without ethnic power-sharing, the average size of the dominant group was 79 percent, while in the 11 power-sharing states the dominant group averaged only 67 percent (64 percent without the exceptional case of Finland). Put differently, only one of the 12 democratic states with linguistic minorities of less than 20 percent (Finland) used power-sharing techniques in its ethnic relations, while 10 of the 14 democratic states with minorities above 20 percent (all but Belize, Cape Verde, Estonia, and Latvia) did so.[16] Clearly accommodation of ethnic groups above this threshold, in an ethnic democracy, ordinarily involves the use of explicit power-sharing techniques that by their nature dilute the prevailing ethnicity of the state. With an Arab minority of about 19 percent, Israel stands near the fulcrum: close to the upper limit on the size of minorities that states have generally been able to incorporate successfully into functioning majoritarian democracies, and beyond which most have found consociationalism more applicable.[17] To judge by experience elsewhere, it would appear that Israel *could* conceivably integrate this minority without wide use of power-sharing techniques, but that such techniques may already be advisable and would have been absolutely essential if Israel had tried to incorporate the occupied territories democratically.

Does the existence of a broader Arab–Israeli conflict make Israel's minority issue unique? One of the more curious defenses of *de facto* discrimination is the argument that Israeli Arabs, as an ethnic minority linked to an external threat, represent a unique security problem. This is not the case. There are Greeks in Turkey and in Turkish Cyprus, Turks in Greek Cyprus, Hindus in Pakistan, Muslims in India, Tamils in Sri Lanka, Arabs in Iran, Albanians in Macedonia, Chinese in Vietnam, Somalis in Ethiopia, and many potentially hostile tribes with cross-border links in Africa. In the past, ethnic Japanese in the United States and Canada, Armenians in Turkey, Germans throughout eastern Europe, and various "suspect" ethnic groups in the Soviet Union, have been a source of concern to these governments.

The treatment of these "enemy minorities" has hardly been auspicious. The experiences of Armenians during World War I, of Japanese in the United States during World War II, and of German minorities during and after World War II, all testify to the corrosiveness of wartime suspicions. In recent decades the expulsion of suspect minorities has been commonplace, long before civil strife in the former Yugoslavia and the attendant "ethnic cleansing." It is noteworthy that among the 26 ethnic states rated as democratic, only the Baltic states parallel Israel in having sizable minorities linked to a potentially hostile neighbor. Clearly such links do put minority groups in a more complicated and vulnerable position.

One useful index related to this pattern is the exclusion of ethnic minorities from military service. Again, Israel is not unique in selective conscription. Among democratic nations, Britain did not apply the draft to Ireland in World War I or to Northern Ireland in World War II, while in Canada the conscription of French Canadians was a contentious issue in both conflicts. Elsewhere minorities have been excluded from the armed forces, in whole or in part, including in Burma, Fiji, Guyana, Iraq, Malaysia, Pakistan, Sri Lanka, and a number of African states.[18] Military service often serves minorities as a path to gaining legitimacy and acceptance, as it has with the Druze community in Israel.

DIRECTIONS OF CHANGE

Given the depth of the ethnic division, lessons from experience elsewhere, and the particular strengths of Israeli politics, the growth of consociationalism in Arab–Jewish relations seems inevitable. Israeli Jews wish to remain Jewish. That, after all, was the basic idea of Zionism. By the same token, Israeli Arabs are a non-assimilating minority with their own culture, language, and identity. Democratic governments – and even many non-democratic regimes – usually achieve long-term stability in such cases by power-sharing based on the explicit recognition of two or more ethnic communities.[19]

Changes in value orientations (see below) may foster development of an overarching identity, a common framework that transcends the division into Jew and Arab. Though the name *Israel* is decidedly Jewish in origin, Arab citizens have often expressed interest in expanding the concept, as a territorial label, to encompass non-Jews as well. This would in essence create the common civic space that has existed only in theory. Israeli Arab novelist Anton Shammas has asked for "a new definition of the word 'Israeli,' so that it will include me as well...." Responding from a Jewish perspective, A. B. Yehoshua, a leading Israeli literary figure, projects a gradual cultural symbiosis leading to a common Israeli identity and notes that during the First Temple period "Jewish religious identity was not at all a necessary element of Israeli identity."[20]

The introduction of power-sharing might be eased by the fact that consociationalism already works on the Jewish side. Power-sharing among Jewish groups, messy and contentious yet effective, already serves as a model of independent organization, collective bargaining, and direct action within the framework of law. On the municipal level, a "system of elite consultations" kept Arab–Jewish peace in Jerusalem over the decades, providing another model.[21] Survey data show that support for consociationalism has risen over the years both among Jews and Arabs.[22]

Whether conceived as consociationalism or as reform of ethnic democracy, specific proposals for Jewish–Arab accommodation tend to be similar. Most involve explicit recognition of Israeli Arabs as a national minority with rights as a group, such as an act of the Knesset affirming that "the Arab minority in the State of Israel is an integral part of the Jewish State and is entitled to full recognition of its specificity within the framework of law."[23] Recognition of Arabs as a minority could involve making state symbols and practices more inclusive, by having "Israeli" holidays that draw in both communities, for example.

Secondly, following from such recognition would be group autonomy in cultural and educational affairs, with election of a representative body for the purpose, and possibly including establishment of an Arab-language university. Functional autonomy in these areas may be necessary to counter the growth of support for territorial autonomy or total separation.

Finally, inter-ethnic consociationalism will get a tremendous boost when Arab parties that accept the framework of a Jewish state are brought into government coalitions. Nothing else would provide as clear an index of the extension of Israeli power-sharing to the Arab community.

This is in addition, of course, to a fair allocation of resources and equality before the law. Nothing in the "Jewish" nature of the state inherently compels discrimination in local government budgets, health and welfare services, education, economic opportunities, or treatment in the courts. In fact all of the above measures could be implemented without renouncing the essential Jewishness of Israel as a nation-state or ethnic democracy. What they involve is some dilution of the relationship between ethnicity and statehood, moving Israel more toward the center of the spectrum on this dimension. There always remains some sense in which an ethnic minority "does not fully belong" in a nation-state with a dominant ethnic group (Swedes in Finland, for example), but Israel would become more of a "normal" nation-state with "normal" minority problems.

A majority in both communities – roughly two-thirds, in fact – believe that a solution based on Israeli statehood and recognition of Arab rights as a national minority is both preferable and workable.[24] This assumes, of course, that the process of delinking the Israeli Arab situation from developments in the West Bank and Gaza continues. The 1988 acceptance by the Palestine Liberation Organization (PLO) of a two-state solution to the Israeli–Palestinian conflict, based on mutual recognition between Israel and a Palestinian state in the West Bank and Gaza, accelerated this process – even at the peak of the *intifada* – by setting clearly different courses for Arabs in the occupied territories and Arabs in Israel. Subsequent progress toward Palestinian self-rule in the territories (the 1993 Declaration of Principles, the 1994 Gaza-Jericho agreement, and the 1995 Interim Agreement) separated the two situations further. The idea of Palestinian statehood or self-governance also helps to legitimize Israel as a Jewish state; a Palestinian state as a homeland for Palestinian Arabs (perhaps with its own "Law of Return") would mirror Israel as a nation-state with a dominant ethnic character. It would lend a sense of symmetry to the situation, helping Israeli Arabs achieve a sense of equality and providing them with an option if they wanted to live in an Arab state.

For Arabs within Israel, the sense that the basic conflict is being resolved also frees them to focus further on their own problems and demands. Resolution of broader Arab–Israel issues could conceivably intensify their struggle, in the sense that they could no longer be put off by security arguments. But on the whole, peace and stability on the international level should reduce tensions within Israel, remove legitimate security issues, help expand civil rights, and make Israelis more willing to accept independent Arab organizations and Arab control of their own education and internal affairs. In such a setting Arabs could also perform military service, or another form of national service, as a path to integration and equality.

FORCES FOR CONVERGENCE

Outside influences of globalization and convergence of value orientations reinforce the trend to "normalization" in Israel's ethnic division. Modernization has brought new technologies, new social patterns, penetration of "westernization" in many guises, and new styles of "mass politics" in public life. At its most fundamental level, "modernization" is said to involve liberation from traditional authority, a new positive attitude toward change, and a turn from cultural orientations or values to social rationality. A civil society autonomous of the state emerges, as do new social strata (particularly professionals), more complex economic division of labor, and general bureaucratization. The weight of tradition, and its associated particularities, decline as objective forces mold all aspects of life. There is a convergence as societies respond to the same forces, a process which accelerates as these forces become internationalized. Of course, we are reminded, the dichotomy between tradition and modernity is not absolute. Traditional societies also can undergo considerable change and modern societies retain considerable diversity, often incorporating traditional elements in a variety of ways. But modernization still involves a number of common universalizing tendencies.[25]

In terms of these basic definitions, Israel has long been a modernizing or modernized society. Zionism was itself part of a broad historical challenge to old identities and value orientations. Jews were to join other peoples in a process of nation-building, creating a new order consonant with the progressive currents of the time. Zionism, and Israeli society, were attuned to, and even fixated on, technological innovation and prevailing models of social and economic development. The Yishuv and the state, like other modernizing societies, underwent increased social mobilization, organizational diversification and proliferation, rationalized regulation and allocation (market mechanisms, voting), greater division of labor and occupational specialization, enhanced social mobility, urbanization, secularization, expansion of media, and diffusion of political power.[26]

This process – long and slow but cumulative – was obscured by ideological habits of thought and revived resistance of traditionalists. But by the 1980s and 1990s, with the decline of ideology, the pressures of modernity were taking center stage. In the third great revolution of the modern era – that of information technology, following the earlier industrial and scientific revolutions – Israel was not only a full participant, but was even at the forefront in certain respects. The electronic age was integrating Israel into the larger world in ways that the founders of Zionism could hardly have imagined, while at the same time rewriting the rules of Israeli politics.

The impact of modernization on politics, as generally understood, is to create a more diversified political structure, to extend the scope of law and administration into all spheres, to spread power to wider groups, to weaken traditional elites and traditional sources of legitimation, and to foster a new accountability in which the ruled participate more directly in selection of the rulers and in setting major policies.[27] In the Israeli case, this has been expressed by diffusion of power within and among parties, decline of party dominance, emergence of new kinds of political actors, a new "mass politics" based more on personalities and less on issues, greater electoral fluidity and volatility, and the strengthening of administrative and legislative regularity.

Increasingly in Israel one sees signs of a blurring in the middle, of a less sharp dichotomy between "Jewish" and "Israeli." The outcome of the two-person Prime Minister's contest in 1996 was decided by appeals to the large group of voters in the middle of the spectrum. Netanyahu was forced to emphasize his commitment to the peace process, while Peres stressed his toughness on security. With the general decline in ideological commitment there is added fluidity in politics, and the emerging center is where the game is won or lost. In the center particularism and universalism meet, and Israel finds it can neither live in isolation nor cut itself off from its Jewish roots.

Similar trends operate in the Arab sector, for example in secularization. According to some estimates, the Islamic Movement had the allegiance of one-quarter to one-third of Israeli Muslims, and was "poised to become the leading force" among Israeli Arabs generally.[28] But in 1995 an Israeli Arab researcher reported that Islamism had peaked and was now waning. In 1988, 28 percent of Israeli Muslims had declared themselves as "very religious," 43 percent as "traditional," and 24 percent as "not religious." In 1995 the respective figures were 22 percent, 27 percent, and 52 percent, not that different from the figures among Israeli Jews.[29] Furthermore, when the Islamic Movement finally did compete in the 1996 Knesset elections in coalition with the Arab Democratic Party (ADP), it won only four seats (the ADP alone had won two in 1992).

CONCLUSIONS

No nation these days can totally ignore the civic principle that all citizens ought to be equal before the law despite racial, ethnic, religious, social, or political differences. This idea is now near-universal as a standard (if not as a practice), and Jews have always been among those foremost in promoting it. Nor can Israel escape being part of an increasingly interdependent and technologically-oriented world. In Israel no less than elsewhere, modernization involves challenges to tradition, the decline of ideology, and convergence with other societies. Some describe contemporary Israel as "post-Zionist," though the term has been used in so many contexts (as loss of ideology, as post-materialism, as critique of Zionist historiography, as attack on pop culture, as argument for a non-ethnic state) that it has no commonly agreed meaning.

Conversely, Israel cannot cut its ties to Jewish tradition. As one secular critic concludes, "a Hebrew national consciousness will always have affinities to Judaism."[30] Without Jewish tradition, what would Israel have of its own? "A few Jewish Agency songs, a bit of Palmach style, some pioneering memories, and the idea of the *kibbutz*...," in the words of Amos Oz?[31] Zionism drew heavily, if selectively, on Jewish tradition, and the human reality of a population *not* in rebellion against this tradition guaranteed the re-emergence of much more of it.

Of what, minimally, does the "Jewishness" of the Jewish state consist? Interestingly the Israeli Supreme Court, in dealing with the eligibility of parties to participate in elections, has tried to answer that question. Acceptance of "Israel as a Jewish state," the court ruled, means at the least: (1) maintenance of a Jewish majority, (2) the right of Jews to immigrate (the Law of Return), and (3) ties with Jewish communities outside Israel.[32] None of these features is inherently inconsistent with liberal democracy, and none of them is in fact unique to Israel.

As for non-Jews in Israel, pluralism may actually mean creating a new distinction between "Israeli" and "Jewish." Is it possible to develop an Israeliness that includes, but is not limited to, Jewishness? Can Palestinian citizens be made a part of "us" on at least one level? No nation-state, indeed, is entirely neutral in matters of particular ethnicity or culture, but this does not mean that a Jewish state by definition must be inhospitable to other ethnic groups. The acid test of Israeli democracy will be whether it can take Arab citizens into full partnership.

This should not be impossible. The genius of Jewish politics has always been its power-sharing, or consociationalism in political science terms. Consociationalism is a concept that itself synthesizes the civic and communitarian dimensions of politics. Its point of departure is a clear recognition of the permanence and legitimacy of diversity within society. In the Jewish context it has functioned reasonably well even where the lifestyles of groups were so diametrically opposed as to defy comparison. It has enabled the *haredi* (ultra-orthodox) community in Israel, for example, to become increasingly involved in the system even while questioning some of its basic premises. A balance of mutual dissatisfaction preserves stability, though it is sometimes hard to perceive this through the clamor of complaint.

Can Israel be both Jewish and democratic? The answer is yes, though there will be continuing tension between the two ideals. Furthermore, there is no precedent for a stable ethnic democracy with a minority of 40 percent or more, as would be the case in an Israel extended over the whole of mandatory Palestine. Successful accommodation of Arab citizens within a Jewish Israel clearly assumes a divorce from broader Israel–Palestinian and Israel–Arab issues, if not an overall resolution of the broader conflict.

NOTES

1. Arend Lijphart, *Democracies: Patterns of Majoritarian and Consensus Government in Twenty-One Countries*, Yale: Yale University Press, 1984, pp.1–9. Peter Medding has also made extensive use of the Lijphart categories in his study of the early Israel statehood period: Peter Y. Medding, *The Founding of Israeli Democracy, 1948–1967*, Oxford: Oxford University Press, esp. pp.4–7, 204–10.
2. Lijphart, *Democracies* (note 1) pp.21–30; Lijphart, "Democratic Political Systems: Types, Cases, Causes, and Consequences," *Journal of Theoretical Politics* 1/1 (1989) pp.33–48; Lijphart, *Democracy in Plural Societies: A Comparative Exploration*, Yale, 1977, pp.25–44.
3. Lijphart, "Israeli Democracy and Democratic Reform in Comparative Perspective," in Ehud Sprinzak and Larry Diamond (eds), *Israeli Democracy under Stress*, Boulder, CO: Lynne Rienner, 1993, p.110.
4. For a fuller discussion of traditional Jewish politics, see Alan Dowty, "Jewish Political Traditions and Contemporary Israeli Politics," *Jewish Political Studies Review* 2 (Fall 1990) pp.55–84, and Dowty, *The Jewish State: A Century Later*, California: University of California Press, 1998.
5. Jacob Katz, *Exclusiveness and Tolerance: Studies in Jewish–Gentile Relations in Medieval and Modern Times*, Oxford, 1961, p.196.
6. Sol Roth, *Halakha and Politics: The Jewish Idea of a State*, New York, Ktav and Yeshiva University Press, 1988, pp.124–5; Haim H. Cohn, *Human Rights in Jewish Law*, Ktav, 1984, pp.164–6. Traditional interpretations accepted Christians and Muslims as observers of the seven Noahide laws; see Aharon Kirschenbaum, "Human Rights Revisited," *Israel Yearbook on Human Rights* 6 (1976) pp.229–31.
7. *Gittin*, 60a; *Avoda Zara*, 26a.
8. Cohn, *Human Rights* (note 6) pp.164–6; Maimonides, *Yad, Hilchot Melakhim*, 1:4–5; Roth, *Halakha and Politics* (note 6) p.134.
9. Ian S. Lustick, *Arabs in the Jewish State: Israel's Control of a National Minority*, Texas, 1980, p.5.
10. David Kretzmer, *The Legal Status of Arabs in Israel*, Westview, 1990, p.176.
11. Smooha, "Minority Status in an Ethnic Democracy: The Status of the Arab Minority in Israel," *Ethnic and Racial Studies* 13 (July 1990) p.391; Smooha, *Arabs and Jews in Israel*, Vol. 2, Westview, 1992, p.13.
12. Peled, "Ethnic Democracy and the Legal Construction of Citizenship: Arab Citizens of the Jewish State," *American Political Science Review* 86 (June 1992) pp.432–43.
13. This includes some states that also recognize *jus solis*; a partial list would include Belgium, Bulgaria, Finland, France, Germany, Hungary, Liberia, Poland, Sri Lanka, Switzerland, and the United Kingdom as well as the Soviet Union and most Soviet successor states. Ruth Donner, *The Regulation of Nationality in International Law*, 2nd ed., Irvington-on-Hudson, NY: Transnational, 1954, pp.32, 69, 114–19; United Nations Legal Department, *Laws Concerning Nationalites*, United Nations

ST/LEG/ser.B/4, 1954, pp.222–4, 386–7.
14. Based on the data in *Maps 'N' Facts*, Broderbund Software, 1994; closely-related languages were grouped together and microstates were eliminated.
15. *Freedom in the World: The Annual Survey of Political Rights and Civil Liberties 1994–1995*, Freedom House, 1995, pp.683–4.
16. To strengthen the observation, linguistic divisions in Belize and Cape Verde do not appear to be politically significant, while the controversy over citizenship for Russians in Estonia and Latvia remains a contentious international issue.
17. At the end of 1994 Arabs constituted 19 percent (1.03 million) of a total population of 5.46 million. This was expected to rise to about 21 percent by 2005. Historically the higher birth rate in the Arab sector has been offset by Jewish immigration, and this birth rate has been declining with improved living standards. Consequently demographers project relative stability in the population balance within Israel. *Israel Statistical Abstract 1994*, p.90; Central Bureau of Statistics, "Israel's Population – 5.46 million," Israel Information Service, Internet, 29 Dec. 1994; Calvin Goldscheider, "The Demographic Embeddedness of the Arab–Jewish Conflict in Israeli Society," *Middle East Review* 21 (Spring 1989) p.21.
18. Cynthia Enloe, *Ethnic Soldiers: State Security in Divided Societies*, Georgia: University of Georgia Press, 1980, pp.54–63, 78–82, 136, 182–3, 189–90.
19. This argument is developed by Oren Yiftachel, "The Concept of 'Ethnic Democracy' and its Applicability to the Case of Israel," *Ethnic and Racial Studies* 15 (Jan. 1992) pp.125–36.
20. The exchange between Shammas and Yehoshua is in David Grossman, *Sleeping on a Wire: Conversations with Palestinians in Israel*, Farrar, Straus, and Giroux, pp.257, 270–71.
21. Alex Weingrod, "Shadow Games: Ethnic Conflict and Political Exchange in Israel," *Regional Politics and Policy* 3 (Spring 1993) pp.190–209.
22. Smooha, *Arabs and Jews* (note 11) p.113.
23. Claude Klein, *Israel as a Nation-State and the Problem of the Arab Minority: In Search of Status*, Tel Aviv: International Center for Peace in the Middle East, 1987, p.24; see also Sammy Smooha, "Class, Ethnic, and National Cleavages and Democracy in Israel," in Sprinzak and Diamond, *Israeli Democracy* (note 3) pp.325–6; Smooha, "Minority Status" (note 11) pp.409–10.
24. Smooha, *Arabs and Jews* (note 11) pp.112, 168; Hanna Levinsohn, Elihu Katz, and Majid Al Haj, *Jews and Arabs in Israel: Common Values and Reciprocal Images*, The Guttman Institute of Applied Social Research, 1995, p.23.
25. Dowty, *Jewish State* (note 4) pp.125–36. For background see Shmuel Eisenstadt, *Tradition, Change, and Modernity*, Wiley, 1973, pp.3–21; see also Karl Deutsch, "Social Mobilization and Political Development," *American Political Science Review* 55 (Sept. 1961) pp.17–24; Daniel Lerner, *The Passing of Traditional Society: Modernizing the Middle East*, New York: Free Press, 1958.
26. Eisenstadt, *Tradition* (note 25) pp.23–5.
27. Ibid., p.24.
28. Steve Rodan and Jacob Dallal, "A Fundamental Gamble," *Jerusalem Post International Edition*, 10 Sept. 1994. See also Elie Rekhess, "Resurgent Islam in Israel," *Asian and African Studies* 27 (March/July 1993) pp.189–206; Grossman, *Sleeping on a Wire* (note 20) p.233.
29. Dr. Massoud Eghbarieh of the Givat Haviva Center for Arab Studies, as reported in Haim Shapiro, "Islamic movement waning," *Jerusalem Post International Edition*, 15 July 1995.
30. Boas Evron, *Jewish State or Israeli Nation?*, Indiana: Indiana University Press, 1995, p.210.
31. Oz, "The Secret of the Zionist Magic," in *Under the Blazing Light*, Sifriat Poalim, 1979, p.155.
32. A.E (Election Appeal) 2/88 Ben Shalom v. Chairman of Central Elections Committee 43(2) P.D. 221.

From What *Edah* are You? Israeli and American Meanings of "Race-Ethnicity" in Social Policy Practices

DVORA YANOW

In the development town where I worked for several years, various groups of children delighted in endlessly asking me, "*Me'ezu edah at?*" The answers they were looking for – membership in what is commonly rendered in English as "tribe" and more common-sensically as "ethnic group" of Moroccans, Indians, Tripolitanis, Romanians, Persians, Yemenites, and so on – did not include "*Americanit*" as a possibility. My answer to them consistently left them puzzled (and their frowns eased only when a passing adult jokingly pointed out to them that I was a "*vuzvuzit*," an Ashkenazia).

That *edah* is an operative term in political, as well as daily, affairs may be seen in an examination of Israel's social policy history. But what does the term mean, not in a dictionary sense, but in policy discourse and its enactments? Is that operative meaning comparable to the concepts of "race" and "ethnicity" as used by other nations? Does the notion of *edah* and its use, like "race" and "ethnicity," affect possibilities for social change?

Racial and/or ethnic divisions among a state's population transcend the common polarities of East/West, developed/developing, capitalist/socialist, and so on. Indeed, even among those western countries that seemingly had created a single national identity out of older race-ethnic differences, such as France and Germany, more recent immigrations have raised once again the national identity questions that characterize immigrant countries such as Australia, New Zealand, Canada, the United States, and Israel. There and elsewhere, legal and enacted definitions of race-ethnicity and the categorization of population groups according to "race-ethnic" characteristics (manifested in censuses and other policies) are also linked closely to common definitions of the "good" citizen.

Dvora Yanow is in the Department of Public Administration at California State University, Hayward.

National identity and citizenship questions are enacted through such social policy issues as immigration, immigrant, and language policies, among others.[1] In the context of the present volume, one might ask whether the changes so visible in other parts of Israeli society are also transpiring in its construction of race-ethnicity. While questions of national identity and the image of the "good" citizen certainly concern Israeli Arabs and Palestinians, my focus here is on the Jewish Israeli. I will touch on the implications for non-Jewish Israeli identity toward the end of the article.

Scholars in the field of ethnic studies argue that "race" and "ethnicity" and their associated categories are created by states and societies to establish and reinforce a hierarchy of population groups with attendant power and status.[2] This process is enacted, among other arenas, in the use of these concepts and categories in various public policy and administrative practices. Much ink has been spilled in attempting to define *a priori* what "race" and "ethnicity" are and are not.[3] As D. T. Goldberg notes, most social science exploring the meaning of race has stipulated its definition in keeping with a sense of what the term *should* mean.[4] But how do contemporary Americans and Israelis understand the concepts of race, ethnicity, and *edah*, not conceptually abstracted from a context of practice and daily life, but in their actual use?[5]

What aids and abets the power of these usages is a common public perception that the concepts "race" and "ethnicity" and their associated categories are scientific. On the face of it, "race" and "ethnicity" appear to be universal, grounded in systematic, objective, scientific observations that mirror the "natural" human world.[6] The social and political "realities" of those categories and their entailments typically possess the quality of "common sense"[7] or of "folk wisdom"[8] bolstered by their presumed scientific grounding, as if the categories represented natural kinds. Despite this common sense understanding, neither the concepts of race-ethnicity nor the categories are scientific: most biologists and anthropologists relinquished that idea long ago. It has been replaced in those and allied fields by the understanding that race, ethnicity, and the categories are social constructions reflecting a particular moment in time and its attendant social and political realities.[9]

But this academic perception has largely not permeated into public knowledge or public policies and their enactments. As the concepts and their specific categories are used in daily speech and other acts, their commonly-accepted ontological status is reified. This imputedly scientific and "factual" bolstering carries over into their use in social justice and redistributive policies.

Arenas where social change appears most self-evident often divert attention from areas on which public discourse is silent.[10] The changing sociocultural arenas attracting attention at the moment in Israel are the divisions between Israeli Jews and Palestinians, religious Jews and non-observant Jews, and Russian and Ethiopian immigrant groups and the rest of the Jewish population. What is largely silenced in the discourse concerning population categories with respect to national identity is the extent of internal divisions among Jews, and especially the experiences and perceptions of *mizrahim*. Kook, for example, notes that the most prominent textbooks discuss ethnicity in terms of two broad, dominant (Jewish) groups, *Ashkenazim* and *S'faradim*.[11] While the more apparent divisions are surely transforming Israeli society, there is a risk that these other, silenced arenas will continue on the margins of social change, precisely because they have not (yet) been able to secure a place in public discourse. We may begin to understand why this is the case through a comparative reading of the meanings-in-practice of *edah*. On the face of it, *edah* may seem to have little in common with the American "race" or even with "ethnicity," but in examining their usages, commonalities emerge.

Since silences in public discourse are, by definition, not readily apparent, it can be quite difficult to make them "speak." Taboos and verboten policy goals[12] are tremendously powerful in supporting public silences. Ideas may be discussed in private (in a living room or a cafe or behind closed doors, among family and friends) and still be *publicly* undiscussable – not part of the explicit public agenda. There is a cultural prohibition against talking about them. The emphasis here is on collective and public, rather than private, practices. Indeed, verboten goals may be the subject of private conversations out of "public" hearing.[13]

Much of our knowledge about race and ethnicity is embedded in daily practices, in the categorical and other language used to talk about and "do" race-ethnicity. But although members of a society or polity possess this knowledge conjointly, much of it is known tacitly.[14] We can attempt to make this tacit knowledge explicit by examining the practices in which it is used. Comparative analysis can be helpful in this: it is somewhat easier to identify the public silences and tacit knowledge in a second polity or society and use these processes to reflect on the first one.

Israel and the United States share a similar dynamic process. Both created a national identity out of immigrants and long-term "native" residents from various national-cultural backgrounds.[15] Aside from the creation of governmental documents, institutions, and processes, this entails the constitution, not always explicitly, of the state's collective image of the "good citizen."[16] This is not a matter of immigration law. It speaks, rather, to the unmarked case: the often undefined, unspoken, yet tacitly known norm that comprises the "unhyphenated" national. That term comes from the American experience, in which those immigrants who did not fit the norm became "hyphenated Americans" (especially in the first two-thirds of this century): Italian-Americans, Irish-Americans, Polish-Americans, Jewish-Americans. The unmarked "American," the "good" citizen, at that time was commonly understood to be White, Anglo-Saxon, and Protestant (and it was also tacitly known that this person was a male, middle class property owner). The hyphenation marked a lesser, not-quite-American identity. The unmarked case, while increasingly less common in the US, is still prevalent in Israel: it is still rare to hear references to a Jewish Israeli as distinct from a Christian Israeli or a Palestinian Israeli; "Israeli" commonly denotes the first.

Both Israel and the US were founded on egalitarian principles, in the classless ideology of socialist Zionism and in the adaptation of "classical" liberalism condensed in the constitutional declaration that "all men are created equal."[17] Yet both have developed striated societies, marked in no small part by "race-ethnic" divisions. After every social demonstration, beginning with the Wadi Salib riots of the 1950s, Israel created social policies based on population categories, in the hope each time that the "social gap" would disappear. And yet, "social gaps" remain, most recently given voice by members of the Russian, Ethiopian, and Moroccan/S'faradi communities. Despite economic growth and other social changes, why have these population divisions not disappeared?

CATEGORIZING: THE MEANINGS OF AMERICAN RACE-ETHNICITY[18]

An examination of how "race-ethnic" concepts and categories are used in American policy and administrative practices sheds light on the characteristics of categorizing. Race-ethnic data collection is done most extensively in the US census. The census was initially developed to assess potential tax and voter bases and labor and military pools, the 1870 census being the first to use "race." The collection of race data by agencies other than the Census Bureau was mandated by civil rights legislation beginning in the 1960s.[19] The US Office of Management and Budget (OMB) defined the set of race-ethnic categories that all federal agencies required to collect such data must use. Statistical Directive No. 15, taking effect on 1 January 1980, names and defines five American race-ethnicities (far fewer than the 41 tabulated in the 1990 census): White, Black, Hispanic, Asian or Pacific Islander, American Indian or Alaskan Native. Data are collected in schools, universities, and job training programs, as well as by employers with a minimum number of employees; in hospitals and police departments (in searching for suspected criminals or missing persons, in tracking crimes or infant mortality and birth weights, and to establish treatment, prevention, and apprehension programs). The data collected by the Census for descriptive purposes have, in the last two decades, come to be used in welfare, health, educational, and other policies to allocate program funds based on proportional representation in local populations (e.g., to rural Indian health centers, Asian community centers, job training programs).

Although "common sense" suggests that the two terms refer to different things, analysis of policy documents and agency practices shows that "race" and "ethnicity" are used interchangeably. The census question that asks about "race" includes as tabulated answers colors (White, Black), "peoples" or cultural groups (Eskimo, Aleut, Hmong), and nationalities (Japanese, Chinese). The "ancestry or ethnic origin" question similarly includes both cultural groups (Afro-American) and nationalities (German, Italian). Such usage intermingles three meanings:

1. *race-as-color*, referring to perceived physical differences: facial and skeletal features (different eye, nose, lip, skull, and body shape and hair texture) and blood (in old, now illegal definitions of African-Americans which are, nonetheless, still ensconced in some present day practices,[20] and in current legal definitions of Native Americans for purposes of tribal enrollment, although the notion of genetic material may be replacing blood in common understandings of race-as-color[21]);

2. *race-as-culture*, referring to perceived differences in language, dress, foods, religious practices, and other customs; and

3. *race-as-country-of-origin*, echoing ancient Greek notions of earth, air, sun, water and their related bodily fluids ("humors"), which were later co-located with both physical and behavioral traits.[22]

All of these meanings are carried in contemporary American uses of "race" and "ethnicity." Dictionaries do not help differentiate between them: the *American Heritage Dictionary*, the *Oxford English Dictionary*, and *Webster's II New Revised University* all define "ethnic" using "race" or "racial;" *Webster's* defines "race" in terms of common history or nationality. In mundane and in policy and administrative usages, then, "race" and "ethnicity" are, for all intents and purposes, undifferentiated, which is why I hyphenate them here and treat them as a single entity.

The policy and administrative cases also reveal the ways in which categories operate and convey social and conceptual meaning. Categories highlight elements that are deemed to be similar within the boundaries they draw and different from elements beyond those boundaries. These perceptions of the sameness of things within categories and differences between things in different categories become the organizing principles around which we create categories: something belongs in Category A because it shares "A-ness" and is not "not-A." Persons belong in one American OMB category and not another because of their geographic "origins" (although Indians and Alaskan Natives have an additional, cultural requirement, one of the categorical problems of this schema). A category and its contents are internally undifferentiated, while at the same time being perceived as clearly distinct from all other categories and their contents in the category set.

A set of category names or labels implies two sorts of things about the world of elements being categorized. First, they suggest that nothing has been left out: the categories are exhaustive; everything in the category world has a place in one of the categories. Second, there is no overlap in category membership: the categories are discrete; no element fits into more than one category. By the logic of categories, then, an individual fits one and only one race-ethnic category. One is either White or Black, but not both.[23] Categories become problematic when either (or both) of these two principles is violated. "Category mistakes," whose race-ethnic identity does not fit any single category (either finding no categorical home or fitting into two or more categories at once), present problems of logic for the category set.[24] Yet until recently the US Census Bureau and many other agencies were reluctant to revise their practices to accommodate these social realities. Their attributed scientific standing protects the categories from scrutiny: it is the individual who is in error, not the category.

Categories blind us to other features that nonetheless remain present in the categorized elements (e.g., American race-ethnic identity rests on elements other than "foreign" origins). The highlighting of selected features lends them, on the surface, an importance denied to the occluded features. Furthermore, when a single category is examined, the similarities of its elements become more central than their differences from elements of other categories. But when a set of categories is examined, it is the differences that become most important. The presumedly scientific, factual nature of the concepts and categories allows several policy and administrative practices. One is the identification of individuals race-ethnically by sight, without asking them.[25] Another arises because the categories are pre-determined by the state through its agencies, and individuals who do not find themselves in one of those categories often feel as if they have no choice in self-determined identity (in a society where "choice" is a central part of the political culture). This highlights an additional problem: categories are not treated by individuals as merely statistical entities, which is how the state (through its agencies) treats them. In recent years, categorical usage has taken on the role of providing opportunities for individuals to self-identify as members of a group.

In the US the categories used in race-ethnic-based social policies have become highly contested. As more and more people, asked to identify themselves or their children by race-ethnic background on employment, school admissions, hospital, census, and other questionnaires, refuse to fit their complex identities into the standard five categories, the accuracy and usefulness of these categories are being challenged. Moreover, the recent spread of "hyphenated identities" from European "ethnics" (Italian-Americans, Irish-Americans, Polish-Americans, Jewish-Americans) to other, larger groups (African-American, Asian-American, Latino/a-American, Native American, and now European-American) has presented a very strong conceptual challenge to the "melting pot" assimilatory model. At the same time, however, these five contemporary categories are becoming institutionalized in redistributive mechanisms, challenging the clarity of the concepts of "race" and "ethnicity" themselves.

EDAH: ISRAELI JEWISH 'RACE-ETHNICITY'

Prescriptively speaking, in terms of dictionary definitions, *edah* does not "mean" race or ethnicity.[26] It is translated as "community; congregation; meeting, assembly; flock, swarm, herd."[27] The first three meanings are shared with the word *k'hila*,[28] lending *edah* the sense of a religious community. This sense is underscored by the academic treatment of *edot* in the context of *minhagim*, customs and ceremonies allied with religious groupings (e.g., "*minhag s'farad*" on a prayer book identifying the order of certain prayers following community customs established several hundred years ago). Such treatment often captures the "tribal" sense of *edah*, as in the book title "*Yalkut minhagim: Mi-minhagei shivtei yisrael*" ("An anthology of Jewish communities' [the literal translation is "tribes'"] customs").[29]

"Race," on the other hand, is translated as *geza, 'am, umah, shevet, min, sug, hulya*;[30] and "ethnic" (there is no entry for "ethnicity") is given as *etni (shel g'za'im o amim), giz'i*.[31] *Geza* itself is translated as "trunk, stem, stock; race,"[32] carrying the same historical origins of the English language "race" as a population with a shared ancestor (the so-called "species chain of being," depicted in early anthropological texts as an inverted tree, the "trunk" "branching" into racial divisions).

However, in daily parlance, and most especially in policy-related discourse, *edah* is used as an organizing concept for the provision of redistributive and social justice programs within Jewish Israel. It is in this sense as an ordering population category that it becomes the conceptual equivalent of "race" and "ethnicity" as used in the US and of their equivalents in other countries and languages. By exploring this usage in light of the category practices discussed above, we can begin to discover the ways in which it is shaping public discourse.

The broad, public "discovery" of the so-called "second Israel" in the mid-1960s presented a major challenge to self-perception as a society founded on principles of equality and classlessness. Social policies developed in response to the 1972 Katz Commission report targeted "underprivileged" children (*te'unei tipuah*) and involved formal and non-formal education (the schools, Home Start pre-school programs, the community centers [*matnassim*]), welfare, job training, housing, and other agencies.[33] The terms used in these policies – *te'unei tipuah, mishpahot m'rubot y'ladim*,[34] even "development town residents" – often were proxies for population designations according to a category scheme based on the notion of "*edah*." The categories most commonly given in these policies and in daily parlance for *edah* are geographic place names referring to nation-states or nationalities: Moroccan, Tunisian, Yemenite, Persian, Indian, Iraqi, Russian, German ("*yekke*"), and so on. The category set also includes "people" (Kurd, Georgian, Bukharan); much more rarely one also hears color ("Black") used in this context. In usage, then, *edah* parallels American race-ethnicity: *edah*-as-country, *edah*-as-culture, and *edah*-as-color.

The use of *edah* to refer to Moroccans, Yemenites, and so forth appears, on initial encounter, non-problematic: its lengthy and widespread usage makes *edah* seem common-sensical, natural. But in terms of its prescriptive meanings or in its "tribal" connotation, what sense *does* it make to speak of membership in the French "community," the Russian "congregation," the Iraqi "assembly," the Polish "tribe"?

That the word is not a reflection of natural categories becomes even clearer in its most widespread usage, denoting a collective identity: there are *edot ha'mizrah*, but not "*edot ha'ma'arav*" (Eastern, but not Western, *edot*). Here it becomes clear that *edah* is a marked term, invoked to denote only a subset of the Israeli Jewish population; the non-*mizrahi* is the unmarked case, the norm.[35] We find an example in a 1912 statement of Ben-Gurion's, referring to "Jews in general with no adjective attached, and ... Yemenite Jews."[36] The marked nature of the term becomes even clearer when we consider another use of *edah*: the *edah haredit*, marked off from the secular, non-observant, Jewish Israeli.

The logic of the category terms is, on the face of it, geographic. But if it were *edah*-as-country alone, there should be separate *edah* terms labeled Canadian, English, Australian, Mexican, Argentinian, and so on. Only some nation-states merit *edah* status, in this schema; logics other than geography are present.

Ashkenazim in Europe developed a highly nuanced hierarchy – e.g., the union of a Litvak and a Galitzianer was considered by some an intermarriage – which is preserved much less distinctly among second and later generation immigrants to Israel and North and South America.[37] The existing *Ashkenazi* distinctions in Israel appear to follow the history of aliyot, settlement patterns, and political party affiliations. For example, the sub-categorical distinction made between Germans and Russian-Polish immigrants would seem to reflect waves of immigration and urban/rural, petit bourgeois/kibbutz-moshav-socialist labor distinctions. Similarly, "*Anglo-Saxim*" is a post-1967 creation as a catch-all for English-speaking immigrants from a wide variety of countries of origin who arrived in large numbers after the war. *Edah*-as-culture operates here as a category binder for people whose greatest cultural tie is different dialects of the same language. *Edah*-as-color has largely been avoided, at least in Israeli public discourse. It figures in American Jewish discourse, however, in its negation: Israel's willingness to absorb Ethiopian immigrants is held up by various agencies as proof of the absence of racism (though drawing on American, not Israeli, notions of race).

"Race-Ethnicity" in Social Policy Practices 191

Category logic also requires rules for dealing with unions across categories and their offspring. In the contemporary Israeli Jewish context "intermarriage" most commonly refers to marriages across the *Ashkenazi–Mizrahi* divide, rather than to marriages across subcategories within each of these two broader groups. There is a common assumption that the *Mizrahi* elements will "disappear" into the marriage, with *Ashkenazi* customs, attitudes, and behaviors prevailing.[38] This is in sharp contrast to American usage, in which intermarriage – referring largely to a Black–White union – is seen as diluting the dominant group and diminishing its numbers, rather than strengthening it, as in the Israeli case.[39] Contrary to American practices, Israeli intermarriages "whiten" the children: they become unmarked "Israelis" without *edah*, which is to say, *Ashkenazim*.[40] These practices (as well as the recent contretemps concerning the Ethiopian community) underscore the continuing importance of race-ethnicity-*edah*-as-color/blood/genes.

Many of the social problems of the Jewish Israeli population from the late 1960s into the 1980s – overcrowded housing, inadequate education, drug use, and juvenile delinquency – were identified as problems of the development towns and urban "neighborhoods" (*shkhunot*). These settlement type names themselves became proxies for *edah* categories. But differences of *edah* map irregularly onto Israeli class and geography: not all development town residents are *edot hamizrah* on welfare support; not all urban residents are middle class *Ashkenazim*. And yet, when public discourse on *edah* is silent, it remains difficult to explore these linguistic entailments and their associated social policies and programs.

That *edah* has been the subject of such public silence has been noted by other policy analysts. One of the social policies initiated in 1965 was school "Reform." Initiated by Minister of Education and Culture Zalman Aranne, this restructured secondary education through the establishment of "junior high schools" on the American model. By absorbing students from various backgrounds, these schools were intended to pull the "disadvantaged" up to the level of their urban cohort. Elad Peled asks why, given that Aranne had been Minister since 1955, he did not raise the ethnic issue prior to the Reform effort. His answer is instructive: "[L]ike his party and most of his colleagues, Aranne was for many years 'ethnic-blind.' For him the unity of the nation, the melting-pot orientation, the pioneer image were the leading educational values."[41] These concerns diverted attention, he seems to say, from Jewish ethnicity, thereby silencing it in public discourse.

This "ethnic blindness" could also be described as a class blindness. The *edah* category schema obscures class: country is privileged over economic standing, occluding the longstanding existence of well-to-do *mizrahim* (much as the American categories occlude the existence of a well-established Black middle- and upper-class). The category focus reflects the utopian ideology of Zionism that anticipated a classless reunification and mixing together of Jewish exiles – *kibutz u'mizug galuyot*. Category logic suggests that the country of one's (parents' or grandparents') origin is the most important feature, in keeping with Zionism's focus on diasporic dispersal. It obscures differences internal to each category that might be salient from another point of view.

In reviewing social science research on Israeli ethnicity in the 1950s, H. Goldberg notes that what is striking is the relative absence of the term "ethnicity." Rather, it is referred to by other variables such as "country of origin" or "cultural background." "The trend," he writes, "was to play down the importance of ethnic differences, ... focus ... on institution-building ... and the process of absorbing immigrants into the existing, and developing, social structure ...."[42] The term "ethnic" implied problematic situations and, hence, was avoided.

Ethnicity retained this connotation even when ethnic discourse became more explicit with the discovery in the late 1960s of the "social gap" – the common English translation of both *p'ar hevrati* and *p'ar adati*. Writes Goldberg: "There was an unexamined premise that ethnic influence in Israeli society was something that had to be neutralized,"[43] a premise that he noted continued into the 1980s. In discourse in the field of education, this public silence was quite clear:

> ...the euphemism, *te'unei tipuah* (those in need of care/nurturing) [i.e., "underprivileged" or "disadvantaged," in American parlance]...[entailed] no explicit mention of a specific ethnic group, nor of the general category, *edot ha-mizrah* – the Eastern (Oriental) Jewish communities. However, it was tacitly understood that the education problems referred to were those in the urban neighborhoods and development towns with a high percentage of children from Middle Eastern backgrounds.[44]

Through these decades, a public focus on intra-Jewish social problems was subordinated to the national demands of security. It is perhaps this myth of security (see Barzilai in this volume) that has led to what Avruch and H. Goldberg have identified as the long-term denial in public discussion of the existence of Jewish "ethnicity" in Israel,[45] a silence that is only slowly dissipating. As in the US today, where public attention to "cultural diversity" is feared as sacrificing the *unum* to the *pluribus*, so in Israel the usage of *edah* provokes a similar fear of splitting a unified Jewish front.

RACE-ETHNICITY AND *EDAH*

The American and Israeli cases illustrate that population categories are social constructions that reflect a particular moment in time and its associated sociopolitical needs. The criteria for naming the categories and for dividing people accordingly reflect the point of view of their creators.

In the US, the "Adam" naming Americans according to their kinds reflects the collective historical memory of a "White" person from the Northeast (extending as far as Chicago) who, because of historic encounters with Africans and slavery, sees the race-ethnic world largely in Black–White terms. The categories are given not in alphabetical order (one way in which categorical equivalence is implied) nor in historical order (American Indians and Hispanics, fifth and third in sequence, long preceded the other three), but in the order in which they presented a challenge to the collective definer. It is a power- and status-based order. As the initial schema that demarcated between free persons (of whatever "race") and slaves (of whatever "race") developed a color-*cum*-status-and-behavior hierarchy, non-Whites, -Blacks, and -Indians were added as they appeared on the scene: Chinese (in 1870), Japanese (1880), Mexicans and Filipinos (1930), Hindus and Koreans (1940), Hawaiians (1960), Eskimos, Aleuts, Asian Indians, Vietnamese, Samoans, and Guamanians (1980). Some of the hierarchical rankings pre-dated "New World" settlement; the English imported their ideas about the Irish and Scots, for example, elaborating these prejudices on new soil.

In Israel the naming "Adam" is a secular Jew of Russian-Polish origins, who sees far more variety among those Jews he has never encountered before – *edot hamizrah* – than among the *Ashkenazim* of whom he had prior knowledge and whose languages and practices are more familiar to him.[46] Like the American system, the Israeli hierarchy originated overseas – in Odessans' notions of Berliners, Bialystokers, and Casablancans, for instance – and was then elaborated out of its own particular history of immigration and settlement and the encounter of the socially, politically, and economically dominant group with the "Other."[47] Changing the categories requires, in this sense, reconceptualizing those population histories and their historically-grounded relationships. This accounts, in part, for the difficulties in making such changes, despite the will to legislate change-oriented social policies.

The comparison allows us to explore the extent to which valuative hierarchies are built in to such population divisions. In English language race theory, "race" has connoted, and at times denoted, a descriptive and prescriptive hierarchy of behaviors and associated class and status rankings. To speak of race and use the term in policy practices still slips notions of hierarchy into public discourse.

The notion of *edah* also ascribes a hierarchy, although it is possibly less disabling a concept than race-ethnicity. To the extent that *edah* as it is used corresponds more to *shevet* (tribe) than to *k'hila* (congregation), it has Biblical roots in the tribes that carry Jacob's sons' names.[48] The sons are characterized by particular behaviors, which are projected onto the tribes; but these characterizations seem to be no more than personality traits along the full spectrum of human foibles, not behavioral traits of the same quality as those denoted and connoted by "race" (laziness, excitability): the tribes camp equally around the traveling *aron hakodesh* (ark). "*Edah*," then, retains more of a sense of difference among equals. This would suggest the equalizing strategy of extending *edah* to all Israeli Jews, rather than seeking to eliminate it (a parallel to the increasing hyphenization of all Americans).[49]

It was formerly taboo to discuss race-ethnicity in US public discourse outside of the confines of one's "own" community. While breaking that taboo has not been easy, it is now being done, reflecting major policy and societal changes over the last 30 years. In contrast, Jewish race-ethnicity continues to be largely an area of public silence in Israeli discourse. The consequence is that policies and programs are aimed at groups identified by abstract sociological terms that serve as proxies for unstated assumptions about the supposed traits – class, geographic, "cultural" – of *edah* groups.

Why is there no "affirmative action" in Israel, especially since so many other American ideas have influenced its social policies?[50] There may be many answers, including the appeal to security that serves to unite all Jews conceptually into a single category, smoothing over internal differences. But certainly one of them has to be that social policy action cannot be taken toward a category of people in the absence of explicit talk about the qualities that constitute that category and differentiate it from other possible category schemas. *Edah* needs to be named in public discourse before that discourse can lead to policy action. While overall economic and social situations for various groups have certainly improved, differential treatment, often of a subtle form, still persists, and objective measures (of income, education, and the like) will not remediate the problems concerning these differences that silences in public discourse support. Such silence enables a political science graduate student to be told not to pursue research on *mizrahim* because she "will not get an academic position" or he "will not pass his thesis defense,"[51] or universities to use sociology textbooks that link *edot* to stereotypic, collective behavioral traits. Without public discourse, groups cannot tell their collective stories, and this renders them publicly invisible. If anything may be learned from the American case, it is that perhaps the greatest potential source of change is the ability to publicly tell one's story in terms of a collective experience, using and sometimes challenging and changing state-sanctioned categories. The image of the unmarked "good" citizen is thereby made more inclusive.[52]

At the broader national level, the *edah* system is, as presently conceived, not usable. The principle of differentiation becomes a complex intersection of land-based religion (Jew / Roman Catholic / Muslim / Greek Orthodox and so on) and "peoplehood" (Jew / Palestinian): race-ethnicity as '*am*.[53] As matters of Palestinian statehood develop, and with it explorations of Israeli national identity and symbols, race-ethnic category schemes are likely to change.[54] Is a Palestinian *edah* unthinkable?

A paradigm shift in perception and the language that expresses it is necessary. The silence on Jewish ethnicity in public discourse must be broken; the point of view from which *edah* is constructed must be made explicit and its use be made all-encompassing or be eliminated altogether. As presently enacted, it maintains a hierarchy of population groups and limits possibilities for social change.

NOTES

1. I am making a distinction here between policies that regulate prospective "immigration" (which, in the US at least, are often closely aligned with foreign policies) and policies toward "immigrants" designed to facilitate their absorption/assimilation after their arrival. Unlike Israel, the US has little, at this time, by way of immigrant policy, and what does exist – mostly in the form of language and citizenship training – is left to local governments, non-profit organizations, and voluntary associations.
2. Cf. Davydd J. Greenwood, *The Taming of Evolution*, Ithaca, NY: Cornell University Press, 1984.
3. In the American context, see, e.g., David Theo Goldberg, "The Semantics of Race," *Ethnic and Racial Studies* 15/4 (Oct. 1992) pp.543–69 for an overview on "race," and J. Milton Yinger, "Ethnicity," *Annual Review of Sociology* 11 (1985) pp.151–80 for a review of "ethnicity" that in current reading reveals changes in understanding over the last decade, as well as Michael Omi and Howard Winant, *Racial Formation in the United States*, 2nd edition, NY: Routledge, 1994, and other referenced sources.
4. D.T. Goldberg, "Semantics" (note 3) p.544.
5. Public policy and administrative practices may be read as texts (or "text-analogues," in Taylor's phrase) to yield an understanding of what these concepts and their associated categories mean for a given polity and to explore the role of race-ethnic processes in state-building and national identity. Charles Taylor, "Interpretation and the Sciences of Man," *Review of Metaphysics* 25 (1971) pp.3–51; see also Paul Ricoeur, "The Model of the Text: Meaningful Action Considered as Text," *Social Research* 38 (1971) pp.529–62. I follow here the methodological approach of Mary Douglas, *Purity and Danger*, London: Routledge & Kegan Paul, 1966 (see Robert Wuthnow, James Davison Hunter, Albert Bergesen, and Edith Kurzweil, *Cultural Analysis*, NY: Routledge & Kegan Paul, 1984, Ch.3: "The cultural anthropology of Mary Douglas") and the conceptual approaches of Murray Edelman, *Political Language*, NY: Academic Press, 1977 and George Lakoff, *Women, Fire, and Dangerous Things*, Chicago: University of Chicago Press, 1987.
6. I have elaborated elsewhere on the presumedly factual, scientific nature of race-ethnic categories and their use in American policy and administrative practices. See Dvora Yanow, "American Ethnogenesis and Public Administration," *Administration & Society* 27/4 (Feb. 1996) pp.483–509; "American Ethnogenesis and the US Census," in Carol Greenhouse (ed.), *Democracy and Difference*, Albany, NY: SUNY Press, 1998; and *"Doing" Race/ethnicity: American Ethnogenesis in Policy and Administrative Practices*, manuscript under review. On category construction from the perspective of cognitive linguistics, see Lakoff, *Women* (note 5); from an anthropological perspective, see Douglas, *Purity* (note 5). On categories and their use in political science, see Edelman, *Political Language* (note 5) and *From Art to Politics: How Artistic Creations Shape Political Conceptions*, Chicago: University of Chicago Press, 1995. On the link between "racial" categories and nature, see Greenwood, *Taming* (note 2).
7. Clifford Geertz, "Common Sense as a Cultural System," in *Local Knowledge*, NY: Basic Books, 1983, Ch. 4.
8. Lakoff, *Women* (note 5).
9. Compare, for example, anthropological texts as late as the 1970s, which claimed that there are 'n' races in the world. The number typically given is 3 – Mongoloid, Negroid, and Caucasoid – but it ranges as high as 200 (Stanley Garn, *Readings on Race*, 2nd edition, Springfield, IL: Charles C. Thomas, 1968, p.9). For social constructionist

arguments, see Greenwood, *Taming* (note 2) or Ian F. Haney Lopez, "The Social Construction of Race," *Harvard Civil Rights Civil Liberties Law Review* 29/1 (Winter 1994) pp.1–62 or *White by Law*, New York University Press, 1995.
10. Dvora Yanow, "Silences in Public Policy Discourse: Policy and Organizational Myths," *Journal of Public Administration Research and Theory* 2/4 (Oct. 1992).
11. Rebecca Kook, "Between Uniqueness and Exclusion," in Michael N. Barnett (ed.), *Israel in Comparative Perspective*, Albany, NY: SUNY Press, p.218.
12. Yanow, "Silences" (note 10).
13. I elaborate on this argument in Dvora Yanow, *How Does a Policy Mean?*, Washington, DC: Georgetown University Press, 1996, Ch.7.
14. As Polanyi meant that term: "We know much more than we can tell"; Michael Polanyi, *The Tacit Dimension*, Doubleday, 1966, p.4.
15. Yael Zerubavel, *Recovered Roots: Collective Memory and the Making of Israeli National Tradition*, Chicago: University of Chicago Press, 1995, presents an interesting discussion of rituals and mythmaking in the creation of Israeli identity. See Oliver Robertson, *American Myth, American Reality*, New York: Hill & Wang, 1980, on the American case.
16. I am drawing here on an idea that emerges from Carole Pateman's work in the last decade concerning what constitutional documents assume about the identity of the "good" citizen. See, for example, her "'God hath Ordained to Man a Helper': Hobbes, Patriarchy, and Conjugal Right," in Mary Lyndon Shanley and Carole Pateman (eds), *Feminist Interpretations and Political Theory*, Pennsylvania State University Press, 1991.
17. See Carole Pateman, *Participation and Democracy Theory*, Cambridge University Press, 1970, on the different strains of "classical" liberalism.
18. The following section is a highly condensed summary of the empirical research and theoretical argument developed in Yanow, "American Ethnogenesis and Public Administration," "American Ethnogenesis and the US Census," and *"Doing" Race/Ethnicity*, which include detailed textual analyses of the 1990 US census questionnaire and its race/ethnic-related analytic categories, OMB Directive No.15 and its definitions of American race-ethnicities, EEOC policy statements relative to identifying employees by race-ethnicity, recently published academic and practitioner articles on managing workplace cultural diversity, and the policies and administrative practices of several local agencies.
19. The 1964 Civil Rights Act created the Equal Employment Opportunity Commission (EEOC) and charged it with implementing Title VII (employment protections) and other guidelines. The Civil Rights Act did not define the meaning of "race" – it was assumed to be common sense knowledge – nor does it mention ethnicity. In 1967 President Lyndon Baines Johnson signed Executive Order 11246 requiring government agencies and contractors to establish affirmative action plans for the inclusion of "minorities" in the workplace; Raymond A. Friedman, *The Balanced Workforce at Xerox Corporation*, Harvard Business School Case No. 9-491-049, Rev. 3/21/91. The US Civil Service Commission, which administered EEO programs from 1965 through 1978 – they were then transferred to the EEOC, under the Civil Service Reform Act of that year – defined "minority-group member" primarily to mean (in the terms most common at that time) blacks, Hispanics (Spanish-surnamed persons), American Indians, and Orientals, and sometimes also Eskimos and Aleuts; David H. Rosenbloom, "The Federal Affirmative-Action Policy," in D. Nachmias (ed.), *The Practice of Policy Evaluation*, New York: St. Martin's Press, 1980, p.171.
20. California hospitals, for instance, identify infants by the race-ethnic backgrounds of their parents. The child follows the father in all cases except the following, when it is assigned its mother's identity: (1) if the father is White and the mother is not (i.e., a child is White only if both parents are White); (2) if the mother is Hawaiian; (3) if the mother is a more specific Asian or Other category than the father (e.g., if the mother is Chinese and the father is unspecified Asian); (4) if the father's background is unknown or the parties refuse to identify his background. See also F. James Davis, *Who is Black?*, University Park, PA: The Pennsylvania State University Press, 1991.
21. This shift from blood to genes as an indicator of "race" is being made through the publication of epidemiological and other medical research that correlates the incidence of disease by demographic group, and is reinforced, I believe, by the work of the Human Genome Diversity Project despite their insistence that genetic changes occur

along a continuum rather than along sharply demarcated demographic lines. In communication to a lay public, the meaning of taking a statistical sample is lost, and the correlation becomes understood as a prototype instead.
22. Cf. Greenwood, *Taming* (note 2).
23. This practice undermines the notion of "race" as a set of traits inherited through blood or genetic material. If race is indeed inherited, then there can be no choosing in the case of "mixed" race: *all* of one's ancestors determine one's race.
24. Examples in an American context come from Blacks who look White (e.g., Judith Scales-Trent, *Notes of a White Black Woman*, University Park, PA: Pennsylvania State University Press, 1995) and from "mixed race" individuals (e.g., Maria P.P. Root (ed.), *Racially Mixed People in America*, Newbury Park: Sage, 1992; Gregory Howard Williams, *Life on the Color Line*, New York: Dutton, 1995; Naomi Zack, "An Autobiographical View of Mixed Race and Deracination," *American Philosophical Association Newsletter on Philosophy and the Black Experience* 91/1 (Spring 1992) pp.6–10 and *American Mixed Race*, Lanham, MD: Rowman & Littlefield, 1995).
25. This, indeed, is the policy of the EEOC: employers are required to identify employees without asking them, according to its Standard Form 100 (rev. 4-89, OMB No. 3046-0007). After listing the definitions presented in OMB No. 15, it tells the employer, who must file Information Report EEO-1 documenting workplace racial composition: "You may acquire the race/ethnic information necessary for this report either *by visual surveys* of the work force, or from post-employment records as to the identity of employees. *Eliciting information* on the race/ethnic identity of an employee *by direct inquiry is not encouraged*" (emphasis added). And it carries the further proviso: "Race/ethnic designations as used by the EEOC do not denote scientific definitions of anthropological origins. For the purposes of this report, an employee may be included in the group to which he or she *appears to belong, identifies with*, or *is regarded in the community* as belonging. However, no person should be counted in more than one race/ethnic group" (first three emphases added). Other agencies follow similar practices.
26. In comparative analysis the issue of translation has to be engaged. The researcher cannot "simply" translate: cultural practices and contexts have meaning; terms are not identical in denotation or connotation. This is particularly true of "race," "ethnicity," and their equivalents. On translation see Mark Rutgers, "The Meaning of Administration: Translating Across Boundaries," *Journal of Management Inquiry* 5/1 (March 1996) pp.14–20.
27. Reuben Alcalay, *The Complete Hebrew-English Dictionary*, Tel Aviv-Jerusalem, Massadah Publishing Company, 1965, p.1854; the entry in Marcus Jastrow, *A Dictionary of the Targumim, the Talmud Babli, and Yerushalmi, and the Midrashic Literature*, London: Luzac, 1903, is similar.
28. Alcalay, *Hebrew-English* (note 27) p.2244.
29. Its author is Avraham ben Yaakov (Jerusalem: Hamadpis hamemshalti, 1967); cited by Zerubavel, *Recovered Roots* (note 15) p.268, n.7.
30. Reuben Alcalay, *The Complete English-Hebrew Dictionary*, Hartford, CT: Prayer Book Press, 1962, p.2982. Rendered in English, these are: (for *geza*, see next sentence) people, nation, tribe, kind, type, chain.
31. Alcalay, *English-Hebrew* (note 30) p.1267. English translation: ethnic (belonging to *geza* [in plural] or peoples).
32. Alcalay, *Hebrew-English* (note 27) p.341.
33. Cf. *Prime Minister's Commission for Children and Youth in Distress*, Jerusalem: State of Israel, Prime Minister's Office, Oct. 1972. An English version was published by the Szold National Institute for Research in the Behavioral Sciences (Publication no. 545, July 1973).
34. Literally, families with many children, this referred initially to a family of 5 or more children; it was later revised downward to 4 or more.
35. There is another line of inquiry that needs to be pursued concerning the changing collective category names for *edot hamizrah* (S'faradi, Oriental, *Mizrahi*) and their different connotations. Joelle Bahloul, "The Sephardic Jew as Mediterranean: A View from Kinship and Gender," *Journal of Mediterranean Studies* (1994) explores the construction of the Sephardic Jew as Mediterranean in the context of European Jewish life. In addition to adding another category name and dimension to the discussion, her analysis reflects some of the history and background to the Israel-based construction, although this is not directly her subject.

36. In context "Jews in general" clearly denotes eastern European Jews. David Ben-Gurion, "A single constitution," *Haachdut* (1912); quoted in Gershon Shafir, *Land, Labor and the Origins of the Israeli–Palestinian Conflict, 1882–1914*, Cambridge, 1989, p.91.
37. The internal distinctions went far beyond just Litvaks and Galitzianers. Sholom Aleichem's *Marienbad* (transl. Aliza Shevrin, NY: Putnam, 1982/1917) captures some of these fine gradations. See also Raphael Patai, *The Vanished Worlds of Jewry*, New York: Macmillan, 1980, for discussion of such hierarchical attitudes.
38. Different Pesah food customs is a concern from another point of view. Rabbinical dictum mandates that the wife is to learn to prepare food according to the husband's customs.
39. This attitude was long institutionalized in many state laws, known collectively as the "one-drop rule." Although it is now illegal, the attitude continues (among African-Americans as well as European-Americans; see Davis, *Who?* (note 20) and it is still institutionalized in some administrative practices (e.g., employers identifying individuals by sight, hospitals identifying infants as "White" only if both parents are "White"; see note 20 and Yanow, *"Doing"* (note 6) Ch.5).
40. That marriage "purifies" taint can be seen in the talmud in Tractate Kidushin, ch.4. For example, the daughter of someone ineligible for priestly support (that is, someone whose parentage violated category separation, such as a cohen and a divorcee) can, herself, be eligible to marry a cohen.
41. Elad Peled, "The Educational Reform in Israel," in E. Ben-Baruch and Y. Neumann (eds), *Educational Administration and Policy Making*, Beersheva: Ben-Gurion University and Unipress-Academic Publications, 1982, p.105.
42. Harvey Goldberg, "The Changing Meaning of Ethnic Affiliation," *The Jerusalem Quarterly* 44 (Fall 1987) p.42.
43. Ibid., p.43.
44. Ibid., emphases added.
45. Kevin Avruch, "The Emergence of Ethnicity in Israel," *American Ethnologist* 14 (May 1987) pp.327–39 (Review article); H. Goldberg, "Changing Meaning" (note 42).
46. Zerubavel, *Recovered Roots* (note 15) p.230 notes that the image of a Russian Jewish hero (Trumpeldor) as the "New Hebrew" was created by secular, eastern European Jews as part of a "shared collective memory" that only now is being challenged by different groups as not quite widely enough "shared." Attempts to preserve Trumpeldor's place in the national mythology is evidence of a desire to perpetuate that hegemonic position. She quotes an Israeli man of Middle Eastern heritage telling her, "Honey, if Trumpeldor were a Yemenite, no street would have been named after him."
47. See, for example, Shafir, *Land* (note 36) Ch.4, a Yishuv-era history of relations between Yemenites and Ashkenazim from a wage labor perspective, noting the various hierarchical and egalitarian attitudes of the latter toward the former and the former's desire to be integrated as equals.
48. The census in Leviticus is counted by these tribal divisions and by families within each of them. The earliest post-Biblical historical record of population categories that I have found to date is in Tractate Kidushin 69a ("*Asara yohasin 'alu mi-bavel...*") in the Talmud. A fascinating discussion ensues about categories and their constitution. It relates to the matter of (inter)marriage as well as to Jewish identity, all articulated from an unnamed, yet presumed, categorizing point of view (those in Babylon) apparently worried about community purity and competition from Jerusalem and elsewhere.
49. For the US this suggests the possibly productive alternative of replacing the term "race" with "community" and to speak of five American "communities" rather than of five American race-ethnicities.
50. The question originally was David Levi-Faur's, asked at the September 1996 conference where this work was first presented.
51. These experiences occurred recently. They were related to me in confidence.
52. We learn this also from the post-war experiences of Holocaust survivors and their children, whose stories were silenced but on behalf of whom action was possible once their stories could be publicly and collectively named and publicly and collectively told. See Dan Bar-On, *Legacy of Silence*, Harvard University Press, 1989, for a variation on this idea, treating the implications for the children of prominent Nazis of familial and public silences.
53. At this level another category schema – *le'om* – takes over. One sign that ethnicity is

"Race-Ethnicity" in Social Policy Practices

not a fixed quality is the extent to which Jews appear or are treated as a single, unified ethnicity (or "race") when living among non-Jews. In this light it is perhaps ironic that internal distinctions have been developed for social policy purposes. But at best, this is only a partial explanation for why a (Jewish) Israeli is an Israeli (or a Jew) outside Israel and, say, French, American or Moroccan inside. Nationality (le'om) and ethnicity are categories operating at different levels of analysis; they are answers to different questions and assumptions. Americans are often ethnics internally (and in communities and families), but a nationality outside their borders, much as Maori are "kiwis" (New Zealanders) when traveling outside their borders.

54. That the central political symbols of the state – the flag, the emblem, the anthem – are built on Jewish elements (the star of David, the menorah, the longing for a return to Zion) that exclude non-Jewish Israelis is only now becoming publicly discussable (see, e.g., Clyde Haberman, "The Arabs in Zion: What symbols for them?," *New York Times*, 6/1/95, national edition p.A3). See also Joel S. Migdal, "Society-formation and the Case of Israel," in Michael N. Barnett (ed.), *Israel in Comparative Perspective*, Albany, NY: SUNY Press, 1996, Ch.7; Kook, "Uniqueness" (note 11) and Zerubavel, *Recovered Roots* (note 15).

Changing Places: Jerusalem's Holy Places in Comparative Perspective

ROGER FRIEDLAND and RICHARD D. HECHT

For much of the past decade we have studied the politics of Jerusalem, a site sacred and sovereign to both Palestinians and Israelis. Merging urban sociology and religious history, we have analyzed the city's politics as a struggle over the organization and meaning of time and space, both in daily life and at the most sacred sites in the city. Much of the literature confirms Michael N. Barnett's observation that

> [F]or many social scientists the Israeli case represents an unapproachable challenge, its rich and complex history producing a case inappropriate for the comparative enterprise. Because Israel is unique in many dimensions, its slips through the cracks of social science inquiry into historical peculiarity.[1]

Often the argument for uniqueness rests squarely on the city of Jerusalem. Implicit in the description of Jerusalem as holy to Judaism, Christianity, and Islam contained in almost every analysis of the city is the argument for incomparability. But few have done more than examine the historical layers of religious meanings ascribed to the city by the three religious traditions. Relying on the classical dichotomy of the sacred and profane, these analyses suggest that Jerusalem's sanctity is incomparable to that of any other city. This incomparability is registered by the claims of three religious traditions whose control or absence of control over the city have meant many different things in their separate and intertwined histories. Jerusalem is thus seen as a unique case.

Some studies locate the incomparability of Jerusalem in more subtle arguments in which theology overcomes the people, cultures, and politics of the city. Karen Armstrong's recent history of Jerusalem, one of the best of the past decade, exemplifies the more subtle, hidden

---

Roger Friedland and Richard D. Hecht are at the Department of Sociology and Department of Religious Studies, University of California, Santa Barbara.

argument for uniqueness. Armstrong writes about the sacred, myth, and symbolism. But in the end, her Jerusalem becomes so unique that it can only be understood within the theological histories of Judaism, Christianity, and Islam. Social justice and compassion, rooted in the unique religious perceptions of the city and in the histories of the three religions, are essential to the city's meaning. When they have been transgressed, the city has fallen. For Armstrong, the functions of faith are to "to help build up a sense of self" and

> the importance of transcending the fragile and voracious ego, which so often denigrates others in its yearnings for security. Leaving the self behind is not only a mystical objective; it is required also by the disciplines of compassion, which demand that we put the rights of others before our own selfish desires.

Salvation, she continues, for the people of Jerusalem, whether they are religious or secular

> must mean more than the mere possession of a city. There must also be a measure of interior growth and liberation.... The societies that have lasted the longest in the holy city have, generally, been the ones that were prepared for some kind of tolerance and coexistence in the Holy City. That, rather than a sterile and deadly struggle for sovereignty, must be the way to celebrate Jerusalem's sanctity today.[2]

This understanding of salvation is highly particularistic and seems to be predicated on an Enlightenment view of religion in which religion becomes an individual experience. Interiority subordinates religion's power to construct the external world and community.

We wish to suggest in this article that Jerusalem's sanctity invites precisely the kind of comparative analysis called for by Michael Barnett in the passage noted above by comparing epochal moments of collective violence in Jerusalem with those of another sacred center in India. When one of India's most sacred sites, the Ramjanmabhumi/Babri Masjid in the city of Ayodhya, became the focal point of a protracted struggle between Hindus and Muslims in the 1980s, we were naturally intrigued. Were there similarities between this sacred place and the conflict over Jerusalem's *har ha-bayit/al-haram as-sharif* contested between Jews and Muslims, Israelis and Palestinians?

Based on the research that developed out of these questions, we will suggest that essentialist readings of sacred places, whether they be in Jerusalem or Ayodhya or in some other locale, cannot apprehend the historical transformation of meanings of those places and the role of politics in constituting those meanings. Historical change in the meaning of a sacred place is a very difficult conclusion for those who adhere to the essentialist model. Admitting that politics, including struggles over sovereignty, affect the formation, maintenance, reproduction, and transformation of the meanings is equally difficult for the essentialists.

We will argue that contests over control of sacred sites like the Ram Temple and Babri Mosque in Ayodhya or the Temple Mount and Noble Sanctuary in Jerusalem are a mechanism for challenging and transforming the definition of citizenship in the modern nation-state. Indeed, these contests are consistent with the ancient function of these sites in centralizing the polity and as platforms for mobilization against foreign rule.

TEMPLES OF DOOM

On the morning of 6 December 1992 more than 300,000 *Rama kar sevaks*, "volunteers in service to Sri Rama" descended upon the city of Ayodhya intent upon destroying the Babri mosque and rebuilding a new consecrated temple marking the birthplace of Rama, the divine avatar of Vishnu, or as he is known in North India, Ram. The Indian Supreme Court had ruled earlier that no Temple should be built on the land partially occupied by the Babri Masjid and that the mosque should remain untouched. Nonetheless, the three major religious nationalist groups[3] had called upon Hindus from all over India to come to Ayodhya to build Lord Ram's Temple.[4] On 5 December, Hindu leaders met in Ayodhya to decide whether to build temple or only symbolically clear and sanctify the ground for construction at a later time. The Indian government had dispatched more than 15,000 paramilitary troops to protect the Babri Masjid and fortify the steel and barbed-wire fencing surrounding it. Shortly before noon on 6 December, 40,000 *kar sevaks* of the RSS youth movement Bajrang Dal filtered through the cordons of military police, who offered little resistance. They were led by a throng of sadhus shouting "Jai Sri Ram" ("Victory to Lord Ram"). Wave upon wave of Hindu holy men and *kar sevaks* brandishing clubs, iron pipes, and swords pushed through the police and army lines, trampling the steel fences and barbed-wire. Once inside the enclave, a specially trained force of some 1,200 climbed to the mosque's domes and began smashing through its ceilings with hammers. In less than six hours, the mob tore down the mosque brick-by-brick using shovels, pickaxes, and their bare hands until nothing remained. That night, the *kar sevaks* entered the Muslim quarter of the city, killed ten Muslims, and razed nearly a hundred houses. Others built a temporary temple on the site of the destroyed mosque. Their building continued into the next day, and on the evening of 7 December, the *kar sevaks* began to leave on specially arranged trains and buses while the army moved in to take control of the temple site.[5]

For the next weeks India was shattered by inter-communal violence. Huge sections of India's major cities were placed under military curfew. As many as 1,200 people died in the violence and over 5,000 were wounded. More than 50,000 homes (this excluding large sections of shanty-towns) were destroyed in fires that burned whole sections of cities. More than 100,000 small businesses and offices were looted or torched. Villages in which there was very little "communalism" suddenly were split into warring camps. This round of communal violence was the worst since partition. The central government outlawed worship of Ram at the site (although the District Magistrate lifted the ban on 2 January 1993) and dismissed the BJP governments in the four states it ruled. The RSS, the Bajrang Dal, and the VHP were temporarily banned, and key leaders of the BJP and VHP were marched off to jail or put under house arrest, though all were released within a month. This was followed by a second wave of even more intense communal violence centered in Bombay a month later. While the press described the violence as consuming "shanty towns," these were in reality the areas where the majority of Bombay's urban population was located. Bal Thackeray's Shiv Sena militants organized large collective rituals, *maharatis*, in Bombay's major temples to contest Friday prayers in the city's mosques.[6] The destruction of the Babri Masjid had international repercussions. In Pakistan, dozens of Hindu temples were attacked, and Muslims demonstrated outside Indian embassies around the world, while Interpol and the FBI braced for assassinations and violence in New York, Paris, and London.[7]

The violence at Ayodhya recalled another deadly confrontation in Jerusalem two years before. On 8 October 1990, as many as 5,000 Palestinians massed on Jerusalem's *al-haram as-sharif* to prevent an incursion into its sacred precincts by a small group of Jewish nationalists who called themselves the "Faithful of the Temple Mount." Formed in the early 1980s, this group was determined to lay the foundation stone of a third Jewish temple. The Jerusalem police had banned the demonstration as a provocation, and the Israeli High Court of Justice upheld the police ban. Sermons in al-Aqsa mosque the preceding Friday had called upon Palestinians to defend the sanctity of *al-haram as-sharif*. At about 8:30 am, the plaza in front of the Western Wall directly below the *haram* was filled with more than 20,000 Jews celebrating Sukkot. At approximately 10:30 am, as the Sukkot service ended, the leader of the Faithful of the Temple Mount, Gershon Salomon, and about 50 followers attempted to enter the *haram* at the Mughrabian Gate above the Western Wall plaza. They were met by Israeli Border Police and Municipal Police who ordered them to turn back. "We shall continue our struggle until the Israeli flag is flying from the Dome of the Rock," Salomon defiantly retorted.[8] The group left carrying a banner which proclaimed "Temple Mount – The Symbol of Our People is in the Hands of Our Enemies."

According to initial press reports, the Palestinians subsequently began, without provocation, to throw rocks over the *haram's* walls onto the Jews below in the plaza of the Western Wall. These press accounts of the attack by the Palestinians massed on the *haram* were contradicted later in the official report of the Zamir Commission, by Palestinian and

Israeli civil rights groups, and in the inquest findings of the Jerusalem Magistrate's Court Judge Ezra Kama. While the police were turning away Salomon's group, Border Police within the *haram* patrolled the periphery of the Palestinian demonstrators. Someone in the patrol accidentally dropped a tear-gas canister which rolled into a group of Palestinian women. The Palestinians responded by throwing stones at the police, which continued as the police retreated. Many of these stones fell on the plaza in front of the Western Wall, but by then most of the Jews had fled, scared by the earlier gunfire. The police regrouped and re-entered the *haram* and began spraying bullets at the crowd. Within a matter of minutes 17 Palestinians had been shot to death and more than 100 seriously wounded.[9] Judge Kama held both the Israelis and Palestinians responsible for the tragedy. Neither had done much to prevent a "trivial incident" from becoming the deadliest confrontation between Palestinians and Israelis in Jerusalem since 1967. Further, Judge Kama concluded that in some cases individual police officers faced "real danger" and were justified in using deadly fire, but in others live ammunition was used "without reasonable need."

In the aftermath of this massacre, the violent clashes between Palestinians who had been engaged in an uprising since December, 1987 and Israeli soldiers and settlers intensified. A number of Jews were subsequently murdered in Jerusalem by Islamic militants intent upon avenging the dead Palestinians and the profanation of the *haram*. Also for the first time, religious Jews, with the support of Ariel Sharon, then Minister of Housing, were able to force through a significant Jewish residential settlement in an all-Arab neighborhood just outside the Old City walls.

CONTESTED SACRED CENTERS

Both Jerusalem and Ayodhya are contested sacred centers, between Jews and Muslims in the first case, Hindus and Muslims in the second. In Jerusalem, the same sixty square acre platform Jews refer to as *har ha-bayit* or the Temple Mount, is known by Muslims and Palestinians as *al-haram as-sharif* or the Noble Sanctuary. For Jews this is the site King David purchased for the Israelite nation's first Temple, built by his son Solomon, a Temple destroyed and rebuilt after their return from the Babylonian Exile. The structure was expanded by Herod the Great in the last quarter of the first century BCE and subsequently destroyed again during the Jewish nationalist revolt against Roman rule in 70 CE.

Jews considered this site, at the center of which stood the Holy of Holies, as the center of the world, the place from which God constructed the cosmos, the rock upon which Abraham had bound his son Isaac for sacrifice. It functioned as the sacrificial site, the locus of order between human and divine worlds, the destination of the annual Jewish pilgrimages of Sukkot, Passover, and Shavuot.

For Muslims, *al-haram as-sharif* is the site identified with the miraculous night journey of the prophet Muhammad described in Sura 17 of the *Qur'an* and the prophet's ascent into the heavens where the daily order of prayer was revealed to him. Later traditions would expand this text and its identification with Jerusalem. As the prophet entered this area, he tethered in mid-air his magical steed, Buraq, to the western wall of the *haram*, known to this day as al-Buraq, the same site Jews hold sacred as the Western Wall, one of the remaining walls of the Temple complex destroyed by the Romans.

Just as Jerusalem is a vast complex of Jewish, Christian, and Islamic shrines, temples, tombs, and sanctuaries, Ayodhya with its population of 40,000, located on the Sarayu River, approximately 300 miles northeast of New Delhi in India's largest state Uttar Pradesh, is a vast complex of Hindu, Buddhist, Jain, and Muslim sacred places. There are some 3000 Hindu temples in Ayodhya. As a *tirtha* (literally a "ford" or "crossing") or place of pilgrimage it draws more than a million pilgrims per year. It is a center for the worship of Ram, one of the most popular deities of North India. Ayodhya is also the center of the Ramanandis, one of India's largest orders of *sadhus* or ascetics. This ascetic order is composed of three different groups. The *tyagis* are wandering "abandoners" who move about among the nine major pilgrimage centers and sacred places dedicated to the worship of Vishnu. The *nagas* or "naked" warriors live in *akharas*, military encampments or fortresses. The *rasiks* are "enjoyers of the bliss" of serving Ram and his consort Sita. They live in the temples dedicated to the two deities, serving them, attending to their ritual needs, and beautifying their temples.

As a *tirtha*, Ayodhya connects heaven and earth, life and death, and the living with the ancestors. Two groups of *pandus* or *tirthpurohits*, Brahman pilgrimage-priests serve pilgrims who visit its temples and the Sarayu to be set free from impurity, from transgressions, and from sickness, to gain merit in the complex ritual venerations of the river itself, to cremate a corpse, to guide the dead across the river of death, or to feed the ancestors. As Peter van der Veer has demonstrated, these two Brahman orders are central to the economy of pilgrimage at Ayodhya and their relationships have not been free of violence.

For Hindus, Ayodhya is the birthplace of Ram, an incarnation of Lord Vishnu, the paradigmatic exemplar of all Hindu virtues. According to the *Rama-katha*, one of two great epics about the creation of a mythical Indian kingdom, Rama is the father of the Hindu nation, the perfect king who brings happiness and prosperity to his whole realm and to all people.[10] His reign, *rama rajya*, is the index by which all existing political structures are to be judged and the utopia toward which Hindu history and the Indian polity must be pushed. As Hans Bakker has shown, the control of Ayodhya is not limited to remembrance, but is equally important as a continuing manifestation of the divine. The mosque then is an encroachment on the divine itself and the struggle to protect the site from a profaning incursion is a divine battle.[11] The place of King Rama's birth was marked with a splendid temple, the Ramjanmabhumi, which remained even after Rama moved his capital to Saketa and the city went into decline. Hindus argue that, while the Ramjanmabhumi was repeatedly lost and recovered throughout the city's history, the Temple was only destroyed in the sixteenth century when a nobleman in the court of the first Moghul Emperor Babur tore its walls down to construct the Babri Masjid in honor of the emperor on the former temple's location.

In a similar manner, the symbolic meanings of Jerusalem's *har ha-bayit* and *al-haram as-sharif* were intensified in the history of Judaism and Islam. For Jews, the Temple Mount was integrated into an increasingly centralized mythical geography surrounding the *even-shetiyyah*, the stone of foundation, which pointed to a messianic future in which the Temple would be rebuilt. For Muslims, Jerusalem will be the site where God will judge the righteous and evil-doers. Likewise, the symbolic meanings of Ayodhya have been expanded, in some cases reworking traditional Hindu myths. According to the Hindi guidebook to Ayodhya, *Ayodhyaji ka Prachin Itihas*, Ayodhya existed before the creation of the profane world. Manu, the first man, brought it from heaven and created the world outward from it. The sites of Hindu sacred geography are identified with the body of Vishnu himself. Ujjain was the feet of Vishnu, Dwaraka his navel, Haridwar his heart, Mathura his neck, Kashi or Banaras his nose, and Ayodhya his head. Ayodhya is considered the source of all worlds: Brahmalok, Indralok, Vishnulok, and Golok.[12]

Recent narratives infuse the history of Ayodhya with the miraculous. Babur himself, it is said, could not build his mosque after the destruction of the Ramjanmabhumi. Each night, the walls he ordered built during the day collapsed. The emperor was informed that Hanuman, Lord Rama's divine monkey servant, would never allow a mosque to be built on its site. He was only successful when he agreed to incorporate Hindu features into his mosque, to allow Hindus to worship in it, and when he would call it Sitapak, recalling not his reign, but Rama's queen Sita.[13]

THEORY OF SACRED CENTERS

Sacred centers have been bread and butter for historians of religions. But the events at Jerusalem's *har ha-bayit/al-haram as-sharif* and Ayodhya's Ramjanmabhumi Temple/Babri Mosque are very difficult to understand within the inherited intellectual traditions.

Mircea Eliade spent his life looking for universal symbolic structures, or metaphors – like center, axis mundi, sacred mountain – which he believed were manifested in all sacred cities and temples. Sacred space and time become unique sites connecting this world to the next, whose organization can be read in parallel with canonical texts. Influenced by this conception of the sacred center as fashioned by forces that break with ordinary historical time, historians of religions have set these sacred sites apart ontologically from other places, and assumed them to be sacred and static for all time. This has allowed students to analyze ritual behavior within these sites in isolation from other behavior in the cities where these sites are located.

The dominant tradition in the study of religions metaphorically "reads" the social organization of these spaces in order to understand the cosmology which, it is assumed, gives rise to the material organization of that space. Paul Wheatley has argued that the world's first cities originated not as markets or fortresses, but as ceremonial centers whose existence made territorial rule by kings possible.[14] In his comparative historical analyses, the construction of the symbolic center was the precondition for the political center. In the cultural geographical tradition, heaven imprints earth, ideas shape landscapes.

But because the sacrality of such centers is treated as phenomenologically and ontologically incommensurable, their social production and reproduction have not generally been seen as part of the interperpretive problematic. Although it is recognized that sacred centers may have multiple meanings, the ways in which conflicts between those meanings are adjudicated has never been systematically addressed. While sacred centers may be understood as sources of enormous social power, sacred places themselves are studied without politics, without power. The ways in which state power may generate sacrality and affect the meaning of that sacrality are therefore overlooked. Jonathan Z. Smith has argued that Eliade's sacred center is neither universal, nor does it have cosmogonic origins. Rather, Smith argues, in the Ancient Near East the cosmogonic text and the construction of the sacred center typically mimicked the social creation of a political, royal center.[15]

In these phenomenological or idealist traditions, the multiple meanings of these sacred sites are a source not of conflict but of alternative, equally genuine interpretations. Mircea Eliade, for example, describes the potential conflict of meanings given to the Temple of Durga at the Kalighat in Calcutta. Some of the pilgrims understand Durga as a goddess of terror to whom goats are sacrificed. But, for the initiated, Durga is the manifestation of cosmic life in constant and violent regeneration. What, he asks, is the true meaning of Durga? Is it the meaning given by the masses or that of the elite? He answers that

> both are equally valuable; that the meaning given by the masses stands for as authentic a modality of the sacred manifested by Durga ... as the interpretation of the initiates. And I can show that the two hierophanies fit together – that the modalities of the sacred which they reveal are in no sense contradictory, but are complementary, are parts of a whole.[16]

Without politics, with an implicit consensus, the history of sacred space can thus become a history of religious ideas.

In the classical sociological and anthropological traditions, earth shapes heaven, the material organization of society, the meaning of its sacred spaces. In reflectionist readings of the Durkheimian tradition, the material organization of space and time is reflected in their symbolic representation, and thus sacred centers symbolize the social power of the collectivity. In the more materialist neo-Weberian traditions, like in the work of Stein Rokkan, power concentrates and the resultant territorial centralization generates its own sacrality, usually understood as an institutional center of legitimation. The sacred center legitimates central authority or may become a rival to other sacred sites or to profane centers of economic or governmental power.[17] Marxist writers like David Harvey, while they have not explicitly tackled sacred centers, have theorized the state's sacralization of territory as a form of aestheticization, a fetishized form of false consciousness, not a reflection of, but a strategic deflection from, class-based interest conflicts. In any event, the sacrality of a center hinges on how it is harnessed to or challenged by state power. Whether in Chichén Itzá, Mecca, Rome, or Santiago de Compostela, pilgrimage and sacrifice belong to the political economy of power.

In this second tradition, the ways in which territories are socially organized shape the kinds of maps by which they are understood. Shifts in the representation of space and time derive from underlying "objective" organization and the political conflicts they make possible. If the first tradition understands the organization of sacred space and time as the materialization of discourse, the second sees it as a discourse by which the material world is understood, even if it is in fact a misapprehension. These latter approaches tend to give short-shrift to the impact of the ideal on the real. Symbols are often understood as malleable resources to be invoked to mobilize, to deflect, to justify, and to motivate. Power has a material base, but lacks a cultural one. Symbols are just so much superstructure. The state's ability to use a sacred center within its jurisdiction may affect its capacities for legitimation, but the content of that legitimation is immaterial to the analysis. And ironically, the second tradition is as bereft of ordinary politics as the first. In these largely societal studies, conflicts, if they are studied at all, are confined to epochal struggles between institutional elites who occupy divergent social and often geographical locations. Tensions between elites and masses are neglected, except sometimes as a problem of central control and peripheral compliance. Curiously, these approaches replicate analytically the same ontological distancing of sacred centers so essential to historians of religions. The actual places and the people who live in them disappear from view.

In both the interpretive and social structural approaches to sacred space and time, territory and map are always exterior, one to the other. Neither approach to sacred space pays much attention to the actual social construction of the specific physical territory or symbolic map, and neither can explain the events at *har ha-bayit/al-haram as-sharif* and the Ramjanmabhumi/Babri Masjid. Power and sacrality must be conjoined.

First, both sites are doubly sacred, holy within two different religions. They are both contested sacred centers. Both, as we shall soon show, have repeatedly been sites of violent conflict over who will control them, conflicts over meaning which cannot be assimilated into a unitary structure. This is true not only between Jews and Muslims and between Hindus and Muslims, but also within each community. For example, the Muslim groups within Jerusalem understand the *haram* in different ways: the Muslim Brotherhood attributes transnational importance to the site, while Hamas gives it a particular national significance, and many Muslim pilgrims see it only as a sacred place. Peter van der Veer has demonstrated a similar range of meanings among the Hindus of Ayodhya or those who visit it on pilgrimage.[18]

Second, in the context of conflict, access to the space and time of both sacred sites has always been conditional upon the exercise of state power. Ritual rights in these sacred centers depend upon the authority of the state. Ritual rites, like appropriation in a capitalist market, require property rights. Given that contemporary possession reflects the exercise of past power, these sites memorialize the political power of those who once conquered them.

Third, not only has access to these sacred centers hinged on state power, but the sacrality of the site itself cannot be divorced from the historical exercise of state power in general and the nation in particular. These sites signify territorial collectivities – ancient Israel in the first case, *aryavarta* ("the land of the Aryans"), *Bharatvarsha* ("country of Bharata"), and more recently *hindu rastra* ("the Hindu nation") in the second. Swami Dayananda Sarasvati (1824–1883), an early Hindu nationalist, taught that the kings of *aryavarta* had ruled the entire world and had taught India's wisdom to all people. Likewise note that Israel's first effective sovereign, King David, who unified the twelve tribes, chose Jerusalem as his capital, just as it is Rama, the first, albeit mythic, Hindu king whose capital Ayodhya originally was. The ritual language of sacrifice began as a language of state.

Fourth, religions anchored in these sacred centers have been essential to the formation of modern nationalist movements and the modern nations hold these sites sacred as nationalist – not just religious – centers. Jerusalem is, of course, the sovereign capital of Israel, and the Zionist claim to Palestine is rooted here. After the Romans destroyed Jerusalem in 70 CE, the Jews adapted to their exile by holding tightly to their map of history, to the repeated and promised cycle of exile and redemption. The Jews survived as a people, Eli Wiesel is fond of saying, because they remembered. As Saul Friedlander and Adam Seligman have recently shown, the Israelis placed the Shoah, the Nazi destruction of European Jewry, into this classic narrative form, the singular evilness of exile followed by national redemption. This sequence could be read both as a "secular" statement of historical cause and reason for nationhood, and as a "religious" statement of God's direction of history. This collective memory was progressively brought to Israel's sacred center as a memorial in Jerusalem and as its legitimating mandate. But, the tension between nationalist history and religious theodicy also opened the way for the religious nationalist right to claim the Shoah and to redefine the state in religious terms.[19]

Jerusalem is also the capital of Palestine. When the Palestinians first declared a state in 1948, they chose Jerusalem as their capital. When the PLO was formed, it held its founding meeting, over the strenuous objections of King Hussein, at the Intercontinental Hotel on the Mount of Olives overlooking Jerusalem, which was technically outside the municipal boundaries of East Jerusalem until 1967. When Faisal Husayni was arrested in 1988 by the Israelis for having prepared the declaration of independence that would ultimately be announced at the Palestine National Council meetings in Algiers, it was said that he intended to make the announcement from atop the *haram* near the grave of his father, Abdul Qadir al-Husayni, the most charismatic Palestinian military figure of the 1930s and 1940s who was killed in 1948 at the battle of Kastel.

Likewise, Indian nationalism is grounded in the history of Hindu tradition. The term "Hindu," a category absent in the ancient Indic period, was, in fact, largely a construction imposed by various conquerors. Although the term may have ancient ethnic connotations, associated with the lighter complected *arya* as opposed to the darker *anarya*, it was first systematically applied throughout South Asia by the Islamic rulers to refer to all those who were not Muslim.[20] Later, during the British Raj, it meant anything that was of India, particularly its heterogenous high cultures and religion which included Aryan, Brahmanical, and Vedic traditions. The British either solidified or refashioned Hindu as a religious category with communal significance, granting representation to those so defined within the colonial state. But this category of Hindu disrupted other particularistic patterns of local loyalties and created a pan-Indian network that would be inherited in its secular form by the Indian national state.[21] Indian national identity is in many ways a secularized religious discourse.

However, there are two critical differences between Jerusalem and Ayodhya, between Judaism and Hinduism. First, Judaism is a transcendental tradition, one in which the divine is generally not available in the phenomenal world, whereas Hinduism is an immanent tradition, one where the divine is accessible as a material presence in the human world. Transcendent religions tend to centralize their representation of the divine, whereas immanent religious traditions are multiple and polycentric. It is for this reason, we would argue, that Protestantism, an eminently transcendent tradition, has been associated with the early formation of nation-states given the relative ease with which emergent states could resacralize the ground around the telos of the nation. In immanent traditions, in contrast, there are a multiplicity of sites through which individuals can approach the divine, making both for unruly and expansive spatiality and making it difficult for the state to counter or harness religion as a cultural force in the making of the nation-state. Jerusalem was *the* sacred center for Judaism, while Ayodhya was one among many sacred sites for Hindus.

A second difference was that while both Jerusalem and Ayodhya represented ancient national centers, British colonial authority was centered in Jerusalem but not in Ayodhya. Jerusalem was a mythic and an actual governmental center; Ayodhya was mythic alone. Jerusalem emerged organically as the center of the Zionist and Palestinian nationalist strivings; Ayodhya was not central to Indian nationalists. While Palestinian nationalism began by politicizing the sacred center in Jerusalem, both the founding Jewish and Indian nationalists were ambivalent about these sites as places in which to ground their national identity, in that both were committed secularists who were opposed by religious communities who held these sites to be most sacred. For the Zionists Jerusalem was both the sign of the sacred and the sovereign. Labor Zionism was opposed by the devout Jews of the old Yishuv, centered in Jerusalem, who saw the Zionists as usurping the Messiah's role by forming a modern nation-state.

Both Jerusalem and Ayodhya were symbolic centers for religious nationalist opponents to the secular socialist dominant regimes. Jerusalem was also a major center for the maximalist Revisionist Zionists for whom Zion was a rallying cry and a bastion of support. The Labor Zionist felt compelled to claim and defend Zion. But, they could never really "have" it either, and the city remained a symbolic resource for their religious Zionist, revisionist Zionist, and anti-Zionist religious opponents, who by fighting over the exercise of public authority in the city sought to change the meaning of the signifier and thus the basis of legitimacy of the state.[22] On the Indian side, a disproportionate number of senior activists in the religious nationalist parties of the 1980s and 1990s cut their teeth in organized Hindu movements in Uttar Pradesh, opposed to both Gandhi's unity politics and Nehru's secularism in the 1940s. While Zionists and Palestinian nationalists in Palestine had to organize around Jerusalem; in India, the nationalists did not have to contend in the same way with Ayodhya. In the Indian case Ayodhya was neither *the* sacred, nor the sovereign center, although it has significance as a religious and a nationalist center.

While Ayodhya's sacral character is established in the mythical reign of King Rama, it is believed that the city was rediscovered and restored in our epoch, the Kali-yuga, by King Vikramaditya. After his death, the city was destroyed by the Muslims and did not return to prominence until the reign of the Nawabs of Awadh in the eighteenth century. Hans

Bakker's archeological study of a number of sites in and around the contemporary city indicates that the Ayodhya of the *Ramayana* became identified with the important North Indian town of Saketa during the reign of the Guptas in the fifth century CE. The Guptas moved their capital from Pataliputra to Saketa and renamed it Ayodhya.

The Gupta period is generally understood as one of the most extensive and culturally creative periods of Indian history prior to the Moghuls, and the Gupta kings Kumaragupta and Skandagupta were both ardent devotees to Vishnu. One of Skandagupta's titles was Vikramaditya, and he likened himself to King Rama. One of the dominant themes of his court was restoring the city to what it had been during the time of Lord Rama.

Valmiki's Ramayana and Tulsidas' *Ramacharitamanas* with their sacralizations of Rama's reign and Ayodhya have been interpreted in many ways prior to our century. Tulsidas' version was extraordinarily popular in north India and led to new devotional movements from the Hindu Middle Ages into the nineteenth century. A particular powerful appropriation of the Rama-katha tradition appeared in the Baba Rama Chander's social movement in Uttar Pradesh in the early decades of this century. The goal of his movement was to support the national movement and to oppose large-scale landlords in the area. Verses from Tulsidas were popularized as part of the resistance to colonial rule. The demons of the epic, the *rakshsasas*, who Rama vanquished, were identified with the landlords, capitalists, and the British.

The rhetoric of the contemporary Hindu nationalist movements often dramatically closes any historical gap between the mythic enemies of Rama and modernity. For example, one of the most prominent figures among the Hindu nationalists is Uma Bharati, a *sadhvi* or female spiritual renunciant. In 1992, as the BJP and VHP pushed for the building of the Ram temple on the site of the Babri mosque, she did not distinguish between mythic and present enemies, suggesting that the holy men who would lay the foundation of the temple would transform "Hindustan" into an authentic Hindu state. They would destroy the tyrant just as Ravana had been vanquished by Rama. "Announce it boldly to the world," she said,

> that anyone who opposes Ram cannot be an Indian. Muslim remember Rahim who longed for the dust of Lord Ram's feet.... Songs of Hindu-Muslim brotherhood were sung by Mahatma Gandhi. We got ready to hear the Azaan along with temple bells, but they can't do this, nor does their heritage permit them to do ... The two cultures are polar opposites. But we still preached brotherhood – We could not teach them with words, now let us teach them with kicks – Let there be bloodshed once and for all.

Just as there was an essential mythological enmity between Rama and Ravana, so there was between Hindu and Muslim. They could not live together in a Hindu nation. Bharati left no doubt with her listeners as to the solution and goal: "Leftists and communist ask me if we desire to turn this land into a Hindu *rashtra*. I say it was declared one at the time of partition in 1947 – Hindustan, a nation of Hindus and Pakistan, a nation of Muslims. ... Declare without hesitation that this a Hindu *rashtra*, a nation of Hindus."[23]

The mass media have aided the intensified Ram devotion and his ascendance as the unitary deity of the nation, creating the same simultaneity Benedict Anderson saw in the coalition of Protestantism and print-capitalism in the formation of the European nation-state.[24] Romila Thapar has noted that the Indian film industry and television have been major vehicles through which Rama devotion has been popularized.[25] Philip Lutgendorf's study of Ramanand Sagar's serialized "Ramayana" on state television in 1987 confirms Thapar's observation and immense role that this media has had on the production of a nationalized Hindu religiosity. Lutgendorf notes that between 40 and 60 million people watched the entire serial, with some of the most popular segments reaching as many as 80 to 100 million avid viewers. Weddings and funerals were delayed, city squares become eerily quiet, towns appeared to be virtually deserted or under martial law on each Sunday morning when the serial was broadcast. Seeing the epic was understood as a *darshan*, an auspicious sight. Television sets were garlanded, decorated with sandalwood paste and vermilion, conch shells were blown. The pedestals upon which the televisions sat were sanctified with cow dung and water from the Ganges, and worshipped with flowers and incense. On one Sunday morning there was a power failure in one of Banaras' suburbs, blacking out a segment of the serial. An angry mob stormed the power station and set it ablaze. The serialization of the epic created an alternative ritual calendar in which Rama's return was celebrated as, one report noted, "an early Divali," and the slaying of Ravana earlier occasioned out-of-season *dashahra* festivals.[26]

THE FIRE LAST TIME

In the West we tend to separate religion from nationalism, thinking of nationalism as a modern phenomenon rooted in the territorial historicity of a state. National identities are thought to be built in opposition to or outside the domain of religion which is conceived of as a supra-national phenomenon. Students of the formation of western nation-states have recognized that the relation to religion marks the cultural logic and partisan structure of a nation. For example, as Stein Rokkan has shown us in the West, those nations able to organize a separate national church were able to form cohesive nation-states earlier than those whose citizens remained obedient to the teachings of the supra-national Catholic Church. In this case, it is understood that the transnational Latin Church operated as a drag on the formation of national loyalties.

We are today confronted by religious nationalism, apparently new fusions of archaic and modern identities. In fact, many national identities in the modern world were built through the political uses of religious identities, by organizing ritual, imagery, and pilgrimage to centers sacred to the religion, and a number of these sites were contested between religions over access to and activity at the site. This was certainly the case in the Israeli–Palestinian conflict where the roots of Zionism and Palestinian nationalism were profoundly shaped by religion, where the sacred sites of Jerusalem were critical to forming the national identities of both peoples. It was also true in the case of Indian nationalism which built on the Hindu cosmologies and Hindu sacred sites to ground the new nation, and where Hindu–Muslim conflict was integral to the formation of the Indian and Pakistani nations.[27] In both cases, the nation was not formed in opposition to religion, but as part of a conflict that was thoroughly suffused with religious meanings. The combatants in these struggles over sacred space and time were predominantly religious nationalists, men who understood the nationalist significance of their religion or the religious significance of their nation. For them, the struggle for ritual rights as the sacred center was one of the most important battlegrounds. Pilgrimage to and political violence around the sacred centers of Jerusalem and Ayodhya is part of the genetic material of Israel/Palestinian and Indian nation formation. Let us begin with the case of Jerusalem.

On Friday, 23 August 1929, thousands of Muslims streamed out of the Noble Sanctuary to begin what would become the bloodiest and most savage communal rioting of the less than decade-old British Mandate over Palestine. Rioting spread throughout Palestine, as Jewish agricultural villages around Jerusalem at Motzah, Har-Tuv, Hulda, and Be'er Tuvia were attacked. The Jewish quarters of Safed were attacked and burned, and in Hebron, mobs went house to house, killing 66 Jews with knives and hatchets. Before the British were able to restore order ten days later, nearly 133 Jews had been killed and 339 had been seriously wounded. The British troops and police killed 116 Arabs and wounded 232. The entire Hebron Jewish community was evacuated.

The violence of August 1929 was a continuation of violence that had flared in Jerusalem in April 1920 and had been confined to the city and sections of Jaffa. Common to both of these cases of violence was the extension of Jewish ritual rights at the Western Wall. The British had inherited from the Turks and before them the Ottomans a labyrinthine corpus of agreements governing the religious communities of Jerusalem and Bethlehem's usage of time and space in Church of the Holy Sepulcher, the Tomb of the Virgin, the Church of the Ascension, the Church of the Nativity and the Western Wall of *har ha-bayit*. At the Western Wall, Jews were allowed customary privileges of praying there, but could not bring any of the equipment of ritual, including readers tables, benches, screens to divide men and women in prayer, and they could not blow the ram's horn or *shofar* on Rosh Ha-Shana or Yom Kippur. By 1929, the British routinely referred to these agreements as the "Status Quo in the Holy Places."

In both cases of violence, two individuals were central; a young Muslim cleric by the name of Muhammad Haj Amin al-Husayni and Ze'ev Jabotinsky, the founder of Revisionist Zionism. In the rioting of April 1920, Haj Amin escaped across the Jordan River and was sentenced in abstentia to ten years in prison for an inflammatory speech he gave just before the violence began. Jabotinsky was sentenced to fifteen years, although the sentence was almost immediately commuted to one year. Haj Amin was pardoned the following September and returned to Jerusalem where he was appointed in 1921 to the position of Grand Mufti, the highest Islamic cleric in Palestine and a post created by the British administration. A year later he was elected to the presidency of the Supreme Muslim Council.

Haj Amin al-Husayni was not just the Grand Mufti with authority over substantial resources under the central control of the Jerusalem *waqf* or pious endowment, the Islamic *shari'a* courts, and a network of mosques and Islamic schools: he was also the leader of the Palestinian nation and mobilized that nation using the Supreme Muslim Council as his central organizing device. Throughout the 1920s until he fled Palestine at the beginning of the first Palestinian revolt in 1936 he used pilgrimage to a site near Jerusalem called Nebi Musa where Muslims believed Moses was buried as a way to consolidate a cross-local Palestinian consciousness. And most importantly for our purposes, he used the defense of Islamic ritual rights at the *haram* as his central rallying cry to mobilize Palestinians against the Zionists. This was ironic because the Labor Zionist movement was not concentrated in Jerusalem, but along the Mediterranean coast and in the north in the Galilee. Jerusalem was, in contrast, a center for Zionists drawn from the Revisionist and Religious Nationalist streams.

The Mufti believed that Zionist efforts to extend their ritual rights beyond those delimited by the "Status Quo" to be indicative of their efforts to ultimately claim the entire *haram* as their own for the site of a third Jewish temple. Indeed, he was well aware of Zionist efforts led by Chaim Weizmann in 1918, in 1926, and again in 1928 to purchase sections of the Western Wall. Weizmann's plan was not necessarily motivated by any religious concerns for the Wall. He thought that its purchase might stimulate enthusiasm for Zionism in western Europe and America. In 1922, the Supreme Muslim Council and the Arab Executive Committee received a copy of a painting dating from the late nineteenth century which hung in the Old City's Torat-Hayyim Yeshivah which showed the Dome of the Rock crowned by a Star of David. The Jews explained that this painting was only a decoration and *mizrach* used in Jewish prayer. They also indicated that the painting was used for purposes of fund-raising abroad. The picture was copied and widely circulated by the Supreme Muslim Council throughout the Muslim world to demonstrate that the real intention of the Jews was nothing short of the occupation of the *haram* itself.

The Revisionists were opposed to what they saw as the traitorous accommodation and gradualism of the Labor Zionists. They were determined to make all of Palestine – Western and Eastern Palestine on both banks of the River Jordan – into a Jewish state. Their efforts to expand Jewish ritual rights at the Western Wall were spearheaded by its youth movement, Betar. In 1930, the Shaw Commission which was convened to determine the causes of the violence in August 1929 found that the Revisionist Zionist demonstrations a week before the outbreak of the violence had set in motion a movement of reciprocal sacrilege. At that time, the Betar youth assembled at the Wall, shouting "The Wall is ours," raised the Jewish national flag, and sang Ha-Tikvah, the Zionist anthem. An unsubstantiated rumor that they had also attacked Muslim residents in the immediate area of the Western Wall and had cursed the name of the Prophet only fanned the flames. The day after the Revisionist demonstrations, approximately 2,000 Muslims marched on the Western Wall, destroyed a Torah scroll and a number of prayer books. We gain insight into what the Status Quo meant to the Revisionists in Menachem Begin's reminiscences of being involved in similar demonstrations in the early 1940s, although these did not have the same violent intercommunal results. Begin rejected any religious or mystical meanings to the Western Wall. The Western Wall was the voice of history which both the British and the Arabs had tried to silence. For Begin, the Status Quo's limitation of Jewish ritual rights was "real slavery." He concluded that

> A people that does not defend its holy places – that does not even try to defend them – is not free, however much it may babble about freedom. People that permit the holiest spot in their country and their most sacred feelings to be trampled underfoot – are slaves in spirit.[28]

In the 1929 conflict in Jerusalem, the Palestinian nationalist movement was led by a Muslim cleric who used the defense of Muslim ritual rights at the *haram* as a vehicle for mobilization against the Zionists. In the process, the Mufti appealed to Islamic forces throughout the world and Islamicized the meaning of Palestinian identity. Ultimately, this contributed to the severity of the civil war within the Palestinian nation in which those forces who wished to accommodate Zionism did violent battle with Haj Amin al-Husayni's supporters, and Christians were the object of particular hatred, leading to the beginning of a massive emigration of Palestinian Christians. The Mufti's opponents within Jerusalem were not the Labor Zionist mainstream, but the minoritarian and territorially maximalist Revisionist movement that seized upon the extension of Jewish ritual rights at the Western Wall to mobilize support for their cause. These forces, largely secular, were ultimately subordinated during the 1948 war.

The violence at Ayodhya in 1992 also has a long pre-history. There is considerable evidence that Hindus and Muslims worshipped together in the Babri Masjid throughout the eighteenth century and well into the nineteenth. Friction between the two communities emerged concurrently with the decline of the Muslim Nawab authority in Ayodhya as the British exercised increasing power over the semi-independent rulers and kingdoms of North India (Ayodhya was annexed in 1856). In 1855, Muslims claimed that there was a mosque in the Hanumangarhi, the Fortress of Hanuman, located near the Babri Masjid. The Hanumangarhi was a total monastic institution for devotees of Rama who were also trained in a military fashion. The Muslims gathered in the Babri Masjid and threatened the Hanumangarhi. This led to a violent confrontation in which the Hindus stormed the mosque and killed 70 Muslims. The killings in the mosque were accompanied by large-scale plundering of the Muslim population of the city. The intercommunal tension was further intensified when the Hindus intentionally slaughtered a number of pigs on the day of the burial of the Muslim casualties. The British responded to this first violent clash by erecting a railing around the Babri Masjid, allowing the Muslims to pray inside the mosque and the Hindus to do their *puja* on a raised platform outside the mosque. There were further incidents of violence in 1912 and 1934 associated with the Cow-Protection Movement. In 1934, several hundred Muslims were massacred before the army could intervene. The British responded by imposing a punitive tax of a few hundred rupees on the Hindu citizenry of Ayodhya.[29]

However, the definitive event in the unfolding violence at the Babri Masjid took place shortly after partition. Some have seen it as the definitive event because it changed the status quo concerning the mosque.[30] On the night of 22 to 23 December 1949 a statue of Rama miraculously appeared in the mosque, which since the violence of partition had been guarded by armed watchmen. The news of the manifestation of Rama spread rapidly. The Hindus interpreted the event as testimony that Rama was directing them after independence to reclaim the center of the nation. The Muslims interpreted the event as an attempt to defile their mosque. It was only with great difficulty that the army and police were able to quell the ensuing riots. In the wake of these riots, leaders from both communities initiated litigation to reassert their claims to the site and the right of entrance which had been closed to both Hindus and Muslims immediately after the violence. The commissioner of Faizabad, the capital of Uttar Pradesh, ordered the district magistrate to remove the image from the mosque. However, the magistrate, who was a supporter of the RSS, chose to retire rather than follow the order of his superior. Since 1949, the image of Rama has remained in the mosque. In 1950, a branch of the RSS in Ayodhya was able to secure legal permission to perform *puja* for the image within the Babri Masjid once a year. Subsequently, they also organized uninterrupted devotional singing at the mosque's gate.

THE CONTEMPORARY CONFLICTS

After the Six Day War of 1967, when Israel achieved sovereignty over Jerusalem, it legally erased any restrictions on Jewish ritual rights at the Western Wall. The Knesset's "Law of Holy Places" provided free, unimpeded access to all religious sites and, more importantly, allowed each religious community to oversee their own sacred places. The "Status Quo" was maintained exactly as it had been during the Mandatory Period for the Christians, but gave Jews new rights at the Western Wall. The Muslims were allowed to maintain the "Status Quo" on top of the *haram* itself. This war unleashed a religious nationalist movement, the Gush Emunim, or "Bloc of the Faithful," who saw the settlement of the conquered lands of the West Bank and Gaza as actions in a messianic drama: the suburbanization of Jerusalem was thus imbued with redemptive significance. They understood the failure of Israel to restore complete ritual access to *har ha-bayit*, let alone cleanse the Mount of Islamic profanation, as indicative of the "normalized" secular nature of Israeli civic culture, reflecting a state which seeks to be like other states, a profane refuge for Jews seeking shelter only from pandemic antisemitism.

Since 1967, the push for expanding Jewish ritual rights on the Temple Mount has been led by religious nationalists and the heirs of the same Revisionist tradition who challenged the "Status Quo" in the 1920s. There have been more than two dozen separate violent assaults on the *haram* since 1967. The great majority of these have been carried out by individuals, but the most serious threat was organized by members of Gush Emunim who believed that the destruction of the Dome of the Rock would lead to national redemption. The plotters stole high explosives from Israel Defense Forces bases. They carried out elaborate reconnaissance missions, and even built life-size models of sections of the *haram* to rehearse the mission. It was only the illness of one of the leaders of the plot that temporarily scraped their plans. Gershon Salomon, the leader of "The Faithful of the Temple Mount" who was turned away from entering the Mughrabian Gate minutes before the violence broke out in October 1990, is also a leading Jerusalemite activist of the Tehiyah or "Renaissance" Party which in many ways sees itself, not Begin's nor Shamir's nor Natanyahu's Likud party, as the true heir of Jabotinsky's Revisionism.

And just as in 1929, when they were confronted by Islamic political leaders, so too, in 1990, the men who organized the massing of Muslims on the *haram* to confront the perceived threat were activists from the Islamic Resistance Movement or as it is better known through its acronym, Hamas, which broke away from the Egyptian dominated Muslim Brotherhood in Gaza and challenged the Jordanian dominated Brothers in West Bank, and has emerged as a rival to the political leadership of the Palestine Liberation Organization. Much like other militant Muslim groups throughout the Middle East and North Africa, their graffito is *al-islam huwa-el-hal*, "Islam is the solution." They reject any partition of Palestine, which has been given by God to Muslims as a trust until the end of time. Since the first days of the Intifada in December 1987 which they take pride in beginning, they have repeatedly used the *haram* as the symbolic site to challenge the Israelis, the PLO, and false Muslims who have cooperated with secularist regimes.

Shortly after the killings on the *haram*, Hamas published a short allegorical story in one of Jerusalem's nationalist newspapers (*A-Sha'ab*, 12 October 1990). In the story, black birds drove off the white doves which had always nested in the Ka'aba in Mecca since the days of the Prophet. The doves fled to Jerusalem where they rebuilt their nests. When Yehuda Litani, a veteran Israeli commentator on Palestinian politics in the occupied territories, asked his contacts within Hamas what they made of the story, he was told that it demonstrated that Allah was preparing to deliver the decisive blow against the idolaters, Israel, and the US which were symbolized by the black birds. But, for Hamas there was an additional meaning to the story and this intensified the symbolic place of *al-haram as-sharif* in their struggle. Mecca and Medina are controlled by idolaters, by the US, and even by the Israelis. Jerusalem's *al-haram as-sharif* through the sacrifice of its martyrs on 8 October had been sanctified as the one and only remaining holy place, free from control by idolaters. For Hamas, Jerusalem had become the very center of the Muslim world.[31]

The Hindu campaign to liberate the Ramjanmabhumi Temple began in the early 1980s with the Visva Hindu Parishad's mass rituals to liberate the birthplace of Rama, to free the god from what they understood to be a Muslim jail. The VHP, unlike either the RSS or the BJP, is dominated by religious leaders and its efforts to mobilize Hindus had distinctive ritual meanings. In 1983, the VHP sponsored the *Ekatmatayajna*, "the sacrifice for unanimity," in which huge processions wound their way across India. Each of these processions had trucks which carried large bronze pots filled with water from the Ganges. As the processions traversed the countryside, the water of the Ganges was distributed in each village and the supply replenished by mixing water from local sources with water of the Ganges. In February 1989, the VHP, BJP, and RSS joined in organizing a convention of Hindu activists who agreed to build a new temple at the site of the Ramjanmabhumi. Villages across India would prepare and consecrate the bricks for the new temple. Even Hindu communities of the diaspora, like Los Angeles, dedicated bricks. Intercommunal tensions rose as the bricks began moving toward

Ayodhya during the summer and early fall. Rajiv Gandhi's efforts to defuse the conflict by suggesting that the temple might be built about 200 meters from the site of Babri Mosque ended by alienating both Hindus and Muslims and contributed substantially to his loss at the polls in November 1989. BJP candidates racked up a record number of parliamentary seats in North India.

The leaders of the BJP and RSS, men like Lal Krishna Advani, tend to describe the conflict over the Babri Mosque in nationalist terms. They argue that the government's unwillingness to take control of the site is indicative of the moral collapse of the Hindus, who are too willing to grant to the Muslim minority rights which they deny to the Hindu majority. The Indian constitution's separation of religion and state has led to corruption which should best by overcome through *hindutva*, the religious-nationalist formulation of Vinayak Damodar Savarkar who sought to define Hindus by organically linking them to the nation. Hindus are inseparably linked to the sacrality of the land (*bharat*), to the fatherland (*pitribhu*), and holy land (*punyabhu*). In an interview in June 1993, Advani suggested that "the BJP is a party with a vision of a new, resurgent and modern India wed to a distinctive concept of Hindutva. It is committed to the secular ingredients of the Indian constitution: rejection of theocracy; equality of all citizens, irrespective of religion; and full freedom of worship."[32] The activists from the VHP understand the struggle to liberate the birthplace of Rama in religious terms. In April 1991, V. H. Dalmia, the president of the VHP, told a New Delhi crowd of half a million Hindus, the largest demonstration since India's Independence, that his party understood the struggle for Ayodhya to be "a continuation of the ancient battle, the *Ramayana*." Uma Bharati, a VHP member of the Indian parliament, told the crowd that religious tolerance was not the most important issue: "Those Ram devotees who sacrificed their lives have washed this temple with their blood. Everyone except us wants the mosque to remain there so that religious harmony remains strong. If this is so, we would like a temple to Hanuman to be built in Mecca and Medina. How good the atmosphere would then be with Muhammad on one side and Hanuman on the other."[33]

The three religious nationalist parties (VHP, BJP, and RSS) also sought to alter the situation at the Babri Mosque through litigation. In 1986, a local court in Uttar Pradesh ruled that there was no compelling reason for the mosque to remain closed as it had been since 1950. The judge had also been assured by the local constabulary that opening the building would not provoke violence. Literally, within hours of his decision becoming public, rioting broke out in six North Indian towns in which 20 people were killed. In October 1990, the VHP organized a mass effort to destroy the Babri Mosque. Prime Minister Vishvanath Singh, who had been on the job for less than a year, ordered the army to arrest as many demonstrators as necessary to protect the mosque. Tens of thousands of paramilitary police were deployed and more than 100,000 people were arrested on the roads. Ayodhya was sealed off, but the assault could not be halted. As the mass of demonstrators pushed forward, Hindu police removed the padlocks on the mosque's gates. In the end, the army opened fire on the demonstrators and over the next few weeks thousands of Hindu and Muslims died in the rioting sparked by this assault. The General Secretary of the VHP, Ashok Singhal, noted that the significance of this first mass assault was

> that the Hindus cannot be taken for granted in this country anymore. Their voice will be heard in this country. This pseudo-secularism of Muslim appeasement has exploded in this country today, and it will explode further.... Now neither the politicians nor the administration can give the Muslims any assurance or guarantee of security. Their security now will depend only upon their relations with the Hindus.[34]

THEATERS OF NATIONALIST STRUGGLE

The fact that these sacred centers are integral to the identity, the territorial claim, and the legitimation of the modern nation state has made them productive sites for those groups within each nation that wish to transform the cultural basis of state power from the universalism of secular democracy to the particularism of a state grounded in religious law. They have provided the best battlegrounds for those who wish to return the modern nation-states that hold these sites sacred to the religious traditions which undergirded their formation and provided their essential pre-history.

The Israeli, Palestinian, and Indian nations were well grounded symbolically at the *har ha-bayit/al-haram as-sharif* and Ramjanmabhumi/Babri Masjid. For Israelis, David and Solomon anchored their united monarchy in Jerusalem's Temple. For Palestinians, the *haram al-sharif* is the heart of the capital of their future state. In 1920s Haj Amin al-Husayni declared the Muslim festival commemorating Muhammad's night journey from Mecca to Jerusalem to be Palestine Day. For Hindus, the Ramjanmabhumi is the beginning point of their national identities, while for India's Muslims it is the zenith of their national history in the subcontinent. What makes these sites so distinctive is that in both cases, the adherents of the majority religion of the sovereign power – Jews in Israel and Hindus in India – do not have full access in the sacred center of the religion in which their authority is at least partially grounded. The site spatializes an anachronistic relation between the two groups, inverting the contemporary relationship where Hindus are subordinate to Muslims in the case of Ayodhya, and Jews to Muslims in the case of Jerusalem.[35]

Given the importance of these sites as symbolic centers of the Israeli, Palestinian, and Indian nations – and given the religious pre-history of the three nations – it should come as no surprise that these contested sacred centers might emerge as particularly productive sites for political mobilization for social movements within the nations who wish to transform the cultural logic of their nation's identity and the legitimacy of the state which speaks in the nation's name. In both Israel and India, the state was governed by parties, Labor Zionists in Israel and the Congress Party in India, who held to a secular basis of nationalism, promulgating as much as politically possible the separation of state and religion. It was thus regimes ruled by these parties that reconfirmed the ritual rights held by Muslims in both states. Challenging Islamic ritual property rights at both sacred centers was a way for religious nationalists in both countries to contest the secular, western basis of authority of their national states.

These contested sacred sites stand as collective representations of the historical conflicts out of which the nation was formed in the first place. For those who want to ground state authority more fully in religion, they stand as inversions of the natural order of things – indicators of the limits of sovereignty, self-inflicted boundaries of state power, manifestations of the state's failure to embrace its religious significance. They are thus perfect theaters in which to replay and recast the historical drama so that it might end appropriately.

CENTER AS SITE AND SYMBOL

Territorial centers are both sites of material control and symbolic orientation. Material centers are foundational signifiers. Center formation is one of the important means by which power is written or inscribed in the Derridean sense. Through centers, the metaphysical basis of power is determined. Centers function as the theater in which that basis is consecrated, affirmed, and displayed. Rituals organized at the center tap the primal social solidarity, the *communitas*, that Turner has argued is the foundational energy of society. Centers are always potential sources of power, for it is at centers that collective identities are grounded. Collectivities are often defined by the common center to which they look. Upon this center, a collectivity is imagined, a people projects its image.

In the case of Jerusalem and Ayodhya, contesting possession of a sacred site has been used by groups who wish to change the basis of governmental authority from a nation grounded in mutual consensus and democratic laws to a religio-ethnic group ground in divine providence, that draws is existence and coherence from the gods.

That power is both symbolized and organized from and through the sacred center implies that the center's social construction will have a politics. Not only will state elites attempt to control or counter the uses to which that sacred is put as Allan Grapard has demonstrated in a series of articles, but conflicts over the social order will ramify in the society's sacred landscape. Indeed, a number of analysts, among them Clifford Geertz, have now pointed to the role of rituals at the center not as mere external instrumental legitimation of governmental authority, but as its internal expressive mechanism. James Duncan, for example, has illustrated how the struggle between two competing discourses and narratives of kingship in nineteenth century Sri Lanka was played out in the politics of the landscape of Kandy, the royal capital.[36]

We would argue that, in its way, our analysis is consistent with the facts presented by David Harvey in his path-breaking analysis of the contest over Sacre Coeur. Harvey argues that identification built on the territorial state represents a reactionary retreat from the political project of modernity and class politics. But the implication of our work is that spatialization and the formation of sacred centers may be critical to the formation and representation of all collectivities. We would argue that many religions are political, not only that power is necessary to regulate access to and control the use of sacred sites, but that the formation of sacred centers is integral to the organization and operation of political power in and of itself. Here, we would part company with historians of religions like Gerardus van der Leeuw and others who argue that a place becomes sacred by the repeated exercise of political power. Sacred centers are not just reflections or traces of political power; they are often instruments and sources of political power. It is striking to point out that when socialist social revolutions take place, they tend not to displace the existing center, but to take it and transform it, precisely because it is the signifier of the collectivity.

The originary act of power is an act of representation. The center always has a dual meaning, as site and sign of power. Representation does not merely legitimate power, it constitutes it. Power does not merely ground representation, it signifies it. Powerful representation is representation that has power. Materiality is meaningful and meaning must be materialized. The center is both a real property and has the property of being a center. Its meaning as a sign of power depends on the capacity of the powerful to control access to it. Ritual rights depend on property rights, sacred space being a property, like any other, which cannot internally produce the conditions of its reproduction. Because the center is the primordial signifier, those who wish to be powerful seek both to control it and to ground their right to control it in their control over it. The monopoly on legitimate violence depends on the state's monopoly on legitimation, or in other words, on representation. National representation is a centered and centering historical process.

NOTES

1. Michael N. Barnett, "The Politics of Uniqueness: The Status of the Israeli Case," in Michael N. Barnett (ed.), *Israel in Comparative Perspective: Challenging the Conventional Wisdom*, Albany, NY: SUNY Press, 1996, p.3.

2. Karen Armstrong, *Jerusalem: One City, Three Faiths*, New York: A.A. Knopf, 1996, pp.421 and 427.
3. The three groups are the Bharatiya Janata Party, the "Indian People's Party" (BJP), the Rashtriya Svayamsevak Sangh, the "National Union of Volunteers" (RSS), and the Vishva Hindu Parishad, the "World Hindu Society" (VHP).
4. The most comprehensive treatment of the major religious nationalist parties and movements in Indian history is Christophe Jaffrelot, *The Hindu Nationalist Movement in India*, New York: Columbia University Press, 1996.
5. Edward A. Gargan, "Hindu Militants Destroy Mosque, Setting Off a New Crisis in India" and "Crowd's Religious Zeal Turns to Physical Abuse," *New York Times*, 7 Dec. 1992. For a chronology of the events see D. Awasthi, "A Nation's Shame," *India Today*, 31 Dec. 1992, W.P.S. Sidhu and D. Awasthi, "Spineless Spectators," *India Today*, 31 Dec. 1992, V. Ramakrishnan, "The Wreaking Crew: in Ayodhya, Demolition and After," *Frontline*, 1 Jan. 1993, "The Tragic Sequence," *Frontline*, 1 Jan. 1993, "Dateline Ayodhya," *Frontline*, 1 Jan. 1993, and "Looting the Ômandir," *Frontline*, 15 Jan. 1993.
6. Stanley J. Tambiah, *Leveling Crowds: Ethnonationalist Conflicts and Colletive Violence in South Asia*, Berkeley: University of California Press, 1996, pp.253–5.
7. See the postscript "December 1992" to Ainslie T. Embree, "The Function of the Rashtriya Swayamsevak Sangh: To Define the Hindu Nation," in Martin E. Marty and R. Scott Appleby (eds), *Accounting for Fundamentalisms: The Dynamic Character of Movements*, Chicago: University of Chicago Press, 1994, pp.645–9, R. Thakur, "Ayodhya and the Politics of India's Secularism: a Double Standard Discourse," *Asian Survey: A Monthly Review of Contemporary Asian Affairs* 33/7 (1993) pp.645–64, Y. Ghimire and R. Pathak, "Too Much, too Late," *India Today*, 31 Jan. 1993, and Y. Ghimire, "The Rise of the Saddhus," *India Today*, 31 Jan. 1993.
8. Daniel Williams, "Israelis Slay 19 Arabs in Clash in Jerusalem," *The Los Angeles Times*, 9 Oct. 1990.
9. The initial accounts of the conflict placed the dead at between 19 and 21. At the press conference of the Jerusalem based Palestine Human Rights Information Center on 15 October, this original number was reduced to 17. Of those who were initially reported to have been killed at *al-haram as-sharif* one died of a heart attack, two individuals who were initially reported to have died were injured and survived, and the fourth had been shot by an Israeli civilian in another part of the city and had died. See "Special File: The Haram al-Sharif (Temple Mount) Killings," *Journal of Palestine Studies* 20/2 (1991) pp.134–59.
10. Bakker, "Ayodhya: A Hindu Jerusalem," *Nvmen* 38/1 (1991) p.90 cites Ramayana 1.1.2–4 as an example of Rama's perfection.
11. Bakker, "Ayodhya: A Hindu Jerusalem," p.96.
12. The classical Hindu cosmos was divided into three worlds. Here, Golok, "the world of sacred cows" provides the fourth world. The addition of Golok may reflect the support Uttar Pradesh during the late nineteenth and early twentieth century for the Gorakshini Sabha, the Cow Protection Society. The society was created in order to protect cows from Muslim slaughter which became one of the prime causes for intercommunal violence. See Anand A. Yang, "Sacred Symbol and Sacred Space in Rural India: Community Mobilization in the 'Anti-Cow Killing' Riot of 1893," *Comparative Studies in Society and History* 22/4 (1980) pp.576–96. It is then very significant that Ayodhya is origin of the sacred world of cows which inverts the Muslim claim to Ayodhya.
13. Neeladri Battacharya, "Myth, History and the Politics of Ramjanmabhumi," in Sarvepalli Gopal (ed.), *Anatomy of a Confrontation: The Babri Masjid-Ramjanmabhumi Issue*, New York: Viking, 1991, pp.134–5. The Hindi term sitapak is an abbreviate for of the Sanskrit, sitapakasthana, "the kitchen of Sita." See Hans Bakker, "Ayodhya: The History of Ayodhya from the 7th Century BC to the Middle of 18th Century – Its Development into a Sacred Centre with Special Reference to the Ayodhyamahatmya and to the Worship of Rama accoridng to the Agastyasamhita," *Groningen* (1986) Part 2, pp.173–5 for a description of the Sita kitchen which formed a part of the earlier temple.
14. Paul Wheatley, *The Pivot of the Four Quarters*, Chicago: Aldine, 1971.
15. For a critique of Eliade's celestial reading of Australian aboriginal narratives as another instance of the sacred pole as cosmic axis connecting the lived topography with cosmogony, see Jonathan Z. Smith, *To Take Place: Toward Theory in Ritual*, Chicago: University of Chicago Press, 1987, esp. pp.1–23.

16. Mircea Eliade, *Traité d'histoire des religions*, Paris, 1948; rpt. 1970, p.20. English, trans. by Rosemary Sheed, *Patterns in Comparative Religion*, New York: New American Library, 1974. Eliade (p.xiv) defines "hierophany" as "anything which manifests the sacred."
17. Stein Rokkan, "Dimensions of State Formation and Nation Building: A Possible Paradigm for Research on Variations within Europe," in Charles Tilly (ed.), *The Formation of National States in Western Europe*, Princeton: Princeton University Press, 1975, pp.562–600.
18. Van der Veer, *Gods on Earth*.
19. Saul Friedlander and Adam B. Seligman, "The Israeli Memory of the Shoah: On Symbols, Rituals, and Ideological Polarization," in Roger Friedland and Deirdre Boden (eds), *Now Here: Space, Time and Modernity*, Berkeley: University of California Press, 1994, pp.356–71.
20. See the recent discussion by Cynthia Kepley Mahmood, "Ayodhya and the Hindu Resurgence," *Religion* 24/1 (1994) pp.73–80.
21. Gerald James Larson, *India's Agony Over Religion*, Albany, NY: SUNY Press, 1995, esp. p.141.
22. For a more extensive discussion of these groups see our *To Rule Jerusalem*, New York: Cambridge University Press, 1996.
23. Quoted in Katherine K. Young, "Women in Hinduism," in Arvind Sharma (ed.), *Today's Woman in World Religions*, Albany, NY: SUNY Press, 1994, pp.99–100. Jan Platvoet, "Ritual as Confrontation: The Ayodhya Conflict," in Jan Platvoet and Karel van der Toorn (eds), *Pluralism and Identity: Studies in Ritual Behavior*, Leiden: E.J. Brill, 1995, pp.217–18 notes that in the contemporary appropriation of the Ramayana, the roles of Rama and Sita were reversed in the most powerful way, forcing the nation to act in order to save Rama from the hands of the Muslims.
24. Benedict Anderson, *Imagined Communities: Reflections on the Origin and Spread of Nationalism*, Revised edition, New York: Verso, 1991, p.40–46.
25. Romila Thapar, "A Historical Perspective on the Story of Rama," in *Anatomy of a Confrontation*, pp.157–8.
26. Philip Lutgendorf, "All in the (Raghu) Family: A Video Epic in Cultural Context," in Lawrence A. Babb and Susan S. Wadley (eds), *Media and the Transformation of Religion in South Asia*, Philadelphia: University of Pennsylvania Press, 1995, esp. pp.218–26.
27. See, for example, Romila Thapar, "Imgained Religious Communities? Ancient History and the Modern Search for a Hindu Identity," *Modern Asian Studies* (May 1989) pp.209–31 and Subrata Kumar Mitra, "Desecularising the State: Religion and Politics in India after Independence," *Comparative Studies in Society and History* 33/4 (1991) pp.755–77.
28. Menachem Begin, *The Revolt*, 1948; rpt., Los Angeles: Nash, 1972, p.88.
29. Bakker, "Ayodhya: A Hindu Jerusalem," pp.93–4, Van der Veer, *Gods on Earth*, pp.38–9, and Peter van der Veer, "God must be Liberated!' A Hindu Liberation Movement in Ayodhya," *Modern Asian Studies* 21/2 (1987) pp.288–9.
30. Van der Veer, "God must be Liberated!", p.289.
31. Meron Benvenisti, *Fatal Embrace*, Jerusalem: Keter Publishing, 1992, pp.15–17 (Hebrew). The most comprehensive account of the struggle over the Temple Mount and the *al-haram as-sharif* since 1967 is Nadav Shagrai, *The Contentious Mountain – The Struggle over the Temple Mount: Jews and Muslims, Religion and Politics since 1967*, Jerusalem: Keter Publishing, 1995.
32. "Ending corruption main plank: BJP," *Times of India*, 19 June 1993.
33. Mark Fineman, "The Wrath of Rama: A Fight Over a Mosque on Ground Holy to Hindus Has Reignited India's Ancient Feud," *Los Angeles Times Magazine*, 19 May 1991.
34. Ibid.
35. Menachem Friedman, "The State of Israel as a Theological Dilemma," in Baruch Kimmeling (ed.), *The Israeli State and Society: Boundaries and Frontiers*, Albany, NY: SUNY Press, 1989, esp. pp.203–4.
36. Clifford Geertz, *Negara: The Theater State in Nineteenth Century Bali*, Princeton: Princeton University Press, 1980, "Centers, Kings and Charisma: Reflections on the Symbolics of Power," in *Local Knowledge: Further Essays in Interpretive Anthropology*, New York: Basic Books, 1983, pp.21–146, and, most recently, James S. Duncan, *The City as Text: The Politics of Landscape Interpretation in the Kandyan Kingdom*, Cambridge: Cambridge University Press, 1990.

Imported Problem Definitions, Legal Culture and the Local Dynamics of Israeli Abortion Politics

NOGA MORAG-LEVINE

INTRODUCTION

The subject of abortion has sparked political and religious controversy in countries all over the world during the past few decades, and Israel has been no exception. Energized by the commitments of transplanted American immigrants and infused with the language of the American controversy, Israeli abortion politics unfolded largely in the shadow of American abortion divisions. Yet despite the significance of this influence, pertinent domestic debates retain fundamental distinctions from their American counterpart. Most notably, these differences are in the salience of abortion problems in the political agendas of the two countries, the relative weight of individualist and collectivist formulations of relevant interests, and the place of law and legal institutions in the definition and resolution of the abortion issue. Whereas abortion in the United States is a recurrent source of deep social divisions, political violence, and constitutional litigation, abortion in Israel is a tangential controversy characterized by a systemic gap between restrictive formal legal norms and liberal abortion practices. This article considers both the impact of the American abortion dispute on the evolution of Israeli abortion politics and the factors responsible for continuing divergence between the political and legal frameworks defining abortion questions in the two countries.

The relationship between problem definitions on the one hand and policy agendas, processes, and outcomes on the other, is the subject of an extensive and diverse political science inquiry. Nevertheless, relatively little attention has been directed at the cross-national dimensions of this issue. Acknowledging this gap, Bosso has contended that "(t)o look harder at how distinct polities define problems to begin with may give us

---

Noga Morag-Levine is in the Department of Political Science at the University of Michigan.

renewed appreciation for the relative distinctiveness of national policy styles amidst problem-induced similarities. Comparative studies of problem definition can go a long way toward separating out what is shared and what remains unique."[1] As an example of the type of insights such research can yield, Bosso cites Yishai's comparison of the distinct problem definitions underpinning abortion politics in Sweden, the US, Ireland, and Israel.[2] Building upon Yishai's work and heeding Bosso's call, this article considers the fit between broader traits of Israeli law and politics and the problem definitions framing the Israeli abortion debate. But instead of a horizontal cross-national comparison between central governing problem definitions, this study adopts a dynamic approach comparing the place of alternative problem definitions across the evolution of Israeli abortion politics. Within this context, particular attention is paid to domestic elements supporting and impeding the implementation of fundamental features of the American abortion dispute within Israel's internal abortion scene.

The limited resonance of US- inspired abortion problem definitions in Israel is indicative of enduring political and legal cultural differences. The American conception of abortion as a universally tragic dilemma pitting a woman's right to choose against a fetus's right to life, conflicts with particularistic Jewish formulations of the question in Israel. At the same time, American constructions of the problem as a constitutional dilemma concerning the limits of legitimate governmental power are inconsistent with two salient Israeli attributes. The first is the continuing, though diminished, deference to nationally defined collective values and the related perceived normalcy of state intervention in one's personal life. The second is a systemic reliance, termed here *de facto legalism*, on various quasi-legal, illegal, and extra-legal mechanisms in mitigating such interferences and mediating fundamental value conflicts. The impact of these differences on the capacity of imported conceptions of the abortion dispute to alter the issue's salience and meaning in Israel is the central concern of this article.

AMERICAN ABORTION INFLUENCE AND THE MECHANISMS OF IMPORTATION

Abortion was among the many political causes carried to Israel by American immigrants. American expatriates and immigrants from other English speaking countries have played a decisive role in mobilizing Israeli abortion activism, on both sides of the issue, and in the introduction of American conceptions of the dispute into Israeli political discourse. This process was most clearly embodied in the career of Marcia Freedman, an American immigrant and Citizens' Rights Party member of Knesset during the early 1970s. Freedman arrived at the Knesset in January 1974, only a few months after *Roe v. Wade* (1973) was decided in the United States. The first piece of legislation she introduced was a Freedom of Choice bill which, following *Roe,* proposed ending all abortion restrictions during the first three months of pregnancy and cited the basic human right of deciding whether or not to bring a child into the world.[3] Four years later when she left the Knesset, Marcia Freedman was still talking about abortion.[4] In the intervening four years Freedman and the disproportionately English speaking Israeli feminist movement she helped found spearheaded a campaign that, for the first time, brought the subject of abortion to Israel's streets and living rooms. Marcia Freedman's abortion bill was defeated by an alternative and more restrictive legislative proposal. But the efforts of Freedman and other US-influenced feminists were crucial in setting Israeli abortion law reform in motion.

To this day, Israeli abortion activism is often expressed with an American inflection. This is especially true of activists calling for greater liberalization of regulatory restrictions but applies also to largely orthodox American immigrants who, through a variety of strategies, have sought to reduce the number of abortions in Israel. Notable in this context were the activities of Haim Hazan, an American born statistician and a one-time special abortion consultant to the Minister of Health appointed under ultra-orthodox pressure.[5] A less militant anti-abortion Jewish American influence is represented in Just One Life, an organization created under the auspices of the Council of Young Israel Rabbis in Israel with the goal of providing economic and social support for alternatives to abortion.

Israeli interest groups on both sides of the issue receive financial support from sympathetic organizations and individuals abroad, and at times even seek direct engagement by outside, most commonly American actors, in their internal struggles. Thus a 1992 campaign organized by an ad-hoc coalition of women and civil rights groups in opposition to a proposed change to Israel's abortion law, requested and received political and financial support from liberal American Jewish groups. A memo written by the coalition made explicit reference to the need within this realm for "both national and international advocacy, including public and private opposition by American Jewish leadership who are known to be committed to reproductive rights."[6] More recently and from the opposite direction, the head of a major Israeli anti-abortion organization quoted a statement made by the American Senator Jesse Helms according to which a "substantial number of senators and congressmen would demand a reduction of foreign aid to Israel" unless the number of abortions in Israel is immediately reduced.[7]

Similarly, developments in American abortion politics are closely followed and viewed as domestically relevant by both sides of the Israeli abortion controversy. Thus, for example, in a 1992 speech before the Knesset, MK Yosef Azran of the religious Shas Party noted in an apparently garbled reference to the US Supreme Court's 1992 *Casey*[8] decision: "a recent decision by the Supreme Court, not ours, but in the

United States, required a medical committee deciding upon an abortion to provide the woman with extensive information regarding the outcome of abortion. ... Why what is common in the United States should not be common in Israel?"[9] On the other side of the arena, women's organizations pay similarly close attention to the evolution of American abortion doctrine. In the wake of the Court's *Webster* opinion, the secretary-general of the large women organization Naamat voiced concern over the potential impact of the decision on anti-abortion forces in Israel and urged Labor Zionist organizations in the United States to add their political muscle to the American pro-choice struggle.[10] For their part, members of the Israel Feminist Movement wrote to President Bush to protest his veto of abortion funding legislation and to announce their intention to hold an Israeli march in support of a planned National Organization of Women Washington, DC reproductive rights rally.[11]

The very reliance of Israeli abortion activists on American energy, funding, and ideological inspiration suggests the extent to which abortion remains foreign to core Israeli concerns. Aided by the general attentiveness of the Israeli media and public to all manner of American trends, efforts to move abortion onto the center stage of Israeli politics and to imbue it with American derived symbolic significance were nevertheless hindered by legal and political-cultural factors which conferred distinctly different meanings and solutions on the abortion question.

A SHORT HISTORY OF ISRAELI ABORTION REGULATION

The following summary of the history of abortion regulation in Israel sets the stage for subsequent discussion of competing problem definitions in the debates surrounding various stages in the development of Israeli abortion policy.

Until 1977, the Israeli criminal code strictly prohibited all abortions, although the courts interpreted the law to exempt abortions performed under medical necessity. Similar in nature to anti-abortion state laws that existed prior to 1973 in the United States, the Israeli law did little to alter widespread illegal abortion practices by private providers.[12] In addition, state subsidized sick funds performed abortions approved by ad hoc committees instituted by the sick funds themselves.[13] This mechanism was the one essentially adopted by the Knesset when Israel reformed its abortion law in 1977.

The new abortion law combined a general criminal prohibition against the performance of abortions with specified procedures for the approval of some abortions by authorized medical committees. The law included a list of legitimate grounds for committee approval of abortion requests. Under the 1977 law these grounds included the age of the woman, her health, marital status, and illegal circumstances surrounding the pregnancy (i.e. rape, incest). An additional provision, known as the

Social Clause, authorized committees to approve abortions on the basis of difficult socio-economic conditions surrounding the woman or her family.

The Social Clause was eliminated from the law in 1980 under pressure from an ultra-orthodox coalition partner. Since that time there have been no further amendments to the law despite periodic demands for the Clause's reinstatement and for stricter abortion restrictions. Problem definitions employed by various interest groups active in this effort are the center of the following discussion.

THE PROBLEM OF ABORTION: ALTERNATIVE ISRAELI DEFINITIONS

The Israeli abortion debate incorporates five central definitions of the problem, three associated with calls for more restrictive abortion policies, and two with more liberal perspectives on the subject. They are abortion as a: (1) religious problem, (2) demographic problem, (3) moral problem, (4) social welfare problem, and (5) feminist cause.

Abortion as a Religious Problem

In Israel, as elsewhere, religious norms and interests have been at the center of demands for greater abortion restrictions. Orthodox religious parties have spearheaded all anti-abortion legislative initiatives. Similarly, as discussed below, groups active in opposition to abortions are directly or indirectly associated with orthodox interests. Nevertheless, the Israeli abortion arena is marked by the relative paucity of explicit religious argumentation, and by what appears to be an intentional effort by anti-abortion activists to distance their campaigns from other secular–religious cleavages in Israel. Thus, Member of Knesset (MK) Avraham Shapira, from the ultra-orthodox party Yahadut Hatorah, began a parliamentary speech urging stricter enforcement of Israel's abortion law with the words: "The multiplicity of abortions in Israel is not a religious subject. ... The subject is totally within the domain of health and education, and ought to be viewed as a first order national priority."[14]

The insulation of the abortion question from direct religion and state conflicts is facilitated by the comparative flexibility of relevant Jewish religious doctrine, and the compatibility of this doctrine with alternative, non-religious Israeli justifications for abortion law. In contrast to the absolutist premises propelling much Christian, especially Catholic, anti-abortion positions, orthodox Judaism allows significant room for compromise. The Torah makes no explicit mention of abortion, removing the issue from the realm of supreme biblical prohibitions. Subsequent rabbinical discussions are vague and inconsistent, but unequivocal in the priority accorded the life of the mother over that of the fetus. The central Talmudic text in this regard concerns a situation in which a woman encounters life-threatening difficulties in labor. The rabbbis' answer regarding abortion under these circumstances distinguishes between two situations. Prior to the emergence of the head, "her life takes priority over his life." But if labor had progressed beyond that point he is not to be touched "because one does not trade one soul with another."[15] Rabbinical responses dating back to the seventeenth century express degrees of disapproval but lack the theological urgency of doctrines viewing life as beginning at conception. Instead, the emphasis shifts to the nature of the circumstances constituting sufficient threat to maternal well-being so as to justify abortion under Jewish law.[16] Differences between this framework and the one propelling the American pro-life position are evident in the language employed by the American ultra-orthodox organization Agudath Israel of America in an Amicus brief submitted to the US Supreme Court in connection with the *Casey* decision. The brief called for replacing the fundamental rights concept of *Roe v. Wade*, with "a framework whereby abortion claims would or would not be accorded 'fundamental rights' status depending upon the circumstances surrounding their assertion."[17] Speaking to the differences between Jewish religious law and Catholic dogma on this issue, Rabbi Pinhas Stolper, executive director of the Union of Orthodox Jewish Congregations, stated in 1989: "We do not identify with those groups that feel all abortion is murder. ... Unlike the Catholic position ... in the Jewish view the supreme need is to consider the life, health and well being of the mother."[18]

A similar contextual approach was advanced by two rabbinical opinions accompanying a 1974 report by a commission charged with providing a blueprint for revising Israel's abortion law.[19] Significantly, the law proposed by this commission and subsequently adopted, with minor revisions by the Knesset, is more in harmony with the traditional Jewish approach than the more absolute prohibition it replaced. The Israeli statute combines principled disapproval of abortion with exemptions under specified circumstances, a solution much in keeping rabbinical case by case decisions on abortion. While Israeli law substituted the secular authority of the committees for the rabbinical, it retained the norms and logic of the traditional religious process.

The primary difference between the 1977 law and Jewish tradition lay in its inclusion of socio-economic conditions among the specified exemptions. The difficulty of reconciling socio-economic exemptions with religious formulations of maternal health led to ultimately successful ultra-orthodox agitation against the Social Clause. Yet, importantly, in keeping with the previously mentioned efforts to insulate the abortion debate from the politics of religion in Israel, that argument has rarely assumed center stage in the ultra-orthodox campaign against the Clause.

Speaking to the incentives to camouflage the religious motivations behind anti-abortion positions, a 1984 editorial in a newsletter published by Efrat, the primary group active in the anti abortion front, stated:

> We should develop ideas and present facts before the general public. We should not use religious arguments in front of them. There are plenty of philosophical, moral, demographic and health reasons to oppose abortions. ... Religious justifications may lead the secular public to think that this is just another religious observance.[20]

First among such alternative formulations has been the presentation of abortions as a threat to the future of a Jewish popular majority in Israel.

Abortion as a Demographic Problem

Otherwise sharply divided factions in Israeli politics share concerns about the stability of a Jewish popular majority in Israel, based on the close link between the country's demographic composition and the Israeli state's precarious Jewish and democratic identity. Demographic constructions of the abortion problem thus gain sympathy not only from those concerned with the state's Jewish future, but also from those committed to the long-term viability of the democratic Jewish formula.

Demographic concerns were, in fact, the context within which abortion first entered Israel's political agenda during the 1960s. In 1962, in response to well publicized declines in the rate of Jewish births, Efrat, the anti-abortion group noted above, was established. Its full name at the time was "Efrat – Association for the Encouragement of Fertility among the Jewish People." Efrat initially promoted general pronatalist policies and social norms, rather than anti-abortion legislation. However, by 1965, Efrat was actively calling for stricter enforcement of dormant abortion prohibitions.

The link between demographic concerns and abortion was likewise reflected in a 1966 report by a "natality problems" commission. The report cited abortion among the factors contributing to declining Jewish birthrates, and proposed a governmental unit that would oversee national demographic policy.[21] Established in 1968, the Demography Center, currently housed within the Ministry of Labor and Welfare, has repeatedly incorporated covert anti-abortion messages in its policy missions and publications.[22] In 1990, the Demography Center hatched a plan for a major survey to identify married and intentionally childless women with the goal of targeting these through a propaganda campaign that would argue that "professional careers are good and nice, but should not conflict with the creation of a family."[23]

The resonance of demographic arguments across the spectrum of Israeli politics is nowhere more evident than in the lip service paid by many abortion rights activists to Jewish natality concerns. Amir and Navon describe a reluctance on the part of a number of women and liberal groups, including the Israeli Association for Civil Rights and the Israeli Family Planning Association, to challenge the abortion-demographic linkage.[24] A 1992 position paper written by Alice Shalvi, the chairwoman of the Israel Women's Network, coupled strong opposition to proposed legislative restrictions with the following statement: "We do not, however, believe that abortion is a desirable mode of birth control and we call on the government and other authorities to develop a demographic policy of family planning which will include ... economic and social incentives for middle and upper income, university educated couples, to encourage them to have larger families."[25]

Abortion as a Moral Problem

The third problem definition employed by anti-abortion activists and the one most directly influenced by American pro-life rhetoric is the equation between abortion and murder. The most recent and direct appearance of this formulation in the context of Israeli legislative politics occurred in December 1996 when the ultra-orthodox party Shas submitted a bill defining the fetus as a person for the purpose of civil and criminal law. The bill which, if passed would have opened the way for the prosecution of abortion as murder, initially garnered the support of 51 members of Knesset including some from the Labor Party. It lost momentum, however, when the opposition mobilized and some of its initial supporters withdrew, claiming that they had not understood its relevance to abortion. Primarily a symbolic gesture, this bill is nevertheless significant as a first attempt to introduce fetus-centered formulations, evocative of American pro-life discourse, into Israeli statutory debates.

Language and symbols characteristic of the American pro-life movement appear in Israel for the first time during the 1980s. A 1985 Efrat newsletter featured Ronald Reagan on its cover and cited the American pro-life movement as a model worthy of imitation. Efrat also began to incorporate in its publications, Hebrew adaptations of American pro-life staples such as "Four Ways to Kill a Baby," and the organization's reference in its subtitle to Jewish natality was substituted with a new name: "The Right to Life."

Since that time, Efrat has emulated the emotional appeal of American pro-life campaigns with graphic images of the fetus and the abortion process. In 1996 Efrat distributed 1.4 million leaflets with an illustrated Hebrew adaptation of the "Diary of a Baby," an American pro-life publication relating the thoughts of a soon-to-be-aborted fetus. In public lectures across the country, Efrat representatives have frequently cast abortion as a dangerous, immoral, and grotesque act. These tactics have met with significant opposition, most interestingly from members of ultra-orthodox communities. After parents in several such communities complained about their children's exposure to pictures included in Efrat's "Diary of a Baby" leaflet, the organization published an apology in the ultra-orthodox press.[26]

Differences in the sensibilities of Israeli and American pro-life supporters and activists are likewise evident in the ambivalence expressed by Efrat's chairman, Dr. Eli Shus-Heim, regarding "Silent Scream," a movie depicting an abortion in graphic detail, and used as a frequent tool of the American pro-life movement. The movie, in Hebrew translation, is distributed and presented to targeted audiences by Efrat but, according to Shus-Heim, the Hebrew version produced by Efrat excludes some of the most disturbing sections included in the English original and is not usually shown to pregnant women considering abortion. Distancing himself from American pro-life language, Shus-Heim articulated his view of the relationship between abortion and murder: "I don't use the word murder, I don't think it adds anything. But it is the cessation of life of a human creature."[27]

Partially the product of differences in style and aesthetic sensibilities, Efrat's reluctant embrace of pro-life language and tactics is, more profoundly, the product of fundamental tensions between the agendas of the two anti-abortion movements. While hard core pro-life activists in the United States see abortion as a matter of life or death, such moral fervor is largely absent from parallel Israeli activism. This difference results from variation in underlying religious motivations. As noted, Jewish religious law does not condemn all abortions, and, indeed, requires them where the mother is endangered. Thus, Jewish abortion prohibitions are difficult to reconcile with pro-life constructions equating all abortions with murder.

In contrast with the American pro-life movement's concern with global protection of fetuses everywhere, efforts in Israel exclusively target abortions performed on Jewish women. This distinction is in part itself a product of differences in underlying religious beliefs, but it also follows from the centrality of nationalistic demographic concerns noted above. A statement on Israeli television by Haim Hazan, the American immigrant consultant to the Ministry of Health, offers a particularly jarring example of the instrumental and particularistic tenor of pro-life rhetoric in Israel: "I do not accept the malignant notion that a woman is master of her body. Her body does not belong to her. The fetus has a right to live. ... He is a potential soldier. In recent years close to 2000 potential divisions have been destroyed."[28] A visit to Efrat's Internet home page is likewise instructive. At the top of the page, which includes links to excerpts from the movie "Silent Scream," and other pro-life documents, a new organizational title suggests growing discomfort with the universalistic premise of the American pro-life manifestos. In contrast to the words "right to life" added to Efrat's name during the 1980s, the new name reads: "International Organization for Saving Jewish Babies."[29]

These tensions derive from conflicts between the logics of local and imported formulations of the abortion problem and are essential to understanding the dynamics underpinning cross-national importation of ideological causes. As the following discussion reveals, similar difficulties were encountered by those who sought to introduce liberal, feminist based definitions of the problem presented by abortion regulation.

Abortion as a Social Welfare Problem

The abortion law enacted in Israel in 1977 was the product of converging pressures from opposite sides of Israel's political spectrum. The first was a coalition of religious-national interests pushing for stricter enforcement of abortion prohibitions. The second was a small group of American inspired feminists, critical of existing abortion prohibitions and eager to invoke the issue's symbolic power to mobilize the women's movement in Israel. They encountered significant resistance from traditional women's organizations in the country who were wary of unsettling an ambiguous, but generally adequately functioning status quo, in which abortions, though legally forbidden, were easily obtainable.[30] Their support was ultimately won through appeals grounded in social welfare rather than purely feminist considerations.

Long-standing pro-natalist commitments began to be qualified during the early 1970s by new awareness of the relationship between large family size and poverty. A 1972 report by the Prime Minister's Committee on Children and Youth in Distress focused public attention on the socio-economic gap between families of Afro, Asian, and European origin, linking this gap to differences in family size.[31] Yishai contends that a "hidden agenda" directed at the reduction of Afro-Asian birth-rates undermined the effectiveness of explicit pro-natalist policies. The role of this mixed agenda was evident in the centrality of poor women's access to abortion for the coalition that ultimately passed abortion reform.[32]

The intended beneficiaries of the Social Clause initially included in the legislation were married, young, and healthy women who could not qualify for abortions under alternative exemption categories. Under this clause, such women could benefit from state-facilitated and even some state-funded abortions. In addition, the clause explicitly recognized socio-economic conditions, conferring some legitimacy upon abortions performed for such reasons. Reflecting upon the centrality of the clause to the ultimate passage of the law, Ora Namir, a Labor Party MK at the time and a former government minister, commented: "The abortion law was primarily enacted because of the socio-economic clause. Well-off women, including religious well-off women, don't need laws, they know where to go and how to protect themselves. We thought it was important ... to aid a population of women that have difficulty dealing with the conditions of their lives."[33] In response to the social welfare rationale of the new legislation, the 1977 law requires that abortion approval committees include a social worker in addition to physicians. Not surprisingly, the Social Workers Union actively opposed the abolition of the Social Clause.[34]

Since the abolition of the Social Clause, liberal abortion activism has centered upon largely ritualistic initiatives directed at the Clause's reinstatement. Such proposals periodically appear before the Knesset, and the Labor Party platform has repeatedly included a principled (but unimplemented) commitment to restore the Clause. This, rather than a demand for elimination of abortion prohibitions as such, has been the central rallying cry of Israeli abortion activism. This trend has been coupled by similar emphasis upon health and immigrant absorption policies, in the rhetoric invoked by women groups faced with subsequent threats to the Israeli abortion status quo. Thus a broad based women's coalition, created in 1990 in response to a pending anti-abortion legislation, framed its campaign in reference to health rather than women's autonomy. This emphasis contrasted with explicit pro-choice rhetoric invoked by American liberal Jewish groups that provided both funding and political support for the coalition's campaign.[35] Similar strategic considerations led the Coalition to emphasize the connection between liberal abortion policies and the needs of new immigrant populations. Due to frequent use of abortion as a substitute for contraception among immigrants from the former Soviet Union, demand for abortion was expected to rise disproportionately in the wake of increased immigration during the late 1980s and early 1990s.[36] The projected effect on successful absorption of these immigrants was invoked by the coalition in general publications and in a letter sent to members of the Knesset Immigration and Absorption Committee.[37]

The thread running through the problem definitions employed by groups favoring liberal abortion policy is an avoidance of feminist language and women's rights formulations. While efforts to recast Israeli abortion politics in a more feminist image have been repeatedly made, they have been politically marginalized.

Abortion as a Feminist Cause

As noted before, during the 1970s American feminist influences introduced a new vocabulary and tactics into Israeli abortion discourse. Carrying banners declaring "We are not the national womb," members of the nascent feminist movement disrupted a 1976 meeting of the Israel Association of Obstetricians and Gynecologists, which then opposed liberalized abortion law. Through the efforts of Marcia Freedman, they also placed an explicit pro-choice agenda before the Knesset. This agenda failed due to tensions between the rights-based focus of the imported feminist agenda and the national collectivist values that many Israeli women continue to hold. Yishai describes the political lives of Israeli women as shaped by the conflicting pulls of collective and individual identities, feminist and nationalist commitments. Difficulties in reconciling these competing goals, Yishai argues, have stymied women's capacity to advance their interests politically.[38] This observation appears especially pertinent to understanding the limited impact of feminist perspectives on the course of Israeli abortion debates. The resonance of demographic concerns across a wide spectrum of Israeli politics was clearly a factor in Israeli women groups' reluctance to promote a free choice agenda. But perhaps more fundamental was the distinctly different meaning of the concept of choice, as such, in Israeli political life.

Amir and Binyamin describe Israeli abortion procedures as rituals of symbolic control. These rituals serve as disciplinary mechanisms for articulating collective disapproval, but do not, in practice, block Israeli women's access to abortion.[39] Israeli women's acceptance of a law requiring them to plead their need for abortion before three strangers is understandable when one realizes that this is part of a much broader pattern of interference by the Israeli state in the most personal spheres of life. In a society in which women undergo both a compulsory draft and pre-marital rabbinate decreed and state-sanctioned inquiries into their menstrual cycle, abortion committees amount to a relatively less invasive affront. But perhaps even more significantly, where the possibility of sacrificing one's child in war is never far from the mind of any parent, a governmental role in procreation decisions is likely to seem less preposterous. Reflecting the complexity of these sentiments, Labor Party MK Yael Dayan made the following statement in support of the Social Clause's return: "The state can send its children to the army, for life or death. ... It can not force us to be mothers. ... [T]here is no compulsory law on motherhood and love."[40] In what may have been a Freudian slip, the liberal MK's own reference to the state's right to send *its* children to the army suggests the gap between the political cultures in which Israeli and American abortion rights activism are planted.

The American focus on rights, whether of the fetus or the woman, was thus countered in Israel with arguments couched in the language of national rather than individual well being. The marginality of rights to definitions of abortion problems in Israel is in part explained by continuing deference to the state as an embodiment of nationally defined collective values. But this marginality is, in addition, the product of the relative irrelevance of legally defined rights to actual state interference in abortion. The gap between abortion law and practice and its place within broader Israeli legal cultural traits is the subject of the following section.

RIGHTS, DE FACTO LEGALISM, AND LEGAL CULTURE

In the United States, delimiting the authority of government to regulate abortion has been the ongoing task of the Supreme Court. So far two lines of decisions have addressed this question. The first established abortion as a constitutionally protected right and severely curtailed the circumstances justifying state intervention in this area, while the second divorced any such abortion rights from constitutional entitlements to state or federal assistance.[41] In Israel, however, the question of governmental powers was immaterial to a debate which, in the absence of constitutional limitations, focused on the terms of state intervention rather than its justification.[42] However, these terms of intervention were only partially reflected in formal legal resolutions of the abortion question. They were instead defined through semi-formal mechanisms grounded in the ambiguous authority of the abortion approval committees.

Law, Mobilization and Abortion Compromises

Despite the sharp controversy that surrounded the Social Clause's abolition, the change had little practical impact on the number of approved abortions which, after a temporary dip, soon returned to their pre-amendment levels.[43] The elimination of the Clause did not reduce the number of abortions because, in the wake of the legislative change, abortion approval committees began to substitute alternative exemption categories, most notably physical or mental risk to the mother, for explicit reliance on socio-economic considerations.[44] The ease with which the abortion committees could effect this change stems from the almost complete autonomy the Israeli abortion law grants abortion approval committees. The Israeli abortion statute offers no rationale for the qualified prohibition it imposes and does not identify the claims it seeks to balance. A woman who is denied an abortion by a committee cannot appeal the decision, but can bring her request before any additional committee or committees. At the same time, a committee's decision to grant an abortion is essentially unreviewable. The Israeli Supreme Court has determined that a husband, and by implication any other third party, does not have a right to appear before a pregnancy termination committee (*Plonit v. Ploni*, 1980).[45]

An important result of this autonomy has been significant diversity among the committees operating in various hospitals in the country. These differences pertain both to the rigidity of relevant bureaucratic procedures and to the leniency with which alternative committees tend to approach requests for abortion approval.[46] This variation results from both the personal beliefs of senior doctors and administrators in each hospital and from the hospital's religious affiliation.[47] The power to bring abortion requests before any committee in the country and resubmit denied requests before alternative committees, coupled with the availability of liberal, often private hospital operated, committees have been the lynchpin of Israeli abortion compromises.

Thus, a 1990 attempt to tamper with this arrangement through legislation regulating such private hospital committees[48] resulted in one of the most visible and well-coordinated abortion access campaigns in Israel. After the proposed amendment passed the first of three required hearings in the Knesset, a broadly based coalition of fifteen women's, and civil rights groups was created to fight the bill. The coalition, largely financed by contributions from American Jewish sources, targeted

Knesset members of both the right and the left, convened press conferences, published a detailed information pamphlet and prepared to launch a mass public campaign including petitions and demonstrations. These plans were rescinded when the political tide shifted and the bill was tabled after ultra-orthodox pressure waned.[49]

The organizational effort spawned by the proposed private hospital amendment was quite unusual. Although members of left-leaning parties have brought many bills seeking the reintroduction of the Social Clause, women's groups have tended not to mobilize behind such actions. Perhaps more significantly, even a proposal to eliminate all abortion restrictions and the entire committee system, initiated in 1987 by Labor Party MK Ora Namir after a young woman died while undergoing an illegal private abortion,[50] failed to arouse much interest among women's organizations.

A similar lack of emphasis upon formal legislative solutions is evident in the strategies of anti-abortion interest groups. Efrat's chairman, Eli Shus-Heim, has indicated his willingness to support a return of the Social Clause to the law in exchange for greater access by Efrat to abortion committees and women facing abortion choices. Efrat has likewise expressed reservations regarding the earlier mentioned 1997 attempt by the ultra-orthodox Shas to define the embryo from conception onward as a person under the criminal code. Addressing differences between American Evangelical pro-lifers and his own organization, Shus-Heim stated: "You cannot save even one baby by passing laws, by trying to force people. We need to respect a woman's rights – she has a right to know exactly what it is that's growing inside her. We believe in education, not confrontation."[51]

This belief, perhaps most profoundly, has led Efrat to reject the civil disobedience tactics endorsed by some American pro-life groups. Efrat's home page now highlights the following statement: "(Efrat) categorically rejects demonstrations and acts of violence against doctors and clinics, and condemns breaking the law."[52] This position is in part the product of tactical concerns regarding the potential backlash that civil disobedience tactics may trigger in Israel. But it more significantly reflects deeper underlying differences between American and Israeli pro-life conceptions of the political and symbolic importance of law within abortion struggles and the urgency of moral justifications for its violation. The reluctance of abortion activists on both sides to engage the law directly indicates fundamental differences in the meaning and impact of law within each of the abortion stories. This phenomenon is perhaps nowhere clearer than in the rhetoric invoked by the Israeli Supreme Court in its few references to the circumstances governing abortion in the country.

De Facto Legalism and Abortion Rights

The status of abortion has, since the enactment of the 1977 law, come before the Court on only two occasions. The first was the earlier mentioned 1980 *Plonit v. Almoni* decision in which a majority concluded that a husband did not have the right to intervene in approval procedures pertaining to his wife's abortion request. The second involved the Court's 1993 and 1996 decisions in *Nahmani v. Nahmani*,[53] which dealt with the right of a husband to veto the implantation into a surrogate mother of fertilized eggs jointly created by him and his now estranged wife. The common denominator linking these cases is Supreme Court language conferring a quasi-legal status on de facto abortion practices contradictory to the letter of the law. The 1980 case, decided after the cancellation of the Social Clause, concerned an abortion request by a married woman who was in the process of separating from her (according to her claim) abusive husband. Although the woman's request was not based in any of the remaining legal exemption categories, the legal grounds for the committee's abortion approval were never discussed in the decision, which focused instead on the husband's claimed right to intervene. In a revealing statement, Justice Ben-Ito acknowledged the precariousness of the legal structures underpinning the abortion status quo when she described the pertinent law as a delicate compromise aimed at determining not whether but how abortions would be performed and cautioned against judicial interference in this fragile equilibrium.[54] In a similar fashion, the existence of a qualified right to abortion in Israeli law served as an important subtext of the judicial and academic debate surrounding the Supreme Court's two *Nahmani* decisions. Both decisions include specific references to the rights of women to control their body and to the contested analogy between the existence of such rights and Mr. Nahmani's right to veto the implementation of the eggs. The Justices' references to a right to abortion, despite the law's explicit prohibition of the practice, suggests the manner in which de facto formulations of abortion rights are embedded within Israeli abortion discourse, reaching even to the Supreme Court.

In contrast to American concerns with dyadic divisions between constitutional and unconstitutional moves, Israel's abortion arena has unfolded along a spectrum marked by much more subtle gradations in legality. Israeli legal rights, whether those of the fetus or the woman, have been marginal to an abortion management process only marginally constrained by its legal shell. Instead, both sides, out of mutual fear of backlash, appear committed to compromise premised upon the circumvention of law. Amir and Navon describe the Israeli abortion scene as a two tiered system shrouded in an air of secrecy aimed at preserving the gap between a restrictive image and liberal reality.[55] The fit between such formulas and similar extra legal religion and state resolutions links the Israeli abortion story to broader traits of Israeli political and legal culture.

The Avoidance of Law and Irreconcilable Differences

Current Israeli abortion resolutions rest upon two opposing concessions. Formal state law accords with pertinent Jewish religious tenets, while actual practices support state-facilitated abortions that are often at odds with religious precepts. It is an arrangement in keeping with similar ad hoc resolutions of potentially explosive political conflicts.

The avoidance of law has been a crucial strategy in Israeli circumvention of direct opposition between the state's Jewish and democratic commitments. The absence of an Israeli constitution articulating the meaning of these commitments and the extra-legal but well entrenched status quo governing the place of religious norms within multiple spheres of public life are the primary examples of such avoidance.[56] Israeli abortion solutions diverge to some extent from extra-legal approaches to the religious status quo because the open ended abortion committee discretion on which they rely constitutes an institutional bypass within the law. Similar solutions have been employed in Israel in a variety of politically sensitive areas ranging from the definition of army service exemptions granted to ultra-orthodox men as "postponements" to state recognition of religiously forbidden marriages performed abroad. The avoidance and circumvention of law converge in Israel with broader illegalist social tendencies. Sprinzak identifies Israeli illegalism as "an instrumental orientation towards the legal order and a conviction that democracy does not depend upon strict adherence to the law."[57] Similar arguments regarding an Israeli propensity towards contingent understandings of law have subsequently been made by Lehman-Wilzig and Rosen-Zvi.[58]

Neither illegalism nor extra-legalism are unique Israeli traits. They exist to some extent in all societies. But the phenomenon may be especially pronounced under conditions of norm competition and dissonance between alternative legal cultures.[59] In a comparison of attitudes toward law among European Union countries, Gibson and Caldeira found cross-national differences in a willingness to tolerate exceptions to the law, and linked these differences to variations in underlying legal cultures.[60] In an investigation of the factors responsible for such legal cultural variations, Bierbrauer connected differences between collectivist and individualist orientations among Kurds, Lebanese, and Germans, with divergent preferences for formal procedure and guidelines.[61] The Israeli case appears to offer further evidence regarding both the existence and the significance of such cross-national differences and the manner in which they influence the definition and negotiation of fundamental social disputes such as abortion.

CONCLUSION

The unique place of abortion in the US follows from two closely linked features of the American debate. The first is a direct competition between two absolutist and mutually exclusive rights-based formulations of the problem. The second is a political and legal cultural framework in which such rights give rise to binding constitutional limitations on the authority of government. Problem definitions supporting rights-based formulations thus pushed the abortion question into the central stage of constitutional law and politics. In contrast, problem definitions grounded in alternative conceptions of state authority and legal culture significantly diminished the salience of abortion in Israel.

Whereas both governing American abortion problem definitions are individualist and absolutist, the Israeli debate reflects a more collectivist and contextual understanding. On the anti-abortion side, this difference is the product of contingency inherent to religious Jewish attitudes towards abortion, and the particularistic focus of national Jewish demographic concerns. Both factors distinguish such Israeli activism from the universalistic and right to life claims of their American counterparts. On the opposite side of the issue, pervasive governmental interference in multiple intimate spheres of Israeli life dictated against the construction of abortion regulation as a unique invasion of a protected autonomous domain. Instead, problem definitions appealing to collective interests in social welfare, women's health, and immigration absorption were employed.

Differences in underlying problem definitions naturally extended to differential emphasis on law centered rhetoric and tactics. Abortion in the United States is constructed, first and foremost, as a constitutional dilemma pertaining to the power of government to enact particular laws. In Israel, such questions are less consequential not only due to differences in conceptions of legitimate state authority, but also due to the lesser significance of law *per se* in resolving of such questions. Incentives for law-centered discourse and tactics are tied to perceptions of the symbolic and direct impact of relevant legal instruments. In Israel, however, the terms of religion and state compromises have often depended upon closely guarded gaps between formal symbolic messages and actual practices. In abortion, as in many other points of conflict between Jewish religious norms and the secular state's democratic commitments, the avoidance of law has served to deflect direct confrontation between what many Israelis fear are irreconcilable fundamental differences. Fear of bringing these differences into the open has sustained ambiguous political resolutions and legal circumvention techniques. American inspired conceptions of what is at stake in abortion ultimately failed to alter the course of Israeli abortion politics because they were incompatible with the terms of this increasingly fragile compromise.

ACKNOWLEDGMENTS

Support provided for this research by the Lady Davis Fellowship Trust is gratefully acknowledged.

NOTES

1. Christopher J. Bosso, "The Contextual Bases of Problem Definition," in David A. Rochefort and Roger W. Cobb (eds), *The Politics of Problem Definition*, Lawrence, KS: University of Kansas Press, 1994.
2. Yael Yishai, "Public Ideas and Public Policy: Abortion Politics in Four Democracies," *Comparative Politics* 25 (1993) pp.207-28.
3. *Roe v. Wade*, 410 U.S. 113 (1973). Marcia Freedman, *Exile in the Promised Land*, Ithaca, NY: Firebrand Books, 1990; Yael Yishai, "The Hidden Agenda: Abortion Politics in Israel," *Journal of Social Policy* 22/2 (1993) pp.193-212.
4. Freedman (note 3).
5. Delila Amir and David Navon, *The Politics of Abortion in Israel*, Tel Aviv: Pinchas Sapir Center for Development, Tel Aviv University, 1989.
6. "Shatil-Sponsored Coalition Opposes Changes in Israel's Abortion Law," (Press release on file at Israel Women's Network, Reproductive/Abortion file).
7. Judy Siegel, "Helms: PM Must Reduce Israeli Abortions," *Jerusalem Post*, 13 Feb. 1997.
8. In *Planned Parenthood of Southeastern Pennsylvania v. Casey* 112 S.Ct. 2791 (1992) the US Supreme Court voted to uphold provisions such as informed consent and a mandatory 24-hour waiting period in the Pennsylvania Abortion Control Act. The decision, of course, did not relate to abortion approval committees which are a feature of Israeli, not US, abortion regulation.
9. *Knesset Minutes 1991*, 13th Knesset, Meeting 8, 3, 279.
10. *Webster v. Reproductive Health Services*, 492 U.S. 490 (1989). Judy Siegel, "Na'Amat Fears Israeli Fallout From U.S. Ruling on Abortion," *Jerusalem Post*, 6 July 1989, p.2.
11. Letter from the Israel Feminist Movement to President George Bush, 10 Nov. 1989 (on file with author).
12. P. Sleiter, D. Wiener and M. Davis, "Denied Abortion Requests in Jerusalem, 1972-5," 20/3 (1978) pp.277-81. Dan Shnit, "Induced Abortion in Israeli Law," *Israeli Yearbook on Human Rights* 15 (1985) p.155.
13. Sleiter *et al.* (note 12).
14. *Knesset Minutes 1993*, 13th Knesset, Meeting 111, 35-32, 6198.
15. Mishna Ohalot.
16. David M. Feldman, *Birth Control in Jewish Law*, New York: New York University Press, 1968; Ratson Arusi, "Formal and Actual Norms Governing Abortion Under Jewish Law," *Diney Yisrael* 8 (1987) p.119.
17. Jewish Law Legal Briefs. *Casey v. Planned Parenthood of Southeastern Pennsylvania*, (http//www.jlaw.com/Briefs/casey.html).
18. Walter Ruby, "The Organized American Jewish Community Takes a 'Freedom of Choice' Line on Abortion," *Jerusalem Post*, 14 March 1989, p.7.
19. Committee for the Investigation of Abortion Prohibitions, "Commission Report: Appendixes D and E – Hallachic Opinions," *Public Health* 17/4 (1974) p.495.
20. Shlomo-Yona Tuaf, "Religious Justifications Ought Not Be Used in Front of the General Public," *Yedion* 17-18 (1984) p.3.
21. Dov Friedlander, "Population Policy in Israel," in Bernard Berelson (ed.), *Population Policy in Developed Countries*, New York: McGraw Hill, 1974.
22. Amir and Navon (note 5).
23. Michal Kedem, "The Ministry of Labor Investigates: Why Married Women Do Not Give Birth," *Hadashot*, 22 Nov. 1990.
24. Amir and Navon (note 5).
25. Alice Shalvi, "Why the I.W.N. Opposes the Proposed Changes in the Abortion Law," (on file at Israel Women's Network, Reproductive Abortion file).
26. Shachar Ilan, "Distribution of Anti Abortion Leaflet Ceased in Ultra Orthodox Neighborhoods," *Ha'aretz*, 1 Sept. 1996.
27. Liat Mashat, "A Horror Show Named Abortion," *Yediot Ahronot (Zmanim Modernim)*, 10 Oct. 1996, pp.4-5.
28. Tali Barzilai-Zonenfeld, "Not All Fetuses Are Equal," *Al Hamishmar*, 29 Jan. 1988, pp.17-19.
29. Http://www.efrat.org.il/back.html, 11/17/97.
30. Lesley Hazleton, *Israeli Women: The Reality Behind the Myths*, New York: Simon & Schuster, 1977.

31. Lotte Salzberger, Sarah Magidor, Amy Avgar, and Janet Baumgold-Land, *Patterns of Contraceptive Behavior Among Jerusalem Women Seeking Pregnancy Counselling 1980–1989*, Jerusalem: Hebrew University of Jerusalem, Paul Baerwald School of Social Work, 1991.
32. Yishai, "The Hidden Agenda" (note 3).
33. *Knesset Minutes 1990*, 12th Knesset, Meeting 181, 28 May.
34. Yitzhak Kadman, "Pregnancy Termination From a Social Perspective," *Society and Welfare* 2 (1979) pp.320–29.
35. Noga Morag-Levine, "Abortion in Israel: Community, Rights, and the Context of Compromise," *Law and Social Inquiry* 19/2 (1994) pp.313–35.
36. Eitan P. Sabattelo, "Early Assessments of an Increased Demand for Abortions Subsequent to the Growth of Immigration From the Soviet Union," *Hevra U'Revacha* (1992) p.185.
37. Protocol of the meeting of the Coalition for the Prevention of Amendment 30 to the Criminal Code, 11 Nov. 1990 (on file at Israeli Association for Civil Rights (ACRI), Abortion file).
38. Yael Yishai, *Between the Flag and the Banner: Women in Israeli Politics*, Albany, NY: State University of New York Press, 1997.
39. Delila Amir and Orly Binyamin, "Abortion Approval As a Ritual of Symbolic Control," in Clarice Feinman (ed.), *The Criminalization of Women's Body*, Binghampton, NY: Haworth Press, 1992, pp.1–25.
40. *Knesset Minutes 1993*, 13th Knesset, Meeting 137, 20 Oct.
41. The absence of a state interest in abortion restrictions aimed at the protection of fetal rights (during the first two trimesters of pregnancy) was established in *Roe v. Wade*, 410 U.S. 113 (1973). The absence of a state duty to provide funding for non-therapeutic abortions was established in *Maher v. Roe*, 432 U.S. 464 (1977) and *Harris v. McRae*, 448 U.S. 297 (1980).
42. Today, following the enactment of Basic Law: The Dignity and Freedom of the Individual (1992), new abortion restrictions would, in all likelihood, face political and legal challenges grounded in the claim that they violate protected fundamental individual rights. Although the fate of such claims, should they be raised either in the Knesset or before the Supreme Court, remains uncertain, there exists in Israel today a potential for a very different debate than the one that framed abortion legislation during the 1970s.
43. Amir and Navon (note 5).
44. Thus, whereas in 1979, 40% of hospital abortions were approved under the social clause and 8.2% were performed under the risk to the mother clause, in 1980, the year in which the social clause was eliminated, 35.1% of abortion approvals were granted under the medical risk clause. Israeli Central Bureau of Statistics figures cited in Amir and Navon (note 5).
45. *Plonit v. Ploni*, Civil Appeal 413/80, PADI 35 (3), 58, 1980.
46. Amir and Navon (note 5); Salzberger *et al.* (note 31).
47. Memorandum from attorney Neta Ziv Goldman to the directors of the Israel Association of Civil Rights (ACRI), May 1987 (on file at ACRI, Abortion file).
48. Draft Amendment No.30 to the Criminal Code, 21 Aug. 1989.
49. Morag-Levine (note 35); Yishai, *Between the Flag and the Banner* (note 38).
50. Private abortion bill submitted by MK Ora Namir to MK Rafi Edri, 26 Jan. 1987 (on file at Israel Women's Network Reproductive/Abortion file).
51. S.A. Osborne, "Bill Sparks Abortion Controversy," *Christianity Today* No.4, 7 April 1997, p.60.
52. Http://www.efrat.org.il/back.html, 11/17/97.
53. The Supreme Court tackled the Nahmani case twice. First, in a 1993 decision, the Court ruled that Mr. Nahmani had a right to stop the process *(D. Nahmani v. R. Nahmani and others*, Civil Appeal 5587/93, Padi, 49(1), 485). In an en-banc rehearing of the case in 1996 the Court reversed the 1993 decision and ruled in favor of Mrs. Nahmani (*R. Nahmani v. D. Nahmani and others*, Diyun Nosaf 2401/95 Tak-Al, Volume 96 (3), 522).
54. *Plonit v. Ploni*, Civil Appeal 413/80, p.60, 85-86.
55. Amir and Navon (note 5).
56. Charles S. Liebman and Eliezer Don-Yehiya, *Religion and Politics in Israel*, Bloomington: Indiana University Press, 1984.

57. Ehud Sprinzak, "Elite Illegalism in Israel and the Question of Democracy," in Ehud Sprinzak and Larry Diamond (eds), *Israeli Democracy Under Stress,* Boulder, CO: Lynne Rienner, 1993, p.175.
58. Sam N. Lehman-Wilzig, *Wildfire: Grassroots Revolts in Israel in the Post-Socialist Era*, Albany, NY: State University of New York Press, 1992. Ariel Rosen-Zvi, "Legal Culture: On Judicial Review, the Enforcement of Law and Inculcation of Values," *Iyunei Mishpat* 17 (1992) pp.689–716.
59. Dai-Kwon Choi, "Western Law in a Traditional Society Korea," and Keith S. Rosenn, "The Jeito: Brazil's Institutional Bypass of the Formal Legal System and Its Development Implications," in Csaba Varga (ed.), *Comparative Legal Cultures*, New York: New York University Press, 1992.
60. James L. Gibson and Gregory A. Caldeira, "The Legal Cultures of Europe," *Law & Society Rev.* 30/1 (1996) pp.55–85.
61. Günter Bierbrauer, "Toward an Understanding of Legal Culture: Variations in Individualism and Collectivism Between Kurds, Lebanese, and Germans," *Law & Society Rev.* 28/2 (1994) pp.243–64.

Israeli Environmental Policy in Comparative Perspective

DAVID VOGEL

INTRODUCTION

This article explores Israeli environmental policy and places it in comparative perspective. The first part traces Israel's environmental policy from statehood though the present. It argues that through the early 1970s, Israeli policies were roughly similar to those of other nations at comparable levels of economic development. However, since the mid-1970s, Israel has accorded environmental protection a lower priority than other rich democracies. The second part of the article examines various explanations for Israel's status as an environmental "laggard." It concludes by noting that as Israel has become a more "normal" post-industrial nation – relatively prosperous, more closely integrated into both the global and regional economy, and at peace with its neighbors – the priority it has accorded to environmental protection has increased.

HISTORICAL OVERVIEW

The First Two Decades

Israeli policy toward the environment during the state's first two decades focused primarily on managing its natural resources to promote economic development. As in the American West, one of the scarcest and most critical of these resources was water, over which the government quickly asserted its control. Between 1955 and 1959, the Knesset enacted legislation that effectively nationalized all surface and sub-surface water sources. None could be used without a government permit and all water use was metered. The nation's water affairs were placed in the hands of the Water Commission, which was responsible for

---

David Vogel is at the Haas School of Business, University of California at Berkeley.

determining who received water, from which sources, and in what quantity. The Commission also controlled the drilling of wells, water prices, and reuse policies.

Israel also established a formal planning system. The Town and Country Ordinance of 1948, which was promulgated under the British Mandate, granted local councils extensive power over land use. The ordinance was significantly strengthened by the Town and Planning Building Law of 1965 which was modeled on the British system of system of town and country planning. This legislation required planning authorities to prepare development plans at local, district, and national levels and required planning permission for both new buildings as well as the modification of existing ones. Yet in Israel, as in Britain through the mid-1960s, pressures for development and the lack of a grass-roots environmental movement meant that, in practice, requests for planning permission were almost invariably granted, regardless of whether they conformed to the provisions of official plans.

Israel's highest priority for land-use was to make land available for housing and agriculture. The former was necessary to accommodate the large-scale immigration that followed independence; the latter reflected the Zionist emphasis on rural settlements and farming. While Zionist ideology has subsequently been criticized for regarding nature as an obstacle to be overcome – indeed to be literally paved over, or, in the case of the Hula swamps, to be drained – there was nothing unique about Zionist attitudes or policies toward nature or land-use.[1] They were typical of other "frontier" societies which faced the challenge of settling a growing population on undeveloped land.

For Jews from the diaspora, like the American pioneers, the primary challenge was to "civilize" what was an extremely hostile physical environment. As one popular pioneer song in Israel during the 1950s put it, "We shall build you, our beloved country, and make you beautiful; we shall cover you with a robe of concrete."[2] "Conquering nature" and "transforming the desert into a green and prosperous land," also had a moral dimension: it was meant to symbolize the creation of a new post-diaspora Jew. As the Israeli writer Izhar Simlanksy put it: "We always believed that if we achieved our aims – if we made the desert bloom, abolished wilderness, settled it, made it civilized ... then all the good things we dreamt of [a change in the Jewish character, a new liberated Jew ...] would come to pass."[3]

However, in one important respect Israel was distinctive among "frontier" societies: both before and after statehood it placed a high priority on reforestation. The Jewish National Fund (JNF), whose establishment predated the State of Israel, was not a conservation body; its aim was to develop the land, not preserve it. It planted trees as part of its political effort to expand and maintain Jewish control over Palestine; much of the land which it reforested was purchased from Arabs. Although many of the trees turned out to be inappropriate for the climate and topography of the Middle East, the JNF did ultimately plant over two hundred million trees, and succeeded in restoring much of the land of Israel to the more hospitable conditions that had existed during biblical times.

Like both Great Britain and the United States, Israel's early environmental initiatives were primarily in the area of nature preservation.[4] In 1963, the Knesset enacted the National Parks, Nature Reserve and National Sites Law which provided legal protection for natural habitats, wildlife, and historical sites. This legislation established a Nature Reserves and National Park System which, under the leadership of Avaham Yoffe, embarked upon an aggressive conservation program. Under the Nature Reserve Law's "Natural Assets Regulation," hundreds of plants and animal species were protected. The priority placed on nature conservation was reflected not only in the work of the quasi-governmental JNF, but also in the establishment, in 1954, of a civic organization, the Society for the Preservation of Nature.

Unlike virtually all other new post-war nations, thanks to the policies of the British occupation, the organizational skills of the Yishuv leaders and the socialist ideology of Mapai, Israel possessed a strong and powerful state bureaucracy at the time of statehood.[5] Not only was 90 percent of the nation's land either owned or operated by the government, but all infrastructure development was publicly controlled and managed as well. Accordingly, the state of Israel had sufficient legal, organizational, and financial resources to shape the direction of economic development. As Richard Laster notes, "Had central and local governments used the [regulatory] power granted them by law, Israel would have been ahead of every other state in the world at the beginning of the environmental revolution of the 1960s."[6]

Yet, not surprisingly, Israeli society had other priorities, most notably meeting the needs of hundreds of thousands of poor refugees for food, shelter, and employment, protecting national security, and socializing and mobilizing a highly pluralistic society. While in the United States, it was the political and ideological influence of business which constrained efforts at environmental protection prior to the 1960s, in Israel this role was played by the institutions and values of Labor Zionism. Israel's lack of a politically independent private sector inhibited environmental regulation because it meant that to the extent that the state sought to regulate the environment, it was largely regulating itself and the labor institutions with which it was closely associated. In light of the priority placed on economic and political development, "Israel's major polluters, the large collectives and corporations of the government, Histradut and mixed sectors, bore the symbol of servants of the public interest."[7]

Mid 1960s – Early 1970s

During the second half of the 1960s and the early 1970s, environmental protection began to occupy a more prominent place on the political agenda in virtually all affluent capitalist nations. This change was in part prompted by the rapid economic expansion that took place in a number of countries during the 1950s and 1960s – a development which also occurred in Israel. Between 1960 and 1972 Israel's economic growth averaged 9.2 percent while GDP per capita grew 5.6 percent, after a similarly strong performance in the 1950s.[8]

This period represents the critical watershed in post-war environmental policy among democratic highly industrialized nations. Public demands for environmental regulation increased significantly. Indeed, for a brief period environmental quality was *the* dominant political issue in the United States, Japan, as well as in much of western and northern Europe.[9] Similar pressures emerged in Israel, though on a somewhat lesser scale, in part because Israel was still in the early phases of industrialization and therefore had experienced less environmental deterioration than other relatively affluent countries.[10]

Between 1965 and 1973, environmental activists in Israel, like their counterparts in western Europe, the United States, and Japan waged a number of highly visible public campaigns.[11] They attempted to prevent construction of an oil refinery in the Red Sea coastal town of Eliat, block construction of an electric power plant on the coast in Tel Aviv, protect the water quality of Lake Kinneret, the country's only freshwater lake and the source of much of its water supply, improve air quality in the desert town of Beersheva, and prevent mining in the Carmel National Park.[12]

The results of these political initiatives were mixed. On one hand, the Tel Aviv power plant was built after the Knesset took the unprecedented step of approving legislation taking control of the site location decision out of the hands of the local planning commission. On the other hand, some additional controls were established to protect water quality in Lake Kinneret, mining was forbidden in the Carmel National Park, and the Beersheva Citizen's Action group was able to prevent the expansion of a chemical plant that had become a major source of air pollution. In addition, the Eliat oil refinery project was halted, though for economic rather than environmental reasons.

A number of these grass-roots mobilizations attracted considerable media attention and substantial public participation. For example, 12,000 Israelis participated in a demonstration led by the Society for the Protection of Nature in Israel to prevent mining in Carmel National Park, making it the largest public demonstration in Israel to date.[13] A petition demanding improved air quality in Tel Aviv attracted 30,000 signatures, while an ad hoc group of Tel Aviv residents opposed to the construction of the coastal power plant claimed a membership of more than 100,000.[14] Israel thus appeared to be on the verge of developing a modern environmental movement roughly comparable to those of other developed democracies.

Like more than one hundred other nations, Israel sent an official delegation to the 1972 Stockholm Convention on the Environment. Upon its return, it requested that the government establish an administrative body to protect the nation's physical environment. Due to the efforts of Deputy Prime Minister Yigal Allon, who wanted to strengthen the government's ability to respond to regional and global environmental issues, the government established the Environmental Protection Service (EPS) as a separate agency in the office of the Prime Minister. It was staffed with 36 people, of whom 30 were professionals. While not a separate ministry, the establishment of this new governmental body marked a significant step in Israel's recognition of the importance of environmental protection and paralleled similar organizational initiatives in a number of countries.

ISRAEL AS AN ENVIRONMENTAL LAGGARD

It is at this point that Israeli environmental policy and politics begins to diverge from those of other relatively developed democratic welfare states. In Europe, the United States, and Japan, the policy and political changes of the late 1960s and early 1970s proved enduring. While the actual balance between environmental protection and other public policy objectives has varied among countries and over time, environmental regulation has remained an important part of the policy agenda in virtually all developed countries. Environmentalists in Europe and the United States, whether mobilized through political parties, national organizations, or local groups, have constituted an ongoing source of political pressure on both business and government and this pressure has been reflected in a steady expansion of the scope and enforcement of regulatory controls.

However, in Israel the political mobilizations of the late 1960s and early 1970s were not sustained. Israel was also unaffected by the "second wave" of global environmental concern that took place during the latter part of the 1980s, a period that witnessed the growth of green parties in Germany and the European Parliament, the significant strengthening of European Community environmental regulation, and the resurgence of environmentalism in the United States, even though by this time Israel had become much more prosperous and its environmental problems correspondingly more serious.[15]

While Israel did finally establish a Ministry of the Environment in 1988, this decision reflected the need of the Shamir government for an additional cabinet position to reward a political ally, not a commitment to environmental protection. Moreover Israel's delay in establishing this ministry made it the 126th country in the world to do so.

Compared to other industrial nations, the power of Israel's Environment Ministry was limited, especially in the area of enforcement. Public authority in Israel is highly fragmented: each Ministry, as well as public bodies such as the Water Commission, operates relatively independently, with its own resources and priorities. Accordingly, the impact of the Environment Ministry on Israeli environmental policy has depended on its ability to influence the policies of other public bodies, agencies and institutions.

However, other governmental bodies whose policies have a major impact on Israeli environmental policy have generally been indifferent to environmental concerns. For example, the Ministry of Agriculture has made little effort to enforce restrictions on pesticide use or encourage the use of biological control techniques, even though many of the latter have been developed in Israel and exported. Nor has the Ministry encouraged farmers to reduce their use of chemical fertilizers, even though fertilizers are the major cause of the high level of nitrates that pollute much of Israel's coastal aquifer – which supplies 40 percent of Israel's groundwater.[16] Likewise, the Water Commission has continued to subsidize the use of water by farmers, even though agriculture consumes 70 percent of Israel's renewable reserves and has contributed to the overpumping of Israel's aquifers.

The Environment Ministry also has no influence over Israeli transportation policy. This remains under the control of the Ministry of Transport which has aggressively pursued additional road and highway construction, with little regard for environmental consequences. For their part, Israeli planning authorities and local governments have done relatively little to discourage urban sprawl. Perhaps most importantly, the Ministry of Housing has frequently resisted the Environment Ministry's efforts to require new housing developments to install adequate sewage treatment facilities.[17]

Because Israeli environmental law is unique in that virtually all violations are considered criminal rather than civil, in principle the government enjoys considerable leverage over polluters and other violators of Israeli environmental standards. But while many Israeli environmental standards are relatively strict – most are based on either EU, American, or WHO standards – they are poorly enforced. According to Alon Tal, the founder and director of the Israeli Union for Environmental Defense, "While many other nations assess stiff fines to industrial polluters and are even sending chief executives to jail, Israeli industries continue to pour toxic chemicals into the Mediterranean, fresh water streams and groundwater, and escape with minimal damages."[18] In fact, many of the main violators of Israeli environmental standards are public bodies, such as municipalities and government hospitals. But under Israeli law, public officials cannot be prosecuted without the consent of the Attorney General and such permission has rarely been granted.

This lack of political will reflects the weakness of environmentalists in Israel's electoral and pressure group system. Unlike other nations whose electoral systems facilitate multiple parties, no "green" party has emerged in Israel. What makes this especially significant is that Israelis form political parties easily, readily, and frequently. For example, in 1996, 20 parties were represented in the Knesset. Their agendas reflect the wide range of issues which preoccupy Israelis. These range from religious–secular relations and policies toward the occupied territories, to the welfare of various ethnic groups, and the treatment of immigrants and Arab citizens.

In 1979, Israel, with a population of three and a half million, had only four environmental associations.[19] Of these, only the Society for the Protection of Nature was a grass-roots body. But its primary focus has been on education and recreation. While segments of the Israeli public have periodically become mobilized over particular environmental issues, for the most part public activism has remained episodic and localized. The Israeli environmental movement has yet to develop either a national political presence or a popular base. Israel's most politically active and effective environmental pressure group, the Israel Union for Environmental Defense, primarily relies on litigation rather than popular mobilization. Significantly, virtually all its funding comes from the diaspora. Other environmental organizations such as the Council for A Beautiful Israel and the JNF do not play an important political role or are dominated by the state.

Over the last decade, press coverage of environmental issues has increased. All major daily newspapers now have reporters covering the environment. Yet, in contrast to the United States or much of Europe, environmental stories rarely appear on the front page. There has been little investigative reporting and even less systematic analysis of the long-term environmental problems confronting Israel. The latter is in part due to the Israeli government itself, which provides the public with relatively little information about the state of Israel's environment, even with respect to such critical issues as drinking water quality. Nor, unlike other countries, does Israel require environmental impact assessments for major projects. For example, the National Planning Board recently refused to conduct an environmental impact assessment for the controversial Trans-Israel Highway. While the Israeli judicial system provides citizens with standing before the High Court of Justice to challenge the government's compliance with its own laws, the impact of this access on environmental policy has been modest.[20]

Israeli land-use policies have favored development over preservation. Less than half of Israel's 190 kilometer-long Mediterranean coastline is open to the public and only a dozen kilometers of beach enjoy protected status. The remaining stretches of open beach are rapidly being displaced by commercial and residential development, which has been encouraged by local governments eager for new sources of revenue. Seventeen marinas have either been constructed or approved, even though they will block the natural flow of Nile basin sand which replenishes Israel's beaches.[21] Rapid development is also threatening the quality of Lake Kinneret as well as the area's extraordinary beauty.

Israeli's water treatment facilities also remain inadequate. A number of urban areas, including Jerusalem, still lack adequate sewerage treatment facilities. In 1995, 120 million cubic meters of raw sewage and 55 million cubic meters of excess treated sewage flowed unchecked into the nation's eco-system, harming the Mediterranean Sea, Lake Kinneret, and the Red Sea, yet the government has yet to draw up a national water and sewage treatment plan.[22] Israel's rivers remain highly polluted, the result of decades of having been used as outlets for poorly treated sewerage and untreated industrial waste.

Because Israel is not a heavily industrialized nation, Israel has not had to contend with significant groundwater contamination by heavy metals, organic solvents, or other hazardous wastes. However, its water supply is threatened by agricultural fertilizers and pesticides.[23] Moreover the widespread use of the latter poses an increasingly serious health problem. Israel continues to permit the use of a number of pesticides banned by other industrialized nations, including DDT.[24] Indeed, while Israel has officially adopted EU food pesticide residue standards, they are only enforced for exported food. As a result, as one official in the Ministry of the Environment recently observed, "German children eating strawberries ingest fewer residues than Israeli kids do."[25]

Solid waste disposal has become one of Israel's most pressing environmental problems: 95 percent of it, amounting to three million tons per year, is buried in 400 landfills. Israel's per capita generation of trash is the third highest of any industrial nation.[26] It recycles only 3 percent of its solid waste, one-tenth the level of western Europe and Japan.[27] While Israel does recycle 25 percent of its paper, both Holland and Japan recycle more than half their paper and the United States nearly one-third.[28] Israel uses 100,000 tons of glass each year, very little of which is recycled. Outside of Tel Aviv sits the most visible symbol of Israel's waste disposal policy: the Hiriya dump, an 82-meter high mountain of garbage collected from the Tel Aviv area which poses a threat to planes at Ben-Gurion airport due to its attractiveness for birds.

To be sure, Israel can claim some important environmental achievements. For example, its drip irrigation systems are among the world's most technically advanced and it has developed the world's most ambitious wastewater recycling program, thus enabling it to make extensive use of waste water for irrigation.[29] More than 70 percent of Israeli households contain solar-powered water heaters, which supply 3.2 percent of Israeli's energy needs. Israel has also made progress in complying with the provisions of the Barcelona Convention, a regional treaty designed to protect the Mediterranean by controlling oil spills and preventing land-based sources of pollution. As a result of strict Israeli regulations, its beaches are among the cleanest and the safest in the Mediterranean: between the 1970s and the early 1990s, tar concentrations declined from an average of 3.5 kilograms per meter of beachfront to 20 grams per meter.[30] Israel's accomplishments in the area of nature conservation and wildlife protection are also noteworthy. And it has prohibited the use of billboards along its highways.

In sum, while Israel's environmental record during its first two decades certainly compares favorably with those of other nations established since World War II, since the early 1970s it has placed significantly lower priority on protecting and improving its physical environment than the United States, Japan, and the Member States of the European Union. In a number of important respects, its environmental priorities have remained mired in the 1950s, with a focus on nature conservation and reforestation rather than on pollution and sold waste disposal. As one observer put it in 1990: "Environmentally speaking, Israel's tendencies lie with developing nations."[31]

EXPLAINING ISRAELI ENVIRONMENTAL POLICY

How can we account for the distinctiveness of Israeli environmental policy? Why did it evolve into an "environmental laggard"?

Culture

One set of possible explanations has to do with the social, cultural, and religious values of Israelis. The harsh experience of many Jews in the diaspora did little to promote an appreciation for nature. While the ancient Jewish tradition was deeply imbued with a sense of reverence and respect for nature and the land, the rituals, rules, and norms that reaffirmed these values lost much of their meaning after the Jews were expelled from their homeland. An indifference to the "sources of life, air and water," was compounded by the conditions of exile. Jews rarely owned land, while in both eastern Europe and the Middle East they generally lived in conditions of rural or urban poverty which hardly was conducive to a benevolent view of "nature."[32] Moreover, the vast majority of Jewish immigrants to Israel came from nations whose cultural and political traditions placed little or no value on the physical environment, including central Europe, and the nations of the former Soviet Union as well as the Middle East. The same holds true for Israel's native Arab population.

To be sure, hiking did become an important part of the Israeli ethos. Each year, the Society for the Protection of Nature, whose 50,000 members make it Israel's largest environmental organization, guides 50,00 day tours in which a total of 750,000 people take part, including half a million schoolchildren.[33] Many of these outdoor activities also involve an educational component; indeed one of Israel's most notable environmental achievements has been to discourage its citizens from picking wildflowers. Israel also celebrates the Jewish holiday of Tu b'Shevat – also known as *hag ha'ilanot* or the "holiday of the trees" – during which schoolchildren plant trees.

But the interest of Israelis in "nature" primarily has to do with staking a claim to the land of Israel, not with preserving or protecting the land itself. As one journalist put it, "we teach our children to love the land of their birth. We take them on trips, and teach them the name of every rock and flower. And yet ... in our daily lives we treat the environment with contempt."[34] The relationship of most Israelis to Eretz Israel does not include an environmental component – with the notable and important exception of reforestation. Indeed, an indifference to preserving or conserving the actual land of Israel for future generations is one of the few issues on which secular and religious Jews agree. Significantly, there are no Israeli or Jewish counterparts to natural symbols of national identity such as Mt. Fuji, the English countryside, the Black Forests of Germany, the Austrian Alps, or the American West.[35] All of Israel's sacred sites are part of the built rather than the natural environment.

Another cultural dimension of Israeli environmental policy is rooted in geography. Israel is part of the Middle East, a region whose citizens are notable for their lack of concern about environmental values. The indifference of Israelis for the cleanliness of public spaces is common throughout the Middle East. Indeed a propensity to litter is one trait which Israelis share with their Arab neighbors. As one journalist writes:

> At the end of a summers' day at Sakhne, one of the most beautiful nature sites in the Beit Shean Valley, the spring-few swimming pools and lush gardens are covered with bottles, paper, plastic, newspapers and diapers left by hundreds of visitors. The bilingual nature of the trash – both Hebrew and Arabic – testify to the similar approach of both Jews and Arabs towards litter.[36]

Of the seas of garbage that periodically surface off Israel's Mediterranean coast, approximately 20 to 30 percent comes from Lebanon; the rest is produced domestically.

But an explanation rooted in Jewish history, or culture, or geography has limited value. After all, Israelis are not simply a composite of the nations and communities from which they came. They are different and distinctive in a number of important respects. To take the two most striking examples, the Jews who came to Israel had virtually no experience in either farming or fighting. And yet this has not prevented Israel from developing either a modern agricultural sector or a highly competent military.

Moreover, national values can change. Contemporary American attitudes toward the environment bear little resemblance to America's frontier ethos, in part because contemporary America is both richer and more urban. The attitudes of Israelis toward their physical environment could have undergone a similar transformation, especially since Israelis have eagerly adopted other contemporary American values. Finally, while Israel is both culturally and geographically a part of the Middle East, in many important respects it is far from a typical Middle Eastern nation. Israel's political institutions are European in origin; there is no reason why its environmental priorities and policies could not also more closely resemble those of the Member States of the EU instead of its Arab neighbors.

In sum, while cultural factors may have contributed to the relatively low priority that Israelis have placed on environment protection compared to other democratic welfare states, they do not adequately explain the distinctiveness of Israeli environmental policy. For such an explanation we have to turn to international politics and economics.

International Politics

There is one dimension on which Israel has remained distinctive among relatively affluent democracies, and that is the salience of security and security-related concerns. It is significant that 1973 marks not only the establishment of the Environmental Protection Service but also the Yom Kipper War. No other developed nation has confronted such continuous and significant threats to its physical security since the 1972 Stockholm conference. "The fact that security is still a major preoccupation for Israelis has been a critical determinant of both the structure of its institutions and its political culture. The acute defense problem produced a 'siege mentality' with strong repercussions on political institutions."[37] A nation preoccupied with its physical existence can hardly be expected to devote significant efforts to its physical environment. From this perspective, Israel might be more appropriately compared not to Europe and the United States, but to South Korea and Taiwan – other affluent nations which have confronted severe security dilemmas throughout most of the post-war period and which until recently have placed a low priority on environmental quality.

In a number of important respects, the energy devoted to the debate over Israel's geographic boundaries and its relations with its Arab population and neighbors has occupied the political space that in other developed countries has been filled up by environmentalism and other variants of post-industrial politics, including feminism.[38] The most enduring political legacy of the mid-1970s in Israel was not environmentalism but the formation of a nationalist movement dedicated to settling and retaining the West Bank – a movement which has in turn spawned a peace movement challenging its goals. In a sense, the ongoing preoccupation of Israelis with the boundaries of the land of Israel has displaced a concern with the land itself. As Yaron Ezrahi notes, "Israelis have been raised to recognize that ... on this battered land ... there is no such thing as pure nature."[39]

At the same time, the privileged role played by the military in Israeli society has also adversely affected the nation's environmental quality. Security considerations have led Israel to repeatedly subordinate environmental concerns to military ones. For example, while the Nature Reserves Authority has overseen the creation of 191 protected nature reserves covering one-seventh of Israel's pre-1967 territory, two-thirds of these reserves are located in the Negev Desert and are used by the army for training and firing ranges. Likewise, the initial Zionist emphasis on constructing housing developments that used as much land as possible was dictated by the need to extend the scope of Jewish political control in Palestine. Since 1967, the pattern of Jewish settlement in the West Bank – featuring low-density housing and often inadequate sewerage and accompanied by a massive road building program – has been similarly informed by political and security considerations.

Economics

There is a second, related, explanation for the nature of Israeli environmental policy: its pattern of economic growth. Following the Yom Kipper War, Israel began to experience severe economic difficulties, due in part to a much higher level of defense spending that was only partially offset by increased American aid. Between 1973 and 1988, Israeli's GDP growth averaged only slightly above three percent while its per capita growth averaged around one percent.[40] Its rate of inflation was among the highest in the industrialized world. It was only in the mid-1980s, following the government's stabilization program and the first major decline in defense spending since the Yom Kippur War, that Israel's economic performance began to improve. Israel's GNP doubled between 1987 and 1992, and its per capita income increased to $13,320. Since then the latter has increased to nearly $16,000 – making Israelis as affluent as the citizens of a number of EU Member States.

Thus, Israel is quite literally a "nouveau riche" nation, and it is not surprising that many of its citizens are preoccupied with increasing their levels of private consumption. In practice, this means living a life-style that approximates that of the suburban United States: relying on automobiles, the number of which has recently doubled, shopping at malls rather than neighborhood stores, living in detached residences rather than apartments, purchasing extensively packaged goods, and generally participating in a "throwaway culture."

The sounder environmental practices that characterized Israeli life through the first decades of statehood – such as reliance on public transportation, living in apartments, shopping with reusable bags and using returnable glass bottles – are identified by the Israeli public with the privations and hardship of this period. In fact, it was only in the late 1980s that Israel switched from using returnable glass bottles for soft drinks and beer to plastic and non-returnable ones.[41] In short, Israelis may not have been sufficiently affluent for a long enough time to be concerned about "quality of life" issues such as environmental quality.

It is also important to note that Israel has historically committed considerable resources to the consumption of public goods, most notably defense. Its citizens have been required to make substantial sacrifices, personal as well as material, in the interests of national security. It is only recently that these burdens have lessened. Until the 1990s it may well have been premature for them to subordinate their new-found individualism for another set of collective goods and disciplines.

THE FUTURE OF ISRAELI ENVIRONMENTAL POLICY

The future of Israeli environmental policy is likely to be shaped by three factors, one domestic and two international.

Economic and Population Growth

A set of factors that will pressure Israelis to pay more attention to environmental issues is the combination of population and economic growth. Israel has the highest rate of population growth in the western world; indeed it is nearly three times that of the United States and western Europe. Between 1990 and 1992, Israel's population grew by nearly 10 percent. While the number of immigrants from the former Soviet Union, the main source of recent population growth, has recently decreased, it is still approximately 70,000 a year. Moreover, since 1992, Israeli economic growth has averaged 7 percent – the highest of any developed nation. Between 1991 and 1996, per capita GNP grew by an average of 2.2 percent.[42]

If present trends continue, early in the twenty-first century the population density of the 8,000 square kilometers north of the Negev and south of the Golan Heights will average 1,000 people per square kilometer. This will make it one of the most densely populated regions in the world. Without any change in the current pattern of suburban-style home construction or reliance on automobile transportation, Israel from Jerusalem to Tel Aviv will be one enormous megalopolis with few green spaces and massive traffic jams. Israel's underground supplies of water will be both strained and polluted, while the region's air quality, which has recently begun to decline, will become steadily worse as automobile usage keeps increasing. If present trends continue, it has been estimated that by the year 2020 there will be three million cars in Israel and 60 percent of the Galilee will be paved over.[43]

On a number of dimensions, the nation's current pattern of economic development is rapidly straining its physical capacities: at some point what has been characterized as "the Los Angelesation of Israel" will begin to interfere with the lifestyles of its middle class. In the short run, the individualism and materialism that characterizes post-Zionist Israel are exacerbating its environmental problems. But in the long run, if more Israelis adopt the post-material values of their counterparts in western Europe and the United States, they will likely demand stricter government controls over land use and pollution. If so, Israeli environmental policy will become more similar to those countries whose citizens enjoy comparable standards of living.

Economic Integration

The future of Israeli environmental policy will also be affected by Israel's increasing integration into the world economy.[44] One consequence of Israel's growing affluence and the peace process has been a significant strengthening of Israel's economic links with the rest of the developed world. While Israel has long traded extensively with both the United States and the EU, the peace process has opened up a number of markets that were previously closed to it. In addition, Israel has begun, for the first time in its history, to receive significant foreign direct investment, primarily from Europe and the United States.

These developments will put increasing pressure on Israel to enforce EU and American environmental standards. Multinationals generally impose host country regulatory standards on their facilities in other developed nations, which will in turn put pressure on Israeli firms to improve their environmental practices. In addition, products produced in Israel for export to the EU and the United States are required to meet the latter's relatively strict regulatory standards, which may in turn encourage Israeli consumers to demand similar standards for products produced for their domestic market. This process has already had an impact on Israel. For example, Israel has recently adopted the automobile emissions standards of the EU as well as the EU's pesticide standards. The former reflects the European origin of many Israeli vehicles, the latter the importance of the EU as a market for Israeli agricultural exports.

More informally, recent Israeli initiatives in the area of recycling have been influenced by European and American practices. Israel has also entered into agreements to exchange environmental technology with the United States and Germany as well as bi-lateral agreements for environmental cooperation with the US, Germany, Egypt, Austria, Sweden, Spain, Turkey, and the European Union. Israel is also poised to become a major exporter of environmental technologies, especially in the areas of water use and agriculture. The resulting economies of scale will make it possible for Israeli firms to produce many of these technologies for the domestic market as well.

The Peace Process

The future of Israeli environmental policy will also be strongly affected by the peace process. Israel and its neighbors constitute a highly interdependent eco-system, especially with respect to water resources. One important consequence of the 1967 War was to give Israel control over much of the region's water supplies, including the headwaters of the Jordan River in the Golan Heights and the aquifers under the West Bank and Israel. As a result, its citizens have been able to consume a disproportionate share of scarce water resources. In part as a result of Israeli policies, the Palestinians face an increasingly severe water crisis, which must be addressed if the West Bank and Gaza are to become economically viable. While it has received relatively little public attention, the framework negotiations between Israel and the Palestinian Authority (PA) include an environmental track. The PA has established an environmental body and has received funds from the European Union to help it address a number of pressing environmental problems.[45]

In addition to official negotiations, there have also been a number of private initiatives. In 1993, the Israel/Palestine Center for Research and Information began to address a number of regional environmental issues. Its Environmental Roundtable, which includes both Israelis and Palestinians, held a conference on "the environmental challenges facing Israel, the West Bank and Gaza" in Jerusalem in December 1994. It marked the first time that Israelis and Palestinians interested in environmental issues had met in an informal context to discuss their mutual concerns.[46] Meetings have also taken place among environmental groups in Jordan, Israel, Egypt, and the Palestinian Authority under the auspices of Eco-Peace, a Middle East Environmental NGO Forum.[47]

Prior to the peace process, regional environmental cooperation was extremely limited; in fact while Israel was a signatory to the Mediterranean Action Plan, established by 16 countries in 1975 under the auspices of the United Nations Action Program, it was unable to be an official participant due to Arab opposition.[48] The peace process has made possible Israeli participation in regional environmental conferences in both Arab and neutral states and has resulted in a various environmental agreements with its neighbors. Those include multilateral plans to protect the Gulf of Eliat and combat pollution in the Gulf of Aqaba, both of which involve Egypt and Jordan. Agreement has also been reached on a regional plan to combat desertification. In 1994, 41 Middle Eastern nations approved the Bahrain Environmental Code of Conduct, which established a cooperative framework for environmental protection in the region.[49] As the region becomes more economically integrated and developed, the number of regional agreements to address common environmental problems is likely to increase, as has occurred in western Europe and North America.[50] This in turn is likely to raise the salience of environmental regulation within Israel.

CONTEMPORARY DEVELOPMENTS

In recent years, public interest in environmental issues has increased.[51] Public opinion surveys report substantial public awareness and concern about environmental quality, especially air pollution.[52] The Ministry of the Environment designated 1994 as the "Year of the Environment" and this was accompanied by increased coverage of environmental issues in the media as well in school curriculum. Yossi Sarid, who served as Environment Minister between 1993 and 1996, was a colorful, highly-visible politician who played an important role in increasing public awareness of Israel's environmental problems. Israel's Environment Ministry now has a staff a more than 400 and a budget of approximately $41 million.

In 1995, the Ministry began offering financial grants to Israeli companies that invest in monitoring and pollution control facilities and in environment-friendly technologies and materials. $160 million has been allocated over a four-year period. In a parallel development, the Society for the Protection of Nature in Israel, Ormat Industries, and the Manufacturers' Association have established an organization called ALVA (the Hebrew acronym for Industrialists for Ecology) to promote ecologically responsible behavior among Israeli firms. Much of its focus will be on designing more environmentally-friendly products to meet the demands of overseas consumers.[53]

There has also been a growth in the number of grass-roots organizations opposing environmentally damaging development projects in their communities, an Israeli version of the Not In My Backyard attitude common in many developed countries. For example, the residents of Ramat Hovav opposed the construction of Israel's first toxic-waste incinerator in their community while an unusual coalition of Orthodox Jews and local Arabs have joined together to block an industrial park in the lower Galilee, one of Israel's last large reserves of green countryside.[54] Significantly, in the 1996 elections, seven of Israel's major political parties included an environmental section in their platforms.[55]

This increase in public concern has led to some important policy changes. In 1991, the Ministry of the Environment issued its first regulations controlling the disposal of hazardous wastes and in 1993, the Knesset approved legislation closing 400 garbage dumps throughout the country, most of which were illegal, and replacing them with five giant landfills.[56] Another new statute required the collection of glass, plastic, and paper by households and businesses. In 1992, Israel finally upgraded and expanded its outdated ambient air quality standards, basing them on 1987 World Health Organization guidelines.[57] Two years later the Knesset adopted a Protection of Animals law and in 1996 it approved legislation facilitating private litigation against polluters. The government also began to re-flood 1,500 acres of wetlands in the Hula Valley in belated recognition of their critical role in filtering nitrates into the Sea of Galilee, Israel's major source of drinking water. In a major victory for environmentalists, in March 1996 an Israel court ruled that a housing development in Safed could not add additional residents until it had established an adequate sewage purification system.[58] In April 1997, the Knesset approved legislation amending five environmental statues by establishing heavier fines for violators. Perhaps most importantly, during the 1990s, Israeli land-use planning began to incorporate environmental concerns to a much greater extent and in a more proactive way.[59] Finally, in 1998, Israel's most infamous garbage dump, Hiriya, was shut down after serving the Tel Aviv region for 50 years.

Still, while these changes in attitudes and policies are important, they represent a far cry from the "greening" of Israel. In marked contrast to many other heads of state, no Israeli Prime Minister has ever publicly expressed any interest in environmental policy. Netanyahu angered environmentalists both by appointing the same individual to head both the Environment and Agriculture Ministries and by continuing construction of the Trans-Israel Highway, an eight to ten lane road through the heart of Israel's countryside.

CONCLUSION

If Israel's position as an environment laggard during the 1970s and 1980s reflected its uniqueness among democratic welfare states, then the increase in environmental concerns during the 1990s reflects its emergence as a more normal post-industrial nation, subject to the same global influences as other developed economies. To the extent that Israel is increasingly affluent, more closely integrated into the global economy, and enjoys the progressive normalization of its relations with both its Arab neighbors and other countries, Israel's environmental policies and politics will gradually become more similar to those of other affluent nations. In part for cultural reasons, Israel is unlikely to ever be classified as among the world's "greenest" countries: at best its environmental politics and policies are more apt to resemble those of its northern Mediterranean neighbors, France and Italy, than the greener nations of northern Europe or the United States.

NOTES

1. For a discussion of Zionist attitudes toward nature, see Avner de-Shalit and Moti Talias, "Green or Blue and White? Environmental Controversies in Israel," *Environmental Politics* 3/2 (Summer 1994) pp.289–91. See also Avner de-Shalit, "From the Political to the Objective: The Dialectics of Zionism and the Environment," *Environmental Politics* 4/1 (Spring 1995) pp.70–87.
2. Quoted in de-Shalit and Talais, pp.289–90.
3. Ibid., p.289.
4. See David Vogel, *National Styles of Regulation: Environmental Protection in Great Britain and the United States*, Ithaca: Cornell University Press, 1986.
5. For an analysis of Israel as a strong, post-colonial state, see Joel S. Migdal, *Strong Societies and Weak States*, Princeton: Princeton University Press, 1988, pp.142–76.
6. Richard Laster, "Environmental Law in Israel Today," in Robin Twite and Jad Issac (eds), *Our Shared Environment*, Jerusalem: Israel/Palestine Center for Research and Information, 1994, p.122.
7. Paulette Mandelbaum, "Pollution and the Making of Public Policy: Israel, 1965–1975," unpublished doctoral dissertation, Department of Political Science, Columbia University, 1997, p.74.
8. Ishac Diwan and Nick Papandreaou, "The Peace Process and Economic Reforms in the Middle East," in Stanley Fischer, Dani Rodrik, and Elias Tuma (eds), *The Economics of Middle East Peace*, Cambridge: MIT Press, 1993, p.31.
9. See David Vogel, "Representing Diffuse Interests in Environmental Policy," in R. Kent Weaver and Bert A. Rockman (eds), *Do Institutions Matter?* Washington, DC: Brookings Institution, 1993, pp.237–71. See also David Vogel, "Environmental Policy

in Europe and Japan," in Norman Vig and Michael Kraft (eds), *Environmental Policy in the 1990s*, Washington, DC: Congressional Quarterly Press, 1990, pp.257–78.
10. Eran Fritelson, "Allowing for Sustainable Growth Under Drastic Immigration Stress in Israel," *Journal of Environmental Planning and Management* 37/4 (1994).
11. This section is based on Mandelbaum (note 7).
12. For a more complete list of environmental disputes between 1966 and 1973, see Mandelbaum (note 7) pp.123–4.
13. Mandelbaum, p.157.
14. Ibid., p.173.
15. See David Vogel, "Environmental Policy in Europe and Japan," in Vig and Kraft, *Environmental Policy in the 1990s* (note 9) pp.257–78.
16. See, for example, Janine Zacharia, "Why is Israel Still Spraying DDT?" *The Jerusalem Report*, 23 Jan. 1997, pp.24–5.
17. See for example, D'vora Ben Shaul, "Court Protects Water in Safed," *The Jerusalem Post*.
18. Quoted in Elaine Fletcher, "Israel's Environment: Government, Media and the Public," in Twite and Issac, *Our Shared Environment* (note 6) p.40.
19. Yishai, "Environment and Development," pp.209–10.
20. See Martin Edelman, "The Judicialization of Politics in Israel," *International Politics Science Review* 15/2, pp.177–86.
21. "Coastal Conflicts," *Jerusalem Post Weekly Edition*, 8 March 1997, pp.28–9.
22. Bill Hutman, "Sewage Flows Unchecked," *The Jerusalem Post*, 1 May 1996. See also Yossi Laster, "The Political Economy of Waste Water in Israel," *Institute for Advanced Strategic and Political Studies – Policy Studies* (Feb. 1996).
23. Liat Collins, "Hazardous Waste Piles Up Untreated," *Jerusalem Post*, 1 May 1996, p.10.
24. See Zacharia (note16) pp.24–5 and Lisa Perlman, "The Environment in Israel," *Israel Environment Report* 13/1, p.22.
25. Perlman, ibid.
26. Fletcher (note 18) p.32.
27. "Israel to Scrap Dumps in Favor of New Landfill," *Engineering News Record*, 13 June, 1994.
28. "Israel Push for Recycling: Going to Waste," *Israel Business Today*, 27 Dec. 1991.
29. "Israel Works its Water," *Engineering News Record*, 1 October 1981.
30. Tom Sawicki, "Bay Watch," *The Jerusalem Report*, 29 June, 1995, pp.18–19, see also Perlman, "The Environment in Israel" (note 24).
31. Perlman, "The Environment in Israel" (note 24).
32. Quoted in Fletcher (note 18) p.26.
33. Stahl, "Educating for Change," p.16.
34. David Newman, "Stop Polluting the Peace," *The Jerusalem Post*, 12 Jan. 1996.
35. For a fascinating discussion of the role of nature in shaping various national identities, see Simon Schama, *Landscape and Memory*, New York: Vintage Books, 1995.
36. Fletcher (note 18) p.38.
37. Yishai, p.21.
38. See Yael Yishai, *Between the Flag and the Banner: Women in Israeli Politics*, Albany, NY: State University of New York Press, 1997, for a discussion of the role of Israeli nationalism in inhibiting the development of feminist politics.
39. Yaron Ezrahi, *Rubber Bullets: Power and Conscience in Modern Israel*, New York: Farrar, Straus and Giroux, 1997, p.55.
40. Jad Isaac, "Environmental Protection and Sustainable Development in Palestine," in *Our Shared Environment* (note 6) p.13.
41. Fletcher (note 18) p.31.
42. Hanan Sher, "Special 1997 Forecast Report," *The Jerusalem Report*, 9 Jan. 1997.
43. Janine Zacharia, "Water expert say Israel will have to desalinate most drinking water," *The Jerusalem Report*, 5 Sept. 1996, p.6; D'vora Ben Shaul, "The More We Develop, the Harder It Gets," *The Jerusalem Post*, 3 June 1996.
44. For an extended discussion of the role of international trade and economic integration in raising regulatory standards, see David Vogel, *Trading Up: Consumer and Environmental Regulation in A Global Economy*, Cambridge: Harvard University Press, 1995.
45. Isabel Kerschner, "A Blueprint for Green," *The Jerusalem Report*, 26 Dec. 1996, pp.32–3.

46. The proceedings of this conference have been published. See Robin Twite and Robin Menezel (eds), *Our Shared Environment: The Conference*, Jerusalem: Israel/Palestine Center for Research and Information. See also Twite and Issac (note 6).
47. See, for example, *Dead Sea Challenges*, Jerusalem: Eco Peace, 1997.
48. See Peter Haas, *Saving the Mediterranean,* New York: Columbia University Press, 1990.
49. See "The Multilateral Track," *Israel Environment Bulletin* 18/1, pp.9–14.
50. See, for example, *An Inventory of New Development Projects* (in the PA, Jordan, Israel, and Egypt) Eco-Peace: Middle East Environmental NGO Forum, Dec. 1995.
52. See Yael Yishai, "The Paradox of the 1996 Elections: 'Old' vs. 'New' Politics," unpublished paper, p.7.
51. Stanton Miller, "Heralding Israel's Environmental Consciousness," *Environmental Science and Technology* 27/7 (1993) p.1254.
53. Ruth Ebenstein, "Responsible Industry," *The Jerusalem Report*, 6 Feb. 1992.
54. Sue Fishkoff, "Toxic Smoke," *The Jerusalem Post*, 16 Feb. 1996, and Netty Gross, "Smoke Signals," *The Jerusalem Report*, 19 Sept. 1996, pp.18–22.
55. Liat Collins, "Parties Present Positions on Environmental Issues," *Jerusalem Post*, 23 April 1996, p.12.
56. "First hazardous waste law in Israel", *Haznews*, Feb. 1991.
57. "Israel's New Ambient Air Quality Standards," *Israel Environment Bulletin* 15/2 (Spring 1992-5752) pp.8–9.
58. D'vora Ben Shaul, "Court Protects Water in Safed," *The Jerusalem Post*, 4 March 1996.
59. Eran Feitelson, "The Israeli Road Toward Sustainability: Incremental Transformation of Environmental Planning," *Israel Environment Bulletin* 19/4, pp.16–23.

The Gender and Pacifism Hypothesis: Opinion Research from Israel and the Arab World

MARK TESSLER, JODI NACHTWEY, and AUDRA GRANT

This research report replicates, extends, and adds a longitudinal dimension to several recently published analyses, including one in a volume on Israel in comparative perspective.[1] Focusing on the relationship between gender and attitudes toward international conflict, and specifically on the gender and pacifism hypothesis which asserts that women are more peace-oriented than men, the present report analyzes data from two public opinion surveys in Israel and from additional opinion surveys in Egypt, Kuwait, Jordan, Lebanon, and Palestine. The dual and interrelated goals of this study are (1) to incorporate the Israeli case into an on-going effort to test a social science hypothesis purporting to have explanatory power in diverse social and cultural contexts; and (2) to compare findings from Israel and other Middle Eastern societies in order to determine whether aggregate societal circumstances affect the applicability of this hypothesis.

THE GENDER AND PACIFISM HYPOTHESIS

The gender and pacifism hypothesis, discussed in a growing body of literature addressing connections between international studies and gender studies, asserts that women are more pacific than men in their approach to international relations, more open to compromise in resolving disputes, and less likely than men to see war as appropriate in particular conflicts. The hypothesis links competition, violence, intransigence, and territoriality to a "male" approach to human relations, including those among sovereign states, while viewing moderation, compromise, tolerance, and pacifism as a "female" perspective. This view is summarized in the following terms in a recent

---

Mark Tessler, Jodi Nachtwey, and Audra Grant are at the Center for International Studies, University of Wisconsin-Milwaukee.

volume on *Global Gender Issues*:

> Throughout history there have been numerous examples of women warriors, and women fighters exist today. In spite of this, there is a pervasive gender dichotomy that divides women and men into "life-givers" and "life-takers".... As life givers, women are not only prevented from engaging in combat, but are also expected to restore "life" after a death dealing war is over. Women are expected to mourn dutifully the loved ones who fell in war and then to produce new lives for the nation to replace its lost members. [Thus] in spite of their participation, women remain associated with war's opposite – peace.[2]

Two perspectives are frequently advanced in support of the gender and pacifism hypothesis, both emphasizing the uniquely female experience of motherhood. The first seeks to establish a link between women, motherhood, and peace by celebrating the traditionally "female" attributes of caring and nurturing. In the sphere of international relations, the "care-giving" perspective emphasizes a universal predisposition toward nurturing and links women's roles as domestic care-givers to a more tolerant attitude toward the resolution of international conflicts.[3]

A second and closely related perspective advances the concept of "moral motherhood," asserting that women have a responsibility to eliminate violence as conflict resolution and substitute "maternal thinking" and "preservative love." Based on the proposition that maternal thinking derives from social practice of mothering, this perspective reflects an effort to counterbalance an international relations discourse favoring such "male" concepts as power, hegemony, and hierarchy.[4]

While care-giving and moral motherhood theories have made a mark on contemporary thought, they have also faced considerable criticism. Critics charge that these perspectives stress the experience of motherhood in forming normative predispositions but fail to differentiate between women who do and do not have children. Equally important, critics argue that these theories ignore the possibility that men as well as women are capable of nurturing behavior and thought. Another criticism is that by reifying their roles as mothers, these discourses obscure the complex origins of a woman's political orientations, including a tendency toward pacifism. Some critics complain that care-giving and moral motherhood approaches are unduly mechanistic, attributing cause and effect but failing to develop a coherent model linking such thinking to tolerance, pacifism, and other supposedly "female" political norms. Still others question whether the hypothesized gender differences even exist, pointing to both the paucity of rigorous and systematic studies testing the hypothesis and inconsistent findings in what research is available. The fact that empirical research is limited almost entirely to the United States is a related concern.

Several studies have found American men to be more supportive of militarism and war involvement than American women by an average of seven to nine percentage points,[5] while other data-based investigations report no sex-linked differences in general militarism. Among the latter is a study by Conover and Sapiro analyzing data from the 1991 American National Election Study Pilot Study.[6] They report that women were less supportive than men of the 1990–91 Gulf War but not of militarism in general, and they speculate that sex-linked differences may surface in relation to concrete rather than hypothetical war situations. Even then, the authors add, the differences are "by no means large enough to divide men and women into different camps, and they are certainly not large enough to warrant making the kinds of statements differentiating women and men that have long been part of [the popular] stereotype."[7]

A similar conclusion is reached by one of the few pertinent studies conducted outside the United States. Reporting on research in Northern Ireland, Morgan states that

> it is not possible to draw a simple distinction between women and men in terms of their attitudes toward the violent conflict [in the country]. In terms of attitudes toward violence, the spread has always been wide, and variables such as social class, age, family background, and geographical location have probably been more important than gender in shaping individual responses.[8]

This echoes the overall conclusion reached by Conover and Sapiro based on their research in the United States: "stereotypes [about male–female differences] turn out to be only partial truths, and the hypotheses [about the explanatory power of gender are] only partially confirmed."[9]

ISRAEL IN COMPARATIVE PERSPECTIVE

Against this background, the present study uses public opinion data from survey research in Israel and five other Middle Eastern societies to test the hypothesis that women are more pacific than men in evaluating international conflict. This study seeks to enhance the empirical foundation for evaluating the gender and pacifism hypothesis, and to incorporate the Israeli case into this cumulative hypothesis-testing. Given the limitations and inconsistent findings of previous empirical research, it is important to provide as much additional evidence as possible about the validity and locus of this widely-debated proposition.

From one point of view, the Israeli case is no more important than any other. The goal is to amass as much information as possible about whether and when women and men express different attitudes toward international conflict. Israeli data contribute to this just as do data from any other country. However, this study is not unrelated to efforts to place the study of Israel into a comparative perspective. On the contrary, it may be thought of as "normalizing" Israel's incorporation into cross-national research; Israel is treated as are all countries – as a source of data to evaluate hypotheses that purport broad applicability but are disputed in scholarly literature. Data from Israel thus become building blocks in the construction of social science theory.

A comparison of findings from Israel and those from other societies will also shed light on the degree to which patterns observed in Israel are unique. This is of interest not only to students of Israel, but also to those evaluating the gender and pacifism hypothesis. Placing the Israeli case in comparative perspective allows us to use Israeli data not only to assess the hypothesis but also to identify specific conditions under which it does or does not apply. Following the logic of comparative analysis, something of value will be learned regardless of whether findings from Israel are similar to or different from those from other countries.

Given the significant differences between Israel and the other countries included in this study, comparing them requires something of a "most different systems" research design. This in turn increases confidence in generalizability if similar findings are reported: if a similar pattern holds in each case, then the varying conditions of the countries studied point to the pattern's broad applicability. This holds whether the pattern confirms or disconfirms the hypothesis. Depending on the findings, similar patterns observed in each country will either significantly confirm or undermine the gender and pacifism hypothesis.

Should gender-based differences appear in some countries but not others, these dissimilar findings can be linked, aggregating political and social system attributes to identify factors associated with the hypothesis. For example, if findings about the link between gender and attitudes are not the same in countries that are more and less developed, more and less democratic, or more and less secular, the characteristics of those national systems where a positive association has been observed may constitute conditions under which gender is of value in accounting for attitudinal variation.

A similar contribution is made possible by longitudinal comparison. This includes a comparison of Israeli data collected at two different points in time, one during the Intifada and before the Gulf War and the other after the Gulf War at a time when the Palestinian uprising had lost much of its momentum. A temporal dimension is also present in the Arab data sets, two of which are from the earlier period and three of which are not only from the latter period but from the period following the Israel–PLO agreement as well. Despite a measure of overdetermination, these longitudinal data allow us to consider the question of generalization – not only across space but also across time. If events such as the Intifada and the Gulf War affect gender-based differences, these events will be identified as additional variables shaping the relationship between gender and attitudes toward international conflict.

It may be noted in passing that these comparisons also shed light on

Gender and Pacifism Hypothesis

the implications of political and social change. The temporal dimension of the data, as stated, will show whether change has occurred over time and will permit any observed changes to be linked to important developments in the Middle East region. Cross-sectional comparison can make a similar contribution, in that differences between countries that are more and less developed, more and less democratic, or more and less secular will suggest what might follow should a country experience movement on one or more of these dimensions.

This dynamic perspective is relevant for within-system as well as between-system comparison, and we pursue it with respect to levels of individual religiosity. We test the relationship between gender and attitudes not only among all respondents surveyed in each country, but also separately among more religious and less religious respondents. Should a difference be found, either in general or under the conditions that characterize particular countries, it will be possible to determine whether changes in personal religiosity affect the link between gender and attitudes toward international conflict.

In sum, this study places Israel in comparative peprspective in three ways. First, it incorporates Israel into a cumulative scholarly endeavor, providing evidence with which to test a prominent hypothesis that claims general applicability. Second, it makes cross-sectional and longitudinal comparisons to examine differences and similarities between Israel and other Middle Eastern societies, thereby identifying system-level variables affecting the hypothesis. Third, it explores political and social change both by assessing variation over time and by examining possible determinants of attitudinal variation.

DATA AND FINDINGS

Detailed information about data sources, research design, and methodology is presented in the publications referenced earlier.[10] Accordingly, only a summary account of these considerations will be presented here.

One of the two Israeli data sets was collected in 1989 and is from a national sample of persons over the age of 18 residing in 400 randomly selected urban Jewish households. Polling was done by the Dahaf Agency, which conducted the survey as part of a broad program of research on women and war designed by Professors Galia Golan and Naomi Chazan of the Hebrew University of Jerusalem. The sample yielded useable responses from 985 individuals, including 534 women and 451 men. The second Israeli data set was collected in 1991 and is from a national random sample commissioned by the German magazine *Der Spiegel*. A total of 993 Jewish Israelis were interviewed.

The Egyptian and Kuwaiti data were collected in 1988 and are from stratified and broadly representative samples of Muslim adults residing in Cairo and Kuwait City respectively. The surveys, which are part of a larger and continuing study of Arab attitudes toward domestic and

TABLE 1
ITEM LOADINGS ON FACTOR MEASURING ATTITUDES TOWARD THE
ISRAELI–PALESTINIAN CONFLICT

Israel 1989:

Would you be willing to return either all or some of the occupied territories in return for a peace agreement with the Arabs? .69419

Do you prefer to address the problem of the West Bank and Gaza by exchanging them for peace, by giving the Palestinians partial autonomy, or by removing the Arab population from these territories? .64914

Do you agree or disagree that Israel should consider permitting the establishment of a Palestinian state? .54507

Do you think the real aim of the Palestinians is to establish a state alongside Israel or to destroy the Jewish state and drive out its population? .52313

Israel 1991:

Use the following 11-point scale, ranging from 5 (highly sympathetic) to -5 (highly unsympathetic) to express the degree of your support for the Palestinian cause. .76550

In your opinion, which of the following solutions, ranging from Palestinian statehood to complete Israeli annexation, is the best way to resolve the status of the West Bank (Judea and Samaria) and Gaza? .74283

Egypt 1988:

Do you believe that the Arab-Israeli conflict can be solved by diplomacy or is a military solution required? .86036

Do you agree or disagree that peace with Israel is both desirable and possible? .62474

Kuwait 1988:

Do you believe that the Arab–Israeli conflict can be solved by diplomacy or is a military solution required? .79864

Do you agree or disagree that peace with Israel is both desirable and possible? .78454

Palestine 1994:

Which political faction do you prefer, one that does or one that does not favor territorial compromise to resolve the conflict with Israel? .77115

Do you support or oppose the conduct of armed operations against Israeli targets in Gaza and Jericho? .76479

Palestine 1995:

Do you agree or disagree that peace negotiations with Israel should continue? .72057

Do you or do you not expect the achievement of a lasting peace with Israel? .60347

TABLE 1 (Continued)

Palestine 1996:

Do you agree or disagree that peace negotiations with Israel should continue?	.76717
Do you support or oppose the current peace process?	.78939
Do you believe that final status negotiations can produce an acceptable solution to the conflict with Israel?	.59224

Jordan 1994:

To what extent do you favor diplomatic relations with Israel?	.91676
To what extent do you approve of the PLO-Israel agreement?	.87477
To what extent are you satisfied with the policies being pursued by Yasir Arafat?	.85009

Lebanon 1994:

To what extent do you favor diplomatic relations with Israel?	.92109
To what extent do you approve of the PLO-Israel agreement?	.93366
To what extent are you satisfied with the policies being pursued by Yasir Arafat?	.45131

foreign policy issues, were conducted under the supervision of Professor Jamal Sanad Al-Suwaidi of the Emirates Center for Strategic Studies and Research, who designed the project in collaboration with Professor Mark Tessler. The interviews with 295 Egyptians and 300 Kuwaitis were conducted by research assistants selected on the basis of previous experience in survey research administration. The Jordanian and Lebanese data were collected in 1994 and are based on random samples in major cities – Amman, Irbid, and Zarqa in Jordan and Beirut, Saidon, and Tripoli in Lebanon. The surveys, which include interviews with 251 Jordanians and 252 Lebanese over the age of 18, were carried out by the Market Research Organization of Amman, Jordan. The data were subsequently purchased off-the-shelf by the Office of Research of the United States Information Service and subsequently exchanged with the senior author of the present study. The Palestinian data, from 1994, 1995, and 1996, were collected by the Center for Palestine Research and Studies (CPRS), which has been using area probability sampling to conduct regular polls of West Bank and Gaza residents since September 1993. The three CPRS data sets employed in the present study are, respectively, from highly representative samples of 1,228, 1026, and 967 Palestinian adults residing in the West Bank and Gaza.

The dependent variable in the present analysis is attitude toward the conflict between Israel and the Palestinians and other Arabs, with

TABLE 2
RELATIONSHIP BETWEEN GENDER AND ATTITUDES TOWARD THE
ARAB–ISRAELI CONFLICT AMONG ISRAELI, EGYPTIAN, KUWAITI,
PALESTINIAN, JORDANIAN, AND LEBANESE RESPONDENTS

Supports Compromise, Diplomacy, and/or Non-Violent Means of Resolving Arab–Israeli Conflict		Female	Male	Total
Israel 1989:	Highly Supportive	35%	33%	34%
$X2 = .44$	Somewhat Supportive	31%	34%	32%
df = 2				
p > .05	Not Supportive	34%	33%	34%
	Total	475	382	857
Israel 1991:	Highly Supportive	35%	32%	34%
$X2 = 1.74$	Somewhat Supportive	37%	35%	36%
df = 2				
p > .05	Not Supportive	28%	33%	30%
	Total	498	495	993
Egypt 1988:	Highly Supportive	83%	90%	87%
$X2 = 3.13$	Somewhat or Not Supportive	17%	10%	13%
df = 1				
p > .05	Total	133	141	274
Kuwait 1988:	Highly Supportive	24%	25%	25%
$X2 = .69$	Somewhat Supportive	33%	29%	31%
df = 2				
p > .05	Not Supportive	43%	46%	44%
	Total	148	136	284
Palestine 1994:	Highly Supportive	51%	53%	52%
$X2 = 1.14$	Somewhat Supportive	35%	35%	35%
df = 2				
p > .05	Not Supportive	14%	12%	13%
	Total	619	609	1228
Palestine 1995:	Highly Supportive	24%	26%	25%
$X2 = .77$	Somewhat Supportive	57%	54%	55%
df = 2				
p > .05	Not Supportive	19%	20%	20%
	Total	504	522	1026

Gender and Pacifism Hypothesis

TABLE 2 (Continued)

Supports Compromise, Diplomacy, and/or Non-Violent Means of Resolving Arab–Israeli Conflict		Female	Male	Total
Palestine 1996:	Highly Supportive	35%	34%	35%
$X2 = .98$ df = 2	Somewhat Supportive	36%	37%	36%
p > .05	Not Supportive	29%	29%	29%
	Total	476	491	967
Jordan 1994:	Highly Supportive	33%	34%	33%
$X2 = 3.78$ df = 2	Somewhat Supportive	15%	26%	21%
p > .05	Not Supportive	52%	40%	46%
	Total	79	83	162
Lebanon 1994:	Highly Supportive	36%	36%	36%
$X2 = 3.26$ df = 2	Somewhat Supportive	19%	28%	23%
p > .05	Not Supportive	45%	36%	41%
	Total	107	103	210

respondents rated according to the degree of their support for, or opposition to, a peaceful resolution based on territorial compromise and mutual recognition between Israelis and Palestinians. As in the earlier studies, we have used a data reduction technique known as factor analysis to identify items from the survey instruments that provide a reliable measure of attitudes toward the conflict. Items that ask about the conflict and have high loadings on a common factor are then combined to form an attitudinal scale. Table 1 lists the items that we used to construct this scale for each of the data sets. The factor loadings of these items are given as well.

Table 2 shows the relationship between gender and attitudes toward the Arab–Israeli conflict for all seven of the data sets. We have trichotomized ratings on the scale measuring the dependent variable, as in the earlier analyses, and computed the chi square in each instance to determine whether a statistically significant difference between male and female attitudes exists. The earlier studies found that neither in the 1989 Israeli sample nor in the Egyptian, Kuwaiti, and Palestinian samples was there a significant difference in the attitudes expressed by men and women toward issues of war and peace. As shown in Table 2, this pattern of no significant relationship characterizes all the additional data sets in this study.

TABLE 3
RELATIONSHIP BETWEEN GENDER AND ATTITUDES TOWARD THE ARAB–ISRAELI CONFLICT AMONG MORE RELIGIOUS RESPONDENTS AND LESS RELIGIOUS RESPONDENTS FROM ISRAEL, EGYPT, KUWAIT, JORDAN, AND LEBANON

Israel 1989:	More religious:	$X2 = 0.63$, $df = 2$, $p > .05$
	Less religious:	$X2 = 0.35$, $df = 2$, $p > .05$
Israel 1991:	More religious:	$X2 = 2.05$, $df = 2$, $p > .05$
	Less religious:	$X2 = 1.52$, $df = 2$, $p > .05$
Egypt 1988:	More religious:	$X2 = 3.14$, $df = 2$, $p > .05$
	Less religious:	$X2 = 0.62$, $df = 2$, $p > .05$
Kuwait 1988:	More religious:	$X2 = 3.04$, $df = 2$, $p > .05$
	Less religious:	$X2 = 0.64$, $df = 2$, $p > .05$
Palestine 1995:	More religious:	$X2 = 0.92$, $df = 2$, $p > .05$
	Less religious:	$X2 = 0.36$, $df = 2$, $p > .05$
Jordan 1994:	More religious:	$X2 = 1.53$, $df = 2$, $p > .05$
	Less religious:	$X2 = 2.34$, $df = 2$, $p > .05$
Lebanon 1994:	More religious:	$X2 = 1.15$, $df = 2$, $p > .05$
	Less religious:	$X2 = 4.28$, $df = 2$, $p > .05$

Table 3 adds a within-system dimension not present in the earlier inquiries, disaggregating each sample on the basis of religiosity and separately examining the gender relationship for more and less religious respondents. Religiosity is measured in both Israeli samples through a self-identification question. There are no items dealing with religiosity in the 1994 and 1996 Palestinian samples, which accordingly are not included in Table 3. The other five Arab samples, including the 1995 Palestinian data set, contained a number of items dealing with religiosity and religious attachments, and in each case we employed factor analysis and dichotomized the item loading highest on a religiosity factor to form the categories used in Table 3. In no instance, neither among more religious respondents nor among less religious respondents, is there a statistically significant relationship between gender and attitudes toward the Arab–Israeli conflict in any of the samples.

The consistent finding of no relationship, while offering fewer possibilities for comparative analysis, provides compelling evidence that the gender and pacifism hypothesis does not apply in the Middle East, or at least not in the case of the Arab–Israeli conflict. Given that debates in the relevant scholarly literature are for the most part pursued with little supporting empirical evidence from any society, these clear and consistent findings may also make an important contribution to discussions about the accuracy of this hypothesis more generally.

THE ISRAELI CONTRIBUTION

With respect to this report's special interest in the Israeli case, particularly in comparative perspective, the following observations and conclusions may be advanced on the basis of the findings presented in Table 2 and Table 3.

First, findings from Israel add incrementally to the base of empirical evidence by which the gender and pacifism hypothesis, like any hypothesis, must be judged. Other things being equal, findings from Israel are not any more important to this cumulative scientific endeavor than are findings from any other society. But neither are they less important. The Israeli case can and should be integrated into this effort, offering, like any individual case, evidence about whether and under what conditions gender is useful in accounting for variance in attitudes toward international conflict. For the time being, systematic empirical evidence bearing on these questions remains limited, which explains the absence of a consensus among scholars working in the area. But studies in Israel can provide some of the data by which present-day scholarly debates will eventually be resolved, and this is one of the contributions that the present research report aspires to make. Specifically, studies conducted in Israel in 1988–89 and 1991 show that gender is not of any use in accounting for observed attitudinal variation, and findings from the Israeli case accordingly provide support for the position of those who do not find the gender and pacifism hypothesis persuasive.

Second, comparisons between Israel and other countries can help identify any system-level attributes that determine whether or not this hypothesis obtains. In the present instance, since the hypothesis does not appear to apply in the Israeli case, any attributes which differentiate Israel from societies where a relationship between gender and attitudes toward international conflict is found will specify variables associated with the salience of that relationship. For example, Israel differs from the United States and western Europe in its continuing state of war, in the official connection between religion and state, and perhaps in other factors as well. To the extent that subsequent research demonstrates a link between gender and attitudes toward international conflict in the US or western Europe, comparisons with Israel can help identify the system-level characteristics forming the locus of that relationship. In this hypothetical example, the gender and pacificism hypothesis will have been shown to hold only in societies not involved in prolonged military conflicts and that do officially separate religion and politics.

Third, the logic of such analyses also applies to comparisons between Israel and other countries in the Middle East, such as that undertaken in the present study. In this instance, findings from Israel and all of the other countries examined are similar, and so this research tells us something about the system-level attributes that do *not* affect the relationship between gender and attitudes toward international conflict.

Those attributes separating Israel from the other cases, such as whether a majority of the country's citizens is Jewish or Muslim or whether the country is more democratic or less democratic, are not variables affecting the validity of the hypothesis. Parenthetically, this logic holds when comparing any combination of the cases examined. Similar findings from Jordan and Egypt indicate, for example, that whether a regime is monarchical or republican has nothing to do with the applicability of the gender and pacifism hypothesis.

Finally, findings from the present research provide insights about the consequences of social and political change. The longitudinal, the between-system cross-sectional, and the within-system cross-sectional analyses all offer specific conclusions about the gender and pacifism hypothesis, while illustrating how survey data can be used to assess the prospects for change in other hypotheses specifying individual-level variable relationships. In this instance, findings point to constancy in gender's lack of explanatory power, suggesting, within the parameters of the available data, that it does not become more relevant as conditions of war and peace change over time, as countries become more developed, democratic, or secular, or as populations become more or less religious.

CONCLUSION

This research report is not offered as a case study focusing on the relationship between gender and issues of war and peace in Israel.[11] Although our findings do have some implications for the Israeli case, the nature and dynamics of this relationship are not considered with any specific attention to politics, associational life, or issues of public policy in Israel. Rather, the report employs survey data from Israel to test a hypothesis that is the subject of considerable debate in theoretical literature concerned with linkages between gender and international studies. This study not only employs Israeli data to add to the accumulated evidence addressing this hypothesis: it also tests the hypothesis with survey data from other Middle Eastern countries and compares the findings from these cases to those from Israel. As such, its primary contribution is to demonstrate how survey research in Israel can be used not only to describe and explain Israeli attitudes, but to advance programs of research, including comparative studies, which have the construction of social and political theory as their principal objective.

In the present instance, findings from Israel and all of the other cases are remarkably clear and consistent. Both in general and under conditions specified by levels of personal religiosity, gender bears no significant relationship to attitudes toward international conflict. These findings provide compelling evidence that the gender and pacifism hypothesis does not apply in a wide range of social and political contexts, including those that characterize the Israeli case. Further, the findings demonstrate that the null hypothesis pattern is stable over time, in Israel and presumably elsewhere, despite the intervention of important events bearing on war and peace in the Middle East. Finally, the similarity of findings from the various cases indicates that social dynamics in Israel resemble those in the Arab world in at least some critical respects. Although Israel and its Arab neighbors are very different from one another in aggregate patterns of politics and society, including the circumstances of women, these differences appear to have no impact on attitude formation in the present analysis.

NOTES

1. Mark Tessler and Ina Warriner, "Gender, Feminism, and Attitudes toward International Conflict: Exploring Relationships with Survey Data from the Middle East," *World Politics* 49 (Jan. 1997) pp.250–81; Mark Tessler and Ina Warriner, "Gender and International Relations: A Comparison of Citizen Attitudes in Israel and Egypt," in Michael Barnett (ed.), *Israel in Comparative Perspective: Challenging the Conventional Wisdom*, Albany, NY: SUNY Press, 1996.
2. V. Spike Peterson and Anne Sisson Runyan, *Global Gender Issues*, Boulder, CO, 1993, pp.81–2. Peterson and Runyan draw heavily on Jean Bethke Elshtain, "Reflections on War and Political Discourse," *Political Theory* 13/1 (1985) pp.39–57.
3. See Patricia Ward Scaltsas, "Do Feminist Ethics Counter Feminist Aims?" in Eve Browning Cole and Susan Coultrap-McQuin (eds), *Explorations in Feminist Ethics*, Bloomington, IN: Indiana University Press, 1992. See also Elshtain (note 2).
4. See Sara Ruddick, *Maternal Thinking: Toward a Politics of Peace*, New York, 1989; and Mary G. Dietz, "Citizenship with a Feminist Face: The Problem with Maternal Thinking," *Political Theory* 13/1 (1985).
5. See Lisa Brandes, "The Gender Gap and Attitudes toward War," paper presented at the 1992 annual meeting of the Midwest Political Science Association, Chicago; Robert Y. Shapiro and Harpreet Mahajan, "Gender Differences in Policy Preferences: A Summary of Trends from the 1960's to the 1980's," *Public Opinion Quarterly* 50 (1986) pp.42–61; and Tom W. Smith, "Gender and Attitudes toward Violence," *Public Opinion Quarterly* 48 (1984) pp.384–96.
6. Pamela Johnston Conover and Virginia Sapiro, "Gender, Feminist Consciousness, and War," *American Journal of Political Science* 37 (Nov. 1993) pp.1079–99.
7. Ibid., p.1095.
8. Valerie Morgan, "Women and the Peace Process in Northern Ireland," *Global Forum Series Occasional Papers*, Durham, NC: Duke University Center for International Studies, 1996, p.6.
9. Conover and Sapiro, "Gender, Feminist Consciousness, and War" (note 6) p.1095.
10. In addition to the publications identified in note 1, methodological information is also presented in Mark Tessler and Jolene Jesse, "Gender and Support for Islamist Movements: Evidence from Egypt, Kuwait, and Palestine," *Muslim World* LXXXVI (April 1996) pp.194–222; and Mark Tessler and Jamal Sanad, "Will the Arab Public Accept Peace with Israel: Evidence from Surveys in Three Arab Societies," in Gregory Mahler and Efriam Karsh (eds), *Israel at the Crossroads*, London: I.B. Tauris, 1994. These publications do not provide information about three of the data sets employed in the present study, that from Israel in 1991 and those from Jordan and Lebanon.
11. For information about the relationship between gender and peace in Israel see Dafna N. Izraeli and Ephraim Taboury, "The Political Context of Feminist Attitudes in Israel," in Yael Azmon and Dafna N. Izraeli (eds), *Women in Israel*, New Brunswick, NJ: Transaction Publishers, 1993; Naomi Chazan, "Israeli Women and Peace Activism,"

and Nurit Gillath, "Women Against War: Parents Against Silence," in Barbara Swirski and Marilyn Safir (eds), *Calling the Equality Bluff*, New York: Pergamon Press, 1991; Roberta Micallef, "Israeli and Palestinian Women's Peace Movements," in Elizabeth Warnock Fernea and Mary Evelyn Hocking (eds), *The Struggle for Peace*, Austin, TX: University of Texas Press, 1992; and Simona Sharoni, *Gender and the Israeli–Palestinian Conflict*, Syracuse, NY: Syracuse University Press, 1994.

The Promised Land of the Chosen People is not all that Distinctive: On the Value of Comparison

IRA SHARKANSKY

Concepts of the Promised Land and Chosen People have served the Jews well. Since biblical times they have been associated with self-esteem amidst adversity. We can surmise that Jewish self-esteem has contributed to communal solidarity and survival, as well as individual success in economics, culture, and politics. Yet the Promised Land and Chosen People may deter accurate self-assessment in modern Israel by emphasizing the uniqueness of the nation and its homeland. Israeli social scientists, journalists, and policy analysts make assertions about national traits that differ significantly from those apparent in comparative analysis.

There is no denying that Israel, like other countries, has traits that truly are distinctive. It is also the case that individual researchers in other countries are parochial, and describe national traits that do not stand up to comparison. For Israeli Jews, however, the temptations may be greater than those of other nations. Biblical doctrines of Promised Land and Chosen People refer to them. They may add to parochialism even among Israelis who do not think of themselves as religious. The dangers of parochialism lie not only in mistaken commentaries, but in distorted political efforts and misdirected economic resources. Policy advocates who do not compare their country with others may contribute to an undue allocation of efforts to problems that are widely perceived to be extreme, but which in reality are no worse or even less severe than in other countries.

The article illustrates Israeli parochialism with respect to three disparate issues where many have claimed distinctiveness, but where cross national comparisons indicate that Israel does not significantly differ from other countries or departs from conventional wisdom. The

---

Ira Sharkansky is at The Hebrew University of Jerusalem.

topics considered here have been prominent in recent disputes. And while Israel has no collection of systematic surveys plotting the issues that most trouble the public, the issues addressed here have been featured in Israel's popular media. Intellectuals and ranking officials have subjected them to special campaigns and government programs. The three issues addressed below are (1) the power of religious interests to shape public policy, (2) economic and social inequality, and (3) the incidence of traffic deaths. This article describes claims made for each issue and assesses them against data from within Israel and cross-national comparisons. I conclude that these findings put the burden of proof on those who claim that Israel, or any other country, has special traits that distinguish it from others.

This article emphasizes the need to test expectations about Israel or any other country, ideally with multi-case comparisons, employing reliable data that lends itself to quantitative analysis. Claims about change should also be bolstered with sophisticated analyses of multinational comparisons over time. As the subsequent discussion indicates, however, problems in assembling comparable data over time often limit multi-national studies of change. In such cases, static cross-national findings must sustitute for reliable analyses of change. Findings about change within Israel about income equality and traffic fatalities which are reported here caution against any simple perception that either the social gap or road safety is getting worse. Knowing the power of religious or anti-religious activists is no less important in judging the quality of Israel's public sphere. But, alas, this issue is even more difficult to define and assess cross-nationally and over time.

THE POWER AND THE LIMITS OF RELIGION

Israel's history assures a prominent role for religion. Founded in 1948 with a declaration of being a Jewish state, Israel stood against the trend of breaking the church–state nexus that had prevailed for more than a century in Europe and North America. Yet religious and secular commentators exaggerate both Israel's distinctiveness on this trait and the capacity of the opposing camp to shape policy.[1] Here the emphasis will be on religion and policy disputes among Israeli Jews. There are also disputes involving Christians and Muslims, but those among Jews are most often on the public agenda.

According to Hebrew University sociologist Moshe Lissak, "The cleavage between the religious and the secular is the deepest one within (Israeli) society."[2] Points of controversy between religious and secular activists include:

- Which aspects of religious law should be enforced by state authorities, and which bodies should have the final say in applying religious law? This cluster of issues includes the application of religious law to the Sabbath and religious holidays; the sale of non-kosher food; rules of modesty and decency; abortion, organ transplants and other medical practices; the treatment of ancient Jewish graves uncovered in construction projects; who should be considered a Jew; and who should be given the designation and authority of "rabbi" to perform marriages, divorces, and conversions to Judaism.

- The rights of non-Jews, including access to public positions and other benefits of public policy.

- The rights of various categories of Jews: religious and secular Jews, ultra-orthodox and non-orthodox, as well as Jews from North Africa, Ethiopia, and Asia have claimed that they have been treated unfairly by other Jews.

- The significance of the biblical Land of Israel, and how much of that imprecise landscape should be insisted on, or bargained away for the sake of peace. Not the least of the issues in this cluster is Jerusalem, with demands by Christians and Muslims, as well as Israeli and diaspora Jews, for a say in its control.

All of these controversies simmer without clear resolution. Individual cases pertaining to a general issue cause brief commotion, and may find some resolution. But before long, another case emerges reflecting the same underlying disagreement.

Groups at different points on the religious–secular spectrum tend to be socially isolated and express antagonistic stereotypes of one another. Both religious and secular Jews suffer, the former because the state and most of its people violate divine commandments, the latter because personal freedom is undermined by religious activists. Divisions and stereotypes are reinforced by separate schools for the ultra-orthodox, orthodox, and secular Jews, by separate military service for the orthodox and total exemption for the ultra-orthodox, and by newspapers for each of the orthodox and ultra-orthodox communities. There is social pressure among ultra-orthodox against listening to radio or television, and kiosk owners in ultra-orthodox neighborhoods may fear to sell secular newspapers. Ultra-orthodox neighborhoods in Jerusalem gave upwards of 70 percent of their vote to ultra-orthodox parties in the 1988 national election.[3]

Stereotypes expressed by religious and secular Israelis indicate that members of the other community are aggressively antagonistic toward them and are making advances in religious–secular disputes.[4] The Israeli media contribute to stereotyping by emphasizing religious conflict and providing access to distinguished Jews in Israel and the diaspora who express strong views about the power of one or another antagonist.[5]

Several problems stand in the way of a systematic reckoning of whether religious or secular interests have been dominant in recent

Israeli history or which camp wins individual confrontations. One problem involves the designation of an issue as religious. More than Christianity or Islam, Judaism combines ethnicity with doctrines in ways that challenge simple analysis. And a great diversity of belief and practice reflects the long history of Judaism and its spread through many cultures. Jewish humanists, agnostics, atheists, and anti-clerics are no less at home in Israel than the ultra-orthodox and mildly religious. Virtually every policy issue that reaches the agenda of Israel's cabinet has a Jewish component. The different sides in an argument about welfare policy, fiscal policy, or defense may refer to the well-being of the *Jewish* state, or wrap their demands in what they call *Jewish* norms or tradition.

Another problem is selecting a "religious" or a "secular" posture to use in judging the outcome of a controversy. Israel's character as a Jewish state appears more in the preoccupation of political activists with Jewish issues than with any consensus about religion or what is good for the Jews. Religious and secular leaders differ among themselves on the formulation of demands and ranking them from the lesser to the greater importance. The lack of unity among religious authorities is also known in Christian and Muslim communities, and may be endemic to issues with a spiritual content.

> One special problem has been the other-worldly orientation of these deeply religious people; another problem has been religious particularism, where theological disputes have inhibited political cooperation.[6]

Details of individual confrontations also confuse the judgment of religious or secular success. How to record an outcome if one side has won the enactment of a law but where the measure is seldom enforced, as in the case of forbidding the sale of non-kosher food,? And how to reach a general conclusion when the same general problem (e.g., public modesty, Sabbath observance, legal definitions of Who is a Jew) returns time and again, with variations in the character of the demands and subtle nuances in the ways that issue is resolved, or when individual episodes disappear from the public agenda without a resolution?

National politics works to blur religious or secular victories. No party has ever won a majority in national elections, and every government has been a coalition among parties that both compete and cooperate with one another. The religious vote is divided between several parties. One or another religious party has been a member of most governing coalitions, and they have occasionally had enough seats in the Knesset to threaten a governmental fall by withdrawing their support. For most of the period between the elections of 1992 and 1996, there was no religious party in the coalition. Yet no Israeli government would lightly take an overt posture against an issue of religion, due to the service of religious parties as coalition partners in the past, and the prospect that they will be needed in the future.

Tie Score, Even in the Holy City of Jerusalem

Taking the city of Jerusalem as a case in point, the record of recent religious–secular policy conflicts suggests that the score is roughtly tied. In recent years, examination of disputes in this most sensitive of Israeli cities shows chronic conflict about religion, with sporadic outbursts of public demonstrations, but with neither religious or secular interests predictably dominant.

In cases involving road construction and a new stadium that were opposed by religious activists, plans were sometimes delayed or altered but rarely reversed. With one new highway, it was decided to close an exit that led through a religious neighborhood on Sabbaths and holidays and to construct a wall to screen the sight and sound of the main artery from the religious neighborhood. Religious activists likewise delayed the completion of a major intersection over the disturbance of ancient graves found at the site. Authorities agreed to alter the roadway to avoid the graves, but construction then went forward despite the discovery of additional graves on the revised route. A more recent controversy reached a confusing compromise: traffic is prohibited during times of prayer on the Sabbath and religious holidays, but permitted at other times on those days, which is confusing since prayer times vary with the season. The compromise, which has been appealed to the Supreme Court, is unsettling to both religious and non-religious communities. Religious activists want to close the road throughout the Sabbath and holidays, while secular activists want it opened entirely.

The issue of "indecent" advertising in bus shelters left the public agenda after a wave of burning shelters and an agreement between the advertising company and religious representatives. Negotiations between the parties seemed futile when a shelter was burned that carried a picture of a mayonnaise jar without any human forms. The Yad Vashem Holocaust Memorial has resisted demands of ultra-orthodox to remove a display of photographs showing nude concentration camp inmates. Yad Vashem officials explain that the pictures are an important part of exhibits that depict the humiliations that were part of Nazi policy. Ultra-orthodox threats to open their own Holocaust Memorial seem to have been rhetorical bluster. It is easy to threaten such actions but costly to implement them.

Secular interests scored some victories with the opening of restaurants, discotechs, and cinemas on the Sabbath. The municipal by-laws which had kept them closed were ruled to be flawed in a 1987 court decision, and religious politicians have not succeeded in enacting a new measure. Secular interests also gain by inaction at times. Laws prohibiting the sale of non-kosher food, for example, are enacted but generally not enforced. A newspaper report of May 1995 indicated a significant increase in the shops selling pork in response to immigration from the former Soviet Union.[7]

Demands by non-orthodox rabbis for recognition and funds for their congregations are another challenge to the orthodox establishment. Here, outcomes have been mixed. The status quo provides orthodox rabbis a monopoly on marriages and divorces performed in Israel, but many Israelis marry or divorce outside of Israel. The Interior Ministry accepts foreign documents in recording personal status, and Israeli courts protect the rights of spouses and children. Meanwhile, there has been an increase in the number of Reform and Conservative synagogues and schools with financial support from government and quasi-governmental organizations.

There has been a continued expansion of ultra-orthodox neighborhoods, with corresponding increases in public resources for schools and other institutions. A great deal of rhetoric surrounds these material benefits, as secular politicians charge that the religious parties inflate their demands and receive excessive material rewards through their importance in governing coalitions. Religious politicians insist that they receive less than a fair share of resources, and what they do receive is the result of legitimate politics. The truth is difficult to nail down. Financial allocations for housing and infrastructure in religious neighborhoods, plus support for religious schools and other institutions come from a variety of ministerial and quasi-governmental budgets, under numerous program headings. Complex bookkeeping discourages a comprehensive and persuasive record of distributive benefits.[8]

How does this stand-off between religious and secular interests in policymaking compare to other western democracies? On the dimension of expressed belief, Israel seems to fit somewhere among other western regimes. Surveys indicate that about 20 percent of Israelis define themselves as ultra-orthodox or orthodox, another 30 percent define themselves as "traditional," and 79 percent place themselves on a continuum between "strictly observant" and "somewhat observant."[9] Surveys from 21 countries (not including Israel), show between 2 and 82 percent reporting that they attend church weekly; 24 and 81 percent who feel religious; 39 and 96 percent who express a belief in God.[10]

On the dimension of government support for religion, Israel also finds itself in company with numerous other countries. The varied modes of support complicate any effort at systematic international comparison. In Israel as elsewhere, material support flows from public authorities to religious bodies in various ways. Even in the United States, despite separation of church and state, religious organizations receive substantial tax exemptions, as well as direct financial support for hospitals, schools, and other religiously affiliated institutions. While there is no established church in the United States, religiosity appears to be the national creed.[11] Coins and currency, as well as the pledge of allegiance, proclaim the importance of God. Religious leaders speak out on issues of policy, and occasionally seem to influence the decisions of government officials.

The prominence of a religious symbol on the national flag puts Israel in a group along with the United Kingdom, Finland, Sweden, Norway, Denmark, Iceland, Switzerland, Greece, Australia, and New Zealand. Perhaps every democracy's list of national holidays is heavily affected by religion, with special prominence for Good Friday, Easter, and Christmas.

ISRAELI INCOME EQUALITY

The salience of income equality in Israel reflects elements of socialism in the Zionist ideology, as well as ancient Judaic doctrines. It also reflects claims of religious and ethnic discrimination that have set Arabs against Jews and Jews of Asian and African backgrounds against those with European backgrounds. Distinguished academics and journalists have criticized what they describe as an intolerable degree of inequality in Israel, but this issue is no less complex than the puzzles about religious or secular power. In both cases, simple assertions about Israeli distinctiveness fail on the dimension of international comparison.[12]

Commentary about a substantial "social gap" is sufficiently widespread to acquire the status of conventional wisdom. A recent book by the Hebrew University political theorist Ze'ev Sternhell argues that Israeli egalitarianism has been an ideological symbol, rhetorical device, rallying cry, or decoration for a Labor Party that failed to take it seriously.[13] A senior columnist with the *Jerusalem Post*, Yosef Goell, has written that "Recent studies have shown that among developed countries, Israel is second only to the United States in income inequality."[14] The Hebrew University political sociologist Michael Shalev has written that Israel falls short of other welfare states in the seriousness and success of its egalitarian policies.[15] Dan Horowitz and Moshe Lissak, as well as Goell and Shalev, have written about increasing inequality between Israel's income groups.[16]

It is no easy task to define or measure economic equality, and there are no universally acceptable comparisons of equality between Israel and other countries. Thus, no claim about empirical findings can be taken as the final word. However, findings derived from some comparative analyses do indicate that Israel may be substantially more egalitarian than suggested in the writings of Sternhell, Shalev, or Goell.

Competing concepts of socio-economic equality include opportunities and achievements in income, education, occupational status, housing, and health, but it is common for scholars to deal with the more narrow and measurable issue of income equality. Yet, experts quarrel about the virtues and problems associated with measurements showing differences between upper and lower income groups, the widely used summary indicator (GINI coefficient), national measures of the "poverty line," and distinctions between income and wealth (important for studies of the aged, who tend to score low on monthly income but higher on accumulated wealth). It is no simple task to distinguish between gross and net income; assign monetary values to the public services received by families; trace the flow of transfer payments; measure how much families in each income class pay for indirect taxes (sales, value added, property, customs duties); evaluate wealth represented by housing, land, savings accounts, pension funds, and other possessions; or untangle the murky but important item of unreported (underground) income. The problems do not stop with assessing the formal legislation concerned with taxes and services, but require an assessment of how different taxes are actually levied and collected, and how services are actually distributed. Most research proceeds only part of the way along the chain of increasing precision. Few compilations struggle with the problems of differential policy implementation from one population sector to another, or questions like, *What is the value of public education received in a slum school compared to that in an upper middle class neighborhood?* or *What about the uneven assessments of taxes, or the discretionary discounts on taxes provided in cases of hardship?*

The analytical problems multiply for those concerned with comparisons across national borders. Countries do not have identical public services, transfer payments, and tax rates. They differ on how they record the exclusion of certain incomes and expenditures from taxation, as well as in their reputations for implementing declared policies and the quality of their economic statistics.[17] What emerges from this collection of problems is a severely limited array of international data. The information available has been collected for some countries on an irregular basis, assembled and partly refined by individual scholars or teams concerned with issues of international comparison.

The result of all these complications is that no analyses can answer the doubts of skeptics with respect to the assessment of income equality in different countries at different points of time. Yet even those rough comparative tools surpass the accuracy of observations scholars or journalists can offer about their own country without an explicit consideration of the comparative dimension.

Equality and Economic Development

One of the lessons that emerges from comparison is that there is an association between equality and a country's level of economic development. A statistical analysis of data assembled for 45 countries in the mid-1980s shows coefficients of simple correlation between GNP per capita and measures of income equality in the range of .5 to .7.[18] Countries with higher levels of GNP per capita tend to have more equal distributions of income. The findings make sense, as equality is expensive. It depends on a national treasury sufficiently wealthy to afford substantial programs in education and other social services; transfer payments to aid the unemployed, incapacitated, elderly, and large families; and an administrative structure sophisticated enough to assess and collect taxes in a progressive manner. A wealthy economy also provides more opportunities for personal advancement in the private sector via higher wages and savings, as well as non-governmental bank loans, educational scholarships, and charitable funds collected for the needy.

The data considered here show that Israel is not among the few most egalitarian societies, but neither is it among the wealthiest. Israel's level of income equality more or less reflects its level of economic development. To the extent that measures of Israel's income equality depart from levels generally associated with its economic development, they show *that Israel is more egalitarian than a number of other countries at or above its level of wealth*. Regression analyses and a consideration of residuals show that Israel's GINI coefficient is lower than predicted by its level of GNP per capita (indicating greater equality than typically associated with its GNP per capita), while the proportions of incomes received by low-income and high-income families are respectively higher and lower than predicted by its level of GNP per capita (also indicating greater equality of incomes than typically associated with its GNP per capita).[19] On absolute comparisons and scores in relation to GNP per capita for various measures of income distribution, Israel appears more egalitarian then Australia, Canada, Denmark, France, Italy, New Zealand, Norway, Sweden, Switzerland, United Kingdom, United States, and West Germany.[20]

Israel Not Alone in Inequality Increases

Those critics who charge that Israel's economy has become less egalitarian in recent years are essentially correct. However, the same point is also true for numerous other national economies. There are several indications that the heyday of the welfare state has passed, or that welfare policies have retreated in the face of political victories by right-wing parties.[21] The homeless appear to be more prominent on the city streets of Europe and North America than Israel.

Data for numerous countries on *changes in equality* are even more scarce and less comparable than data about equality in individual countries at fixed points in time. National governments alter their distributions of taxes, program benefits, transfer payments, and statistical concepts without reference to what the changes mean for social scientists concerned with stable data sets. GINI coefficient for the United States increased (in the direction of inequality) from .376 in 1947 to .392 in 1986.[22] The percentage of American families below the poverty line increased from 24 in 1969 to 36 in 1991.[23] There was a lessening of equality among Israel's income classes between 1985 and 1993. However, the changes were not consistently in the direction of greater inequality. There was a narrower gap between lowest and highest income groups in 1992–93 than in any year since 1986–87.[24] A spurt towards inequality from 1988 to 1991 may reflect a period of sizable immigration and the unemployment experienced by new arrivals rather than any deliberate policy on the part of the government.

Whatever the causes of Israeli inequality, it has been ameliorated by progressive rates of taxation. Pre- and after-tax figures show that the Israeli tax system substantially narrows the income gaps. In the United States, in contrast, the gaps are widened by a tax system that is regressive in the aggregate.[25]

TRAFFIC SAFETY

The picture is similar in the field of traffic safety: claims of severe conditions contrast with comparative findings that include Israel along with numerous other countries. Media reports have focused on highway "carnage" and "bloody outrage," and the "eleventh plague."[26] Policymakers devote special resources to their war against "slaughter on the roads." A permanent governmental commission (National Council for the Prevention of Road Accidents), with a staff and budget, and previously headed by a justice of the Supreme Court, is charged with coordinating police, road construction, and education activities for the sake of road safety. The *Jerusalem Post* reported in a front page story that Chief Sephardi Rabbi Eliahu Bakshi-Doron urged Prime Minister Yitzhak Rabin to declare an "emergency situation" on the nation's roads and do everything possible to stop accidents.[27] Another *Jerusalem Post* article reported that as bad as highway safety has been, it has gotten worse in recent years.[28]

When the subject is examined comparatively, Israel's record of road deaths appears to be normal with respect to a group of countries appropriate for comparison, or even to be *low* by international standards. Moreover, data from a 20 year period indicates a substantial *decline* in Israeli road fatalities in relation to population.

It should be no surprise that the level of economic development is important for road safety. The incidence of highway deaths in relation to the number of motor vehicles shows a strong negative correlation (–.82) with GNP per capita. Economic resources work to lower accidents via the quality of vehicles and roads, the level of drivers' education, and the length of driving experience accumulated by a nation's citizens. Israel shows a higher incidence of traffic deaths in relation to motor vehicles than the more wealthy countries of western Europe and North America. However, a regression analysis of traffic deaths per vehicle and GNP/capita, shows Israel with a *lower* incidence of traffic deaths than expected for its level of economic development. With respect to the alternate measure of traffic deaths in relation to total population, Israel shows a lower incidence of fatalities than Germany, Belgium, the United States, France, Austria, Canada, Australia, Italy, Finland, Switzerland, Denmark, and Japan. Israel's incidence of fatal accidents has declined substantially: from 21 per 100,000 population in 1974 to 9 per 100,000 in 1991.[29]

This is a field where at least some Israeli officials realize that the situation is not all that bad. The head of the Transport Ministry's Road Safety Administration told a Cabinet meeting that Israelis may be among the world's worst drivers, but not among the most dangerous. He listed Israel as the fifth *lowest* in a list of 23 developed countries with respect to the per-capita rate of road deaths (i.e., in a position better than 17 other developed countries). On his list Israel scores better than Switzerland (which many Israelis see as a bastion of law and order), the United States (a symbol for all that is modern and desirable), as well as France, Germany and Italy.[30] When the Minister for Domestic Security said at the end of 1995 that the year had seen a decrease in road fatalities, however, an official of the Transportation Ministry accused him of exaggerating and said that "the situation was far from satisfactory."[31] When an official with responsibility for road safety went before the Finance Minister with a request for funding, he admitted that Israel scored relatively well among developed countries, and had seen a decrease in traffic deaths in relation to population. Nonetheless, he felt obliged to press for an emotional campaign against the minister's skepticism.[32]

DISCUSSION

There are no final answers or simple conclusions about the power of religion, economic equality, or road safety in Israel. For a social critic, it may be enough to proclaim that religious or secular groups are oppressive, that the degree of economic equality is not sufficient, or that too many people die as a result of road accidents. A social scientist should take account of the conceptual and operational complexities in these issues, and – insofar as it is possible to array international comparisons – how each country performs in relation to others with which it is reasonable to compare it.

Comparative analysis suggests results that are reasonable to expect. If a country scores on a trait similar to other countries to which it may be compared (that is, similar on characteristics likely to affect the issue being considered) it is fair to conclude that its performance is acceptable within the level of resources that states generally are inclined to allocate to the issue. For those who assert that comparison is not an appropriate standard of judgment, the only solution may be access to a Paradise where resources and opportunities are unlimited and justice is the prime value.

In sum, it appears that Jewish religious interests are strong enough to put their issues on Israel's agenda, but not powerful enough to dominate policymaking. When considered comparatively, the role of religion in the Jewish state resembles the situation in western democracies generally.

Likewise with respect to income equality and traffic safety. On these traits, perhaps to the dismay of those who think of themselves as the Chosen People of the Promised Land, Israel scores within the normal range. On the two issues that lend themselves most clearly to quantitative analysis (i.e., income equality and traffic safety), the picture belies the conventional wisdom: Israel scores a bit more egalitarian and its road are safer than nations with which it might fairly be compared.

The concept of the Chosen People may lead Israelis to feel themselves different from others. On some measures, such feelings may be justified. Israel is, after all, the only country with a Jewish majority. It also may be the case that there is a high incidence of physicians in relation to population, large outlays on defense in relation to GNP, and amounts of foreign aid from governments and non-governmental organizations that are high by international standards.

Parochialism can have serious implications. For those who are not satisfied with a reasonable level of aspirations, as defined by the achievements of countries that are similar on important traits, a parochial insistence on ever greater achievements in a favored policy field can produce a distortion of resource allocations. The results may be the failure of other public policies that are not currently fashionable, or damage to the private sector from higher taxes relative to competitors in international markets.

Israeli parochialism has an additional danger. The centrality of the Promised Land to religious and nationalist Jews produces an intensity and rigidity about issues currently on the national agenda. The vilification of Prime Minister Yitzhak Rabin for bargaining away parts of the Promised Land and his assassination are extreme representations of emotions whose incidence in the population is not possible to gauge accurately. They represent a threat not only to the flexibility that is important to international negotiations, but also to the sanity of the political culture and the democratic character of Israel's regime.

NOTES

1. This section relies on the author's *Rituals of Conflict: Religion, Politics, and Public Policy in Israel*, Boulder, CO: Lynne Rienner, forthcoming.
2. *Jerusalem Post*, 24 Nov. 1995, p.8.
3. Maya Choshen, "The Elections to the Knesset in Jerusalem: Statistical Outlook," Jerusalem: Jerusalem Institute for Israel Studies, 1990 (Hebrew).
4. Ephraim Tabory, "Avoidance and Conflict: Perceptions Regarding Contact between Religious and Nonreligioius Jewish Youth in Israel," *Journal for the Scientific Study of Religion* 31/2 (1992) pp.148–62.
5. For example, *Jerusalem Post*, 12 April 1994, p.6; 11 Jan. 1991, p.6; 15 April 1990, p.4; 26 Oct. 1989, p.1; 25 Nov. 1988, p.6.
6. John C. Green, "The Christian Right and the 1994 Elections: A View from the States," *PS: Political Scence & Politics* 27/1 (March 1995) pp.5–8.
7. *Ha'aretz*, 3 May 1995, p.1.
8. *Ha'aretz*, 19 April 1995, p.6.
9. *Jerusalem Post*, 17 Jan. 1992, p.1B and 7 Jan. 1994, p.4B. For a discussion of nuances

among categories of Israeli Jews, see Eliezer Don-Yehiya, "Does Place Make a Difference? Jewish Orthodoxy in Israel and the Diaspora," in Chaim I. Waxman (ed.), *Israel as a Religious Reality*, Northvale, NJ: Jason Aronson, 1994, pp.43-74.
10. Robert A. Campbell and James E. Curtis, "Religious Involvement Across Societies: Analysis for Alternative Measures in National Surveys," *Journal for the Scientific Study of Religion* 33/3 (1994) pp.215-29.The countries covered in the surveys were Australia, Belgium, Britain, Canada, Denmark, Finland, France, Germany, Hungary, Iceland, Ireland, Italy, Japan, Mexico, Northern Ireland, Netherlands, Norway, South Africa, Spain, Sweden, and United States.
11. David C. Leege and Lyman A. Kellstedt (eds), *Rediscovering the Religious Factor in American Politics*, Armonk, NY: M.E. Sharpe, 1993; Kenneth D. Wald, *Religion and Politics in the United States*, Washington, DC: CQ Press, 1992; Stephen D. Johnson and Joseph B. Tamney (eds), *The Political Role of Religion in the United States*, Boulder, CO: Westview Press, 1986; Robert Wuthnow, *The Restructuring of American Religion*, Princeton: Princeton University Press, 1988; R. Laurence Moore, *Selling God: American Religion in the Marketplace of Culture*, New York: Oxford University Press, 1994; and Michael J. Lacey (ed.), *Religion and Twentieth-Century American Intellectual Life*, New York: Cambridge University Press, 1989; Harold Bloom, *The American Religion: The Emergence of the Post-Christian Nation*, New York: Simon & Schuster, 1992; Daniel Bell, "The Return of the Sacred? The Argument on the Future of Religion," *British Journal of Sociology* 28/4 (Dec. 1977) pp.419-49; Rodney Stark and William Sims Bainbridge, *The Future of Religion: Secularization, Revival, and Cult Formation*, Berkeley: University of California Press, 1985; Jon Butler, *Awash in a Sea of Faith: Christianizing the American People*, Cambridge: Harvard University Press, 1990; Barry A. Kosmin and Seymour P. Lachman, *One Nation Under God: Religion in Contemporary American Society*, New York: Crown Publishers, 1993.
12. This section relies on the author's "Israeli Income Equality," *Israel Studies* 1/1 (Spring 1996) pp.306-14.
13. Ze'ev Sternhell, *Nation-Building or a New Society? The Zionist Labor Movement (1904-1940) and the Origins of Israel*, Tel Aviv: Am Oved, 1995 (Hebrew).
14. *Jerusalem Post*, 26 Nov. 1993, p.4A.
15. Michael Shalev, *Labour and the Political Economy in Israel*, New York: Oxford University Press, 1992, pp.245-6.
16. Dan Horowitz and Moshe Lissak, *Trouble in Utopia: The Overburdened Polity of Israel*, Albany: State University of New York Press, 1989, p.83f.
17. Timothy M. Sneeding, Michael O'Higgins, and Lee Rainwater (eds), *Poverty, Inequality and Income Distributin in Comparative Perspective: The Luxembourg Income Study (LIS)*, New York: Harvester Wheatsheaf, 1993.
18. Analysis performed by the author with data from Denny Braun, *The Rich Get Richer: The Rise of Income Inequality in the United States and the World*, Chicago: Nelson-Hall, 1991, pp.55-7, 75-6.
19. Israel's ratios of actual to predicted values for Household GINI are .83; for the proportion of total income in families in the lowest 20 percent of income 1.11; for the proportion of total income in families in the highest 20 percent of income .85; for the proportion of total income in families in the highest 10 percent of income .73.
20. Data supporting these conclusions appear in the author's "Israeli Income Equality."
21. See, for example, Martin Rein, Goesta Esping-Andersen, and Lee Rainwater (eds), *Stagnation and Renewal in Social Policy: The Rise and Fall of Policy Regimes*, Armonk, NY: M.E. Sharpe, 1987.
22. Braun (note 18) p.186.
23. *Statistical Abstract of the United States, 1993*, Table 735.
24. *Statistical Abstract of Israel*, Jerusalem: Central Bureau of Statistics. Detailed Tables are available from the author.
25. *Statistical Abstract of the United States, 1993*, Washington, DC: US Government Printing Office, 1993, Table 750. This table shows that some transfer payments have the effect of making the American distribution of income more progressive. Israeli data appear in *Statistical Abstract of Israel*. Detailed tables are available from the author.
26. *Jerusalem Post*, 8 Nov. 1993, p.1; 29 Dec. 1994, p.6; 24 Nov. 1995, p.10. Ten plagues figure in the biblical story that stands at the center of the Passover holiday.
27. *Jerusalem Post*, 2 Aug. 1995, p.1.
28. *Jerusalem Post*, 24 Nov. 1995, p.10.

29. *Statistical Abstract of the United States, 1993,* Table 1396; *Statistical Abstract of Israel,* 1992 and 1975, Tables 18.25 and 29.8. As in other fields of policy analysis, policy advocates argue in behalf of one or another conception and indicator. The data employed here come from reliable public sources and employ widely-used indicators.
30. *Jerusalem Post,* 2 June 1995, p.11.
31. *Ha'aretz,* 1 Jan. 1996, p.7.
32. As told to the author.

Abstracts

Courts as Hegemonic Institutions:
The Israeli Supreme Court in a Comparative Perspective
Gad Barzilai

This article deals with the hegemonic power that supreme courts may have in democracies. From that comparative perspective, I analyze the change that the Israeli Supreme Court has experienced from being a rather secondary political institution in the 1950s, and 1960s, to being a major political institution, even a hegemonic one, since the 1970s, and principally in the 1980s and 1990s. I exhibit that this change has many similarities to growing adjudication in other democracies. Based on a theoretical analysis and exploration of the institutional and public status of the Israeli Supreme Court until nowadays, I raise two explanations as to its prime role in Israeli politics. The first explanation focuses on fragmentation and polarization of other political power foci. The second explanation focuses on cultural and social changes in the Israeli society, especially its Americanization and more prevalence of liberal norms among several segments in Israeli society. I show how the Court has transformed public sources of legitimacy and has become hegemonic. This article concludes by exploring the costs of broad adjudication for judicial legitimacy, and the social costs concerning judicial legitimacy for segments like Arab-Palestinians and ultra-orthodox Jews who do not enjoy the liberal discourse.

Israeli Constitutional Politics: The Fragility of Impartiality
Menachem Hofnung

The power of courts to engage in constitutional politics and to apply judicial review derives, in most countries, from a provision of formal authority and from extension of that authority by the courts. Is it possible, though, that a formal provision of judicial review may lead to a consequent reduction in judicial power to engage in constitutional politics? The powers of judicial review are currently used more frequently than before in striking down laws and administrative actions. European governments, parliaments, and administrators interact differently as a result of this judicial activity. In Europe and the US, the courts usually base their constitutional review on an accepted yardstick, (e.g. a written constitution or the European Community legislation), when interfering with sensitive political decisions. By contrast, the history of judicial review in Israel offers an interesting case, where, in the absence of a written constitution, the Supreme Court, especially when acting as the High Court of Justice, has been a very active actor in national constitutional politics. I will argue here that a grant of formal authority in Israel, in 1992, created a situation in which the courts' power to review future legislation and executive policies is in jeopardy. This is the case because this grant of formal authority has caused the courts to be publicly perceived as partisan actors in the political arena, whereas previously, they were viewed as neutral unbiased judicial organs. Furthermore, this shift has induced minority groups to attempt to introduce their own exceptions to the law and thus avoid the implications of judicial review.

Structural Change and Leadership Transformation
Gabriel Sheffer

This article examines the nexus between political structural change and leadership development in Israel. It also demonstrates that the development of Israel's regime and political leadership is in many ways comparable to other western democracies. Third, it contributes to the largely neglected comparative study of leadership in democratic and democratizing states. The Israeli case is pertinent since Israel has experienced a movement from a collectivist and elitist, to a pluralist and corporatist, and, more recently, to a democratic regime in which individuals are more assertive and freer from the state's bonds.

This analysis assumes that political culture and arrangements answer social needs. I suggest that, due mainly to shifting social loyalties and inclinations, Israel's consociational arrangement carried over from the pre-state period was replaced in the late 1960s by neo-corporatism, and that the latter is now being transformed into a multicultural private-liberal arrangement. The transition from a neo-corporatist to liberal-private market regime in Israel and other democratic states has been marked by the emergence of transactional, meteoric, and bargaining leaders, whose strengths are pragmatism, a cautious and flexible reformism, and clever use of the media.

Interest Politics in a Comparative Perspective: The (Ir)regularity of the Israeli Case
Yael Yishai

Systems of interest groups constitute complex configurations that are subject to cross-cultural and cross-national variability. This article attempts to place interest politics in Israel in a comparative perspective in order to reveal in which respects it resembles, or alternatively differs from, other democratic societies. Cross-national studies of interest group systems have centered on three fundamental theories: pluralism, corporatism, and elitism (partyism). The paper shows first how Israel fits into these models. The paper focuses on the changes taking place in interest group politics. The scope of the change, its pace, its direction, and its determinants are analyzed. Changes are noticeable in every aspect of interest group politics: groups are no longer mobilized to the national cause or attached political parties. State power is gradually shrinking; organizational concentration of interests group has weakened; the associational arena has turned more diverse, and access has widened. These changes are evoked by alterations in the economy, in society, and in the polity.

The Social Organization of the Israeli Economy: A Comparative Analysis
Daniel Maman

The social organization of the Israeli economy has been shifting, since the mid-1960s, from a pluralist to a dual economy, in which a multitude of small firms coexist with big business. At the top of the Israel's big business are several business groups, a feature that is shared with many other countries both developed and developing. This paper studies the factors which have contributed to the emergence and dominance of business groups in the Israeli economy. Studies on other societies where business groups prevail suggest several explanations. These include market imperfections, cultural heritage, and political economy. This paper suggests that in the Israeli context a combination of political and economic factors has led to the emergence and dominance of business groups. State organizations have played a decisive role in these processes. The Israeli state apparatus itself, as in other newly industrializing countries, directs the economic development; it was responsible for the industrialization in the 1950s onwards, the emergence of the military-industrial complex in the mid 1960s, and the privatization policy in the 1980s. The economic processes which have strengthened the concentration trend and the central role of business groups are the business collapse after the recession of the 1960s, the hyper-inflation of the late 1970s, the economic crisis in the mid 1980s, and the rapid growth from the early 1990s.

Business in Politics: Globalization and the Search for Peace in South Africa and Israel/Palestine
Gershon Shafir

This paper seeks to understand the reasons behind the politicization of the white South African and Israeli Jewish business communities expressed through their support for peacemaking with Africans and Palestinians repectively. Positions taken by the business communities and their allies converged with security concerns and underwrote the redefinition of the white–black and Israeli–Palestinian conflicts as obstacles to economic modernization. The new perspective resonated with an acute consciousness concerning the difference between "winning" and "losing" countries.

Have Globalization and Liberalization "Normalized" Israel's Political Economy?
Michael Shalev

The cold winds of economic liberalization appear to have chilled the longstanding dominance of the state in Israel's political economy. This is notable, given the continued relevance of ideologies and practices associated with Zionism and the Arab–Israeli conflict, the essential underpinnings of the state's remarkable record of economic interventionism. Following a brief historical introduction, this paper presents an empirical survey of the scope and significance of changes since 1985 in critical loci of potential liberalization: internationalization (flows of goods and capital); public expenditure; concentration and control of capital; privatization and deregulation; and labor market transformations. It concludes that Israel's political-economic regime is in the advanced throes of policy reforms, institutional shifts, and structural changes that are directly at odds with its long record of *embedded illiberalism*. Yet, liberalization has not occurred evenly, consistently, or completely. Despite dramatic changes in the public sector, "normalization" of the Histadrut and the ascendancy of market-oriented culture, the legacy of Zionist collectivism persists. The role of the state – especially its management of the national conflict – remains crucial to the political economy even though it is less obvious. From a comparative standpoint, the broad outlines of the Israeli story are similar in essence to trends elsewhere, yet the Israeli case also supports the generalization that politics of liberalization are to some extent nationally specific and potentially contradictory to global economic "imperatives."

Warfare, Polity-Formation and the Israeli National Policy Patterns
David Levi-Faur

This paper offers a comparative analysis of the interaction between warfare, polity-formation, and the consolidation of national patterns of policy making in Israel. The comparative perspective offers the American pluralism, the French etatism, and the Dutch corporatism as a framework of reference for the study of polity-formation, for the institutionalization of national policy patterns, and for the extent of change. War and war preparations resulted in the formation of a strong and centralized military machine on the one hand, and an autonomous and strong Israeli state on the other. In addition, they contributed to both the consolidation of the Jewish labor movement and the political decline of the Jewish middle class. Without denying the importance of change, this paper contends that continuity in the basic characteristics of the Israeli policy pattern will prevail over the normative tendency of dominant social groups to adopt a more "American" type of pluralism in Israeli policy making and will constrain the converging effects of globalization over the Israeli political economy.

Consociationalism and Ethnic Democracy: Israeli Arabs in Comparative Perspective
Alan Dowty

The case of Israeli citizens who are ethnically Arab is of special interest because of Israel's commitment to democratic institutions and the intensity of the Arab–Israeli conflict. The position of the Arab minority in Israel is the weakest aspect of Israeli democracy, but this can be explained in part by security considerations; in part, it is also a function of Jewish political experience and traditions. Comparison of this experience to other cases suggests that "consociational" democracy is, as observers have generally claimed, better equipped in general to cope with serious divisions within a country. There are, however, clear limits in its application to ethnic minorities not identified with the dominant ethos, at least where a tradition for sharing power with other national groups does not exist.

From What *Edah* are You? Israeli and American Meanings of "Race-Ethnicity" in Social Policy Practices
Dvora Yanow

"Race," "ethnicity," and their equivalents are social constructions, created and used by states in social policy and administrative practices to establish and maintain status and power hierarchies. In the US they are, however, commonly understood and treated as universal, objectively observable, and measurable scientific facts. This enables their usage in policy and administrative contexts. I argue here that *edah* has been understood and used in similar ways, contributing to silences in public discourse that impede social change.

Changing Places: Jerusalem's Holy Places in Comparative Perspective
Roger Friedland and Richard D. Hecht

This essay challenges the essentialist interpretations of sacred places which deny the historical transformation of the meanings attributed to those places and the role of politics in the constitution of those meanings. Here we compare the conflict between Hindus and Muslims in the destruction of the Ram Temple and Babri Mosque in Ayodhya in 1992 and conflict between Jews and Muslims over Jerusalem's Temple Mount and Noble Sanctuary, especially in one violent confrontation in 1990 between Israelis and Palestinians. In both cases we attempt to show the long history of conflicts in both sites. We argue that control over sacred sites like Ayodhya's Ramjanmabhumi/Babri Masjid and Jerusalem's *har ha-bayit/al-haram as-sharif* proves the avenue and mechanism for challenging and transforming the definition of citizenship in the modern nation-state. In both cases, this represents a continuation of the ancient function of sacred sites, to centralize the polity. But, it also means that changing the constituent elements of the nation-state, in this case citizenship, through the center accelerates the rapidity of that change. Sacred real estate becomes a highly productive and potentially violent venue for the articulation of change. In this comparative analysis we are able to determine five factors involved in the social construction of physical territory and the symbolic map of the nation-state. First, sites like these are contested within the traditions which hold them to be sacred. Second, access to ritual space and time in sacred sites is conditional upon the exercise of state power. Third, the sacrality of the site cannot be separated from the historical exercise of state power in general, and the nation in particular. Fourth, the religions anchored in these sites have been essential to the formation of modern nationalist movements. Fifth, since the legitimacy of the state is grounded in claims to these sites, they also become the battlegrounds for those who wish to challenge and ultimately transform the state itself.

Imported Problem Definitions, Legal Culture and the Local Dynamics of Israeli Abortion Politics
Noga Morag-Levine

Through analysis of the evolution of Israeli abortion politics, this study examines the impact of interconnections between legal culture and local policy problem definitions on the reception of imported policy paradigms. Despite efforts to infuse Israeli abortion politics with American-derived pro-life and pro-choice formulations, these definitions remain at the margin of relevant Israeli debates. The article attributes this phenomenon to two related factors: (1) dissonance between the absolutist, individualist, and universalist underpinnings of the American problem definitions and contextual, collectivist, and particularistic Jewish understandings of the issue in Israel; and (2) incompatibility between American limited government and related constitutionalist framing of the legitimacy of abortion regulation on the one hand, and salient Israeli political- and legal-cultural traits on the other. Especially important in this regard is the place of traditional Israeli deference to the state as an embodiment of shared values, and a systemic reliance on circumvention mechanisms, termed here de facto legalism, as an alternative to explicit articulation of these increasingly contested values. In abortion, as in many other domains where conflicts between Israeli Jewish and democratic commitments are implicated, the avoidance of law has served to deflect what Israelis increasingly fear may be irreconcilable differences. American-inspired conceptions of what is at stake in abortion ultimately failed to alter the course of Israeli abortion politics because they were incompatible with the terms of this increasingly fragile compromise.

Israeli Environmental Policy in Comparative Perspective
David Vogel

This article explores Israeli environmental policy and places it in comparative perspective. While Israel's policies were roughly similar to those of other nations at comparable levels of development through the early 1970s, since the mid-1970s, Israel has accorded environmental protection a lower priority than other rich democracies. After a number of explanations for Israel's status as an environmental "laggard" are explored, the paper concludes by noting that as Israel has become a more "normal" post-industrial nation, the attention it has accorded to environmental protection has gradually increased.

The Gender and Pacifism Hypothesis:
Opinion Research from Israel and the Arab World
Mark Tessler, Jodi Nachtwey, and Audra Grant

This research report replicates, extends, and adds a longitudinal dimension to several recently published analyses, one of which appears in a volume on Israel in comparative perspective. Focusing on the relationship between gender and attitudes toward international conflict, and specifically on the gender and pacifism hypothesis which asserts that women are more peace-oriented than men, the present report analyzes data from two public opinion surveys in Israel and from additional opinion surveys in Egypt, Kuwait, Jordan, Lebanon, and Palestine. The dual and interrelated goals of this study are (1) to incorporate the Israeli case into an on-going effort to test a social science hypothesis purporting to have explanatory power in diverse social and cultural contexts; and (2) to compare findings from Israel and other Middle Eastern societies in order to determine whether aggregate societal circumstances affect the applicability of this hypothesis.

The Promised Land of the Chosen People is not all that Distinctive: On the Value of Comparison
Ira Sharkansky

Ideas about the Promised Land and Chosen People may deter accurate self-assessment in modern Israel by emphasizing the uniqueness of the nation and its homeland. A consideration of three issues on the national agenda shows that Israel is not clearly distinctive from other countries on these traits. On the dimensions of income inequality and traffic deaths, some measurements challenge the conventional wisdom: they show Israel scoring *more desirable* than international norms. By implication to other fields, the findings put the burden of demonstration on those who would claim that Israel or any other country has special traits that distinguish it from others. Parochialism may have serious consequences if it leads to distortions of resource allocations to fields where policymakers think there are shortfalls, but where the country actually does well by international standards. In Israel's case, moreover, a parochial insistence on land thought to be promised by the Almighty may get in the way of agreements that would increase a measure of worldly peace.

Index

administrative review, 38–9
Afrikaner, 105, 107–110
American, 15, 18, 21, 26–7, 30, 38, 44, 88, 109, 111, 158, 163–5, 185, 186, 187, 190–1, 226, 228, 231, 233–4, 239, 242, 246, 251, 255, 267, 287
apartheid, 106, 109–13, 118–19
Arab, 2, 20–1, 25–6, 29, 57–8, 78, 104, 106, 112–13, 115–17, 123–4, 126, 131, 139, 147, 161, 169, 172, 173, 175–81, 184, 216, 247, 255, 260, 261, 265, 271, 277, 285
Arab boycott, 115, 162
Arab–Israeli conflict, 59, 118, 158–60, 162–3, 175, 214, 270–4
Arafat, Y., 103
Austria, 18, 57, 59–60, 68–9
authority
 horizontal, 92
 vertical, 91–2, 99
autonomy of state, 13, 48, 74, 77, 122, 125–127, 131, 138, 143, 156, 162–3, 165

Barak, A., 28, 30, 64
Barak, E., 64, 68
Basic Law, 18, 28, 37, 40–2, 46–9
behavioral approach, 3
Belgium, 57, 68–9
Ben-Gurion, D., 65–6, 159–60, 190
bourgeoisie, 123, 159–61, 190
Britain, 37, 103, 248
British, 5, 36, 124, 158, 161, 169, 210–11, 217
 Mandate, 90, 113, 172, 214, 247
business groups, 87–99
bureaucracy, 61, 74, 76, 77, 79–80, 84, 94, 99, 126, 134, 139–40, 145, 157–8, 238, 248
bureaucratization, 164, 178

capitalism, 4, 59, 61, 87–8, 107, 135, 213
capitalist, 159, 183, 209, 249
centralization, 97, 157–9, 164, 170, 208
China, 88
civic bloc, 58–9, 66
colonization, Jewish, 123
collectivism, 62–3, 70, 83, 144, 208
 collective, 81, 85, 123, 159, 170, 172, 190, 226, 236–7, 242, 258
 consensus, 40, 48, 62, 75, 105–6, 222, 275, 282
 collectivist, 77, 123, 226
 consensual, 28
consociationalism, 57, 60–1, 66, 69, 172–3, 175–7, 180
constitutional
 court, 18, 34
 dialogue, 46–7
 reform, 18
 review, 35–6, 42, 48
constitutionalism, 18
convergence, 4, 12, 111, 122, 127, 156, 169, 178, 180
corporatism, 74, 84, 156, 165
 liberal, 74, 78–9
 corporatist, 73–4, 81, 124
 neo-corporatism, 57, 60–2, 66–7, 69
culture, political, 56
Cultural Theory of Leadership, 56

Dahl, R., 75, 78
Declaration of Independence, 36–7, 42
decentralization, 60, 80–1, 164, 170
deflation, 140

Our acknowledgements to Michal Sommer for preparing the index.

democratization, 56
demographic, 232, 237, 242
deregulation, 127, 136–8, 142, 146–7
devaluation, 126
direct election, 57, 64, 83
dirigisme, 113, 135
Durkheimian tradition, 208
edah, 183–5, 189–95
elitism, 49, 70, 73, 74, 79, 84
elite, 55, 57, 59–60, 62–4, 67–8, 79–80, 83, 104–5, 107–8, 113–14, 118, 143, 147, 171–2, 179, 207–8, 222
Elon Moreh, 38, 47
embedded illiberalism, 123, 142
England, 5
   English, 26–7, 43, 107–9, 113
equality, 285–7, 289
etatism, 156–7, 159, 163, 165
etatist, 57, 59, 158, 165
Ethiopia, 62
   Ethiopian, 78, 82
ethnic, 57, 62–3, 121, 169, 172, 183, 285
   ethnic democracy, 173–4, 176–7, 181
   ethnicity, 174, 180, 183–5, 187, 191–2, 195
   race, ethnicity, 183–4, 186, 188–9, 192–4
ethnocentric, 2, 83
Europe, 5, 18, 21, 27, 36–7, 42, 44, 69–70, 82, 88, 107, 116, 128, 157–8, 162–3, 165, 170, 188, 190, 249–50, 254, 275, 287–8
   European Community, 250
   European market, 128
   European policy, 34
   European Union 60, 129, 241, 251, 254, 256–7, 259

fragmentation, 15, 26, 28, 30, 63, 157, 164
France, 5, 15–6, 28, 95, 107, 156, 158–9, 163
   French policy, 164
functionalist, 56

Gaza, 119, 126, 141, 177, 218–9, 260
gender, 29, 265, 268, 271–2, 274
Germany, 1, 5, 15–16, 18, 26–8, 30, 124
   German reparations, 95, 125
globalization, 2–3, 13, 105–6, 118, 122–3, 136, 144, 165, 178
   global, 2, 12, 55, 80, 103, 113, 156, 262, 265
guest worker, 140–2, 145

Hamas, 219
Harrari Resolution, 36–7
hegemony, 20, 77, 148, 160, 165
   hegemonic, 15, 19, 28, 31, 159
Hindu, 202, 204–6, 209, 212–14, 217, 219–21

Histadrut, 63–4, 77, 79, 81, 84, 90, 92, 107, 112–14, 116, 124, 126–7, 135–6, 139–44, 159, 248
historical-institutional approach, 6
Holland, 57, 69
hyperinflation, 90, 94, 97–8, 126–7, 138

immigration, 59, 85, 95, 98, 106, 113, 124, 125, 145, 159, 184, 190, 193, 247, 283, 288
   absorption, 115, 124, 134, 147, 190, 192, 242
   immigrants, 3, 62, 75–6, 78, 84, 108, 139, 185, 226, 228, 236, 254, 258
Independence, War of, 161
India, 202, 205, 210–12, 217, 220–1
individualism, 63, 68, 83–5, 258
industrialization, 94, 96, 112, 117, 135, 156, 249
inflation, 83, 96, 98, 114, 133, 161–2
inter-group ties, 91, 93
intermarrige, 191
internationalization, 89, 128, 136, 142, 178
international relations, 266
Intifada, 104, 117–18, 142, 177, 219
Israel Defense Forces (IDF), 21, 67, 95, 158, 218
Italy, 15–16, 30

Japan, 1, 87–9, 92, 94–5, 99, 249–50, 254
Jerusalem, 26, 45, 176, 200–6, 209–11, 214–16, 218–19, 221–2, 253, 260, 281, 283
Jewish, 2, 17, 20–1, 26, 28–30, 40, 57, 59, 65–6, 77–8, 81, 83, 90, 105, 107–8, 112–13, 121, 123, 126, 131, 134–5, 139, 142, 147, 159–61, 165, 170–1, 174, 176–7, 179, 181, 184, 189, 203, 226, 230, 232, 241–2, 255, 269, 276, 282, 289–90
Jewishness, 121, 172–3
   law, *halachah*, 26–7, 29, 231, 234, 281
Jewry, Diaspora, 64, 68, 130, 161, 172, 247, 254
Jews, 63–4, 104, 172, 180, 194, 204, 206, 209, 215, 279, 285
judicial activism, 12, 19, 39, 43, 48
judicialization of politics, 34
judicial review, 16, 18, 20, 25, 27–8, 30, 34–40, 42, 46, 49

Kahane, Meir, 26
Keynesian capacity, 4
Knesset, 17–18, 20, 25–6, 28–9, 36–8, 40–2, 47–8, 58, 64, 82, 170, 176, 179, 218, 228–9, 231, 236, 238, 246, 248, 261
   members of, 227–8, 230, 237, 239

Index

Labor, 40, 43, 57–61, 64, 67–8, 80, 83, 131, 134, 159, 186, 211, 215
  Labor Party, 28, 48, 76, 116, 118, 123, 140–1, 144, 233, 235–6, 285
labor
  market, 77, 139, 145
  movement, 66, 112–13, 123, 160, 165
laissez-faire, 125
Latin America, 88, 106
leadership
  meteoric, 68–70
  political, 55–6
  transactional, 65, 67–70
  transforming, 65–6, 69–70
Lebanon, war in 1982, 40
legitimacy, 16, 20, 25, 30, 67, 80, 127, 147, 222
  diffuse (support), 15, 17, 21, 25, 29, 31
  mythical (support), 15–17, 21, 23, 25, 29–31
  specific, 15, 17, 21, 25, 31
  legitimation, 74, 118, 125, 179, 208, 223
liberal, 15, 26, 30, 42, 48, 58, 63, 67, 70, 110, 170, 173, 226, 230, 235–6
  neo, 114, 121, 137
  semi, 57
  liberalism, 186
liberalism, economic, 61, 63, 65, 122
  liberalization, 2, 60, 63, 68–9, 116–17, 122–3, 125, 127–8, 131, 134, 139, 142–8, 228
  liberalizers, 136
  liberalizing, 126–7
Likud, 30, 40, 45, 64, 67–8, 80, 116, 118, 124, 137–8, 140, 218
Lijphart, A., 169, 170, 174

majoritarianism, 169, 171, 173, 175
Mandela, N., 103, 111–12
Marxism, 4, 208
Middle East, 2, 95, 113, 117, 219, 248, 254–5, 260, 267, 269, 274, 276
military-industrial complex, 94, 98, 107, 125, 162
mitun, 125–6, 144
Monetarism, 4
monopolization, 77–8, 81
Muslims, 179, 201–6, 209, 212, 214–8, 220–1, 269, 276

nationalism, 83, 211, 213–14, 222
  Jewish, 123
  nationalist, 148, 290
  nationalization, 164
nation-states, 190, 202, 211, 213, 221
Netanyahu, B., 30, 45, 64, 68, 179
Netherlands, 59–60, 156, 159, 163
New Deal, 17
Northern Ireland, 103

orthodox, 29, 42, 58–9, 78, 180, 228, 290, 231, 261, 281, 284
  ultra, 233, 239, 241, 281–3
ownership
  family, 92
  private, 80
  public, 124
  state, 77, 96, 136, 162

pacifism, 265
Palestinian, 19–21, 25–6, 29, 57, 59–60, 62, 64, 104–6, 113–17, 123, 141–2, 177, 180, 184, 194, 200–1, 203–4, 211, 221, 259–60, 271
Palestine, 66, 103, 107, 113, 147, 159–60, 172, 181, 209–10, 215–16, 247, 257
participatory society, 82
party-state, 76
Patinkin, D., 121
Palestine Liberation Organization – PLO, 103, 114, 177, 210, 219, 268
Peres, S., 179
pluralism, 74–5, 79, 82, 84, 156, 158, 165, 170, 180
  pluralist, 73, 78, 99, 248
polarization, 15, 26, 28, 30, 95
policy
  economic, 140
  environmental, 262
  social, 124,140
political activism, 76
political parties, 76, 80, 83–4, 252
politicization, 49, 111, 128
  politicized, 139
primaries, 80
privatization, 63, 65, 68–9, 80, 94, 96–7, 114, 127, 134, 136–7, 140, 142, 145, 147, 157
protectionism, 114, 126, 164
public opinion, 20, 69, 118, 127, 260, 265, 267

Rabbinical Court, High, 39–40
Rabin, Y., 64, 67, 103, 115, 288, 290
reasonableness, doctrines of, 35, 43
recession, 97–8
  recessionary, 125
reform Jews, 82
regime
  judicial, administrative, 18
  policy, 122, 143
  political, economic, 122, 125–6, 142, 144
regulation, 34, 42, 74–7, 107, 114, 128, 138, 163, 178, 223, 228–9, 237, 248, 259
  environmental, 249–50
  economic, 125
  regulated, regulating, 125, 142, 238
  regulatory, 136

religiosity, 274, 276, 284
religious parties, 30, 36, 40, 45, 47–8, 59, 68, 230, 282–3
rights
  homosexual, 29–30
  human, 40, 42, 171, 228
  individual, 26, 39, 172
  civil, 18–19, 25–6, 110, 173, 178, 204, 228, 232

sacralization, 212
secular, 1, 26, 29, 36, 48, 62, 78, 82, 193, 210, 218, 230, 242, 252, 268, 280–4
  secularization, 178–9, 210–11, 221
security, 29, 38, 43, 64, 75, 103, 117, 175, 178–9, 192, 248, 256
segmentation, 57
settler society, 147
Shas, 28, 40, 48, 68, 228, 233, 239
Six Day War (1967), 60, 90, 95, 125, 138, 144, 218, 259
1967 borders, 19
Smooha, S., 173
socialism, 156, 285
  parliamentary, 123
  socialization, 6, 66, 80, 162, 248
  socialist, 2, 66, 110, 116, 123, 183, 186
South Africa, 21, 103–14, 118–19
South Korea, 87–9, 92, 94–5, 99
Soviet Union, former, 62, 78, 98, 104, 115, 236, 258
stabilization plan, 96, 114, 126, 134–5, 138, 141, 144, 257
stagflation, 126
stagnation, 127
State Comptroller, 21
state contraction, 127–8, 147
Status Quo, 59, 215–18, 235–6, 284
statutory interpretation, 38–9

Taiwan, 87–9, 92, 94–5, 99
territories, the (occupied), 20–1, 26, 29, 44, 47, 62, 84, 119, 175, 177, 252
terrorism, 142
Tilly, C., 157, 165
transportation policy, 251

United States – US, 1, 16, 28, 30, 36, 40, 43, 68–9, 80, 83, 129–30, 146, 156, 159, 163, 185–6, 188, 193–4, 219, 226, 229, 231, 241, 248–50, 254, 259, 275, 284, 288
  aid, 126–7, 130–1
  guarantees, 131
  Supreme Court, 16–18, 38, 228
urbanization, 106, 178

veto power, 61, 170, 174, 240

welfare state, 123, 132–5, 147, 262, 285, 287
West Bank, 38, 117, 119, 126, 141, 177, 218–19, 256–7, 260, 271
Wildavsky, A., 70

Yishuv, 57–8, 65–6, 90, 108, 112–13, 118, 160–1, 172, 178, 211, 248

Yom Kippur War (1973), 67, 90, 96, 106, 132, 135, 138, 256–7

Zionism, 123, 176, 178–9, 186, 191–2, 214–15
Zionist, 30, 66, 75, 92, 131, 143, 147–8, 157, 160, 180, 209, 211, 247, 257–8, 285
  Labor Zionist, 216, 222, 229, 248
  Revisionist Zionist, 216
Zionist movement, 58, 65, 107, 113, 123, 159, 172

Other Books in the Israeli History, Politics and Society Series

Israel at the Polls, 1996
Daniel J Elazar and **Shmuel Sandler**, *both at Bar-Ilan University* (Eds)

'... well put together, lucid and provides a detailed account of one of the most important Israeli election campaigns in recent times.'
Israeli Perspectives

The 1996 Israeli elections were the first elections by direct vote for the position of prime minister in which a newcomer – Binyamin Netanyahu – defeated the most veteran Israeli politician, Shimon Peres. The result indicated not only a transition of power from the left-centre to the right-centre, but also the decline of the major parties and the ascendance of the smaller parties. *Israel at the Polls, 1996* looks at the parties, election campaigns and the processes that determined this outcome.

288 pages 1998
0 7146 4864 7 cloth
0 7146 4421 8 paper

In Search of Identity
Jewish Aspects in Israeli Culture
Dan Urian, *Tel Aviv University* and
Efraim Karsh, *King's College London* (Eds)

After 50 years of Israeli statehood, Israeli society faces a deepening crisis of identity. This is particularly evident in Israeli culture which, for quite some time, has been effectively disintegrating into several simultaneous sub-cultures. This process has gained momentum during the 1990s, due to the relaxation of national cohesiveness following the Arab–Israeli peace negotiations on the one hand, and to the growing post-modern influences on Israeli culture on the other. This in turn has brought to the fore a whole range of questions which have hitherto been ignored, not least the interrelationship between the Hebrew and Jewish aspects of Israeli culture. This problematic continuum between past and present, between Israeliness and Jewishness, lies at the core of this volume.

Contributors: *Eliezer Schweid, Charles S Liebman, Baruch Kimmerling, Gershon Shaked, Dan Miron, Avraham Shapira, Gad Ufaz, David Zisenwine, Eli Rozik-Rosen, Nurit Gertz, Mordechai Omer, Shimon Levy, Dan Urian and Dalia Manor.*

296 pages 1999
0 7146 4889 2 cloth
0 7146 4440 4 paper

FRANK CASS PUBLISHERS
Newbury House, 900 Eastern Avenue, Ilford, Essex, IG2 7HH
Tel: +44 (0)181 599 8866 Fax: +44 (0)181 599 0984 E-mail: info@frankcass.com
NORTH AMERICA
5804 NE Hassalo Street, Portland, OR 97213 3644, USA
Tel: 800 944 6190 Fax: 503 280 8832 E-mail: cass@isbs.com
Website: www.frankcass.com

Revisiting the Yom Kippur War

P R Kumaraswamy, *The Hebrew University of Jerusalem* (Ed)
Foreword by **Efraim Karsh**, *King's College, London*

By looking at the political, military and intelligence components of the war, the volume offers new interpretations to Israel's conflict with the Arabs. The contributors, leading Israeli academics, some of them involved in the war, make a unique contribution to an understanding of this painful chapter in Israel's history.

By making use of hitherto unpublished materials, including the recently declassified portions of the findings of the Agranat Commission that inquired into the intelligence failure, the volume contributes to a deeper understanding of the Yom Kippur War and its impact on Israeli society.

200 pages 2000
0 7146 5007 2 cloth
0 7146 8067 2 paper

Peacemaking in Israel after Rabin
Sasson Sofer

This is an interdisciplinary study of Israeli society in one of the defining moments in the history of Israel. Prominent scholars of Israel's politics and foreign affairs discuss the critical aspects of the political order, economics, the military, the role of the media and legal reform that are shaping a new Israel. The book reflects the profound changes in foreign policy analysis taking place in recent years, the delicate interplay between the domestic, the regional and the global, and the divided nature of Israeli politics.

The study provides a profile of the overlapping network of cleavages of Israeli society – ethnic, political and ideological. Despite the breakthroughs achieved by Israel with its neighbours it remains to be seen whether the internal divides will prove to be an insurmountable obstacle in realizing a lasting peace.

256 pages 2000
0 7146 5010 2 cloth
0 7146 8064 8 paper

FRANK CASS PUBLISHERS
Newbury House, 900 Eastern Avenue, Ilford, Essex, IG2 7HH
Tel: +44 (0)181 599 8866 Fax: +44 (0)181 599 0984 E-mail: info@frankcass.com
NORTH AMERICA
5804 NE Hassalo Street, Portland, OR 97213 3644, USA
Tel: 800 944 6190 Fax: 503 280 8832 E-mail: cass@isbs.com
Website: www.frankcass.com